Child & Adult Care Professionals

Instructor Resource Guide

McGraw Hill **Glencoe**

New York, New York   Columbus, Ohio   Chicago, Illinois   Peoria, Illinois   Woodland Hills, California

Contributors:

Marlene S. Lobberecht, M.S., CFCS
Family and Consumer Sciences
Teacher & Laboratory School Director
Cypress Creek High School
Houston, Texas

Eleanor L. Keppler, M.S., CFCS
Family & Consumer Sciences
Department Head
Director, Lawrence Central Child
Care Center
Lawrence Central High School
Indianapolis, Indiana

Lowell E. Hedges, Ph.D.
Educational Consultant
Ohio State University
Columbus, Ohio

A special thank you to *The Council for Professional Recognition* for granting permission to reproduce the CDA Competency Goals and Functional Areas. *All CDA information is available on the official CDA website on the Internet.*

Internet Disclaimer

The following Internet listings are a source of extended information related to our text. We have made every effort to recommend sites that are informative and accurate. However, these sites are not under the control of Glencoe/McGraw-Hill, and therefore Glencoe/McGraw-Hill makes no representation concerning the content of these sites. We strongly encourage teachers to preview Internet sites before students use them. Many sites contain links to other sites, and following such links may eventually lead to exposure to inappropriate material. Internet sites are sometimes "under construction" and may not always be available. Sites may also move or have been discontinued completely by the time you or your students attempt to access them.

Safety Notice

The reader is expressly advised to consider and use all safety precautions described in this textbook or that might also be indicated by undertaking the activities described herein. In addition, common sense should be exercised to help avoid all potential hazards and, in particular, to take relevant safety precautions concerning any known or likely hazards involved in caring for children or older adults, or in use of the procedures described in *Child & Adult Care Professionals*, such as the risk of back injuries when lifting children or assisting older adults.

Publisher and Authors assume no responsibility for the activities of the reader or for the subject matter experts who prepared this book. Publisher and Authors make no representation or warranties of any kind, including but not limited to the warranties of fitness for particular purpose or merchantability, nor for any implied warranties related thereto, or otherwise. Publisher and Authors will not be liable for damages of any type, including any consequential, special or exemplary damages resulting, in whole or in part, from reader's use or reliance upon the information, instructions, warnings or other matter contained in this textbook.

The McGraw-Hill Companies

Send all inquiries to:
Glencoe/McGraw-Hill
3008 W. Willow Knolls Drive
Peoria, IL 61614-1083

ISBN 0-07-829017-1
Printed in the United States of America
1 2 3 4 5 6 7 8 9 10 024 07 06 05 04 03 02

Table of Contents

The Child & Adult Care Professionals Program

Child & Adult Care Professionals has all of the right elements for your high school early childhood or adult care programs. The authors provide a current and practical workplace view reflecting the trends in quality early childhood education and care, older adult day care, and intergenerational care. *Child & Adult Care Professionals* is packed with great charts, illustrations, and features. The direct, yet descriptive writing style is easy to understand and full of need-to-know information. Students will gain valuable information regarding developmental issues that impact children and older adults along with learning how to set up educational and recreational activities that are inclusive and culturally diverse. Phonetic pronunciation guides will help your students learn the vocabulary. *Child & Adult Care Professionals* also includes:

- *Intergenerational Interactions* features in every chapter that offer ways of bringing the generations together.
- *How To…* features that reinforce essential skills in working with children or older adults.
- *Ethics in Action* features sprinkled throughout the text that address ethical dilemmas students often face in the workplace.
- *Safety First* features provide need-to-know information about safety issues that arise when caring for children and older adults.
- *Independence Skills* features offer ways for children and older adults to retain independence.
- *Boosting Brain Power* highlights information that impacts brain development.
- *Section Knowledge Checks* and *Mini Labs* help students capture the key elements of each section.
- *Chapter Review & Activities* pages helps students review content and assess performance skills. *Building Your Portfolio* activities in the chapter review help students focus on developing essential workplace skills for careers related to early childhood or older adult care.

Lab Manual

Your high school students will gain a real workplace view with practical labs that introduce them to the world of caring for and educating young children and older adults.

Lab Manual IAE

The **Instructor Annotated Edition** contains answers directly on the student page!

These 50 laminated, 8½- by 11-inch full-color cards showcase 96 learning activities for infants, toddlers, preschoolers, and school-age children. Including art, language, social studies, music and creative movement, math, science, and activity play, these cards provide step-by-step instructions for completing these activities with young children. The *Activity Cards for Children* are included in the **Student Motivation Kit** (see page 9). They can also be purchased separately as ISBN 0-07-830517-9.

These 25 laminated, 8½- by 11-inch full-color cards offer 47 activities in areas such as memory retention, food and nutrition, arts and crafts, independent living, and health and fitness. Each activity offers background information, step-by-step instructions, and ideas for discussion. The *Activity Cards for Older Adults* are included in the **Student Motivation Kit** (see page 9). They can also be purchased separately as ISBN 0-07-830518-7.

This box of tempting resources will add depth and meaning to your program. Use ISBN 0-07-829018-X to order your **Student Motivation Kit**. The kit includes:

- **Activity Cards for Children** include 96 step-by-step activities. These full-color, 8½- by 11-inch laminated cards will help your students prepare engaging activities for infants, toddlers, preschoolers, and school-age children. The *Activity Cards for Children* can also be purchased separately as ISBN 0-07-830517-9.

- **Activity Cards for Older Adults** showcase 47 activities in such areas as memory retention, food and nutrition, arts and crafts, independent living, and health and fitness. Each activity offers background information, step-by-step instructions, and ideas for discussion. The *Activity Cards for Older Adults* can also be purchased separately as ISBN 0-07-830518-7.

- **Child & Adult Care Applications** keep reinforcement in mind. These activities offer students an opportunity to strengthen their knowledge and skills.

- **Child & Adult Care Observations** offer students an opportunity to observe children and older adults in a laboratory setting.

- **Child & Adult Care Career Profiles** provide detailed biographical and career information for foundational leaders and researchers in the early childhood and older adult care professions. Additional career profiles feature key information on early childhood and older adult careers with strong occupational growth expectancy.

- **Child & Adult Care Study Guides** help students take notes as they read the text and listen to instructor presentations on each section of the book. *Child & Adult Care Study Guides* are intended to be used with the PowerPoint® slides found on the *Effective Instruction CD-ROM*.

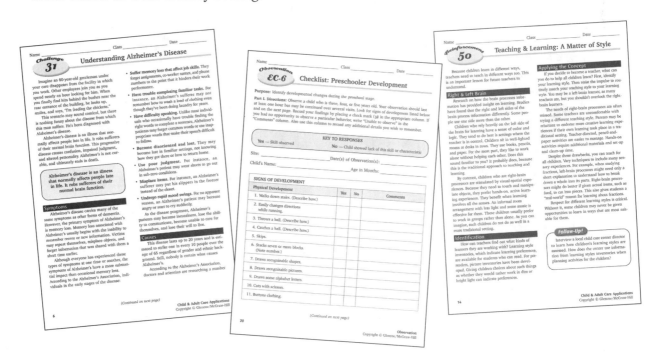

Instructor Resource Guide

This powerful resource provides numerous teaching aids and activities to help you deliver well-rounded lessons and labs. The **Instructor Resource Guide** includes an extensive listing of early childhood education and care, older adult care, and intergenerational care resources; a CDA Competency Checklist on which students can track their progress in meeting the competencies; the *Child & Adult Care Professionals* Correlation to the CDA Competency Goals and Functional Areas; information and activities on safety practices, portfolio development, and employability skills; instructional plans for each section of the text (including the text and test answers); and section tests.

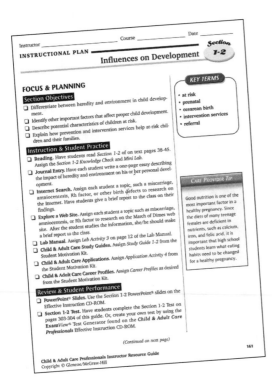

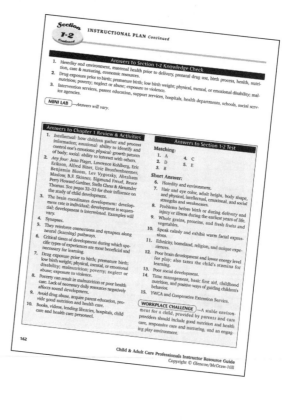

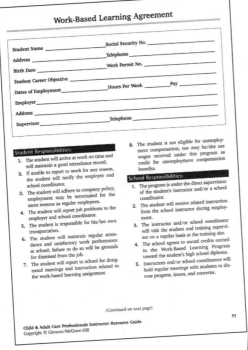

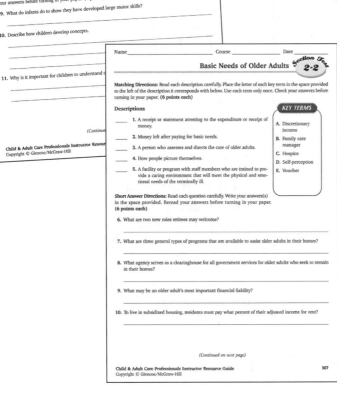

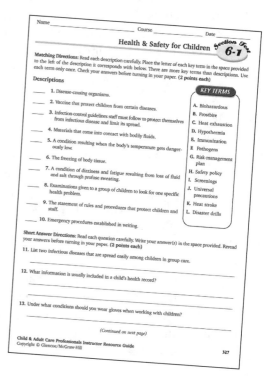

- **Portfolio Development** provides instructor and student information on creating effective career portfolios.
- **Employability Skills** activities highlight topics, such as work-based learning, successful employee characteristics, and entrepreneurship.
- **Section Tests** assess students' knowledge of key terms, concepts, and skills necessary for early childhood and older adult care professions.

Additional Child & Adult Care Resources

The following Web site list contains resources for you and your students in regard to early childhood care and education, older adult day care, and intergenerational care.

Early Childhood Resources

Child Care Bureau (CCB)
http://www.acf.hhs.gov/programs/ccb/

As part of the U.S. Department of Health and Human Services, the Child Care Bureau (CCB) is dedicated to enhancing the quality, affordability, and availability of child care for all families.

Council for Professional Recognition
www.cdacouncil.org

The Council works to improve the professional status of early childhood workers and helps to meet the growing need for qualified child care staff. The Council sponsors the Child Development Associate (CDA) credential.

National Association for the Education of Young Children (NAEYC)
www.naeyc.org

NAEYC is primarily devoted to assuring the provision of high-quality early childhood programs for young children. NAEYC also focuses on the improvement of professional preparation and training for individuals who care for and educate children, birth through age eight.

National Association for Family Child Care (NAFCC)
http://222.afcc.org

NAFCC is a nonprofit organization that is dedicated to promoting high-quality child care by strengthening the profession of family child care.

National Child Care Association (NCCA)
http://www.nccanet.org

NCCA is a professional trade association that focuses on the needs of licensed, private child care and education programs. One of its goals is high-quality affordable child care.

Accreditation & Staff Development

Child Care Information Exchange
www.childcareexchange.com

The Child Care Information Exchange Web site is associated with the director's magazine of the same name. This Web site contains a multitude of resources for early childhood professionals.

National Child Care Information Center
http://www.nccic.org

The National Child Care Information Center (NCCIC), a project of the Child Information Bureau, is a national resource that links information and people to complement, enhance, and promote the child care delivery system, working to ensure that all children and families have access to high-quality comprehensive services.

The Center for Early Childhood Leadership
http://www2.nl.edu/twal/

The Center for Early Childhood Leadership is dedicated to enhancing the management skills, professional orientation, and leadership capacity of early childhood administrators. The activities of the Center include four areas: training, technical assistance, research, and public awareness.

Curriculum, Teaching & Administration

Developmentally Appropriate Practices
www.naeyc.org

This NAEYC Web site focuses on developmentally appropriate teaching practices for early childhood providers.

(Continued on next page)

ERIC Clearinghouse
http://ericps.ed.uiuc.edu/eece/ed2link.html

The Clearinghouse on Elementary and Early Childhood Education Web site contains a wealth of information and Web links for early childhood professionals.

Head Start
http://www2.acf.dhhs.gov/programs/hsb/about/index.htm

Head Start and Early Head Start are comprehensive child development programs that serve children from birth to age 5, pregnant women, and their families. They are child-focused programs and have the overall goal of increasing the school readiness of young children in low-income families. This Web site contains information regarding programs and services of the Head Start Bureau.

National Coalition of Campus Children's Centers (NCCCC)
http://www.campuschildren.org/

The NCCCC is a nonprofit educational membership organization. It supports research and activities affecting college and university early childhood education and service settings, family and work issues, and the field of early childhood education in general.

The Project Approach
http://www.project-approach.com/

The Project Approach refers to a set of teaching strategies that enable teachers to guide children through in-depth studies of real world topics. The Web site contains a wealth of information about all aspects of The Project Approach.

The High/Scope® Approach
http://highscope.org/EducationalPrograms/EarlyChildhood/homepage.htm

On its Web site, the High/Scope® Educational Research Foundation outlines a wealth of information concerning this educational approach to active learning.

The Reggio Emilia Approach
http://ericeece.org/reggio.html

This section of the ERIC/EECE Web site contains information and resources related to the approach to early childhood education developed in the preschools of Reggio Emilia, Italy.

Children's Health

American Academy of Pediatrics
http://www.aap.org/

This Web site contains information regarding the health and welfare of children. The members of the American Academy of Pediatrics dedicate themselves is to attain optimal physical, mental and social health and well-being for all infants, children, adolescents, and young adults.

American Dental Association
http://www.ada.org/public/topics/parents/index.html

The American Dental Association Web site contains consumer news regarding numerous oral health topics, tips for teachers, and educational games.

Centers for Disease Control
http://www.cdc.gov/health/nfantsmenu.htm

The Centers for Disease Control Web site contains information regarding numerous issues related to the health and safety of young children.

Ecolab
www.Ecolab.com

Ecolab, an international cleaning and sanitation company, offers product and service information on its Web site.

GloGerm™
www.glogerm.com/

The GloGerm™ Web site offers information on the GloGerm™ kit and teaching materials concerning the contamination/transmission of germs.

(Continued on next page)

KidsHealth
http://www.kidshealth.org/

This Web site provides doctor-approved health information about children from prenatal development through adolescence. This site has separate locations for children, teens, and parents—each with its own design, age-appropriate content, and tone. It contains a wealth of in-depth information developed by experts in child and teen health.

Children's Mental Health

American Psychological Association
http://www.apa.org/

The American Psychological Association (APA) Web site contains a wealth of mental health information about children and others.

Children, Stress and Natural Disasters
http://www.ag.uiuc.edu/~disaster/disaster.html

This article from the University of Illinois Extension contains a set of resources for teachers to help prepare them for working with children who have been through a disaster. It includes *A Resource Guide for Teachers* that describes what teachers can do to help during the recovery period, a set of *Classroom Activities for Teachers* that can be used following a disaster, and a *Disaster Bibliography* of children's books on floods and natural disasters.

Mr. Rogers/Family Communications, Inc.
http://www.misterrogers.org/families/

This Web site contains the article *Helping Children Deal with Scary News* from Mr. Rogers/Family Communications, Inc.

National Association for Self-Esteem
http://www.self-esteem-nase.org/

The National Association for Self-Esteem Web site contains a wide variety of self-esteem related educational resources.

The Food Allergy Network
www.foodallergy.org

The Web site for the Food Allergy Network offers information about food allergies.

Children's Safety

National Resource Center for Health and Safety in Child Care
http://nrc.uchsc.edu/

The National Resource Center is funded by the Maternal and Child Health Bureau, U.S. Department of Health & Human Services, HRSA. NRC's primary mission is to promote health and safety in out-of-home child care settings throughout the nation.

National Safe Kids Campaign
http://www.safekids.org/

This Web site contains a wealth of information regarding child safety. The National SAFE KIDS Campaign is the first and only national non-profit organization dedicated solely to the prevention of unintentional childhood injury—the number one killer of children ages 14 and under.

U.S. Consumer Product Safety Commission (CPSC)
http://www.cpsc.gov/

The CPSC Web site contains information regarding the safety of children along with product safety and recall information.

Children's Nutrition

Child and Adult Care Food Program
http://www.fns.usda.gov/cnd/care/cacfp/

The USDA's Child and Adult Care Food Program plays a vital role in improving the quality of day care and making it affordable for many low-income families. About 2.6 million children receive daily meals and snacks through CACFP.

(Continued on next page)

Child Care Nutrition Resource System
http://www.nal.usda.gov/childcare/

The Web site for The Child Care Nutrition Resource System provides recipes, resources, and information on preparing nutritious meals and food safety. Day care providers can use this helpful information in conjunction with the Child and Adult Food Program.

Children's Literature & Literacy

Caldecott Award for Children's Books
http://www.ala.org/alsc/caldecott.html

This informative Web site focuses on the Caldecott Medal that was named in honor of nineteenth-century English illustrator Randolph Caldecott. It is awarded annually to the *artist* of the most distinguished American picture book for children. The Web site contains a listing of Caldecott winners along with other resources.

Early Literacy
http://www.earlyliterature.ecsd.net/

The Early Literacy Web site offers useful information in promoting early literacy in young children. Topics include issues, such as whole language, phonics, development, natural environment, direct teaching, and intervention.

Newbery Award for Children's Literature
http://www.ala.org/alsc/newbery.html

The Newbery Medal was named for eighteenth-century British bookseller John Newbery. It is awarded annually to the *author* of the most distinguished contribution to American literature for children. The Web site contains a list of Newbery winners along with other resources.

The Children's Literature Web Guide
http://www.acs.ucalgary.ca/~dkbrown/

This Web Guide contains a number of Internet resources on books for children and young adults.

Advocacy for Children, Programs, and Child Care Staff

Americans with Disabilities (ADA)
http://www.usdoj.gov/crt/ada/adahom1.htm

The ADA home page contains a wealth of resources concerning accessibility for people with disabilities. The site contains information about ADA regulations, education, employment, and parks and recreation, etc. Information about developing accessible play yards can be found at this site.

Children's Defense Fund
http://www.childrensdefense.org/

The Web site for the Children's Defense Fund contains numerous resources to help ensure the healthy growth and development of children to a successful passage to adulthood. The Children's Defense Fund is a private, nonprofit organization that is supported by foundations, corporation grants, and individual donations.

I Am Your Child Foundation (IAYC)
http://www.iamyourchild.org/

The I Am Your Child Foundation is a national, non-profit organization that raises awareness about the importance of early childhood development and school readiness. IAYC has variety of resources for parents, early childhood professionals, child advocates, health care providers, policymakers, and the media.

National Black Child Development Institute (NBCDI)
http://www.nbcdi.org

The Web site for the National Black Child Development Institute (NBCDI) provides information about this nonprofit organization. NBCDI provides and supports programs, workshops, and resources for African American children, their parents, and communities in early health and education, health, elementary and secondary education child welfare, and parenting.

(Continued on next page)

Prevent Child Abuse America
http://www.preventchildabuse.org

The focus of Prevent Child Abuse America is to build awareness, provide education, and inspire hope in the effort to prevent the abuse and neglect of our nation's children. The organization promotes and implements prevention efforts at local and national levels.

Interactive Web Sites for Children

100 Top Kids, Sites
http://www.100topkid.com/

This Web site contains 100 top sites for children. Examples include: Dr. Seuss's Seussville™ (Dr. Seuss™ site), Muppet™ World (the official Muppet site from the Jim Henson Company), How Stuff Works™ (hundreds of cool articles that explain "How Stuff Works"), National Geographic® Kids, plus 95 more.

National Wildlife Federation for Kids
http://www.nwf.org/kids/

This interactive Web site is for those children interested in wildlife. The site is divided into sections according to the age of the child: 1-3; 3-7; 7-13; and 13 and up. A newsletter is also available.

Smithsonian Institute's Kids' Collections
http://kids.si.edu/collecting/>

This Web site is related to "Collecting" rocks and minerals, stamps, coins, and unusual collections. This Web site requires the "Flash" and "Real Player" plug-ins.

Scholastic Kids' Games and Contests
http://www.scholastic.com/kids/home_flash.asp

The Kids Fun Online Home includes: Book Central, Card Factory, Games and Contests, Book Beat, Word of the Week, Kids Poll, Kids Council, Scholastic News Online, Software Station, Speak UP!, and TV Tune-in.

US Mint Just for Kids
http://www.usmint.gov/kids/

This Web site is designed to be a fun, educational tool—for students and teachers—that promotes interest in coins, the Mint, and U.S. history. It contains information about coins and games.

Older Adult Care Resources

AARP, Inc.
http://www.aarp.org/

AARP is a nonprofit membership organization dedicated to addressing the needs and interests of persons 50 and older. Through information and education, advocacy and service, AARP seeks to enhance the quality of life for all people by promoting independence, dignity and purpose.

Administration on Aging
www.aoa.gov/

The Administration on Aging (AoA), an agency in the U.S. Department of Health and Human Services, is one of the nation's largest providers of home- and community-based care for older persons and their caregivers. The AoA mission is to promote the dignity and independence of older people, and to help society prepare for an aging population. This site contains a wealth of information and links to related sites.

Adult Day Services Fact Sheet
(National Association of Adult Day Services)
www.ncoa.org/nadsa/ADS_factsheet.htm

For more than fifty years, NCOA has worked to promote the dignity, self-determination, and well-being of older persons through a wide variety of services and programs.

(Continued on next page)

Checklist on Adult Day Care Centers
(Metropolitan Area Agency on Aging, Minneapolis/St. Paul, Minnesota)
www.tcaging.org/com_adck.htm

Links people to information; assists community groups and providers with planning, coordination and development; and improves the quality of life for seniors and their families through local and regional initiatives.

Child and Adult Care Food Program
http://www.fns.usda.gov/cnd/care/cacfp/

The USDA's Child and Adult Care Food Program plays a vital role in improving the quality of day care and making it affordable for many low-income families. Over 70,000 adults in adult day care centers receive meals and snacks daily through CACFP.

DOROT
www.dorotusa.org

DOROT is a non-profit, multi-service agency that extends a lifeline of support to homebound and homeless elders.

Elder Abuse Prevention
http://www.aoa.gov/factsheets/abuse.html

This Administration on Aging fact sheet contains important information regarding the incidence and prevention of elder abuse.

Elderhostel
www.elderhostel.org

The nation's first and the world's largest educational and travel organization for adults age 55 and over.

National Association of Adult Day Services Association
www.ncoa.org/nadsa/directory/index.html

This directory will help you in your search for quality, community Adult Day Services. NADSA provides a wide range of adult day services to an ever-growing number of older Americans.

Ohio Association of Adult Day Services
www.seorf.ohiou.edu/~xx140

The mission of OAADS is to strengthen the ability of members to offer quality adult day services by providing education, advocacy, and leadership.

Orange County, California
www.oc.ca.gov/aging/Adult%20Day%20Care.htm

This Web site describes two distinct models of adult day care.

Pennsylvania Adult Day Services Association
www.padsa.org

The mission of the Pennsylvania Adult Day Service Association is to serve the interests of its members and to enhance the quality and professionalism of adult day service through advocacy, education, technical support, networking, research, and marketing.

South Dakota Adult Day Care
www.state.sd.us/social/ASA/Caregiver/Adult/daycare.htm

As an advocate for the elderly, Adult Services and Aging's mission is to foster and promote community-based and in-home services, so that elderly South Dakotans can avoid premature or inappropriate institutional care.

Wisconsin Adult Day Care
www.dhfs.state.wi.us/rl_DSL/AdultDayCare/AdultDCintro.htm

A day program that provides the elderly and other adults with services when their caregivers are at work or need relief.

Your Guide to Selecting an Adult Day Services Center
(National Association of Adult Day Services)
www.ncoa.org/nadsa/guide_2_ADS.htm

Promotes the concept of adult day services as a viable community-based option for disabled older persons within the larger constellation of long-term care services.

(Continued on next page)

Intergenerational Resources

Birmingham Public School System
www.birmingham.k12.mi.us/intergenerational.html

A dynamic and supportive network which anticipates, identifies, and meets the needs of older adults, promotes lifelong learning and independence, and encourages participation to enhance the quality of life for all.

Center for Intergenerational Learning
(Temple University)
www.temple.edu/CIL

This center is dedicated to strengthening communities by bringing generations together to meet the needs of individuals and families throughout the life cycle. This center:

- Creates opportunities for youth and elders to contribute to their communities.
- Promotes partnerships among organizations serving young people, families, and older adults.
- Helps organizations integrate intergenerational approaches into their program services.

Experience Corps
www.experiencecorps.org

Provides tutoring, homework assistance, and other supports to children, promotes the continued learning and growth of volunteers through training, team meetings, lectures, and reflection opportunities.

From the AARP Grandparent Center
www.aarp.org/getans/consumer/grandparents.html

The membership of AARP serves the broader community, improving the quality of life for all people as they get older. AARP focuses its efforts and resources in four areas: health and wellness; economic security and work; long-term care and independent living; and personal enrichment.

Generation Connection Society
www.genconn.ca

A non-profit society whose purpose is to develop educational programs and resources which foster positive intergenerational communication, help increase self esteem and promote greater personal and social responsibility.

Generations of Hope
www.hope4children.org

The long-term goal of Generations of Hope is to become a model for policy, legislation, and practice regarding the establishment of diverse, intergenerational neighborhoods which enfold our country's most endangered children into networks of caring, long-term relationships.

Generations Together
(University of Pittsburgh)
www.gt.pitt.edu

As an international center for intergenerational studies, Generations Together is dedicated to the development and understanding of programs that bring the young and the old together to share experiences that promote mutual growth and foster understanding between the generations.

Generations United (GU)
www.gu.org

This Website holds the nation's largest database of intergenerational programs. GU has been designated as the national clearinghouse for intergenerational Learn and Serve Programs.

Grand Parents as Caregivers—Questions on 2000 Census
(U.S. Administration on Aging)
www.aoa.gov/factsheets/grandparents.html

Provides leadership, technical assistance, and support to the national aging network of 57 State Units on Aging.

(Continued on next page)

Grandparent Caregivers
(Generations United)
www.gu.org/projg&o.htm

An organization focused on promoting inter-generational programs and policies, GU addresses the issue of relatives raising children from the perspectives of both the young and old.

Grand Parents and Grandchildren
(Population Division, Fertility & Family Statistics Branch, U.S. Census Bureau)
www.census.gov/population/www/socdemo/grandparents.html

This Web site focuses on volunteer service to one population: children with special or exceptional needs. Volunteers offer emotional support to child victims of abuse and neglect, tutoring children who lag behind in reading, mentoring troubled teens and young mothers, and caring for premature infants and children with physical disabilities and severe illnesses.

Grandparents and Relatives Raising Children
(New York Department for the Aging)
http://aging.state.ny.us/caring/grandparents/index.htm

The state funded Targeted Caregiver Initiative (TCI) was started in 1992 to address the needs of isolated caregivers in New York State, who are of frail family members and also raising young grandchildren.

Grandparents Resource Center
www.grc4usa.org

Provides advocacy and support services to grandparents raising grandchildren, and those seeking custody and visitation rights of their grandchildren.

Illinois Intergenerational Initiative
(Southern Illinois University)
www.siu.edu/offices/iii

Promotes an understanding of issues across generations is the goal of a small group of leaders and decision makers representing education, aging, and human services.

Intergenerational Child Care
(U.S. Administration for Children & Families)
http://nccic.org/pubs/intergen/igen-toc.html

A national resource that links information and people to complement, enhance, and promote the child care delivery system, working to ensure that all children and families have access to high-quality comprehensive services.

Intergenerational Education Program
(California Department of Education)
http://www.cde.ca.gov/cyfsbrach/Isp/intr-fact.htm

This educational program provides instructional and support services to K-12 students through the use of senior citizen volunteers (55+ years of age).

Intergenerational Innovations
www.intergenerate.org

A non-profit organization based in Seattle, that develops and implements creative programs and activities that bring children, youth, and elders together in volunteer service to each other and to our community through tutoring, mentoring, service learning, and computer activities.

Intergenerational Programs
(Delaware Division of Services for Aging and Adults)
www.dsaapd.com/intergen.htm

This Web site provides information focusing on providing support to grandparents and relative caregivers who are raising others' children.

Intergenerational Programs
(Illinois Department on Aging)
www.state.il.us/aging/intergen.htm

The Illinois Department of Aging spearheads a variety of intergenerational programs, one of which relies on older volunteers who help young children, kindergarten through third grade, with reading and other activities.

(Continued on next page)

Intergenerational Service Project
(Kansas State University)
www.ksu.edu/gerontology/ksuigsl.html

KSU coordinates and develops educational and training programs in aging, stimulates aging research, coordinates outreach activities, and serves as a referral center for information on aging resources in Kansas.

Intergenerational Subcommittee
(American Library Association)
www.ala.org/olos/intergenerational.html

This organization recommends, supports, and develops projects that encourage mutually beneficial, enjoyable library programs linking generations.

Massachusetts Intergenerational Network
http://home.earthlink.net/~toyateach/min.html

This network promotes quality intergenerational programming through education, training, and development activities.

Nanas N Papas
www.nanasnpapas.com

This Web site provides information on the best possible child care as well as exceptional career opportunities for mature caregivers. Offers unique career opportunities for individuals who enjoy children but not the stresses of day care or classroom environments.

National Academy for Teaching and Learning (North Texas State University)
www.unt.edu/natla/index.html

This academy promotes a lifespan approach to increasing understanding about aging issues through education and intergeneration. It educates youth about the sources that perpetuate ageist myths and stereotypes, age discrimination, and gerontophobic behavior.

National Family Caregivers Support Program—Grants to States
(Services for grandparents age 60 and over)
(U.S. Administration on Aging)
www.aoa.gov/oaa/status/faq%2Dcaregiving.html#24

The AoA Web site provides information about services, assistance with access to services, individual counseling, organization of support groups, and caregiver training, respite care, and supplemental services, on a limited basis.

National Grandparents Day
www.grandparents-day.com

Enlarging and enhancing the celebration of Grandparents Day by cultivating intergenerational activities throughout the year is the focus of this Web site.

OASIS Intergenerational Tutoring
www.oasisnet.org/institute/volunteer/tutor.html

OASIS is a national nonprofit educational organization designed to enhance the quality of life for mature adults. It creates opportunities for older adults to continue their personal growth and provide meaningful service to the community.

Wisconsin Intergenerational Network
www.wi-win.org/resources.htm

The Wisconsin Intergenerational Network is a statewide network of organizations and individuals who believe that interaction and cooperation among generations contribute to the health and well-being of individuals and society.

Perkins III Legislation

The Carl D. Perkins Vocational and Technical Education Act of 1998 (Perkins III) provides financial support for vocational-technical education programs that prepare students for further learning and for a wide range of high-skill, high-wage careers. Perkins III focuses on high-quality programs that:

- **Integrate academic and vocational education.** Solving the problems facing industry involves the use of applied communications, mathematics, and science.

- **Provide students with strong experience in, and understanding of, all aspects of industry.** If vocational-technical skills are limited to narrowly defined job tasks, it is difficult to integrate advanced academic skills. Covering all aspects of the industry provides a more complete academic context.

- **Promote student attainment of challenging academic and vocational and technical standards.** Perkins III helps ensure that students learn the skills and knowledge they need to meet challenging state standards, as well as industry-recognized skill standards. Meeting both kinds of standards will increase students' successes on the job.

- **Address the needs of individuals who are members of special populations.** Students in special populations need equal access to activities. The goal is to address the needs of these individuals to prepare them for further learning and for high skill, high wage careers.

- **Involve parents and employers.** Through advisory councils, parents, students, teachers, and representatives of business and industry, labor organizations, special populations, and other interested individuals are involved in developing, implementing, and evaluating vocational and technical education programs.

- **Provide strong linkages between secondary and postsecondary education.** Cooperation between secondary and postsecondary education and institutions can be a win-win situation for all concerned. Articulation agreements for transferring credit, usually between high school and vocational-technical centers, support students in acquiring the skills they need for future success.

- **Develop, improve, and expand the use of technology.** Today's workforce is driven by advanced technology and fast-paced innovation. Experience with high technology and communications will prepare students to adapt to a continually changing workforce.

- **Provide professional development for teachers, counselors, and administrators.** Opportunities for professional development, such as workplace internships for business experience or training in all aspects of industry, strengthen vocational-technical programs. Opportunities are provided for both vocational-technical and academic personnel.

Tech Prep

Perkins III reauthorized Tech Prep, a program that prepares students for careers by combining two years of secondary education with two years of postsecondary education or an apprenticeship program (referred to as 2+2 articulation). Perkins encourages work-based learning, new technologies, and partnerships among business, industry, labor, and education.

Workforce Investment Partnership Act

Perkins III works in conjunction with the Workforce Investment Partnership Act of 1998. This legislation created a "one-stop" coordinated system for Federal aid programs for vocational education and other types of education and job training. Programs under Perkins are partners in this one-stop delivery system. The most important aspect of the Act is its focus on meeting the needs of business for skilled workers, as well as the training, education, and employment needs of individuals.

(Continued on next page)

Accountability

To promote continuous program improvement, Perkins III created a performance accountability system. The system uses "core indicators" for annual levels of performance. Core indicators include:

1. Student attainment of specific academic and vocational-technical skill proficiencies.
2. Student attainment of a secondary school diploma or its recognized equivalent, a proficiency credential in conjunction with a secondary school diploma, or a postsecondary degree or credential.
3. Placement in, retention, and completion of postsecondary education or advanced training, placement in military service, or placement or retention in employment.
4. Student participation in and completion of vocational and technical education programs that lead to nontraditional training and employment. Nontraditional employment refers to an occupation or field of work that employs less than 25 percent of people from one gender.

Funding Uses

Funds made available to an eligible recipient under this title may be used to:

1. Involve parents, businesses, and labor organizations in the design, implementation, and evaluation of vocational and technical education programs.
2. Provide career guidance and academic counseling for students participating in vocational and technical education programs.
3. Provide work-related experience, such as internships, cooperative education, school-based enterprises, entrepreneurship, and job shadowing that are related to vocational and technical education programs.
4. Provide programs for special populations.
5. Provide for local education and business partnerships.
6. Assist vocational and technical student organizations.
7. Provide mentoring and support services.
8. Lease, purchase, upgrade or adapt equipment, including instructional aides.
9. Provide teacher preparation programs that assist individuals who are interested in becoming vocational and technical education instructors, including individuals with experience in business and industry.
10. Improve or develop new vocational and technical education courses.
11. Provide support for family and consumer sciences programs.
12. Provide vocational and technical education programs for adults and school dropouts to complete their secondary school education.
13. Provide assistance to students to find an appropriate job and continue their educational pursuits.
14. Support nontraditional training and employment activities.

Integrating Academic & Vocational Education

Perkins Act

The Carl D. Perkins Vocational and Technical Education Act of 1998 (Perkins III) requires vocational-technical programs to integrate vocational and academic education. Such integration relates academic knowledge and skills to "real-world" career and technical skills. This integration allows students to relate information gained in academic courses to the knowledge and skills developed in vocational-technical courses. The development of "integrated" skills provides students with a wider range of career opportunities and expands their continuing education options.

The Changing Workplace

The need to integrate vocational-technical programs was prompted by dramatic changes in the workplace. Skillful hands, while still important, are no longer sufficient in today's technolgy-driven work environment. Jobs today require people with the ability to read complex manuals, analyze data, organize information, work in teams, solve problems, and make decisions.

The changing nature of the workplace calls for a new kind of worker—one who must be prepared to work differently. Workers who have job-specific skills, but lack the academic foundations of mathematics, science, communications, and all aspects of industry, will be left behind as technology advances. Likewise, employees entering the workplace with strong academic skills but who lack technical abilities will be of little value to their employer. The need for an educational strategy that provides workers with the right mix of technical skills and academic skills is clear.

Integrated Programs

Many employers have always thought that education and training should be a "total" experience. That educational strategy is found in the integration of vocational and academic education. A successfully integrated program has the following features:

- It includes the academic areas of science, mathematics, and communications (reading, writing, speaking, and listening). Stellar programs also include social studies and the arts.
- Basic as well as advanced skills are addressed in each of the academic areas.
- Academic skills are taught in the context of the occupational area being studied.
- Integration requires that the content of the vocational curriculum and the content of the academic curriculum be coordinated to reinforce one another.

Establishing an Integrated Program

Instructors seeking to establish an integrated program sometimes encounter resistance from peers, administrators, students, and sometimes parents. This initial resistance can lead to frustration. It is important to remember that integrated programs require the cooperation and support of many people. However, you will find that it is worth the effort when your students succeed. A successfully integrated program depends on:

- Collaboration between vocational and academic teachers.
- The development of integrated curricula.
- Integrated instructional strategies.
- Administrative support of integrated programs.

Developing Cooperation

Integration can motivate students and provide them with a practical understanding of problems and opportunities. It can prompt them to be more attentive to the skills that they will need to move into college or the workplace. Also, by fostering communication between academic and vocational-technical instructors, it will increase cooperation.

(Continued on next page)

The key element in an integrated program is the working relationship between academic and vocational-technical instructors. To take the first step, you will need to make sure the academic teachers are fully aware of the goals and advantages of an integrated program. Here are some useful strategies to follow:

- Invite your fellow academic instructors to your classroom, office, or lab.
- Provide them with copies of your textbooks, instructional materials, courses of study or course outlines, and any vocabulary lists or special projects that you have students complete each term.
- Invite them to attend your advisory committee meetings.
- Invite them to participate in vocational student organization activities.
- Visit your fellow academic instructors' classrooms upon invitation.
- Ask to see the academic textbooks your students are using.
- Work with the academic instructors as equal partners when planning curriculum.

These are only first steps in bridging the gap between vocational-technical and academic education. You should continue the process by:

- Engaging academic instructors in serious discussions regarding how each can be mutually supportive of what the students are expected to learn.
- Discussing how content can be applied in a relevant and meaningful way.
- Familiarizing your academic colleagues with the related communications, mathematics, and science applications found in the ***Child & Adult Care Professionals*** textbook.
- Encouraging your peers to incorporate academic applications into their teaching.
- Gaining administrative support for the integration of vocational-technical and academic curricula by involving administrators in the planning process.

Persistence Pays Off!

In obtaining the cooperation of your fellow instructors, persistence is important. Your colleagues need to be convinced that an integrated program will be of benefit to everyone. They need to know that the aim of integration is to improve the communications, mathematics, and science skills of your students. Remember, integration is bringing vocational and academic teachers together. Cooperation is needed for curriculum development, scheduling, team teaching practices, and the development of assessments. The success of an integrated program also depends on the cooperation and organization, as well as the support, of the administration. The following strategies will be of assistance:

- **Instructional material must be a natural part of course content.** Such material should not appear to be special or unusual. The materials should relate naturally to the subject matter and be "integrated," as a natural part of the course content.
- **Encourage teamwork.** All student activities should be conducted in teams. This is important for laboratory activities as well as for program presentations. Use of such teams also helps students develop interpersonal skills. It also helps mirror the modern workplace, where problem solving in a team framework has been proven to be effective. Remember, though, that the use of teams may also create conflict and disagreements within the team. You should be prepared to help resolve these.
- **Encourage student entries in science fairs and other competitions.** This will help develop support for integration. It will also validate your approach.

(Continued on next page)

- **Encourage students to develop portfolios.** Instruct students to use their portfolios to organize information related to career planning, their course of study, results of student assessments, and student-produced materials.

- **Organize public presentations.** This is an effective public relations strategy. Such presentations can be made before professional organizations, conferences, and individual schools. Organize selected students into a "traveling team." These students can present and demonstrate the project work they completed in class. They can also present their portfolios.

- **Encourage simulation.** For example, you might ask a team of students to set up a company to develop and market a product. The team might then develop a business plan and product idea. The team would then make a formal marketing presentation to school administrators, asking permission to carry out their plan to simulate industry at work.

Measuring Success

The integration of vocational and academic education usually results in an individual who is better prepared to enter the workforce. Research has also shown that students make dramatic gains in achievement when they are given more challenging work that integrates vocational academic education. The success of an integrated program can be measured by the following factors:

- Expanding enrollment.
- Fewer discipline problems.
- Respect of your peers and administration.
- Student success in competitive events, such as FCCLA Competitive Events and SkillsUSA Championships.
- Requests by teachers, students, and community members to visit your program.
- Identification of your program by the state as an exemplary program.
- Requests to make presentations to other schools and at state and national conferences.

The Advisory Committee

The most important resource a technical instructor has is an active local advisory committee. Such a committee is recommended or even mandated by many state vocational technical education boards. The purpose of the advisory committee is to assist in the overall planning and implementation of an early childhood or older adult care curriculum that meets the needs of the industry and leads to job placement of students.

Career and technical education programs need to collaborate with the business community. The advisory committee provides this necessary link and can help:

- Determine the occupational needs in your area.
- Set up long-term and short-term goals for the program.
- Keep the curriculum current in terms of job requirements.
- Give advice concerning work and health standards.
- Create good rapport between businesses and the school's career and technical education program.
- Help find suitable work experiences.
- Assist in securing job placements for students.
- Assist in the evaluation of the program.
- Provide in-service training for instructors.

To organize an advisory committee, consider the following steps:

1. Check with your school board for policies regarding advisory committees.

2. Secure the names of people who are important in various aspects of the human service industry.

3. Write each potential advisory committee member a letter asking for his/her service.

4. When the replies are received, another letter should be sent thanking them for their willingness to serve and give a time and location for the first meeting.

It is usually wise to ask advisory committee members to serve for a minimum of one year. That way, those members whose attendance is lacking or are noncontributing, may be dropped after one year. Remember to send a letter thanking them for their service, and then secure someone else to take their place. Those members who have been active may be continued by mutual agreement. Committee membership should be rotated so that you are never working with a totally "new" committee.

Once the advisory committee has been formed, the first meeting is of vital importance. The meeting should be well-organized and short in duration. Within three days following the meeting, a copy of the minutes should be sent to each advisory committee member.

The use of an advisory committee can be one of the most effective means of keeping the community informed, keeping courses up-to-date, and selling the school board on the importance of career and technical education.

Work-Based Learning

In order to provide real work experience, schools and businesses team together to provide students with work-based learning related to a chosen career. The chart below shows types of work-based learning opportunities you may encounter. More detailed information follows the chart.

Type of Program	Description	Purpose
Service Learning	Students participate in an organized work experience that meets the needs of the community.	Apply classroom learning to real-life situations in communities; for personal growth and learning civic responsibility.
Job Shadowing	A student follows someone on the job.	Learn about a career through watching and listening.
Co-op	Students are employed in a job directly related to their program of study. Schedules vary with time split between school and the job.	Apply classroom learning to work situations.
Internships	Students work alongside current workers, gaining experience while completing general courses required for high school graduation.	Supervised practical training, usually near the end of academic preparation.
School-to-Apprenticeship	Students complete high school studies and, at the same time, participate in more structured on-the-job training.	Prepares people for professional employment in a skilled occupation.
Apprenticeship	Combines structured, paid work and on-the-job training.	Prepares people for professional employment in a skilled occupation.
On-the-Job Training	Employees attend training on new products and tools.	Helps workers maintain high professional standards.
Mentoring	An adult worker or supervisor introduces the student or new employee to a job, a profession, or a skill area.	Model workplace behavior and skills. Students can turn to mentor for feedback, support, and career guidance.

(Continued on next page)

Service Learning

Service Learning programs combine meaningful community service with academic learning, personal growth, and civic responsibility. In these programs, students apply classroom learning to real-life situations in the community. They are exposed to the world of work in a setting where they experience firsthand the needs of the real world. They experience a setting in which they can improve their communities, learn skills they can use at future worksites, and develop a sense of caring for others.

Service programs provide structured time for students to reflect on what they did and saw during the community service activity. Students often keep a journal throughout the experience. Service Learning programs provide opportunities for:

- Exploration of new roles and interests.
- Taking responsibility for and accepting consequences of your own actions.
- Seeing how classroom learning is needed for real life.
- Acquiring practical skills.
- Developing insight, judgment, caring, and understanding.
- Knowledge and exploration of careers.
- An opportunity to relate to people.

Job Shadowing

Some employers may provide job-shadowing experiences in order to expand awareness of a related field. *Job shadowing* involves brief student visits to a variety of workplaces, during which time students "shadow," observe, and ask questions of individual workers. Classroom exercises conducted prior to and following the job shadowing help students connect their experience to their coursework, career pathways, related skills requirements, and future educational options.

Job shadowing:
- Provides a realistic view of a specific job.
- Allows students to observe employees on the job.
- Allows students time to ask questions.

Cooperative Education

Some schools offer cooperative education programs. These are school-based programs that combine classroom study with hands-on experience. Following a carefully developed plan, students work in jobs related to their major field of study while attending school. They can relate or apply what they are learning in class to their major field of study while attending school. Likewise, they can relate the work experiences to what they are learning in class.

Both students and employers benefit from cooperative education programs. While at work, students have the opportunity to develop their technical skills and gain experience in working with other employees and clients. At the same time, they are often paid for their work, which helps to offset their school expenses. Students also receive graded academic credit. Employers benefit because most students have a genuine interest in the field and are motivated to do a good job and learn all they can.

Internships

Many schools offer programs in which students can serve internships at local businesses. An *internship* is supervised practical training. Students work alongside current workers, gaining experience while completing the general courses required for high school graduation.

Internships may be paid or unpaid. Internships allow students to observe the world of work and develop work skills targeted to their chosen career field. Students also learn work-related terminology and the culture and expectations of the workforce.

(Continued on next page)

School-to-Apprenticeship

An internship can be formalized into a school-to-apprenticeship program. An *apprenticeship* is a training program that prepares people for professional employment in a skilled occupation. School-to-apprenticeship programs allow student apprentices to complete their high school studies and, at the same time, participate in more structured on-the-job training.

In the student apprentice program, a sponsor and the apprentice sign an apprenticeship agreement. This type of agreement provides that the apprentice does the work and completes related studies. The sponsor must do everything possible to keep the apprentice employed and must meet apprenticeship standards.

After graduation from high school, the apprentice goes to work full time for the sponsor and continues training on the job, taking any additional instruction required to perform the work.

Apprenticeship

Apprenticeship programs are designed to help people develop the skills needed by industries today. These are operated much like the school-to-apprenticeship programs previously discussed but with broader applications and usually on a post-secondary level. They may be sponsored by labor groups, employers, employer associations, or a combination of these. Formal apprenticeship programs typically last three or four years.

Apprentices participating in a registered apprenticeship program enter into an agreement with the sponsor. The apprentice agrees to perform the work and complete the related study. The sponsor agrees to make every effort to keep the apprentice employed and to comply with the standards established for the program.

Upon entry into the apprenticeship program, apprentices are paid a progressively increasing schedule of wages. As the apprentices demonstrate satisfactory progress in both the on-the-job training and related instruction, they are advanced in accordance with the wage schedule as outlined in the registered apprenticeship standards.

On-the-Job Training

To stay current, employees must continue their training. Employers sponsor training programs or send representatives to the workplace to teach employees about new products and tools. These learning opportunities help workers maintain high professional standards.

Mentoring

Mentors often work with supervisors and classroom teachers to guide students in the work experiences described previously. *Mentors* are usually experienced workers who have the skills and knowledge that the students need to learn to be effective on the job. They might also be other adults such as work-study coordinators, work experience counselors, or job coaches.

Mentors work on-to-one with each student. Mentors can often:

- Serve as coaches and on-the-job instructors.
- Provide students with feedback.
- Provide instruction in the culture and expectations of the workplace.
- Serve as role models for students.
- Provide occupational information related to a particular industry.

Working with Employers

Work-based learning programs such as internships, apprenticeships, and cooperative education programs provide valuable work experience for students. In addition, mentors work with supervisors and classroom instructors to guide students in these work experiences. As students see the connections between school work and the knowledge and skills required by good careers, they understand the importance of learning and can make better decisions about their future. The extent of work experience and mentoring depends on the arrangements made between the school and the employers. For an apprenticeship, which might last several years, the mentoring relationship will be more involved and require more planning.

Written Agreements

Once businesses have committed to providing work experiences or mentoring, agreements should be established. Topics to address include:

- What is expected from the employer.
- How students will get to and from the job.
- The hours students will work per day and per week.
- Expectations regarding attendance.
- On-the-job supervision and risk insurance.
- What the employer can expect from the school site (numbers of visits by school personnel to the job site during a term; who to contact in case of a problem or emergency).

Once both parties have agreed on how these issues will be handled, draw up a written training description that will be signed by the employer, a school official, the student, and the student's parent or guardian.

Aligning Work & School Learning

Once the work-related issues have been worked out, discuss with employers the knowledge and skills the students will be able to take from the classroom to the work site. If employers feel that skills are missing, instructors may be able to add them to the classroom curriculum. Ask employers to detail the experiences they will provide for each student, and the new skills the student will develop. At this time, provide suggestions for creating an optimal work experience.

It is also important to conduct periodic meetings regarding the effectiveness of the program and the need for occasional adjustments for continued improvement. Teamwork between teachers, mentors, and employers will lead to success for all.

Recruiting & Training Mentors

A good mentoring program will enhance the success of work experiences, and this success depends on recruiting good mentors—sometimes a difficult task. Some people may be shy about volunteering but may readily agree to serve when asked and given guidance by the school personnel and employer setting up the program.

Each semester, or whenever there is another group of employers providing mentors, school site personnel may want to conduct a brief training program. In this program (which is best limited to no more than four hours), instructors and program coordinators can discuss the role of mentors and the school's expectation of the mentoring program.

Work-Based Learning Agreement

Student Name _____ Social Security No. _____

Address _____ Telephone _____

Birth Date _____ Work Permit No. _____

Student Career Objective _____

Dates of Employment _____ Hours Per Week _____ Pay _____

Employer _____

Address _____

Supervisor _____ Telephone _____

Student Responsibilities:

1. The student will arrive at work on time and will maintain a good attendance record.

2. If unable to report to work for any reason, the student will notify the employer and school coordinator.

3. The student will adhere to company policy; employment may be terminated for the same reasons as regular employees.

4. The student will report job problems to the employer and school coordinator.

5. The student is responsible for his/her own transportation.

6. The student will maintain regular attendance and satisfactory work performance at school; failure to do so will be grounds for dismissal from the job.

7. The student will report to school for designated meetings and instruction related to the work-based learning assignment.

8. The student is not eligible for unemployment compensation; nor may he/she use wages received under this program as credit for unemployment compensation benefits.

School Responsibilities:

1. The program is under the direct supervision of the student's instructor and/or a school coordinator.

2. The student will receive related instruction from the school instructor during employment.

3. The instructor and/or school coordinator will visit the student and training supervisor on a regular basis at the training site.

4. The school agrees to award credits earned in the Work-Based Learning Program toward the student's high school diploma.

5. Instructors and/or school coordinators will hold regular meetings with students to discuss progress, issues, and concerns.

(Continued on next page)

Employer Responsibilities:

1. The employer will adhere to all state and federal regulations regarding employment including child labor laws, minimum wage laws, and worker's compensation.

2. The student will be given a variety of work assignments and will be supervised by an experienced employee.

3. The employer will make a periodic evaluation of job progress on a rating form provided by the school.

4. The employer will arrange a conference with the school coordinator when a student problem arises.

5. The employer will provide necessary safety instruction throughout the student's training period.

6. The employer will not employ a student learner to displace a regular worker.

7. The employer is not liable to the unemployment compensation fund for wages paid to the student while under the training program.

8. The employer agrees to follow the training plan developed by the program's school-site instructors and on-the-job supervisors.

9. The employer agrees to notify the school coordinator if the student is absent without notification.

10. The employer agrees to permit the school's representatives to visit the student and supervisor at the place of employment to determine progress, obtain direct feedback, and to make adjustments in the training plan whenever necessary.

11. The employer will hold regular meetings for student learner and supervisor to discuss progress, issues, and concerns.

12. The employer agrees to provide adequate equipment, materials, and other facilities required in order to provide an appropriate learning experience for the student learner.

We, the undersigned, agree to the conditions and statements contained herein.

Student _____ **Date** _____

Parent/Guardian _____ **Date** _____

Employer _____ **Date** _____

Instructor/Coordinator _____ **Date** _____

Articulation Agreements

The goal of career and technical education is to prepare students for rewarding careers once they have completed their formal education. Preparation for a successful job today almost always requires some form of postsecondary education or training. Cooperation between secondary and postsecondary educators and institutions makes provides a more effective means of preparing students for high-skill, high wage careers. This form of cooperative communication is called *articulation*.

Usually, articulation is between high school and vocational-technical centers and one or more postsecondary institutions. A postsecondary institution could be an apprenticeship program, a public or private community or technical college, or a four-year college or university.

Articulation Agreements

Articulation occurs when agreement is reached on the identified competencies, or course curricula, and performance levels that will be recognized for credit between the institutions involved. Articulated courses may receive partial or complete course credit. Often, a high school will articulate with one or more postsecondary institutions.

Articulation lessens the duplication of curriculum and therefore, makes it easier for students to make the transition from high school to higher education. Some of advantages of articulation include:

• Decreases duplication of instruction.
• Fosters communications among faculty members.
• Improves program quality.
• Can increase program enrollments.

A Win/Win Proposition

Articulation can be a win/win proposition for institutions as well as students at both levels. To make articulation successful, there are some essential practices that should be considered:

1. **Mutual benefits for all.** Each institution should set mutual goals and identify how students will benefit from an articulated program.
2. **Leadership and commitment.** There must be a strong commitment from members of both educational systems, including:
   • School Boards
   • Boards of Trustees
   • Administrators
   • Placement Coordinators
   • Counselors
   • Curriculum Directors
   • Faculty Members
   • Parents
   • Students
3. **Constant facility involvement.** Communications channels should be identified early in the process and kept open at all times.
4. **Competency-based curricula.** Standards for validating competencies and granting equivalencies must be established.
5. **Written articulation agreements.** There should be signed commitments from all institutions involved so that there is a formal record of understanding.

All Aspects of Industry

The Carl D. Perkins Vocational and Technical Education Act of 1998 (Perkins III) supports programs that provide students with strong experience in, and understanding of, all aspects of industry. This includes the following issues, as they relate to the trade:

- planning
- management
- finances
- technical and production skills
- underlying principles of technology
- labor/personnel
- community issues
- health, safety, and environmental issues.

By providing students with an understanding of all aspects of an industry, such an approach will help you to:

- **Empower students to make career choices.** Programs that provide the skills for only one job do not always provide students with career choices. Students may be unprepared to change career goals or to cope with labor market changes. Teaching all aspects of industry gives students transferable skills, such as planning and management. These skills expand their opportunities.

- **Enable students to adapt to technology change.** Students who have skills in all aspects of industry, together with academic skills, are better prepared to adapt to changes in technology throughout their careers.

- **Involving students in economic development.** If programs prepare students only to fill current job openings, then students will compete for a limited number of jobs and have a limited income potential. However, students who have experience in areas such as planning, management, and community issues will be presented with more career choices.

Aspect of Industry	Description
Planning	Various forms of ownership; relationship of the industry to economic, political, and social context.
Management	Methods typically used to manage enterprises.
Finances	Accounting and financial decisions.
Technical and Production Skills	Production techniques.
Underlying Principles of Technology	Study of the mathematical and scientific principles of technology.
Labor Issues	Worker rights and responsibilities.
Community Issues	The impact of the enterprise and the industry on the community.
Health, Safety, and Environmental Issues	Consider these as they relate to both the workers and the community.

Performance Assessment

Performance assessment is perhaps best defined by what it is *not*. Performance assessment is not a testing strategy. Rather, it is a reflection of the way performance is assessed in the real world. In that world—the world of work—employee evaluations are not determined on the basis of a test. The quality of their performance rather is measured through observation and evaluation of tasks relevant to the work being done.

The outcome, similarly, is not a "grade" in the traditional classroom sense of the word. Rather, the observer fills out a questionnaire—a rubric—and submits a report to the person in charge of promotions and salary increases. Performance assessment attempts to apply this model to the teaching/learning environment.

Authentic Use of Information

A common model of assessment in the classroom is to teach the chapter, then stop and test the students. Performance assessment changes this pattern. The textbook becomes a resource for learning; it becomes a means to an end rather than the end in itself.

When students leave school they will need to use books and other sources to find information on specific subjects. Perhaps they will need to make an oral presentation to a specific audience, design a display, produce a video, or research a consumer question and write a persuasive letter. These kinds of tasks all use information in an "authentic," or real-world, way.

The same is true of performance assessment. Students are engaged in tasks in which they craft products. The instructor is the coach who guides the students' work. He or she provides models of excellent work and gives feedback along the way. Performance assessment tasks get students highly involved in constructing all types of products, and this active involvement results in meaningful learning. The result of this way of teaching and learning is, thus, both process *and* product.

The word *authentic* used with performance assessment means that the performance uses information, concepts, and skills in ways that people use them in the larger world. School should be a valid preparation for what is required in the larger world.

Performance Assessment & Thinking Skills

Thinking skills provide the "verbs" that drive the action in performance assessment tasks. These skills include getting information, processing it, and using it to make a product. Thinking skills include those activities related to understanding the audience (the "target market" for the product in the real-world analog) and crafting a product that fulfills a certain purpose with that audience. The assessment of the student's work should not only look at the final product but should also assess the processes that lead to the final product.

A performance task can be broken down into a process that requires the following thinking skills:

- **Getting the information:** Finding, completing, counting, collecting, reading, listening, defining, describing, identifying, listing, matching, naming, observing (using all the senses), recording, reciting, selecting, scanning.
- **Working with the information:** Comparing, contrasting, classifying, sorting, distinguishing, explaining why, inferring, sequencing, analyzing, synthesizing, generalizing, evaluating, making analogies, making models, and/or reasoning.
- **Using the information for a purpose:** Informing, persuading, motivating.
- **Using information to craft a product/presentation:** Speaking, debating, singing, writing, surveying, designing, drawing, computing, constructing, demonstrating, acting out.
- **Using information to communicate with specific audiences:** Such as peers, younger, older, informed, uninformed, friendly, hostile, apathetic, homogeneous, or diverse groups.

(Continued on next page)

Different Learning Styles & Preferences

Some learners prefer to understand the connections between ideas and excel in the skills of critical analysis. These students are good at predicting, comparing and contrasting, and analyzing. Other learners enjoy organizing information and excel in remembering the details. A third group of learners engages in creative problem solving and uses productive, divergent thinking skills. A fourth group is best at tasks that require interpersonal skills. This group is good at interviewing and working in teams. They focus on attitudes, motivations, feelings, and opinions and are more self-aware than most. Some students prefer to write while others like oral presentations; still others enjoy constructive things. All learning styles are important and students should not use only the style in which they excel, but should work on tasks that require other styles so that they can expand their competency.

Emphasis on Teamwork

Although performance assessment provides chances for both individual and team learning, there is a particularly strong emphasis on cooperation, or teamwork. Teamwork is highly valued in the world. Businesses assess employees on interpersonal skills defined as the ability to:

- Establish and maintain positive working relationships within/outside the employees' team.
- Work toward department goals.
- Work well in a team environment.
- Display an ability/willingness to understand viewpoints of others.

Performance assessment provides an opportunity for students to experience and nurture these vital skills. As a bonus, teamwork is often an initial step to getting students actively engaged and allows for a diversity of ideas to emerge.

Sometimes, an entire project is done through teamwork, with individual students assuming responsibility and accountability for their specific tasks. For example, if the team's task is to create a thematic unit plan, each person on the team should have a lesson activity to create. The whole team can work together to plan all of the elements of the thematic unit. The individual's assessment is for each student's contribution to the project as a whole. There is no team grade for the unit plan. Individuals are accountable for their work and the team has a goal for overall quality.

Attitudes and Mental Habits

A student's success will depend as much on his or her attitudes and mental habits as on the use of information and appropriate thinking skills. Performance tasks allow both students and instructors the opportunity to observe what attitudes and habits are operating as work on a task progresses. Examples of these include individual responsibility; valuing teamwork; showing initiative, diligence, and self-confidence; integrity and behaving ethically; intellectual risk-taking; persistence, flexibility, and adaptability; concern for accuracy, precision, and quality of thought and action; a questioning and problem-posing view of learning; respect for the democratic process; empathy, tolerance, and caring for others; and respect for diverse human endeavors, including academic arts and technical skills.

The Performance Task

While knowledge can be assessed by a written test, skills must be assessed by performance. A performance assessment does just what the term implies—it is an instrument to determine whether or not the student can actually perform the competency in a job-like setting to a minimum standard.

Following are some steps to take in developing and conducting performance assessments.

1. **Determine exactly what should be tested.**
2. **Determine whether process, product, or both are critical.** Process is how the learner performs the task; product is the end result.
3. **Design the assessment tasks.** The assessment task should be designed to require the student to demonstrate attainment of the performance objectives.

(Continued on next page)

4. **Specify the performance criteria.** In most cases the criterion or standards components of the student performance objectives will be specific enough to serve as the criteria for the performance test.

5. **Determine how the performance criteria or test items will be scored.** Two common methods are used to evaluate the learner's degree of competence: a rating scale and a checklist. Performance checklists have several advantages over rating scales. They are easier to score and are also more objective.

6. **Determine the minimum acceptable score.** One approach that may make it easy is to include only essential process- and product-related items. If all of the items are essential, the learner must demonstrate achievement of each performance criterion.

7. **Draft the test.** Three sections are important to a performance test: preparation, student instruction, and the scoring guide.

8. **Try out the test.** Try out the test with a colleague and one or two students before using it to evaluate all students. It is important that items to be evaluated are precise, observable, and clearly worded.

9. **Conduct the performance test.** Prepare the work area and provide students with all necessary equipment, tools, materials, instruments, references, drawings, and other items required to complete the test. The testing situation should require the same equipment, content, sequence, and conditions used in the instruction.

10. **Plan for feedback.** Provide students with an opportunity to ask questions and discuss their experiences after testing is completed. Discuss with students their individual strengths and weaknesses.

Assessing Tasks

Attention should be focused on how the performance tasks are helping build an understanding of housing and design concepts. Rubrics and classroom assessment lists can be the main criteria used to assess performance tasks.

Rubrics

A rubric is a set of descriptions of the quality of a process and/or a product. It is designed to lay out a continuum of quality from very excellent to poor. If two or more instructors are assessing the same type of performance, then using the same rubric will help them both view the assignments in the same way. A rubric for assessing portfolios can be found on pages 129-130 of this guide.

Classroom Lists

The rubric is not a tool for students. Each teacher who uses the rubric makes his or her own classroom assessment list. That classroom assessment list uses terms the students can easily understand. Classroom lists are guidelines. If a student meets every guideline of a classroom list in an excellent manner, the instructor would likely assess the product at the highest rubric level.

While the rubric remains unchanged from instructor to instructor, the classroom assessment lists likely will change. Each instructor, in other words, will decide how best to translate the rubric into a useful list of guidelines for a particular class of students. It should be noted that after a few experiences using classroom assessment lists, students can make their own list of guidelines.

Students' Self-Assessment

The ability to self-assess and plan for improvement is an important life skill. Through self-assessment, students learn to study their own work thoughtfully and identify what they have done well and where they need improvement. When students are taught to use the instructions in the performance task, the assessment list, and examples of excellent work, they learn to become true self-starters and critical thinkers.

Portfolios as Assessment

A portfolio is a collection of samples of a person's work, carefully selected and refined in order to reflect the individual's skills and knowledge. *See pages 114 to 130 of this guide for more information on career portfolios.*

(Continued on next page)

Assessment Strategies Chart

Strategies	Advantages	Disadvantages
Objective Measures • Multiple choice • Matching • Item sets • True/false	• Reliable, easy to validate • Objective, if designed effectively • Low cost, efficient • Automated administration • Lends to equating	• Measures cognitive knowledge effectively • Limited on other measures • Not a good measure of overall performance
Written Measures • Essays • Restricted response • Written simulations • Case analysis • Problem-solving exercises	• Face validity (real life) • In-depth assessment • Measures writing skills and higher level skills • Reasonable developmental costs and time	• Subjective scoring • Time consuming and expensive to score • Limited breadth • Difficult to equate • Moderate reliability
Oral Measures • Oral examinations • Interviews	• Measures communications and interpersonal skills • In-depth assessment with varied stimulus materials • Learner involvement	• Costly and time consuming • Limited reliability • Narrow sample of content • Scoring difficult, need multiple raters
Simulated Activities • In-basket • Computer simulations	• Moderate reliability • Performance-based measure	• Costly and time consuming • Difficult to score, administer, and develop
Portfolio & Product Analysis • Work samples • Projects • Work diaries and logs • Achievement records	• Provides information not normally available • Learner involvement • Face validity (real life) • Easy to collect information	• Costly to administer • Labor and paper intensive • Difficult to validate or equate • Biased toward best samples or outstanding qualities
Performance Measures • Demonstrations • Presentations • Performances • Production work	• Observation • Job-related • Relatively easy to administer • In-depth assessment • Face validity	• Rater training required • Hard to equate • Subjective scoring • Time consuming if breadth is needed
Performance Records • References • Performance rating forms • Parental rating	• Efficient • Low cost • Easy to administer	• Low reliability • Subjective • Hard to equate • Rater judgment
Self-evaluation	• Learner involvement and empowerment • Learner responsibility • Measures dimensions not available otherwise	• May be biased or unrealistic

Special Populations

The Carl D. Perkins Vocational and Technical Education Act of 1998 (Perkins III) includes addressing the needs of special populations in order to make sure they have equal access to all activities provided in educational programs. The definition of *special populations* includes people with disabilities and other barriers to educational achievement, such as limited English proficiency (LEP) and learning disabilities.

Perkins III programs must submit plans for how they will identify and adopt strategies to overcome barriers that result in limited access to vocational-technical education programs. The plan also must include a description of how programs will be designed to enable members of special populations to meet required performance measures. School districts or technical colleges must track and report special population student attainment of performance measures.

Individuals with Disabilities

Perkins III uses the American Disabilities Act (ADA) definition of individuals with disabilities. Such an individual has a physical or mental impairment that substantially limits one or more major life activities, has a record of such an impairment, or is regarded as having such an impairment. Major life activities are those that an average person can perform with little or no difficulty such as walking, breathing, seeing, hearing, speaking, learning, and working. Educational services must be designed to meet individual needs, and students with disabilities must be educated with nondisabled students.

Individuals with Limited English Proficiency

An individual with "limited English proficiency" refers to a secondary school student, an adult, or an out-of-school youth who has limited ability in speaking, reading, writing, or understanding the English language; whose native language is a language other than English; or who lives in a family or community environment in which a language other than English is the dominant language.

Learning Disabilities

In addition to the ADA, the Individuals with Disabilities Education Act (IDEA) provides for people with difficulties related to learning. The IDEA strengthens expectations and accountability for children with disabilities and bridges the gap that sometimes occurs between what children with disabilities learn and what is required in a regular classroom. Under IDEA, a student with a disability may have a physical, emotional, learning, or behavioral problem that is educationally related and requires special education and related services. The categories include autism, deaf-blindness, developmental delay, emotional/behavioral disorder, hearing impairment, mental impairment, multiple impairment, orthopedic impairment, other health impaired, specific learning disability, speech and/or language impairment, traumatic brain injury, and visual impairment/blindness.

Individualized Education Program (IEP)

The IDEA requires that each public school child who receives special education and related services for a disability must have an Individualized Education Program (IEP). The IEP creates an opportunity for teachers, parents, school administrators, related services personnel, and students (when appropriate) to work together to improve educational results for children with disabilities. The IEP guides the delivery of special education supports and services for the student with a disability.

(Continued on next page)

The writing of each student's IEP takes place within the larger picture of the special education process under IDEA. Here are the steps taken to establish an IEP:

Step 1. Child is identified. The state must identify, locate, and evaluate all children with disabilities in the state who need special education and related services. A school professional or parent may ask for an evaluation. Parents must approve the evaluation.

Step 2. Child is evaluated. The evaluation must assess the child in all areas related to the child's suspected disability.

Step 3. Eligibility is decided. A group of qualified professionals and the parents look at the child's evaluation results. Together, they decide if the child is a "child with a disability," as defined by IDEA. Parents may ask for a hearing to challenge the eligibility decision.

Step 4. Child is found eligible for services. If the child is found to be a "child with a disability," as defined by IDEA, he or she is eligible for special education and related services. The IEP team meets to write an IEP for the child.

Step 5. IEP meeting is scheduled. The school system schedules and conducts the IEP meeting.

Step 6. Services are provided. The school makes sure that the child's IEP is being carried out as it was written. Parents are given a copy of the IEP. Each of the child's teachers and service providers has access to the IEP and knows his or her specific responsibilities for carrying out the IEP. This includes the accommodations, modifications, and supports that must be provided to the child, in keeping with the IEP.

Step 7. Progress is measured and reported to parents. The child's progress toward the annual goals is measured, as stated in the IEP.

Step 8. IEP is reviewed. The child's IEP is reviewed by the IEP team at least once a year, or more often if the parents or school ask for a review.

Step 9. Child is reevaluated. At least every three years the child must be reevaluated. Its purpose is to find out if the child continues to be a "child with a disability," as defined by IDEA, and what the child's educational needs are. However, the child must be reevaluated more often if conditions warrant or if the child's parent or teacher asks for a new evaluation.

Inclusion

An instructor's challenge is to ensure that all students learn as well as possible. In addition to choosing the most effective strategies for achieving learning objectives, planning for student diversity will enrich the learning experiences for all. Students vary widely in their level of experience with a subject area, their abilities, and their learning preferences.

Students who are unresponsive to instruction may have serious learning disabilities that require attention or may only need minor adjustments in order to succeed. See the chart titled "Meeting Special Needs" for helpful resources and strategies for learning and other types of disabilities.

Meeting Special Needs

Subject	Description
Limited English Proficiency (LEP)	Some students speak English as a second language, or not at all. Customs and behavior of people in the majority culture may be confusing for some of these students. Cultural values may inhibit some students from full participation in the classroom.
Behaviorally Disordered	Children with behavior disorders deviate from standards or expectations of behavior and impair the functioning of others and themselves. These children may also be gifted or learning disabled.
Visually Impaired	Children who are visually disabled have partial or total loss of sight. Individuals with visual impairments are not significantly different from their sighted peers in ability range or personality. However, blindness may affect cognitive, motor, and social development.
Hearing Impaired	Children who are hearing impaired have partial or total loss of hearing. Individuals with hearing impairments are not significantly different from their peers in ability range or personality. However, the chronic condition of deafness may affect cognitive, motor, social, and speech development.
Physically Challenged	Children who are physically disabled fall into two categories—those with orthopedic impairments (use of one or more limbs severely restricted) and those with other health impairments.
Gifted	Although no formal definition exists, these students can be described as having above average ability, task commitment, and creativity. They rank in the top five percent of their classes. They usually finish work more quickly than other students, and are capable of divergent thinking.
Learning Disabled	All learning disabled students have a problem in one or more areas, such as academic learning, language, perceptions, social-emotional adjustment, memory, or ability to pay attention.

(Continued on next page)

Subject	Tips For Instruction
Limited English Proficiency (LEP)	• Remember that students' ability to speak English does not reflect their academic ability or their I.Q. level. • Try to incorporate students' cultural experiences into your instruction. The help of a bilingual aide may be effective. • Include information about different cultures in your curriculum to help build students' self-image. • Avoid cultural stereotypes. • Encourage students to share their cultures in the classroom.
Behaviorally Disordered	• Work for long-term improvement; do not expect immediate success. • Talk with students about their strengths and weaknesses, and clearly outline objectives and tell how you will help them obtain their goals. • Structure schedules, rules, room arrangement, and safety for a conducive learning environment. • Model appropriate behavior for students and reinforce proper behavior. • Adjust group requirements for individual needs.
Visually Impaired	• Modify assignments as needed to help students become more independent. • Teach classmates how to serve as guides for the visually impaired; pair students so sighted peers can assist in cooperative learning work. • Tape lectures and reading assignments for the visually impaired. • For the benefit of the visually impaired, encourage students to use their sense of touch; provide tactile models whenever possible. • Verbally describe people and events as they occur in the classroom for the visually impaired. • Limit unnecessary noise in the classroom.
Hearing Impaired	• Provide favorable seating arrangements so hearing-impaired students can see speakers and read their lips (or interpreters can assist); avoid visual distractions. • Write out all instructions on paper or on the board; overhead projectors enable you to maintain eye contact while writing. • Avoid standing with your back to the window or light source.
Physically Challenged	• With the student, determine when you should offer aid. • Help other students and adults understand physically disabled students. • Learn about special devices or procedures and if any special safety precautions are needed. • Allow students to participate in all activities including field trips, special events, and projects.
Gifted	• Emphasize concepts, theories, relationships, ideas, and generalizations. • Let students express themselves in a variety of ways including drawing, creative writing, or acting. • Make arrangements for students to work on independent projects. • Utilize public services and resources, such as agencies providing free and inexpensive materials, community services and programs, and people in the community with specific expertise. • Make arrangements for students to take selected subjects early.
Learning Disabled	• Establish conditions and create an environment that leads to success. • Provide assistance and direction; clearly define rules, assignments, and duties. • Allow for pair interaction during class time; utilize peer helpers. • Practice skills frequently. • Distribute outlines of material presented in class. • Maintain student interest with games. • Allow extra time to complete tests and assignments.

Multiple Intelligences

Eight Ways of Learning		
Type	**Description**	**Likes to...**
Verbal/Linguistic Learner	Intelligence is related to words and language, written and spoken.	Read, write, tell stories, play word games, and tell jokes and riddles.
Logical/Mathematical Learner	Intelligence deals with inductive and deductive thinking and reasoning, numbers, and abstractions.	Perform experiments, solve puzzles, work with numbers, ask questions, and explore patterns and relationships.
Visual/Spatial Learner	Intelligence relies on the sense of sight and being able to visualize an object, including the ability to create mental images.	Draw, build, design, and create things, daydream, do jigsaw puzzles and mazes, watch videos, look at photos, and draw maps and charts.
Naturalistic Learner	Intelligence has to do with observing, understanding, and organizing patterns in the natural environment.	Spend time outdoors and work with plans, animals, and other parts of the natural environment; good at identifying plans and animals and at hearing and seeing connections to nature.
Musical/Rhythmic Learner	Intelligence is based on recognition of tonal patterns, including various environmental sounds, and on sensitivity to rhythm and beats.	Sing and hum, listen to music, play an instrument, move body when music is playing, and make up songs.
Bodily/Kinesthetic Learner	Intelligence is related to physical movement and the brain's motor cortex, which controls bodily motion.	Learn by hands-on methods, demonstrate skill in crafts, tinker, perform, display physical endurance, and challenge self physically.
Interpersonal Learner	Intelligence operates primarily through person-to-person relationships and communication.	Have lots of friends, talk to people, join groups, play cooperative games, solve problems as part of a team, and volunteer help to others in need.
Intrapersonal Learner	Intelligence is related to inner states of being, self-reflection, metacognition, and awareness of spiritual realities.	Work alone, pursue own interests, daydream, keep a personal diary or journal, and think about starting own business.

CDA Competency Checklist	Completion Date		
COMPETENCY GOAL I: **To establish and maintain a safe, healthy learning environment.**	Reading	Observation	Practice
1. Functional Area: Safe—Candidate provides a safe environment to prevent and reduce injuries. Examples include the following:			
Keeps the inside of the center and the outdoor play area free of debris; structural hazards; unguarded space heaters; tools and dangerous substances, such as medicine, cleaning products, matches, chipped paint, toxic plants, small objects, balloons, and plastic bags.			
Ensures that safety equipment, such as fire extinguishers and smoke detectors, is in place and operable and someone knows how to use it.			
Maintains a current list of telephone numbers for contacting parents and emergency services, such as poison control, fire company, and medical help.			
Plans and practices monthly fire drills with the children.			
Checks the safety of all outdoor equipment daily.			
Responds immediately and sympathetically to a child's injury or fear of injury, and encourages the same response by the children.			
Takes safety precautions in a reassuring manner without overprotecting or making children fearful.			
Plans measures to prevent potentially dangerous situations, such as leaving sleeping children unattended.			
Maintains first aid supplies—gauze, tape, syrup of ipecac, tweezers, scissors, and soap—and knows basic first aid procedures appropriate for young children, such as how to handle choking and treat cuts.			
Uses safe auto and bus travel procedures, including car seats for children.			
Discusses safety information with parents and tells them about resources, such as poison control centers.			
Explains cause and effect of dangerous situations in simple language.			
Teaches safe use of playground equipment.			
Supervises all children's indoor and outdoor activities.			
Keeps current on information about safety standards for toys and equipment and shares with parents and the center staff.			
Adapts indoor and outdoor equipment to enhance independence of children with disabilities.			
Requires written parental authorization before allowing people other than parents to pick up children from the center.			

Child & Adult Care Professionals Instructor Resource Guide

Name_____ Course _____ Date _____

CDA Competency Checklist	Completion Date		
COMPETENCY GOAL I: (Continued) **To establish and maintain a safe, healthy learning environment.**	*Reading*	*Observation*	*Practice*
2. Functional Area: Healthy—Candidate promotes good health and nutrition and provides an environment that contributes to the prevention of illness. Examples include the following:			
Learns about good nutrition for children from 3 to 5 years old and provides age-appropriate, nutritious meals and snacks. While respecting family customs and habits, the caregiver shares nutrition information with parents and encourages any food contributions to be nutritious.			
Conducts activities in a positive, relaxed, and pleasant atmosphere to reduce tension and stress.			
Washes hands after toileting a child, helping child blow nose, and before food preparation and eating.			
Attends to each child's physical needs, such as toileting, eating, exercising, and napping.			
Provides affection for all children.			
Provides adequate ventilation and lighting, comfortable room temperatures, and good sanitation.			
Makes sure play areas and materials are cleaned daily.			
Establishes procedures for care of sick children; for example, isolating a child with a contagious illness from well children, contacting parents and medical providers, and administering medicine.			
Helps children develop basic health habits.			
Keeps handy current emergency telephone numbers for each child's parent(s), nearest relative, and medical providers.			
Communicates frequently with parents about children's health, nutrition, communicable diseases and medications, and cooperates with parents and health specialists.			
Follows center procedures for maintaining health records and administering medication and first aid and cooperates with health and nutrition staff.			
Establishes a mealtime routine that makes eating pleasant for each child.			

(Continued on next page)

CDA Competency Checklist

	Completion Date		
COMPETENCY GOAL I: (Continued) To establish and maintain a safe, healthy learning environment.	Reading	Observation	Practice
2. Functional Area: Healthy (Continued)			
Limits sugar, salt, processed foods, unnecessary chemical additives, and artificial coloring and flavoring in meals and snacks and encourages parents to do the same.			
Informs parents about health resources, such as physicians or community clinics that provide services to families in their primary language.			
Recognizes symptoms of possible abuse and neglect and is alert to play or behavior that indicates abuse. If physical or sexual abuse is suspected, seeks out resources for information and support, and follows state laws in response. The Candidate responds sensitively to child and family's needs, and cooperates with treatment plans.			
Uses role-playing, modeling, visual material, and real objects to teach healthy physical, mental, dental, and nutritional practices.			
Plans health care and educational activities that integrate health and nutrition information from the children's cultures with medically accepted health and nutrition practices.			
Supports children in developing self-help skills in eating, toileting, washing hands, tooth brushing, etc.			
Includes children in food preparation and provides other nutrition-education activities for children.			
Provides opportunities for children to learn about health care by discussing health care visits, reading books, and encouraging pretend play.			
Recognizes unusual behavior and physical symptoms in children and encourages parents to obtain appropriate treatment.			
Works cooperatively with health professionals and parents to meet the needs of children with disabling conditions.			
Recognizes the signs of a health crisis that children with special needs may have and respond appropriately (e.g., seizures).			
Bilingual Specialization: Provides written health information for parents in both languages.			
Bilingual Specialization: Utilizes cultural values and practices in providing health and nutrition education.			

Child & Adult Care Professionals Instructor Resource Guide
Copyright © Glencoe/McGraw-Hill

Name_____ Course _____ Date _____

CDA Competency Checklist	Completion Date		
COMPETENCY GOAL I: (Continued) **To establish and maintain a safe, healthy learning environment.**	Reading	Observation	Practice
3. Functional Area: Learning Environment—Candidate uses space, relationships, materials, and routines as resources for constructing an interesting, secure, and enjoyable environment that encourages play, exploration, and learning. Examples include the following:			
Uses materials, books, and equipment that are stimulating to each child and suitable to individual learning styles, including disabled children.			
Uses materials that demonstrate acceptance of each child's sex, family, race, language, and culture.			
Provides easily accessible learning materials (e.g., puzzles, crayons, markers, and books) that children can explore themselves as well as putting some materials away for special times or for use at later stages of development.			
Organizes space into identifiable areas that encourage appropriate and independent use of materials.			
Balances active and quiet, free and unstructured, individual and group, indoor and outdoor activities.			
Provides many opportunities for children to develop their senses and ability to cooperate.			
Varies routines spontaneously to take advantage of unusual opportunities (e.g., goes outside in the snow, lets the children watch workers and machinery on the street, or plays with one child for an extra period of time when additional adults are available to care for group).			
Adapts the daily schedule to accommodate children with special needs rather than requiring them to fit the schedule.			
Bilingual Specialization: Uses objects, music activities, and celebrations that are meaningful to young children and encourage development of both languages and cultures.			
Bilingual Specialization: Helps parents identify resources in their homes, families, and community that will support the development of both languages.			
Bilingual Specialization: Establishes and maintains a routine for use of the second language in daily activities.			

CDA Competency Checklist	Completion Date		
COMPETENCY GOAL II: **To advance physical and intellectual competence.**	*Reading*	*Observation*	*Practice*
4. Functional Area: Physical—Candidate provides a variety of equipment, activities, and opportunities to promote the physical development of children. Examples include the following:			
Arranges and encourages physical activities, knowing how children's physical development affects their cognitive, social, and emotional development.			
Observes and evaluates children's developmental levels in order to provide activities for physical skills and development of the senses at the appropriate level for each child.			
Plans and participates daily in appropriate large-muscle activities (e.g., playing ball, running, climbing with children, both indoors and outdoors).			
Provides a variety of activities from children's culture(s), such as dances, music, finger plays, and active games.			
Provides opportunities for children to develop their senses by noticing colors, smelling odors, distinguishing sounds, feeling and touching a variety of objects, and tasting different foods.			
Communicates to children and their parents the importance of outdoor play and physical activity for healthy growth and development.			
Plans for and supports children's changing needs for active play, quiet activity, and rest.			
Supports and encourages, but never forces, children who are fearful of physical activity.			
Observes and evaluates children's physical development, recognizes signs of possible physical disabilities and developmental delays, refers parents to appropriate services; follows up on referrals/individual development plans.			
Adapts the program to meet the special needs of children with disabilities, taking into account the importance of physical development to self-concept and social development.			
Avoids overprotecting children with disabilities, supports their independence, includes them in physical activities with other children (making modifications only when necessary), and encourages parents to do the same.			

Child & Adult Care Professionals Instructor Resource Guide

CDA Competency Checklist	Completion Date		
COMPETENCY GOAL II: (Continued) **To advance physical and intellectual competence.**	Reading	Observation	Practice
5. Functional Area: Cognitive—Candidate provides activities and opportunities that encourage curiosity, exploration, and problem solving appropriate to the developmental levels and learning styles of children. Examples include the following:			
Observes children's play frequently to assess their cognitive development.			
Uses techniques and activities that stimulate children's curiosity, inventiveness, and problem-solving and communication skills.			
Provides opportunities for children to try out and begin to understand the relationships between cause and effect and means and ends.			
Understands the importance of play and often joins children's play as a partner and facilitator.			
Uses the center environment, everyday activities, and homemade materials to encourage children's intellectual development.			
Helps children discover ways to solve problems in daily activities.			
Supports children's repetitions of the familiar and introduces new experiences, activities, and materials as children are interested and ready.			
Recognizes differences in individual learning styles and finds ways to work effectively with each child.			
Encourages active learning, rather than emphasizing adult talking and children's passive listening.			
Provides equipment and materials that children can explore and master by themselves.			
Is alert to the task a child is attempting and provides appropriate support.			
Encourages children to ask questions and seek help and responds to them in ways that extend their thinking; for example, "That's a good question; let's see if we can find out."			
Asks open-ended questions, encouraging children to wonder, guess, and talk about their ideas.			
Encourages children to talk about their experiences and observations.			
Provides opportunities to organize and group, compare and contrast thoughts, words, objects, and sensations.			

(Continued on next page)

Child & Adult Care Professionals Instructor Resource Guide

Name _____ Course _____ Date _____

CDA Competency Checklist	Completion Date		
COMPETENCY GOAL II: (Continued) To advance physical and intellectual competence.	Reading	Observation	Practice
5. Functional Area: Cognitive (Continued)			
Involves children in such projects as cooking and gardening as possible.			
Reduces distractions and interruptions so that children have opportunities to extend their attention span and work on one activity, such as block building or water play, for a long period of time.			
Helps children understand concepts such as space, time, shape, and quantity through many different activities.			
Uses field trips as opportunities to expand children's knowledge and understanding of their world, when possible.			
Obtains (or makes) and uses special learning materials and equipment for children whose disabilities affect their ability to learn.			
Recognizes learning problems and collects good observational examples to support concerns.			
Uses written observational examples of children to make and support referrals according to center policy.			
Bilingual Specialization: Provides learning experiences that lead to the understanding of basic concepts in the language most familiar to each child.			
Bilingual Specialization: Encourages learning of both languages through everyday experiences and activities.			

CDA Competency Checklist	Completion Date		
	Reading	Observation	Practice
COMPETENCY GOAL II: (Continued) **To advance physical and intellectual competence.**			
6. Functional Area: Communication—Candidate actively communicates with children and provides opportunities and support for children to understand, acquire, and use verbal and nonverbal means of communicating thoughts. Examples include the following:			
Has realistic expectations for each child's understanding and use of speech based on knowledge of language development of each child.			
Talks often with individual children and stimulates conversation among children and with adults in the room.			
Provides activities that encourage children to develop listening and comprehension skills.			
Helps children connect word meaning(s) to experiences and real objects.			
Respects the language of non-English-speaking families, encourages them to communicate freely with their children in the language parents prefer, and helps them find opportunities to learn English.			
Is aware of the caregiver's role as a language model for children and uses affectionate and playful tones, clear speech, and responsive conversation.			
Listens attentively to children, tries to understand what they want to communicate, and helps them to express themselves.			
Shares children's communication/language achievements with parents.			
Uses a variety of songs, stories, books, and games—including those from the children's cultures—for language development.			
Talks with children about special experiences and relationships in their families and home lives.			
Uses conversations with children to enrich and expand their vocabulary.			
Provides opportunities for children to represent their ideas nonverbally through activities such as painting, music, and creative movement.			
Helps children learn, understand, and use words to express thoughts, ideas, questions, feelings, and physical needs.			
Writes children's "stories" and labels their drawings showing the relationship between spoken and printed words.			
Introduces longer storybooks gradually as children become interested.			

(Continued on next page)

Name ______________________ Course ______________ Date ______________

CDA Competency Checklist

COMPETENCY GOAL II: (Continued) **To advance physical and intellectual competence.**	Completion Date: Reading	Observation	Practice
6. Functional Area: Communication (Continued)			
Encourages children to take turns talking and listening instead of interrupting each other or adults; ensures that each child has a chance to talk.			
Recognizes possible impairments or delays that affect hearing and speech, helps families find resources, cooperates with treatment plans, and finds ways to communicate positively with children.			
Bilingual Specialization: Shows ability to understand, speak, read, and write both languages.			
Bilingual Specialization: Understands the principles and characteristics of bilingual language development in children and explains these to parents.			
Bilingual Specialization: Assesses each child's language abilities and uses activities that are appropriate to the child's level of development in each language.			
Bilingual Specialization: Allows children opportunities to express themselves in the language of their choice.			
Bilingual Specialization: Uses lullabies, songs, games, stories, books, and finger plays, from both languages, asking parents for examples from their childhood.			

CDA Competency Checklist	Completion Date		
COMPETENCY GOAL II: (Continued) To advance physical and intellectual competence.	Reading	Observation	Practice
7. Functional Area: Creative—Candidate provides opportunities that stimulate children to play with sound, rhythm, language, materials, space, and ideas in individual ways and to express their creative abilities. Examples include the following:			
Recognizes that the process of creating is important—and sometimes more important—than the product.			
Understands that each child's creative expression is unique and does not encourage uniformity.			
Allows time for spontaneous and extended play within the daily routine.			
Includes a variety of music, art, literature, dance, role-playing, and other creative activities from the children's culture(s) in program activities.			
Participates in make-believe games with children.			
Models and encourages children's creativity in language; for example, through rhymes, imaginative stories, and nonsense words.			
Provides unstructured materials (such as blocks, paint, or clay).			
Encourages thorough, repeated exploration of creative materials whenever possible.			
Models creativity by using homemade materials and found objects.			
Helps parents understand the importance of creative expression in children's development and the need to provide children with opportunities for creative activities.			
Provides for "messy" activities with children, such as water and sand play, finger painting, and drawing with markers.			
Encourages children to try new and different activities.			
Provides and rotates a variety of male and female dress-up clothes and other "props," including those from the children's culture(s).			
Keeps informed about and uses cultural community resources.			
Provides crayons, paper, paste, and scissors in a place where children can use them independently.			
Bilingual Specialization: Helps children develop creative abilities through activities and discussion both languages.			
Bilingual Specialization: Helps children identify and imitate creative forms found in the art, music, and dance of their cultures.			

CDA Competency Checklist	Completion Date		
COMPETENCY GOAL III: To support social and emotional development and provide positive guidance.	Reading	Observation	Practice
8. Functional Area: Self—Candidate provides physical and emotional security for each child and helps each child to know, accept, and take pride in himself or herself and to develop a sense of independence. Examples include the following:			
Treats each child as an individual with his or her own strengths and needs and unique characteristics.			
Is sensitive to differing cultural values and expectations concerning independence and expression of feelings.			
Addresses each child by name, talks with every child every day, and encourages each child to call other children and adults by name.			
Has affectionate and appropriate physical contact with each child daily in ways that convey love, affection, and security.			
Helps children through stress, separations, transition, and other crises.			
When possible, offers children choices in activities, materials, and foods, and respects their choices.			
Encourages and helps children practice skills when eating, getting dressed, using toys and equipment, cleaning up, and helping others.			
Gives one-to-one attention to each child as much as possible.			
Enjoys children and directly expresses the enjoyment to them.			
Delights in each child's success, expresses kindness and support when a child is having trouble, and helps him/her learn from mistakes.			
Helps children recognize and accept their feelings and express feelings in culturally appropriate ways.			
Models the recognition and expression of feelings by naming his/her own feelings while expressing them.			
Supports child's developing awareness of him/herself as a member of a family and of an ethnic or social group by talking about families and by celebrating cultural events with children.			
Uses books, pictures, stories, and discussion to help children identify positively with the experiences in their lives.			
Comments directly, sincerely, and positively to children about their performance and ideas.			
Helps children recognize and appreciate racial, ethnic, and ability differences and similarities.			

(Continued on next page)

CDA Competency Checklist

COMPETENCY GOAL III: (Continued) To support social and emotional development and provide positive guidance.	Completion Date		
	Reading	Observation	Practice
8. Functional Area: Self (Continued)			
Emphasizes cooperation in games and activities so that each child experiences success.			
Provides opportunities for all children, including those with disabilities, to feel effective, experience success, and gain positive recognition.			
Understands the effect of abuse and neglect on children's self-concept and works sensitively with such children.			
Bilingual Specialization: Supports the child's attempts to use the second language.			

Child & Adult Care Professionals Instructor Resource Guide

CDA Competency Checklist	Completion Date		
COMPETENCY GOAL III: (Continued) To support social and emotional development and provide positive guidance.	Reading	Observation	Practice
9. Functional Area: Social—Candidate helps each child feel accepted in the group, helps children learn to communicate and get along with others, and encourages feelings of empathy and mutual respect among children and adults. Examples include the following:			
Learns about children's stages of social development and helps children and parents deal with typical issues.			
Has a realistic expectation for young children's social behavior based on their level of development.			
Serves as a social model by building a positive relationship with each child and parent and by maintaining positive relationships with other adults in the center.			
Responds quickly and calmly to prevent children from hurting each other.			
Helps children learn to respect the rights and possessions of others, in light of local expectations regarding sharing.			
Encourages children to ask for, accept, and give help to one another.			
Encourages children to make friends.			
Helps the children become aware of their feelings and those of others by talking about feelings with each child.			
Encourages play and relationships among all children across racial, language, ethnic, age, gender, and special-needs groupings.			
Encourages children to express their feelings and assert rights in socially acceptable ways.			
Encourages children to comfort and help each other.			
Encourages children's attempts to use words to resolve conflicts.			
Encourages cooperation rather than competition.			
Helps children recognize their own and others' feelings, similarities, and differences and helps them develop empathy.			
Helps all children feel valued as members of the group.			
Encourages children to share stories and activities from their families and cultures.			

(Continued on next page)

CDA Competency Checklist

COMPETENCY GOAL III: (Continued) To support social and emotional development and provide positive guidance.	Completion Date		
	Reading	Observation	Practice
9. Functional Area: Social (Continued)			
Uses stories, pictures, and other materials to help children deal with issues such as sharing, separation, negative behavior, and disabilities.			
Bilingual Specialization: Understands that the social roles and expectations for bilingual children in their family setting may be different from those of the child care program and helps the children to behave appropriately in each.			

Child & Adult Care Professionals Instructor Resource Guide
Copyright © Glencoe/McGraw-Hill

CDA Competency Checklist	Completion Date		
	Reading	Observation	Practice
COMPETENCY GOAL III: (Continued) **To support social and emotional development and provide positive guidance.**			
10. Functional Area: Guidance—Candidate provides a supportive environment in which children can begin to learn and practice appropriate and acceptable behaviors as individuals and as a group. Examples include the following:			
Knows a variety of positive guidance methods—such as listening, reinforcement, and redirection—and uses each appropriately.			
Relates guidance practices to knowledge of each child's personality and level of development.			
Avoids negative methods, such as spanking, threatening, shouting, isolating, or shaming children.			
Establishes guidelines for children's behavior that encourages self-control and that are simple, reasonable, and consistent.			
Alerts children to changes in activities or routines well in advance and handles transitions between activities with clear directions and patience.			
Is able to modify play when it becomes overstimulating for any of the children, including children with disabling conditions.			
Builds a trusting relationship with children as a foundation for positive guidance and self-discipline.			
Anticipates confrontations between children and defuses provocative behavior.			
Addresses the problem behavior or situation rather than labeling the child.			
Helps parents develop realistic expectations for children's behavior in ways that help avoid disciplinary problems.			
Knows parents' disciplinary methods and expectations and selects those appropriate for use in the center.			
Has realistic expectations about the children's attention spans, interests, social abilities, and physical needs, including disabled children.			
Gives children real choices and accepts the choices made.			
Lets children solve their own problems whenever possible.			
Explains/demonstrates the reasons for limits in simple words.			

(Continued on next page)

Child & Adult Care Professionals Instructor Resource Guide
Copyright © Glencoe/McGraw-Hill

CDA Competency Checklist	Completion Date		
COMPETENCY GOAL III: (Continued) **To support social and emotional development and provide positive guidance.**	Reading	Observation	Practice
10. Functional Area: Guidance (Continued)			
Uses firm and friendly techniques, such as reminding and persuading, when rules are forgotten or disobeyed.			
Uses positive language with children: for example, "walk" rather than "don't run."			
Involves children in establishing guidelines and limits.			
Recognizes that at times serious behavior problems are related to developmental or emotional problems and works cooperatively with parents towards solutions.			
Is aware of each child's limitations and abilities, uses guidance techniques accordingly, and explains rules at the child's level of understanding.			
Bilingual Specialization: Uses the language in which each child understands expectations, limits, and guidance.			

Child & Adult Care Professionals Instructor Resource Guide

CDA Competency Checklist

	Completion Date		
COMPETENCY GOAL IV: To establish positive and productive relationships with families.	Reading	Observation	Practice
11. Functional Area: Families—Candidate maintains an open, friendly, and cooperative relationship with each child's family, encourages their involvement in the program, and supports the child's relationship with his or her family. Examples include the following:			
Recognizes that children's primary caregivers may be single mothers or fathers, both parents, stepparents, grandparents, uncles, aunts, sisters, brothers, foster parents, or guardians.			
Helps parents understand the development of their child and understand the child's point of view.			
Provides opportunities for parents and other family members to share their skills and talents in the program.			
Recognizes that caregivers can support parents in their role.			
Offers parents information about health and social services and other resources in the community.			
Respects each family's cultural background, religious beliefs, and childrearing practices.			
Observes strict confidentiality regarding children and families and makes parents aware of this policy.			
Suggests activities and materials that parents can share with their children at home.			
Encourages parents to talk about important family events and their children's special interests and behavior at home. Shares information frequently with parents about the child's experiences in the center.			
Is able to discuss problem behavior with parents in a constructive, supportive manner.			
Encourages parents to visit the center, participate in activities, and make suggestions for the daily program.			
Respects and tries to understand the parents' views when they differ from the program's goals or policies and attempts to resolve the differences.			
Tells parents about children's achievements and shares their pleasure in new abilities.			

(Continued on next page)

CDA Competency Checklist	Completion Date		
COMPETENCY GOAL IV: (Continued) **To establish positive and productive relationships with families.**	Reading	Observation	Practice
11. Functional Area: Families (Continued)			
Helps parents with separations from child, recognizing parents' possible concerns about leaving their child.			
Supports children and families under stress, working cooperatively with other professionals, as appropriate.			
Sends home projects made by the children.			
Shares information with parents about the learning opportunities for children in everyday household tasks and routines.			
Helps parents identify resources to diagnose and treat children with disabilities.			
Encourages and assists parents to communicate confidently about their children with government and other community agencies.			
Bilingual Specialization: Helps parents understand the program goals for bilingual development.			
Bilingual Specialization: Supports families' desire to communicate their language and cultural heritage to their children through cultural practices.			

Child & Adult Care Professionals Instructor Resource Guide

CDA Competency Checklist	Completion Date		
COMPETENCY GOAL V: To ensure a well-run, purposeful program responsive to participant needs.	Reading	Observation	Practice
12. Functional Area: Program Management—Candidate is a manager who uses all available resources to ensure an effective program operation. The candidate is a competent organizer, planner, record keeper, communicator, and a cooperative coworker. Examples include the following:			
Works with parents to identify the strengths and needs of each child.			
Develops skills in observing and recording information about children and their families in a nonjudgmental manner for use in planning and carrying out daily program.			
Maintains up-to-date records concerning the growth, health, behavior, and progress of each child and the group and shares the information with parents and appropriate center personnel.			
Considers goals and objectives for each child and for the group. Develops realistic plans responsive to the needs of all.			
Implements plans for each child by identifying developmentally and culturally appropriate activities and materials for each day.			
Has a clear understanding of her/his responsibilities within the program.			
Discusses issues that affect the program with appropriate staff and follows up on their resolution.			
Works as team member with others in the classroom and the program, including substitutes, parents, and volunteers.			
Supports other staff by offering assistance and supervision when needed.			
Makes or obtains materials and equipment appropriate to the developmental needs of the children.			
Coordinates program plans (including guidance and discipline techniques) with parents, specialists, and program personnel, when appropriate.			
Works with appropriate staff to choose substitutes carefully, requiring experience with children of the same ages whenever possible.			

(Continued on next page)

CDA Competency Checklist	Completion Date		
COMPETENCY GOAL V: To ensure a well-run, purposeful program to participant needs.	Reading	Observation	Practice
12. Functional Area: Program Management (Continued)			
Orients new or substitute caregivers and volunteers to routines and special needs and abilities of each child.			
Implements procedures that help children make a smooth transition from one group to another.			
Knows the social-service, health, and education resources of the community and uses them when appropriate.			
Recognizes possible learning problems and works with parents and specialists to develop plans specific to the needs of each child. Implements recommended treatment.			
Establishes liaison with community services that respond to family violence (e.g., Parents Anonymous, Child Protective Services, and shelter programs).			
Bilingual Specialization: Recognizes and helps others recognize the needs of children and families who speak a different language and operate in a different cultural context.			

Child & Adult Care Professionals Instructor Resource Guide

CDA Competency Checklist	Completion Date		
COMPETENCY GOAL VI: **To maintain a commitment to professionalism.**	*Reading*	*Observation*	*Practice*
13. Functional Area: Professionalism—Candidate makes decisions based on knowledge of early childhood theories and practices; promotes quality in child care services; and takes advantage of opportunities to improve competence, both for personal and professional growth and for the benefit of children and families. Examples include the following:			
Enjoys working with young children in a group setting and demonstrates positive attitude in her/his role.			
Understands the philosophy of the program and can describe its goals and objectives to others.			
Continues to gain knowledge of physical, cognitive, language, emotional, and social development as a basis for planning program goals.			
Keeps all personal information about children and families confidential.			
Continually evaluates own performance to identify needs for professional growth.			
Participates in peer evaluation and is able to accept comments and criticism from colleagues, supervisors, and parents in a constructive way.			
Takes advantage of opportunities for professional and personal development by joining appropriate professional organizations and attending meetings, training courses, and conferences.			
Keeps informed about child care practices, research, legislation, and other developments in early childhood education.			
Keeps current on regulatory, legislative, and workforce issues, and knows how they affect the welfare of young children and families.			
Seeks information relevant to the needs of the children she/he is serving—for example, information on school readiness, bilingual development, and special needs—from professional magazines, community colleges, community services, other caregivers, and community members.			

(Continued on next page)

COMPETENCY GOAL VI: (Continued) To maintain a commitment to professionalism.	Completion Date		
	Reading	Observation	Practice
13. Functional Area: Professionalism (Continued)			
Recognizes that caregiver fatigue, low morale, and lack of work satisfaction decrease effectiveness and finds ways to meet her/his own needs and maintain energy and enthusiasm.			
Works cooperatively with other staff members, accepts supervision, and helps promote a positive atmosphere in the center.			
Learns about new laws and regulations affecting center care, children, and families.			
Advocates quality services/rights for children and families.			
Works with other professionals and parents to develop effective strategies to communicate to decision makers the needs of the children and families.			
Develops the ability to state needs for additional resources for individual children or some aspect of the program.			
Is aware that some of the normal developmental characteristics of children (e.g., crying, messiness, dependency, willfulness, negative behavior, curiosity about gender differences, etc.) often make adults uncomfortable. The caregiver can acknowledge these feelings in her/himself, coworkers, and parents while minimizing negative reactions toward children.			
Seeks information about sexual abuse and child abuse and neglect, keeps current on laws and policies concerning reporting and treatment of abuse, and learns effective ways of working with affected children and families.			
Bilingual Specialization: Demonstrates the ability to understand, speak, read, and write in both languages and uses these skills in all aspects of the program.			
Bilingual Specialization: Increases knowledge about bilingual education by reading, attending workshops, and consulting professionals.			
Bilingual Specialization: Maintains and works to increase fluency in her/his second language.			
Bilingual Specialization: Consistency provides opportunities for all children to acquire a second language.			
Bilingual Specialization: Promotes the effective functioning of the bilingual program by attempting to clarify issues relating to bilingualism and multiculturalism.			

Child & Adult Care Professionals Instructor Resource Guide

Becoming a Child Development Associate (CDA)

CDA Eligibility Requirements

Personal
- At least eighteen years of age with a high school diploma.
- Ability to speak, read, and write well enough to fulfill all requirements.
- Must sign a statement of ethical conduct.

Setting
- Must be in a state-approved center.
- Candidate must work as a lead caregiver for a group of at least eight children ages three to five.
- At least ten children must be enrolled in the program with at least two caregivers present.
- No more than twenty percent of those enrolled can be children with special needs.

Experience
- At least 480 hours work experience with three- to five-year-olds in a group setting five years prior to CDA application.

Education
- 120 clock hours with at least ten in each of the eight prescribed areas ranging from planning an environment that is healthy and safe to principles of child growth and development.

As a student in an occupational early childhood program, you might be wondering, "Why should I work toward acquiring the Child Development Associate (CDA) credential?" The internal and external rewards are numerous and include:

- Growing as a professional in knowledge and skill.
- Improving yourself in ways that benefit children.
- Developing a support network of professionals experienced with early childhood development and care.
- Evaluating your knowledge and skills against national standards.
- Acquiring a credential that is nationally recognized by early childhood care providers and educators alike.

The information above offers you an overview of the CDA requirements and assessment process. The training and education required, along with the credential itself, can be a real asset in obtaining gainful employment.

CDA Competency Goals

The Council for Early Childhood Professional Recognition is the sponsoring agency for the CDA credential. As a way to assure families about quality care, the Council created the CDA credentialing program.

The CDA Competency Goals identify the necessary skills for qualified early childhood professionals. They assess the skills necessary in a variety of early childhood settings that include center-based programs for infants, toddlers, and preschoolers; family day care; and home visitor programs. The six CDA Competency Goals include:

A special thank you to *The Council for Professional Recognition* for granting permission to reproduce the CDA Competency Goals and Functional Areas. *All CDA information is available on the official Council for Professional Recognition website on the Internet.*

(Continued on next page)

- **Goal I:** To establish and maintain a safe, healthy learning environment.
- **Goal II:** To advance physical and intellectual competence.
- **Goal III:** To support social and emotional development and provide positive guidance.
- **Goal IV:** To establish positive and productive relationships with families.

- **Goal V:** To ensure a well-run, purposeful program responsive to participant needs.
- **Goal VI:** To maintain a commitment to professionalism.

All individuals desiring to receive the CDA credential must demonstrate their competence in these six areas. Candidates may also receive endorsement in areas of specialization, such as bilingual education.

The Assessment Process

The process for becoming a CDA involves six steps. It is designed to thoroughly assess each candidate in terms of his or her professional skill. The six steps are described below.

Step 1—Inquiry. Once eligibility requirements as outlined in the chart on page 67 are met, candidates can order an application packet from the *Council for Early Childhood Professional Recognition*.

Step 2—Documentation. Next, the candidate must put together the required documentation showing his or her skills. This documentation includes:

- *Professional Resource File.* This file includes an autobiographical statement, written examples showing the candidate's skills in the CDA Competency Standards, and a collection of resource materials (curriculum and activity ideas) that will be of use to the candidate on the worksite.
- *Parent Opinion Questionnaires.* The parent of each child in the candidate's care completes a questionnaire giving his or her perceptions about the candidate's skill and knowledge.
- *Formal Observation.* A formal observation is completed by an advisor of the candidate's choice—often a program director or college instructor. The observation follows the criteria established by the *Council for Early Childhood Professional Recognition*.
- *Early Childhood Studies Review.* This exam is given during the final assessment visit.
- *Oral Interview.* As a final step in the assessment process, the council representative presents the candidate with ten structured child care situations. The interview is designed to show how the candidate uses knowledge acquired through experience and training.

Step 3—Application. After the candidate and his or her advisor collect the necessary documentation, the application for final assessment is sent (along with the fee) to the *Council for Early Childhood Professional Recognition*. You can locate the council's address and telephone number on the Internet.

Step 4—On-Site Visit. A council representative will visit the candidate and the candidate's work site to look at documentation, give the written exam, and conduct the oral interview.

Step 5—Credential Award or Denial. A committee from the *Council for Early Childhood Professional Recognition* reviews all of the candidate's documentation. If all of the documentation is favorable, the council awards the CDA credential to the candidate. If for some reason the candidate needs further education and training, he or she will be notified concerning the specifics of that education and training.

Step 6—Renewing the CDA Credential. Once an individual has received the CDA credential, the initial credential is valid for three years. After the first renewal, the credential can be renewed every five years.

Correlation to the CDA Competency Goals & Functional Areas

Note: Some of the functional area examples have been slightly abbreviated for this chart. CDA correlations to all components of the *Child & Adult Care Professionals* program can be found on the Effective Instruction CD-ROM.

Text & Lab Manual Page Location	Competency Goal I: To establish and maintain a safe, healthy learning environment.
Text: 18, 121-124, 160, 168-180, 186-187, 286-287, 304, 317, 319, 327, 329-331, 336, 354, 432, 444, 450, 463-466, 468, 625-626, 628, 630, 648 **Lab Manual:** 45-50, 53-64, 95-98, 101-107, 109-120	**1. Functional Area: Safe—Candidate provides a safe environment to prevent and reduce injuries. Examples include the following:**
Text: 121-124, 304, 319, 625-626, 628 **Lab Manual:** 60-62	Keeps the inside of the center and the outdoor play area free of debris, structural hazards, unguarded space heaters, tools, and dangerous substances, such as medicine, cleaning products, matches, paint, toxic plants, small objects that could be swallowed, balloons, or plastic bags.
Text: 170 **Lab Manual:** 57	Ensures that safety equipment, such as fire extinguishers and smoke detectors, is in place and operable and knows how to use it.
Text: 160, 172 **Lab Manual:** 53-57, 62	Maintains an easily accessible and current list of phone numbers for contacting parents and emergency services, including poison control, fire company, and medical help.
Text: 186-187, 468 **Lab Manual:** 57-58	Uses diagrams, pictures, and words understood by children and adults to post instructions and practice procedures for fires and other emergencies, including safety procedures for children with disabling conditions.
Text: 169-180, 186-187 **Lab Manual:** 57-58	Plans and practices monthly fire drills for moving all children in care to safety as quickly as possible.
Text: 314-318 **Lab Manual:** 103-104	Ensures outdoor play equipment is safe for small children and in good repair.
Text: 165-166 **Lab Manual:** 62	Responds immediately and sympathetically to a child's injury or fear of injury and encourages the same response by the children.
Text: 18, 286, 304, 317, 432, 444, 450, 468, 630, 648 **Lab Manual:** 53, 101-105	Takes safety precautions in a reassuring manner without overprotecting or making children fearful.

(Continued on next page)

Text & Lab Manual Pages	1. Functional Area: Safe (Continued)
Text: 168-169 **Lab Manual:** 53-54	Anticipates and makes plans to prevent potentially dangerous situations, such as children being left alone or separated while on a field trip.
Text: 165, 327 **Lab Manual:** 55-62	Maintains first aid supplies; knows basic first aid procedures appropriate for young children.
Text: 170-171 **Lab Manual:** 115	Uses safe auto/bus procedures, including the use of appropriate car seats for children under 4 years and seat belts for self and other children.
Lab Manual: 150	Discusses safety information with parents and tells them about resources that provide services to families in their own language.
Text: 169-170, 331 **Lab Manual:** 63-64, 68, 107, 137-138, 145-148, 153-154	Supervises all children's activities indoors and outdoors.
Text: 329-331, 336, 354 **Lab Manual:** 101-104, 109-110	Keeps informed about safety standards for toys and equipment and shares this information with parents.
Text: 463-466 **Lab Manual:** 95-98	Helps preschoolers stop dangerous actions toward themselves and others.
Text: 286-287 **Lab Manual:** 95-98	Explains cause and effect in dangerous situations in simple language, demonstrating as much as possible.
Text: 329, 331, 336 **Lab Manual:** 103-104	Teaches safe use of playground equipment.
Lab Manual: 95-98	Talks and role plays with preschoolers about safety precautions.
Lab Manual: 101-104, 109-110	Adapts the indoor and outdoor areas so that children with disabilities can maximize their independence.
Text: 171-172 **Lab Manual:** 53-54	Requires parents to authorize in writing all persons allowed to pick up children from the program.
Lab Manual: 150	**Bilingual Specialization:** Explains and practices safety procedures such as fire drills, using the language best understood by the children.
Lab Manual: 150	**Bilingual Specialization:** Utilizes cultural values and practices in providing safety education.

(Continued on next page)

Text & Lab Manual Page Location	Competency Goal I: (Continued) To establish and maintain a safe, healthy learning environment.
Text: 15, 43-45, 77-78, 92, 131-132, 159-160, 164-167, 171, 183, 213-219, 235-236, 249-257, 259, 328, 405, 408-409, 432, 480-481, 500 **Lab Manual:** 59-61, 87-94, 115-119	**2. Functional Area: Healthy—Candidate promotes good health and nutrition and provides an environment that contributes to the prevention of illness. Examples include the following:**
Text: 249-257 **Lab Manual:** 87-94	Learns about good nutrition for children from 3 to 5 years old and provides age-appropriate, nutritious meals and snacks. While respecting family customs and habits, the caregiver shares nutrition information with parents and encourages any food contributions to be nutritious.
Text: 77-78, 217, 480-481 **Lab Manual:** 125-127, 175	Conducts activities in a positive, relaxed, and pleasant atmosphere to reduce tension and stress.
Text: 160, 162 **Lab Manual:** 59-61	Washes hands after toileting a child, helping child blow nose, and before food preparation and eating.
Lab Manual: 79-82	Attends to each child's physical needs, such as toileting, eating, exercising, and napping.
Text: 216-217 **Lab Manual:** 79-82	Provides affection for all children.
Text: 160 **Lab Manual:** 61, 101-102, 105-106	Provides adequate ventilation and lighting, comfortable room temperatures, and good sanitation.
Text: 259, 328, 432	Makes sure play areas and materials are cleaned daily.
Text: 159-160, 164-166 **Lab Manual:** 55-56	Establishes procedures for care of sick children; for example, isolating a child with a contagious illness from well children, contacting parents and medical providers, and administering medicine.
Text: 164 **Lab Manual:** 79-82	Helps children develop basic health habits.
Text: 160 **Lab Manual:** 55-56	Keeps handy current emergency telephone numbers for each child's parent(s), nearest relative, and medical providers.
Text: 15, 165, 183, 256 **Lab Manual:** 133	Communicates frequently with parents about children's health, nutrition, communicable diseases and medications, and cooperates with parents and health specialists.
Text: 92, 160 **Lab Manual:** 53-56, 61, 87-94	Follows center procedures for maintaining health records and administering medication and first aid and cooperates with health and nutrition staff.
Text: 253-257 **Lab Manual:** 89-90, 93-94	Establishes a mealtime routine that makes eating pleasant for each child.

(Continued on next page)

Text & Lab Manual Pages	2. Functional Area: Healthy (Continued)
Text: 251-252 **Lab Manual:** 89-92	Limits sugar, salt, processed foods, unnecessary chemical additives, and artificial coloring and flavoring in meals and snacks and encourages parents to do the same.
Text: 408-409 **Lab Manual:** 133, 150	Inform parents about health resources, such as physicians or community clinics, that provide services to families in their primary language.
Text: 171, 213-219 **Lab Manual:** 69-70, 73	Recognizes symptoms of possible abuse and neglect and is alert to play or behavior that indicates abuse. If physical or sexual abuse is suspected, seeks out resources for information and support, and follows state laws in response. The candidate responds sensitively to the child's and family's needs, and cooperates with treatment plans.
Text: 159, 256 **Lab Manual:** 171-174	Uses role-playing, modeling, visual material, and real objects to teach healthy physical, mental, dental, and nutritional practices.
Text: 131-132 **Lab Manual:** 181-182, 187-188	Plans health care and educational activities that integrate health and nutrition information from the children's cultures with medically accepted health and nutrition practices.
Text: 235-236 **Lab Manual:** 141-145	Supports children in developing self-help skills in eating, toileting, washing hands, tooth brushing, etc.
Text: 249-253 **Lab Manual:** 189-190	Includes children in food preparation and provides other nutrition-education activities for children.
Lab Manual: 187-189, 195-196	Provides opportunities for children to learn about health care by discussing health care visits, reading books, and encouraging pretend play.
Text: 166-167 **Lab Manual:** 68, 133, 165-166	Recognizes unusual behavior and physical symptoms in children and encourages parents to obtain appropriate treatment.
Text: 43-45, 405, 500 **Lab Manual:** 159-166	Works cooperatively with health professionals and parents to meet the needs of children with disabling conditions.
Text: 500 **Lab Manual:** 159-160	Recognizes the signs of a health crisis that children with special needs may have and respond appropriately (e.g., seizures).
Lab Manual: 150	**Bilingual Specialization:** Provides written health information for parents in both languages.
Text: 255 **Lab Manual:** 150, 89-90	**Bilingual Specialization:** Utilizes cultural values and practices in providing health and nutrition education.

(Continued on next page)

Child & Adult Care Professionals Instructor Resource Guide
Copyright © Glencoe/McGraw-Hill

Text & Lab Manual Page Location	Competency Goal I: (Continued) To establish and maintain a safe, healthy learning environment.
Text: 74, 145, 231-235, 280, 303, 305-308, 315-317, 326-327, 332-333, 437, 466, 481-482, 572, 574-575, 581, 632 **Lab Manual:** 63, 68,101-107, 109-112, 135-165, 179-182, 185-190, 193-204	**3. Functional Area: Learning Environment—Candidate uses space, relationships, materials, and routines as resources for constructing an interesting, secure, and enjoyable environment that encourages play, exploration, and learning. Examples include the following:**
Text: 327-331, 303 **Lab Manual:** 109-112	Uses materials, books, and equipment that are stimulating to each child and suitable to individual learning styles, including disabled children.
Text: 575 **Lab Manual:** 151-152, 197-198	Uses materials that demonstrate acceptance of each child's sex, family, race, language, and culture.
Text: 307, 326-327 **Lab Manual:** 109-110	Provides easily accessible learning materials (e.g., puzzles, crayons, markers, and books) that children can explore themselves as well as putting some materials away for special times or for use at later stages of development.
Text: 307-308, 332-333 **Lab Manual:** 101-102, 107, 109-110	Organizes space into identifiable areas that encourage appropriate and independent use of materials.
Text: 231-234 **Lab Manual:** 75-85	Balances active and quiet, free and unstructured, individual and group, and indoor and outdoor activities.
Text: 305-306 **Lab Manual:** 139-140, 143-144, 173-174, 187-188	Provides many opportunities for children to develop their senses and ability to concentrate.
Text: 632 **Lab Manual:** 151-152, 171-172	Varies routines spontaneously to take advantage of unusual opportunities (e.g., goes outside in the snow, lets the children watch workers and machinery on the street, or plays with one child for an extra period of time when additional adults are available to care for the group).
Text: 235, 315-317 **Lab Manual:** 159-160	Adapts the daily schedule to accommodate children with special needs rather than requiring them to fit the schedule.
Text: 74, 145, 437, 466, 481-482, 572, 574-575, 581 **Lab Manual:** 150, 195-196, 202-204	**Bilingual Specialization:** Uses objects, music activities, and celebrations that are meaningful to young children and encourage development of both languages and cultures.
Text: 280 **Lab Manual:** 133	**Bilingual Specialization:** Helps parents identify resources in their homes, families, and community that will support the development of both languages.
Text: 280 **Lab Manual:** 150, 133-134	**Bilingual Specialization:** Establishes and maintains a routine for use of the second language in daily activities.

(Continued on next page)

Text & Lab Manual Page Location	Competency Goal II: To advance physical and intellectual competence.
Text: 27-28, 38-42, 79-82, 193-194, 315-319, 326, 329, 441-444, 459-460, 466, 475-476, 495-500 **Lab Manual:** 103-107, 109-112, 135-147, 153-156, 193-194	**4. Functional Area: Physical—Candidate provides a variety of equipment, activities, and opportunities to promote the physical development of children. Examples include the following:**
Text: 27-28 **Lab Manual:** 171-174, 193-196	Arranges and encourage physical activities, knowing how children's physical development affects their cognitive, social, and emotional development.
Text: 27-28, 318-319 **Lab Manual:** 63-64, 67-68, 145-148, 153-154	Observes and evaluates children's developmental levels in order to provide activities for physical skills and development of the senses at the appropriate level for each child.
Text: 326, 329, 617 **Lab Manual:** 193-194	Plans and participates daily in appropriate large-muscle activities (e.g., playing ball, running, climbing with children, both indoors and outdoors).
Text: 466 **Lab Manual:** 179-182, 193-198	Provides a variety of activities from children's culture(s), such as dances, music, fingerplays, and active games.
Text: 441-444, 459-460, 475-476 **Lab Manual:** 187-190	Provides opportunities for children to develop their senses by noticing colors, smelling odors, distinguishing sounds, feeling and touching a variety of objects, and tasting different foods.
Text: 315-317 **Lab Manual:** 133, 193-194	Communicates to children and their parents the importance of outdoor play and physical activity for healthy growth and development.
Text: 317-319 **Lab Manual:** 75-85	Plans for and supports children's changing needs for active play, quiet activity, and rest.
Lab Manual: 79-82, 193-194	Supports and encourages, but never forces, children who are fearful of physical activity.
Text: 27-28, 42 **Lab Manual:** 159-166	Observes and evaluates children's physical development, recognizes signs of possible physical disabilities and developmental delays, refers parents to appropriate services; follow up on referrals/individual development plans.
Text: 38-42 **Lab Manual:** 159-166	Adapts the program to meet the special needs of children with disabilities, taking into account the importance of physical development to self-concept and social development.
Text: 495-500 **Lab Manual:** 159-166	Avoids overprotecting children with disabilities, supports their independence, includes them in physical activities with other children (making modifications only when necessary), and encourages parents to do the same.

(Continued on next page)

Child & Adult Care Professionals Instructor Resource Guide

Text & Lab Manual Page Location	Competency Goal II: (Continued) To advance physical and intellectual competence.
Text: 29, 42, 79-85, 95-98, 103, 116, 118, 131, 135-136, 149-152, 170-171, 187-188, 194-200, 277-466, 498-499, 534, 540-541, 543, 452, 463-465, 561, 563, 567, 569, 591-608, 617-619 **Lab Manual:** 133-149, 151-157, 171-175, 179-182, 185-189, 193-204	**5. Functional Area: Cognitive—Candidate provides activities and opportunities that encourage curiosity, exploration, and problem solving appropriate to the developmental levels and learning styles of children. Examples include the following:**
Text: 29, 200, 278 **Lab Manual:** 147-148, 151-152	Observes children's play frequently to assess their cognitive development and readiness for new learning opportunities.
Text: 103, 325 **Lab Manual:** 171-175, 179-180	Uses techniques and activities that stimulate children's curiosity, inventiveness, and problem-solving and communication skills.
Lab Manual: 95-98, 187-188	Provides opportunities for children to try out and begin to understand the relationships between cause and effect and means and ends.
Text: 465-466 **Lab Manual:** 151-152	Understands the importance of play and often joins children's play as a partner and facilitator.
Text: 603-608 **Lab Manual:** 79-82, 101-107, 109-110	Uses the center environment, everyday activities, and homemade materials to encourage children's intellectual development.
Text: 103, 325 **Lab Manual:** 79-82	Helps children discover ways to solve problems in daily activities.
Text: 540-541 **Lab Manual:** 63-64, 79-85	Supports children's repetitions of the familiar and introduces new experiences, activities, and materials as children are interested and ready.
Text: 461, 534, 561 **Lab Manual:** 63-64, 171-174	Recognizes differences in individual learning styles and finds ways to work effectively with each child.
Text: 277-464 **Lab Manual:** 149, 179-180	Encourages active learning, rather than emphasizing adult talking and children's passive listening.
Text: 617-619 **Lab Manual:** 101-107, 109-112	Provides equipment and materials that children can explore and master by themselves.
Lab Manual: 97-98, 135-136	Is alert to the task a child is attempting and provides appropriate support.
Text: 567, 569 **Lab Manual:** 97-98, 149, 171	Encourages children to ask questions and seek help and respond to them in ways that extend their thinking; for example, "That's a good question; let's see if we can find out."

(Continued on next page)

Text & Lab Manual Pages	5. Functional Area: Cognitive (Continued)
Text: 116, 118 **Lab Manual:** 97-98, 149, 171, 179-180	Asks questions that have more than one answer, encouraging children to wonder, guess, and talk about their ideas.
Text: 279-280 **Lab Manual:** 97-98, 149, 179-180	Encourages children to talk about their experiences and observations.
Text: 591-596 **Lab Manual:** 179-180, 187-188	Provides opportunities to organize and group, compare, and contrast thoughts, words, objects, and sensations.
Text: 600-602 **Lab Manual:** 189-190	Involves children in such projects as cooking and gardening as possible.
Text: 286 **Lab Manual:** 101-102, 107, 109-110	Reduces distractions and interruptions so that children have opportunities to extend their attention span and work on one activity, such as block building or water play, for a long period of time.
Text: 597-600 **Lab Manual:** 173-174, 185-186	Helps children understand concepts such as space, time, shape, and quantify through many different activities.
Text: 170-171, 543 **Lab Manual:** 129-130	Uses field trips as opportunities to expand children's knowledge and understanding of their world, when possible.
Text: 498-499 **Lab Manual:** 159-166	Obtains (or makes) and uses special learning materials and equipment for children whose disabilities affect their ability to learn.
Text: 42, 200, 498-499 **Lab Manual:** 159-160, 165-166	Recognizes learning problems and collects good observational examples to support concerns.
Text: 194-200 **Lab Manual:** 63-64, 67-68	Uses written observational examples of children to make and support referrals according to center policy.
Text: 131, 135, 452, 463-465, 563 **Lab Manual:** 149-152	**Bilingual Specialization:** Provides learning experiences that lead to the understanding of basic concepts in the language most familiar to each child.
Lab Manual: 79-85, 135-137, 149-152	**Bilingual Specialization:** Encourages learning of both languages through everyday experiences and activities.

(Continued on next page)

Child & Adult Care Professionals Instructor Resource Guide

Text & Lab Manual Page Location	Competency Goal II: (Continued) To advance physical and intellectual competence.
Text: 131, 133-134, 145, 147, 176, 357-358, 396, 403, 408, 468, 477, 487-488, 496-499, 563-570, 636 **Lab Manual:** 63-64, 95-98, 135-151, 179-182	**6. Functional Area: Communication—Candidate actively communicates with children and provides opportunities and support for children to understand, acquire, and use verbal and nonverbal means of communicating thoughts. Examples include the following:**
Text: 563-564 **Lab Manual:** 63-64, 147-150	Has realistic expectations for each child's understanding and use of speech based on knowledge of language development of each child.
Text: 396, 566, 636 **Lab Manual:** 129-132	Talks often with individual children and stimulates conversation among children and with adults in the room.
Text: 565-570 **Lab Manual:** 149	Provides activities that encourage children to develop listening and comprehension skills.
Text: 468, 477, 563-564 **Lab Manual:** 149	Helps children connect word meaning(s) to experiences and real objects.
Text: 131, 145 **Lab Manual:** 150	Respects the language of non-English-speaking families, encourages them to communicate freely with their children in the language parents prefer, and helps them find opportunities to learn English.
Text: 563-564 **Lab Manual:** 23-32	Is aware of the caregiver's role as a language model for children and uses affectionate and playful tones, clear speech, and responsive conversation.
Text: 487-488, 564-567, 569-570 **Lab Manual:** 23-32, 97, 149	Listens attentively to children, tries to understand what they want to communicate, and helps them to express themselves.
Lab Manual: 133-134, 176	Shares children's communication/language achievements with parents.
Text: 565 **Lab Manual:** 101-102, 109-112	Uses a variety of songs, stories, books, and games—including those from the children's cultures—for language development.
Text: 147, 357-358, 403, 408 **Lab Manual:** 27-28	Talks with children about special experiences and relationships in their families and home lives.
Text: 567-570 **Lab Manual:** 97-98, 149	Helps children learn, understand, and use words to express thoughts, ideas, questions, feelings, and physical needs.
Lab Manual: 149, 155-156, 171-174, 176	Writes children's "stories" and labels their drawings showing the relationship between spoken and printed words.
Lab Manual: 155-158	Introduces longer storybooks gradually as children become interested.
Text: 567-569 **Lab Manual:** 97-98	Encourages children to take turns talking and listening instead of interrupting each other or adults; ensures that each child has a chance to talk.

(Continued on next page)

Text & Lab Manual Pages	6. Functional Area: Communication (Continued)
Text: 496-499 **Lab Manual:** 159-166	Recognizes possible impairments or delays that affect hearing and speech, helps families find resources, cooperates with treatment plans, and finds ways to communicate positively with children.
Text: 452, 463-464, 465 **Lab Manual:** 150	**Bilingual Specialization:** Shows ability to understand, speak, read, and write both languages.
Text: 452, 463-464 **Lab Manual:** 150	**Bilingual Specialization:** Understands the principles and characteristics of bilingual language development in children and explains these to parents.
Text: 452, 463-464 **Lab Manual:** 171-174	**Bilingual Specialization:** Assesses each child's language abilities and uses activities that are appropriate to the child's level of development in each language.
Text: 452, 463-464 **Lab Manual:** 149-150	**Bilingual Specialization:** Allows children opportunities to express themselves in the language of their choice.
Text: 452, 463-464 **Lab Manual:** 134, 150	**Bilingual Specialization:** Uses lullabies, songs, games, stories, books, and fingerplays, from both languages, asking parents for examples from their childhood.

(Continued on next page)

Text & Lab Manual Page Location	Competency Goal II: (Continued) To advance physical and intellectual competence.
Text: 547-548, 641-643, 645-647 **Lab Manual:** 101-102, 105, 179-180, 133-134, 181-182, 193-204	**7. Functional Area: Creative**—Candidate provides opportunities that stimulate children to play with sound, rhythm, language, materials, space, and ideas in individual ways and to express their creative abilities. Examples include the following:
Text: 547, 644 **Lab Manual:** 199-201	Recognizes that the process of creating is important—and sometimes more important—than the product.
Text: 641-642 **Lab Manual:** 195-204	Understands that each child's creative expression is unique and does not encourage uniformity.
Lab Manual: 75-85	Allows time for spontaneous and extended play within the daily routine.
Text: 644-647 **Lab Manual:** 75-78, 173-174, 193-204	Includes a variety of music, art, literature, dance, role-playing, and other creative activities from the children's culture(s) in program activities.
Lab Manual: 195-198	Participates in make-believe games with the children.
Lab Manual: 171-174, 179-182, 195-197	Models and encourages children's creativity in language; for example, through rhymes, imaginative stories, and nonsense words.
Text: 645-647 **Lab Manual:** 109-110, 139-143, 197-201	Provides unstructured materials (such as blocks, paint, or clay).
Lab Manual: 109-110, 171-174	Encourages thorough, repeated exploration of creative materials whenever possible.
Text: 548 **Lab Manual:** 197-198	Models creativity by using homemade materials and found objects.
Lab Manual: 133-134, 173-174, 176	Helps parents understand the importance of creative expression in children's development and the need to provide children with opportunities for creative activities.
Text: 645-647 **Lab Manual:** 199-201	Provides for "messy" activities with children, such as water and sand play, finger painting, and drawing with markers.
Text: 241 **Lab Manual:** 195-204	Encourages children to try new and different activities.
Lab Manual: 195-198	Provides and rotates a variety of male and female dress-up clothes and other "props," including those from the children's culture(s).
Lab Manual: 133-134	Keeps informed about cultural resources in the community and uses them.
Text: 642-643 **Lab Manual:** 101-102, 179-180, 199-201	Provides crayons, paper, paste, and scissors in a place where children can use them independently.
Lab Manual: 133-134, 150	**Bilingual Specialization:** Helps children develop creative abilities through activities and discussion in both languages.
Lab Manual: 133-134, 105, 181-182, 199-204	**Bilingual Specialization:** Helps children identify and imitate creative forms found in the art, music, and dance of their cultures.

(Continued on next page)

Text & Lab Manual Page Location	Competency Goal III: To support social and emotional development and provide positive guidance.
Text: 216-217, 237-283, 253, 369, 435-436, 452-453, 466, 469, 488-489, 541-545, 548, 571, 572, 574-576, 634-637 **Lab Manual:** 12, 23-25, 27-32, 69-70, 79-82, 95-98, 109-110, 133-134, 149-150, 159-160, 173-174, 179-182	**8. Functional Area: Self—Candidate provides physical and emotional security for each child and helps each child to know, accept, and take pride in himself or herself and to develop a sense of independence. Examples include the following:**
Text: 572 **Lab Manual:** 23-25, 27-32, 79-82	Treats each child as an individual with his or her own strengths, needs, and unique characteristics.
Text: 571, 575-576 **Lab Manual:** 23-25, 27-32, 79-82	Is sensitive to differing cultural values and expectations concerning independence and expression of feelings.
Lab Manual: 79-82	Addresses each child by name, talks with every child every day, and encourages each child to call other children and adults by name.
Text: 435-436, 452-453, 469, 488-489 **Lab Manual:** 79-82, 95-98	Has affectionate and appropriate physical contact with each child daily in ways that convey love, affection, and security.
Text: 216-217, 237-283, 572 **Lab Manual:** 79-82, 95-98, 175	Helps children through stress, separations, transition, and other crises.
Text: 541-542, 544-545, 548 **Lab Manual:** 97-98, 151-152	When possible, offers children choices in activities, materials, and foods, and respects their choices.
Text: 253, 442, 445 **Lab Manual:** 79-85	Encourages and helps children practice skills when eating, getting dressed, using toys and equipment, cleaning up, and helping others.
Lab Manual: 79-82	Gives one-to-one attention to each child as much as possible.
Lab Manual: 97-98	Enjoys children and directly expresses the enjoyment to them.
Text: 435-436, 452-453, 469, 488-489 **Lab Manual:** 12, 97-98	Delights in each child's success, expresses kindness and support when a child is having trouble, and helps him/her learn from mistakes.
Text: 574-575 **Lab Manual:** 97-98	Helps children recognize and accept their feelings and express feelings in culturally appropriate ways.
Lab Manual: 97-98	Models the recognition and expression of feelings by naming his/her own feelings while expressing them.

(Continued on next page)

Child & Adult Care Professionals Instructor Resource Guide
Copyright © Glencoe/McGraw-Hill

Text & Lab Manual Pages	8. Functional Area: Self (Continued)
Lab Manual: 133-134, 179-182	Supports child's developing awareness of him/herself as a member of a family and of an ethnic or social group by talking about families and by celebrating cultural events with children.
Text: 565, 572 **Lab Manual:** 109-110, 179-180	Uses books, pictures, stories, and discussion to help children identify positively with the experiences in their lives.
Lab Manual: 97-98	Comments directly, sincerely, and positively to children about their performance and ideas.
Text: 369, 466 **Lab Manual:** 181-182	Helps children recognize and appreciate racial, ethnic, and ability differences and similarities.
Text: 634-637 **Lab Manual:** 95-98	Emphasizes cooperation in games and activities so that each child experiences success.
Lab Manual: 95-96, 159-160, 173-174	Provides opportunities for all children, including those with disabilities to feel effective, experience success, and gain positive recognition.
Text: 216-218 **Lab Manual:** 69-70, 159-160	Understands the effect of abuse and neglect on children's self-concept and works sensitively with such children.
Lab Manual: 149-150	**Bilingual Specialization:** Supports the child's attempts to use the second language.

(Continued on next page)

Text & Lab Manual Page Location	Competency Goal III: (Continued) To support social and emotional development and provide positive guidance.
Text: 31, 87, 277-280, 430, 436, 447-448, 464-466, 481-482, 571, 573-574, 575-576, 626-629, 632-633 **Lab Manual:** 12, 49-50, 63-64, 67-68, 95-98, 133-134, 142, 147-152, 155-158, 170-172, 193	**9. Functional Area: Social**—Candidate helps each child feel accepted in the group, helps children learn to communicate and get along with others, and encourages feelings of empathy, and mutual respect among children and adults. Examples include the following:
Text: 31, 575-576 **Lab Manual:** 12, 133-134, 170-172	Learns about children's stages of social development and helps children and parents deal with typical issues.
Text: 430, 436, 447-448, 464-466, 481-482 **Lab Manual:** 12, 63-64, 67-68	Has realistic expectations for young children's social behavior based on their level of development.
Text: 87, 277-280 **Lab Manual:** 49-50, 95-98, 133-134	Serves as a social model by building a positive relationship with each child and parent and by maintaining positive relationships with other adults in the center.
Lab Manual: 95-98	Responds quickly and calmly to prevent children from hurting each other.
Text: 571, 575-576 **Lab Manual:** 95-98	Helps children learn to respect the rights and possessions of others, in light of local expectations regarding sharing.
Text: 573 **Lab Manual:** 12, 95-98	Encourages children to ask for, accept, and give help to one another.
Lab Manual: 95-98, 151-152, 155-158	Encourages children to make friends.
Text: 572 **Lab Manual:** 95-98	Helps the children become aware of their feelings and those of others by talking about feelings with each child.
Text: 626-629 **Lab Manual:** 12, 151-152, 159-160	Encourages play and relationships among all children across racial, language, ethnic, age, gender, and special-needs groupings.
Text: 632-633 **Lab Manual:** 95-98	Encourages children to express their feelings and assert rights in socially acceptable ways.
Text: 277 **Lab Manual:** 97-98	Encourages children to comfort and help each other.
Lab Manual: 95-98	Encourages children's attempts to use words to resolve conflicts.

(Continued on next page)

Child & Adult Care Professionals Instructor Resource Guide

Text & Lab Manual Pages	9. Functional Area: Social (Continued)
Lab Manual: 12, 79-82, 153-156, 193	Encourages cooperation rather than competition.
Text: 573-574 **Lab Manual:** 95-98, 142	Helps children recognize their own and others' feelings, similarities, and differences and helps them empathize with others.
Lab Manual: 12, 142	Helps all children feel valued as members of the group.
Lab Manual: 147-152	Encourages children to share stories and activities from their families and cultures.
Lab Manual: 133-134	**Bilingual Specialization:** Understands that the social roles and expectations for bilingual children in their family settings may be different from those of the child care program and helps the children to behave appropriately in each.

(Continued on next page)

Text & Lab Manual Page Location	Competency Goal III: (Continued) To support social and emotional development and provide positive guidance.
Text: 237-238, 279-288, 479, 633-634 Lab Manual: 9-10, 49-52, 63-64, 68, 95-98, 69-70, 75-85, 115-116, 133-134, 150, 151-152, 159-160, 171-172, 175, 176	**10. Functional Area: Guidance—Candidate provides a supportive environment in which children can begin to learn and practice appropriate and acceptable behaviors as individuals and as a group. Examples include the following:**
Text: 281-283 Lab Manual: 95-98	Knows a variety of positive guidance methods—such as listening, reinforcement, and redirection—and uses each appropriately.
Text: 633-634 Lab Manual: 63-64, 68, 95-98	Relates guidance practices to knowledge of each child's personality and level of development.
Lab Manual: 69-70, 115-116	Avoids negative methods, such as spanking, threatening, shouting, isolating, or shaming children.
Text: 282-283 Lab Manual: 95-98	Establishes guidelines for children's behavior that encourages self-control and that are simple, reasonable, and consistent.
Text: 237-238 Lab Manual: 175	Alerts children to changes in activities or routines well in advance and handles transitions between activities with clear directions and patience.
Lab Manual: 75-82, 159-160	Is able to modify play when it becomes over stimulating for any of the children, including children with disabling conditions.
Lab Manual: 95-98	Builds a trusting relationship with children as a foundation for positive guidance and self-discipline.
Lab Manual: 95-98	Anticipates confrontations between children and defuses provocative behavior.
Text: 283-285, 479 Lab Manual: 95-98	Addresses the problem behavior or situation rather than labeling the child.
Lab Manual: 9-10, 133-134, 176	Helps parents develop realistic expectations for children's behavior in ways that help avoid disciplinary problems.
Text: 279-280 Lab Manual: 133-134	Knows parents' disciplinary methods and expectations and selects those appropriate for use in the center.
Lab Manual: 9-10, 12, 63-64, 68, 165	Has realistic expectations about the children's attention spans, interests, social abilities, and physical needs, including disabled children.
Text: 238 Lab Manual: 95-96	Gives children real choices and accepts the choices made.
Text: 285 Lab Manual: 151-152, 171-172	Lets children solve their own problems whenever possible.

(Continued on next page)

Child & Adult Care Professionals Instructor Resource Guide
Copyright © Glencoe/McGraw-Hill

Text & Lab Manual Pages	10. Functional Area: Guidance (Continued)
Text: 286 **Lab Manual:** 95-98	Explains and demonstrates the reasons for limits in simple words.
Text: 286-287 **Lab Manual:** 95-98	Uses firm and friendly techniques, such as reminding and persuading, when rules are forgotten or disobeyed.
Text: 282-284 **Lab Manual:** 95-98	Uses positive language with children: for example, "walk" rather than "don't run."
Text: 283-288 **Lab Manual:** 95-98	Involves children in establishing guidelines and limits.
Lab Manual: 51-52, 95-98	Recognizes that sometimes serious behavior problems are related to developmental or emotional problems and works cooperatively with parents towards solutions.
Text: 288 **Lab Manual:** 95-98	Is aware of each child's limitations and abilities, uses guidance techniques accordingly, and explains rules at the child's level of understanding.
Lab Manual: 150	**Bilingual Specialization:** Uses the language in which each child understands expectations, limits, and guidance.

(Continued on next page)

Text & Lab Manual Page Location	Competency Goal IV: To establish positive and productive relationships with families.
Text: 35, 74, 134-136, 193-194, 196, 279-280, 282-283, 289, 305, 404-406, 465, 469, 505, 573 **Lab Manual: 79-82, 133-134**	**11. Functional Area: Families—Candidate maintains an open, friendly, and cooperative relationship with each child's family, encourages their involvement in the program, and supports the child's relationship with his or her family. Examples include the following:**
Text: 74 **Lab Manual: 79-82, 133-134**	Recognizes that children's primary caregivers may be single mothers or fathers, both parents, stepparents, grandparents, uncles, aunts, sisters, brothers, foster parents, or guardians.
Text: 35 **Lab Manual: 133**	Helps parents understand the development of their child and understand the child's point of view.
Text: 404-405 **Lab Manual: 133-134**	Provides opportunities for parents and other family members to share their skills and talents in the program.
Lab Manual: 79-82, 133-134	Recognizes that caregivers can support parents in their role.
Text: 405-406 **Lab Manual: 133**	Offers parents information about health and social services and other resources in the community.
Text: 194, 469 **Lab Manual: 79-82, 133**	Respects each family's cultural background, religious beliefs, and childrearing practices.
Text: 193-194 **Lab Manual: 49-54**	Observes strict confidentiality regarding children and families and makes parents aware of this policy.
Lab Manual: 133, 175-176	Suggests activities and materials that parents can share with their children at home.
Text: 573 **Lab Manual: 133, 175**	Encourages parents to talk about important family events and their children's special interests and behavior at home. Shares information frequently with parents about the child's experiences in the center.
Text: 282-283, 289 **Lab Manual: 79-82, 95-96, 133**	Is able to discuss problem behavior with parents in a constructive, supportive manner.
Text: 305, 404 **Lab Manual: 133-134**	Encourages parents to visit the center, participate in activities, and make suggestions for the daily program.
Text: 279-280 **Lab Manual: 51, 133-134, 175**	Respects and tries to understand the parents' views when they differ from the program's goals or policies and attempts to resolve the differences.
Text: 196 **Lab Manual: 133, 176**	Tells parents about children's achievements and shares their pleasure in new abilities.
Lab Manual: 79-82	Helps parents with separation from child, recognizing parents' possible concerns about leaving their child.

(Continued on next page)

Text & Lab Manual Pages	11. Functional Area: Families (Continued)
Text: 405-406 **Lab Manual:** 125-128, 133	Supports children and families under stress, working cooperatively with other professionals, as appropriate.
Lab Manual: 29, 133	Sends home projects made by the children.
Text: 134-136 **Lab Manual:** 133	Shares information with parents about the learning opportunities for children in everyday household tasks and routines.
Text: 505 **Lab Manual:** 159-166	Helps parents identify resources to diagnose and treat children with disabilities.
Lab Manual: 133	Encourages and assists parents to communicate confidently about their children with government and other community agencies.
Text: 465	**Bilingual Specialization:** Helps parents understand the program goals for bilingual development.
Lab Manual: 134, 150	**Bilingual Specialization:** Supports families' desire to communicate their language and cultural heritage to their children through cultural practices.

(Continued on next page)

Text & Lab Manual Page Location	Competency Goal V: To ensure a well-run, purposeful program responsive to participant needs.
Text: 43-45, 83, 103, 191-200, 215, 302-304, 325-326, 351-353, 355-356, 359, 405-406, 408-409 **Lab Manual:** 45-62, 73, 75-85, 101-120, 125-128, 133-134	**12. Functional Area: Program Management**—Candidate is a manager who uses all available resources to ensure an effective program operation. The candidate is a competent organizer, planner, record keeper, communicator, and a cooperative coworker. Examples include the following:
Lab Manual: 117-119, 133, 175	Works with parents to identify the strengths and needs of each child.
Text: 191-200 **Lab Manual:** 23-25, 29-32, 49-50, 53-56, 63-64, 67-68	Develops skills in observing and recording information about children and their families in a nonjudgmental manner for use in planning and carrying out daily programs.
Text: 83, 196 **Lab Manual:** 49-56, 61-62, 115-119	Maintains up-to-date records concerning the growth, health, behavior, and progress of each child and the group and shares the information with parents and appropriate center personnel.
Text: 302-304, 325-326 **Lab Manual:** 112, 137-156, 159-166	Considers goals and objectives for each child and for the group as a whole. Develops realistic plans responsive to the needs of all.
Lab Manual: 171-174, 179-182	Implements plans for each child by identifying developmentally and culturally appropriate activities and materials for each day.
Lab Manual: 23, 29-32, 45-47, 83-86, 107, 115-120, 157	Has clear understanding of her/his responsibilities within the program.
Text: 103, 325, 351-353 **Lab Manual:** 117-119	Discusses issues that affect the program with appropriate staff and follows up on their resolution.
Lab Manual: 45-47	Works as a member of a team with others in the classroom and the program, including substitutes, parents, and volunteers.
Lab Manual: 45-47	Supports other staff by offering assistance and supervision when needed.
Lab Manual: 61, 93-94, 109-112	Makes or obtains materials and equipment appropriate to the developmental needs of the children.
Text: 355-356 **Lab Manual:** 49-52, 91-92, 133-134	Coordinates program plans (including guidance and discipline techniques) with parents, specialists, and program personnel, when appropriate.
Lab Manual: 115-120	Works with appropriate staff to choose substitutes carefully, requiring experience with children of the same ages whenever possible.
Lab Manual: 115-120	Orients new or substitute caregivers and volunteers to routines and special needs and abilities of each child.

(Continued on next page)

Text & Lab Manual Pages	12. Functional Area: Program Management (Continued)
Lab Manual: 175	Implements procedures that help children make a smooth transition from one group to another.
Text: 356, 359, 405-406, 408-409 **Lab Manual:** 133	Knows the social-service, health, and education resources of the community and uses them when appropriate.
Text: 406 **Lab Manual:** 159-166	Recognizes possible learning problems and works with parents and specialists to develop plans specific to the needs of each child. Implements recommended treatment.
Text: 43-45, 215, 405 **Lab Manual:** 74, 133	Establishes liaison with community services that respond to family violence (e.g., Parents Anonymous, Child Protective Services, and shelter programs).
Lab Manual: 150	**Bilingual Specialization:** Recognizes and helps others recognize the needs of children and families who speak a different language and operate in a different cultural context.

(Continued on next page)

Text & Lab Manual Page Location	Competency Goal VI: To maintain a commitment to professionalism.
Text: 74, 76-78, 82, 83, 106, 111-112, 120-123, 124-125, 136-138, 143-147, 148, 150-155, 341-349, 360, 410-411 **Lab Manual:** 11, 23-32, 37-51, 61-64, 67-70, 73, 75-85, 87-98, 101-107, 109-120, 133-134	**13. Functional Area: Professionalism**—Candidate makes decisions based on knowledge of early childhood theories and practices; promotes quality in child care services; and takes advantage of opportunities to improve competence, both for personal and professional growth and to the benefit of children and families. Examples include the following:
Text: 76-77 **Lab Manual:** 45-47, 128	Enjoys working with young children in a group setting and demonstrates a positive attitude in her/his role.
Text: 341-346 **Lab Manual:** 23-26, 29-32, 107, 113-119	Understands the philosophy of the program and can describe its goals and objectives to others.
Lab Manual: 9-10, 12, 113-119	Continues to gain knowledge of physical, cognitive, language, emotional, and social development as a basis for planning program goals.
Text: 83, 146 **Lab Manual:** 23-25, 49-52	Keeps all personal information about children and families confidential.
Lab Manual: 27-28, 48, 115-119	Continually evaluates own performance to identify needs for professional growth.
Text: 124-125 **Lab Manual:** 27-28, 45-50	Participates in peer evaluation and is able to accept comments and criticism from colleagues, supervisors, and parents in a constructive way.
Text: 82, 106, 111-112, 143-145 **Lab Manual:** 11-12, 48, 113-120	Takes advantage of opportunities for professional personal development by joining appropriate professional organizations and attending meetings, training courses, and conferences.
Text: 74, 150-152 **Lab Manual:** 115-119	Keeps informed about child care practices, research, legislation, and other developments in early childhood education.
Text: 145-146, 346-349 **Lab Manual:** 115-119	Keeps current on regulatory, legislative, and workforce issues, and knows how they affect the welfare of young children and families.
Text: 152-153 **Lab Manual:** 133, 159-166	Seeks information relevant to the needs of the children she/he is serving—for example, information on school readiness, bilingual development, and special needs—from professional magazines, community colleges, community services, other caregivers, and community members.
Text: 77-78 **Lab Manual:** 125-128	Recognizes that caregiver fatigue, low morale, and lack of work satisfaction decrease effectiveness and finds ways to meet her/his own needs and maintain energy and enthusiasm.

(Continued on next page)

Child & Adult Care Professionals Instructor Resource Guide

Text & Lab Manual Pages	13. Functional Area: Professionalism (Continued)
Text: 120-123, 136-138, 148 **Lab Manual:** 113-121, 125-128	Works cooperatively with other staff members, accepts supervision, and helps promote a positive atmosphere in the center.
Text: 74, 145-146, 151, 410-411 **Lab Manual:** 26, 115-120	Learns about new laws and regulations affecting center care, children, and families.
Text: 145-147 **Lab Manual:** 27-28, 45-47	Advocates quality services and rights for children and families.
Text: 148, 150-155 **Lab Manual:** 23-32, 43-44, 159-160	Works with other professionals and parents to develop effective strategies to communicate to decision makers the needs of the children and families.
Text: 107-108, 153-155 **Lab Manual:** 27-28, 51-52, 68, 159-160	Develops the ability to state needs for additional resources for individual children or some aspect of the program.
Text: 198-200 **Lab Manual:** 9-10, 12	Is aware that some of the normal developmental characteristics of children (e.g., crying, messiness, dependency, willfulness, negative behavior, curiosity about gender differences, etc.) often make adults uncomfortable. The caregiver can acknowledge these feelings in her/himself, coworkers, and parents while minimizing negative reactions toward children.
Text: 83, 219-219 **Lab Manual:** 69-70, 73, 159	Seeks information about sexual abuse and child abuse and neglect, keeps current on laws and policies concerning reporting and treatment of abuse, and learns effective ways of working with affected children and families.
Text: 131 **Lab Manual:** 150	**Bilingual Specialization:** Demonstrates the ability to understand, speak, read, and write in both languages and uses these skills in all aspects of the program.
Lab Manual: 27-32, 48	**Bilingual Specialization:** Increases knowledge about bilingual education by reading, attending workshops, and consulting professionals.
Lab Manual: 150	**Bilingual Specialization:** Maintains and works to increase fluency in her/his second language.
Text: 360 **Lab Manual:** 149-150, 179-182	**Bilingual Specialization:** Consistently provides opportunities for all children to acquire a second language.
Text: 148 **Lab Manual:** 133-134, 150	**Bilingual Specialization:** Promotes the effective functioning of the bilingual program by attempting to clarify issues relating to bilingualism and multiculturalism.

Name_____ Course _____ Date _____

Performance ✓ Checklist

<table>
<tr><td>

Performance Standards

Level 4—Performs skill without supervision and adapts to problem situations.
Level 3—Performs skill satisfactorily without assistance or supervision.
Level 2—Performs skill satisfactorily, but requires assistance or supervision.
Level 1—Performs parts of skill satisfactorily, but requires considerable assistance or supervision.
Level 0—Cannot perform skill.

</td><td>

Attempt (circle one): 1 2 3 4

Comments: _____

_____

_____

_____

PERFORMANCE LEVEL ACHIEVED: _____

</td></tr>
</table>

_____ 1._____

_____ 2._____

_____ 3._____

_____ 4._____

_____ 5._____

_____ 6._____

_____ 7._____

_____ 8._____

_____ 9._____

_____ 10._____

_____ 11._____

_____ 12._____

_____ 13._____

_____ 14._____

_____ 15._____

Instructor's Signature _____ Date _____

Child & Adult Care Professionals Instructor Resource Guide

Planning Thematic Units

Directions: Thoroughly develop one thematic-focused curriculum unit. Be sure to include activity titles, materials and equipment needed, and safety precautions that you must keep in mind. You may be required to write additional curriculum units throughout your course. Complete all parts of the activity. Have your instructor complete the performance checklist at the end of this activity.

Unit Title: _____

Week Number: _____ **Age of Children:** _____ **Curriculum Number:** _____

Thematic Concepts to Teach: _____

_____

_____

_____

_____

_____

Skill Emphasis (things you do): _____

_____

_____

_____

_____

_____

Letter: _____ **Number:** _____

Shape: _____

_____

_____

Subject: Learning Centers—Suggested Activities:

1. _____

_____

Activity Reference: _____

2. _____

_____

Activity Reference: _____

3. _____

_____

Activity Reference: _____

(Continued on next page)

Subject: Learning Centers—Suggested Activities (Continued)

4. _____

_____

Activity Reference: _____

5. _____

_____

Activity Reference: _____

6. _____

_____

Activity Reference: _____

Subject: Math—Suggested Activities:

1. _____

_____

Activity Reference: _____

2. _____

_____

Activity Reference: _____

3. _____

_____

Activity Reference: _____

Subject: Music (Title in Quotations)—Suggested Activities:

1. _____

_____

Activity Reference: _____

(Continued on next page)

Child & Adult Care Professionals Instructor Resource Guide
Copyright © Glencoe/McGraw-Hill

Subject: Music—Suggested Activities (Continued)

2. _____

_____

Activity Reference: _____

3. _____

_____

Activity Reference: _____

Subject: Motor/Outdoor Play—Suggested Activities:

1. _____

_____

Activity Reference: _____

2. _____

_____

Activity Reference: _____

3. _____

_____

Activity Reference: _____

Subject: Art—Suggested Activities:

1. _____

_____

Activity Reference: _____

2. _____

_____

Activity Reference: _____

(Continued on next page)

Subject: Art—Suggested Activities (Continued)

3. _____

_____

Activity Reference: _____

Subject: Science/Sensory—Suggested Activities:

1. _____

_____

Activity Reference: _____

2. _____

_____

Activity Reference: _____

3. _____

_____

Activity Reference: _____

Subject: Story (Underline Title)—Suggested Activities:

1. _____

_____

Activity Reference: _____

2. _____

_____

Activity Reference: _____

3. _____

_____

Activity Reference: _____

(Continued on next page)

Child & Adult Care Professionals Instructor Resource Guide
Copyright © Glencoe/McGraw-Hill

Subject: Circle Time/Communication—Suggested Activities:

1. _____

_____

Activity Reference: _____

2. _____

_____

Activity Reference: _____

3. _____

_____

Activity Reference: _____

Subject: Fingerplay (Title in quotations)—Suggested Activities:

1. _____

_____

Activity Reference: _____

2. _____

_____

Activity Reference: _____

3. _____

_____

Activity Reference: _____

Classroom Management Suggestions: (Bulletin board, Speakers, Field trips, Helpful hints)

1. _____

_____

_____

Activity Reference: _____

(Continued on next page)

2. _____

_____

_____

Activity Reference: _____

3. _____

_____

_____

Activity Reference: _____

Performance ✓ Checklist

Performance Standards
Level 4—Performs skill without supervision and adapts to problem situations.
Level 3—Performs skill satisfactorily without assistance or supervision.
Level 2—Performs skill satisfactorily, but requires assistance or supervision.
Level 1—Performs parts of skill satisfactorily, but requires considerable assistance or supervision.
Level 0—Cannot perform skill.

Attempt (circle one): 1 2 3 4

Comments: _____

_____

_____

_____

PERFORMANCE LEVEL ACHIEVED: _____

_____ **1.** Student clearly develops a thematic unit plan outlining activities for each content area listed.

_____ **2.** Student identifies age-appropriate thematic concepts to teach which effectively develop thematic unit.

_____ **3.** Student incorporates an activity to address each skill to be emphasized within allowed time.

_____ **4.** Student incorporates an activity to address each thematic concept to be emphasized within allowed time.

_____ **5.** Student provides adequate activity description to clearly summarize activity.

_____ **6.** Student incorporates age-appropriate basic academic concepts with thematic concepts.

_____ **7.** Student selects and plans activities considering all plausible safety issues.

_____ **8.** Developmentally appropriate practice strategies included in classroom management suggestions.

_____ **9.** Student identifies materials and equipment that are needed to complete the unit activities.

_____ **10.** Student utilizes correct grammar, sentence structure, and reference information throughout thematic unit plan.

Instructor's Signature _____ **Date** _____

Name_____ Course _____ Date _____

Lesson/Activity Plan Form

Directions: Using print or Internet resources, plan an activity addressing goals, concepts, and related skills as directed by your instructor.

- Complete the lesson/activity plan on page 100 and teach the activity to a small group of preschool children or a small group of older adults.
- Consider the performance checklist criteria as you plan. Your instructor will use the checklist to evaluate your lesson plan and performance.
- On a separate sheet of paper, create and attach to the lesson plan a concept map or flow chart listing concepts and sub-concepts explained in your lesson.
- Upon completion, place a lesson plan with attached samples and a copy of your performance checklist in your portfolio.

Performance ✓ Checklist

Performance Standards
Level 4—Performs skill without supervision and adapts to problem situations.
Level 3—Performs skill satisfactorily without assistance or supervision.
Level 2—Performs skill satisfactorily, but requires assistance or supervision.
Level 1—Performs parts of skill satisfactorily, but requires considerable assistance or supervision.
Level 0—Cannot perform skill.

Attempt (circle one): 1 2 3 4

Comments: _____

_____

_____

_____

PERFORMANCE LEVEL ACHIEVED: _____

_____ 1. Lesson plan is complete, safe, and thorough; accurately details materials/procedures.

_____ 2. Strategies emphasize appropriate activity concepts and related skills.

_____ 3. Activity is developmentally appropriate, safe, and accommodates diverse learners and individual differences. Appropriate pace, methods, and strategies for teaching were implemented

_____ 4. The student used effective strategies to increase child participation and positive reinforcement.

_____ 5. Uses gestures, animated explanations, and child involvement/interest to illustrate a concept or skill.

_____ 6. The student is cooperative and establishes positive rapport with children, teacher, older adults, and others in the program.

_____ 7. The student is knowledgeable about various classroom control techniques and uses them.

_____ 8. The student conducts self in a professional manner and accepts and implements constructive criticism.

_____ 9. The student demonstrates imaginative and creative qualities in lesson implementation.

_____ 10. Student obtains and uses materials/resources appropriately.

_____ 11. Evaluation strategy effectively determines learning outcomes.

_____ 12. Environment set up prior to activity and clean up immediately follows, as schedule permits.

Instructor's Signature _____ **Date** _____

(Continued on next page)

Lesson/Activity Plan

Age Group: _____

Activity Title: _____ Activity Type: _____

Objectives: _____

_____

_____

Concepts/Skill Emphasis: _____

Materials Required: _____

_____

References Used: _____

Activity Procedure:

1. Physical location to begin activity: _____

_____

2. Focus/introduction: _____

_____

3. Step-by-step (use additional paper for explanation if needed): _____

_____

_____

_____

4. Open-ended questions: _____

_____

_____

5. Closure: _____

_____

Evaluation: _____

_____

_____

Student Emergency Information Sheet

Safety
ON THE JOB

Student's Name _____

List person(s) to contact in case of emergency:

Name: _____ Relationship to Student: _____

Home Address: _____

Home Phone: _____ Work Phone: _____

Name: _____ Relationship to Student: _____

Home Address: _____

Home Phone: _____ Work Phone: _____

List any special needs (e.g., medications, allergies, disabilities, etc.).

_____

_____

If you cannot be located in case of serious injury to this student, indicate a physician for emergency treatment:

_____

_____

Preferred Hospital: _____

Signature of Parent or Legal Guardian: _____

Date: _____

Safety
ON THE JOB

Fire Safety Procedures

Tools & Equipment: Fire extinguishers; storage containers or cabinets for flammable or explosive materials; and disposal containers for flammable or explosive materials.

PROCEDURES: Observe the safety demonstrations provided by your instructor or a safety professional. Read the safety materials provided by your instructor. Then complete the following tasks, as assigned by your instructor.

_____ 1. Describe the procedure for responding to a fire.

_____ 2. Demonstrate the Stop, Drop, and Roll technique.

_____ 3. Locate fire extinguishers.

_____ 4. Demonstrate how to operate a Type A fire extinguisher.

_____ 5. Demonstrate how to operate a Type B fire extinguisher.

_____ 6. Demonstrate how to operate a Type C fire extinguisher.

_____ 7. Demonstrate how to operate a Type D fire extinguisher.

_____ 8. Locate the exits to be used in case of emergency.

_____ 9. Read and interpret labels on containers of flammable and explosive materials.

_____ 10. Explain precautions required when using flammable and explosive materials.

_____ 11. Locate storage containers/cabinets for flammable and explosive materials.

Performance ✓ Checklist

Performance Standards
Level 4—Performs skill without supervision and adapts to problem situations.
Level 3—Performs skill satisfactorily without assistance or supervision.
Level 2—Performs skill satisfactorily, but requires assistance or supervision.
Level 1—Performs parts of skill satisfactorily, but requires considerable assistance or supervision.
Level 0—Cannot perform skill.

Attempt (circle one): 1 2 3 4

Comments: _____

_____

_____

_____

PERFORMANCE LEVEL ACHIEVED: _____

_____ 1. Safety rules and practices were followed at all times regarding this job.

_____ 2. Tools and equipment were used properly and stored upon completion of this job.

_____ 3. This completed job met the standards set and was done within the allotted time.

_____ 4. No injury or damage to property occurred during this job.

_____ 5. Upon completion of this job, the work area was cleaned correctly.

Instructor's Signature _____ **Date** _____

Reading a Material Safety Data Sheet

Material Safety Data Sheet
May be used to comply with OSHA's Hazard Communication Standard,
29 CFR 1910.1200. Standard must be consulted for specific requirements.

U.S. Department of Labor
Occupational Safety and Health Administration
(Non-Mandatory Form) Form Approved OMB No. 1218-0072

Identity (As Used on Label and List)	Note: Blank spaces are not permitted. If any item is not applicable, or no information is available, the space must be marked to indicate that.

Section I

Manufacturer's Name	Emergency Telephone Number
Address (Number, Street, City, State, and ZIP Code)	Telephone Number for Information
	Date Prepared
	Signature of Preparer

Section I. This section includes information about the manufacturer of the product, who can be contacted if there are questions.

Section II – Hazardous Ingredients/Identity Information

Hazardous Components [Specific Chemical Identity; Common Name(s)]	OSHA PEL	ACGIH TLV	Other Limits Recommended	% (Optional)

Section II. This section describes the ingredients in the product that may be hazardous. Common names are indicated, which helps to eliminate confusion.

Section III – Physical/Chemical Characteristics

Boiling Point		Specific Gravity (H_2O = 1)
Vapor Pressure (mm Hg)		Melting Point
Vapor Density (AIR = 1)		Evaporation Rate (Butyl Acetate = 1)
Solubility in Water		
Appearance and Odor		

Section III. Information needed to identify the hazardous material is listed in this section.

Section IV – Fire and Explosion Hazard Data

Flash Point (Method Used)	Flammable	LEL	UEL
Extinguishing Media			
Special Fire Fighting Procedures			
Unusual Fire and Explosion Hazards			

Section IV. Is the material flammable or explosive? If so, those data are given here, including the best type of extinguisher to use and whether special procedures are required.

(Continued on next page)

Child & Adult Care Professionals Instructor Resource Guide
Copyright © Glencoe/McGraw-Hill

Section V – Reactivity Data

Stability	Unstable		Conditions to Avoid
	Stable		

Incompatibility (*Materials to Avoid*)

Hazardous Decomposition of Byproducts

Hazardous Polymerization	May Occur		Conditions to Avoid
	Will Not Occur		

Section V. What conditions should be avoided when using the product, and are there any materials that should not come in contact with it? List that information here.

Section VI – Health Hazard Data

Route(s) of Entry	Inhalation?	Skin?	Ingestion?

Health Hazards (Acute and Chronic)

Carcinogenic?	NTP?	ARC Monographs?	OSHA Regulated?

Signs and Symptoms of Exposure

Section VI. What happens if the product comes in contact with skin? What happens if vapors are inhaled? What symptoms should be watched for, and what kind of first aid is required? List that information here.

Medical Conditions
Generally Aggravated by Exposure

Emergency and First Aid Procedures

Section VII – Precautions for Safe Handling and Use

Steps to Be Taken in Case Material Is Released or Spilled

Waste Disposal Method

Section VII. This section should be read before using the product. It also includes information on waste disposal.

Precautions to Be Taken in Handling and Storing

Other Precautions

Section VIII – Control Measures

Respiratory Protection (*Specify Type*)

Ventilation	Local Exhaust	Special
	Mechanical (*General*)	Other

Protective Gloves	Eye Protection

Other Protective Clothing or Equipment

Section VIII. Ventilation, hygiene, and protective equipment required are listed here.

Work/Hygienic Practices

First Aid Can Save Lives

It is important for everyone to learn basic first aid. Do you know the sequence of first aid actions recommended by the Red Cross?

1. Rescue victim and yourself.
2. Restore or maintain breathing and heartbeat.
3. Control heavy bleeding.
4. Treat for poisoning.
5. Prevent traumatic shock.
6. Examine victim carefully to evaluate injury.
7. Seek medical help.
8. Keep checking and assisting victim until medical help is obtained.

When dealing with an injured person, remember that the first rule is to do no harm. Careless treatment can worsen the injury. Also remember the following:

- Keep an injured person lying down.
- Do not try to give liquids to someone who is unconscious.
- If the person is not breathing, perform mouth-to-mouth resuscitation.
- Keep pressure on the wound to control bleeding.
- Keep broken bones from moving.
- Cover burns with thick layers of cloth.
- Keep heart attack victims quiet.
- For eye injuries, pad and bandage both eyes.

Urgent Condition	Basic Symptoms	Basic First Aid Treatment
Traumatic shock	Pale or bluish skin; general weakness; rapid, weak pulse; and rapid, shallow breathing.	Have the victim lie down and raise feet and legs if that does not cause pain. Cover the victim. Get medical help as soon as possible.
Second-degree burns	Burn appears red and spotty and produces blistering, considerable swelling, and great pain. Burned area has a wet appearance.	Submerge area in cold water or apply cold, wet cloths until pain eases. Gently blot dry with clean cloths. Apply sterile dressing. Get medical help as soon as possible.
Third-degree burns	Charred or white appearance. Deep tissue damage. Less pain because nerves have been destroyed.	Treat for shock. Apply cold, wet cloths. Blot dry and apply sterile dressing. Immobilize burned area as much as possible. Get victim to hospital as soon as possible!
Foreign substance in the eye	Red irritated eye that is painful.	Flush eye with gentle stream of room-temperature water for at least 15 minutes. Place sterile gauze over eye. Get victim to a hospital as soon as possible.
Closed fracture	Broken bone beneath the skin but with no open wound.	Immobilize the joints above and below the area. Move the bones as little as possible. Elevate the limb slightly to reduce swelling. Treat to prevent shock. Get the victim to a hospital.

Name _____ Course _____ Date _____

First Aid Procedures

Tools & Equipment: Telephone, First Aid Kit, and MSDS sheets.

> **PROCEDURES:** Observe the safety demonstrations provided by your instructor or a safety professional. Read the safety materials provided by your instructor. Then complete the following tasks, as assigned by your instructor.

_____ 1. Locate the telephone and posted emergency phone numbers.

_____ 2. Locate the eyewash station.

_____ 3. Locate the safety showers.

_____ 4. Locate the First Aid Kit.

_____ 5. Locate the MSDS sheets for hazardous substances.

_____ 6. Explain the precautions required when a victim is bleeding.

_____ 7. Identify the symptoms of exposure to cleaning solvents.

_____ 8. Explain the precautions required when a victim has a back injury.

_____ 9. Locate the main power disconnect and explain the procedure recommended when you observe someone receiving an electric shock and the person cannot let go of the source of electricity.

_____ 10. Perform first aid demonstrations as directed by your instructor.

Performance ✓ Checklist

Performance Standards

Level 4—Performs skill without supervision and adapts to problem situations.
Level 3—Performs skill satisfactorily without assistance or supervision.
Level 2—Performs skill satisfactorily, but requires assistance or supervision.
Level 1—Performs parts of skill satisfactorily, but requires considerable assistance or supervision.
Level 0—Cannot perform skill.

Attempt (circle one): 1 2 3 4

Comments: _____

_____

_____

_____

PERFORMANCE LEVEL ACHIEVED: _____

_____ 1. Safety rules and practices were followed at all times regarding this job.

_____ 2. Tools and equipment were used properly and stored upon completion of this job.

_____ 3. This completed job met the standards set and was done within the allotted time.

_____ 4. No injury or damage to property occurred during this job.

_____ 5. Upon completion of this job, the work area was cleaned correctly.

Instructor's Signature _____ **Date** _____

Child & Adult Care Professionals Instructor Resource Guide

Rescue Maneuver for a Conscious Choking Infant

Safety
ON THE JOB

A quick reaction on the part of a care provider when an infant or child is choking can make the difference between life and death. This handout provides a quick overview of how to give help to a conscious choking infant under 12 months of age; however, special training in first aid and artificial respiration by a certified instructor is recommended for all early childhood professionals.

In order to protect children and care providers, care providers should wear latex or vinyl gloves when providing any first aid treatment. When giving artificial respiration, care providers should use a mask designed for artificial respiration rather than direct mouth-to-mouth contact. Several types of masks are available for this purpose. Check with your local chapter of the American Heart Association, the American Red Cross, or other rescue agency for suggestions on the best type of mask to use in your child care situation.

A. If infant is conscious, but cannot cry or cough:

1. Hold the infant face down over your thigh with your hand and forearm supporting the head, neck, and trunk. The infant's legs will straddle your upper arm.
2. Keep the infant's head lower than the trunk.
3. With the heel of your free hand, give five firm back blows between the infant's shoulder blades.

B. If infant does not begin to cough:

4. Turn the infant face up on your thigh and support the head with your hand and forearm.
5. Keep the infant's head lower than the body.
6. Place third and fourth fingers of your free hand on the infant's chest, one on each side of the breastbone, just below the nipples.
7. Give five quick chest thrusts on the sternum, compressing chest about one inch (too much pressure can cause injury to a child).
8. Alternate with back blows until the object is dislodged or professional medical assistance arrives and takes over.

> **CAUTION:** To learn this rescue maneuver, you must be trained by qualified professionals. Injury can be caused if this technique is administered incorrectly.

One Year & Older

A quick reaction on the part of a care provider when a child is choking can make the difference between life and death. This handout provides a quick overview of how to give help to a conscious choking child one year of age and older; however, special training in first aid and artificial respiration by a certified instructor is recommended for all early childhood professionals.

In order to protect children and care providers, care providers should wear latex or vinyl gloves when providing any first aid treatment. When giving artificial respiration, care providers should use a mask designed for artificial respiration rather than direct mouth-to-mouth contact. Several types of masks are available for this purpose. Check with your local chapter of the American Red Cross or other rescue agency for suggestions on the best type of mask to use in your child care situation.

If the child is conscious, but cannot speak or cough:

1. Stand or kneel behind the child.
2. Make a fist with one hand.
3. Press the thumb-side of your fist against the child's abdomen between the navel and the bottom tip of the breastbone.
4. Grasp your fist with your other hand.
5. Give quick, inward and upward thrusts until the object is dislodged and the child begins to breathe on his or her own or professional medical assistance arrives and takes over.

> **CAUTION:** To learn the Heimlich Maneuver, you must be trained by qualified professionals. Injury can be caused if this technique is administered incorrectly.

Child & Adult Care Professionals Instructor Resource Guide
Copyright © Glencoe/McGraw-Hill

CPR for Young Children

Safety ON THE JOB

> **CAUTION:** To learn CPR, you need to be trained by qualified professionals, such as those from the American Heart Association or the American Red Cross. Injury can be caused if CPR is administered incorrectly. NEVER attempt CPR on a person who is breathing.

CPR for Infants Up to 1 Year

1. If an infant does not have a heartbeat and has stopped breathing, call 911. Then begin CPR.
2. Support the infant's head and neck without tilting it back too far. This may block the air passage rather than keep it open.
3. Cover the infant's nose and mouth with your mouth. Breathe slowly and use enough volume and pressure to make the infant's chest rise—about 1 to 1½ seconds per breath.
4. Check for the infant's pulse. Feel for the pulse on the inside of the upper arm about halfway between the shoulder and elbow.
5. If there is no pulse or heartbeat, begin chest compressions. Use two or three fingers to compress the chest on the breastbone (sternum) the width of one finger below the nipples.
6. Depress the breastbone about 1 to 1½ inches depending upon the infant's size.
7. The rate of the chest compressions should be about 100 times per minute.
8. Give two breaths after every five chest compressions.

CPR for Children 1 to 8 Years

1. If the child does not have a heartbeat and has stopped breathing, call 911. Then begin CPR.
2. Support the child's head and neck without tilting it back too far.
3. Pinch a child's nose and cover the child's mouth with your mouth. Breathe slowly and use enough volume and pressure to make the child's chest rise—about 1 to 1½ seconds per breath.
4. Check for the child's pulse. To feel for the pulse, put your fingers along the groove in the neck beside the Adam's apple (or voicebox). Feel for the pulse for 10 seconds.
5. If there is no pulse or heartbeat, begin chest compressions. With the fingers of your hand closest to the child's legs, locate the notch where the two halves of the rib cage meet. Place the heel of your other hand next to the fingers that located the notch. Take the hand closest to the legs and put it on top of the hand that is in position on the sternum. Interlock your fingers to keep them off of the chest wall.
6. Align your shoulders with the child's sternum. Depress the breastbone about 1½ to 2 inches while keeping your arms straight.
7. Allow the child's chest to rise to the normal position between the compressions without removing your hands from the child's chest.
8. Give two breaths for every five chest compressions. The rate of the chest compressions should be about 100 times per minute.

> For information about CPR courses, contact your local American Heart Association or the American Red Cross.

CPR for Adults

Cardiopulmonary resuscitation (CPR) is a procedure designed to help a victim breathe and restart the heart. It is a skill everyone should learn, especially those who work with or near hazardous materials or machines.

> **CAUTION:** To learn CPR, you need to be trained qualified professionals. Injury can be caused if CPR is administered incorrectly. NEVER attempt CPR on a person who is breathing.

Basic Steps in CPR

Although CPR is not complicated or difficult to learn, it must be done correctly to prevent further injury to the victim. In general, it involves the following steps.

1. Shake the victim gently and shout, "Are you okay?"

2. If the person does not respond, point to a bystander and shout, "Call 911!" If you are alone, make the call yourself.

3. Place the victim flat on the back while supporting the head and neck.

4. Tilt the head back by lifting the person's chin with one hand while pushing down on the forehead with your other hand.

5. Place your ear over the victim's mouth and listen and feel for breathing. Note if the chest rises and falls.

6. If the victim is breathing, do NOT attempt CPR. Roll the person on his or her side and apply any other first aid that may be required.

7. If the victim is NOT breathing, continue lifting the chin and pinch the victim's nostrils shut.

8. Cover the victim's mouth with your mouth, making as airtight a seal as possible. Be sure the person's head remains tilted back.

9. Breathe into the victim's mouth 2 times while watching for the chest to rise.

10. Remove your mouth and allow the victim's chest to deflate.

11. While maintaining the chin lift, check for a pulse. If there is a pulse, continue helping the person breathe. If there is NO pulse, begin chest compressions.

12. Place your middle and index fingers at the bottom of the rib cage. Move up to find the bottom of the bone that connects the ribs. Measure up 2 to 3 finger widths from this point. This is the location of the heart.

13. Position the heel of one hand at this spot. Place your other hand on top and interlace your fingers.

14. Elbows straight, apply pressure with the heel of your hand, delivering 15 compressions within 10 seconds.

15. Repeat steps 7-10 to aid breathing.

16. Deliver another set of compressions.

17. Check for a pulse. If a pulse is present, check for breathing.

18. If the victim is breathing, roll the person on his or her side and monitor pulse and breathing until help arrives.

19. If there is a pulse, but the victim is NOT breathing, repeat steps 7-10 to aid breathing until help arrives.

20. If there is NO pulse, alternate sets of compressions with steps 7-10 until help arrives.

> **Contact Information**
> For information about CPR courses, contact your local American Heart Association.

Using an Automated External Defibrillator

When a child or an older adult goes into cardiac arrest, care providers are often the first source of lifesaving assistance. As a care professional, you should be trained in both conducting cardiopulmonary resuscitation (CPR) and using an automated external defibrillator (AED). Knowing what to do can mean the difference between life and death for those under your care.

CPR, as described on page 110, involves providing mouth-to-mouth breathing and manual heart stimulation as needed to an unresponsive victim. An AED is used in conjunction with CPR and provides electrical heart stimulation.

> **CAUTION:** To learn to use an AED, you need to be trained by qualified professionals. Injury can be caused if an AED is administered incorrectly. NEVER attempt using an AED on a person who is breathing and who has a heartbeat.

Saving Lives

According to the American Red Cross, use of AEDs could prevent 50,000 of the estimated 220,000 annual deaths associated with sudden cardiac arrest in America.

Most AEDs are designed to be used by non-medical personnel in a variety of environments. Currently, AEDs are located in corporate offices, shopping malls, airports, sports arenas, schools, day care facilities, retirement centers, and other places where people gather.

According to the American Heart Association, AEDs can be used on older adults and children over the age of eight who weigh more than 55 pounds.

Although AEDs typically use voice prompts and pictures to walk users through safe automatic external defibrillation, it's still important to receive proper training before attempting to use these devices.

Training will not only teach you how to use an AED safely and effectively, it will also teach you to recognize the signs of sudden cardiac arrest and perform CPR as needed. Contact your local American Heart Association and/or the American Red Cross chapters for more information about AED instructional courses.

The steps below outline the processes you will learn through formal AED training.

1. **Confirm unresponsiveness.**
2. **Call 911**, or your local emergency phone number.
3. **Locate the AED** and bring it to the victim's side.
4. **Open the victim's airway** and check for breathing. If there is no breath or breathing is abnormal, provide two short breaths.
5. **Check for a pulse.** If there is no pulse or heartbeat and another rescuer is present, ask her or him to begin CPR while you prepare the AED. Turn on the AED.

(Continued on next page)

6. **Bare the victim's chest.** Make sure the victim's chest is dry, then attach the adhesive-backed electrode pads to the chest as illustrated on the package.

7. **Analyze the rhythm.** Make sure nobody is touching the victim while the AED evaluates the victim's heart rhythm. If the AED advises shocking, go to Step 8. If no shock is advised and the victim still has no pulse, resume CPR for one minute. Repeat this sequence until the victim is revived, the AED prompts you to shock the victim, or emergency help arrives.

8. **Shock the victim.** If the AED indicates "shock advised," make sure nobody is touching the victim. Announce "Shock indicated.

Stand clear." Then press the shock button. The machine will then re-analyze and prompt you to shock again. If the victim has no pulse after three shocks, resume CPR for one minute. If there is still no pulse, conduct additional sets of three quick shocks followed by one minute of CPR until the AED prompts that no shock is necessary or emergency assistance arrives.

For more information regarding the use of an AED, contact the American Red Cross.

Managing Stress & Substance Abuse

Stress Management

In school, on the job, and in your personal life there are situations that can cause stress. You cannot avoid stress, but you can control your response to it. It's up to you. Here are some tips for dealing with stress positively.

- **Talk with a trusted relative or friend about your problems.**
- **Keep a journal.** Writing about events, thoughts, and feelings can provide an emotional outlet.
- **Set priorities.** Recognize that it is unlikely you will ever be able to do everything on time. Focus on the most important things.
- **Keep your perspective.**
- **Make time for rest and relaxation.**
- **Learn and practice relaxation techniques, such as deep breathing or meditation.**
- **Exercise regularly.** Exercise can relieve stress by releasing tension and making your muscles more flexible. It also helps you stay physically strong and healthy.
- **Eat healthy.** Your body needs good nutrition to deal with the effects of stress.
- **Limit your intake of caffeine.** Too much caffeine can make you nervous, and it can interfere with sleep.
- **Avoid alcohol and other drugs.** Using drugs to cope with stress only increases your problems.
- **Help others.** It will make you feel good, and it will take your mind off your own troubles.
- **Be assertive, not aggressive.** Deal with problems in a direct, positive manner.
- **Set realistic goals that reflect your values.**
- **Encourage a sense of humor.** Laughter can relieve tension.

Substance Abuse

Substance abuse can lead to many negative effects in your life. It can harm you emotionally, physically, and socially. Using drugs can lead to:

- **Inability to concentrate.** Whether you are in school or at a job, you need to be focused on the job at hand. Lack of concentration, one of the many side effects of drug use, can cause your grades to be lower in school or make you fall behind on the job. If you work with machinery, chemicals, or other dangerous equipment or products, a lack of focus can endanger your safety or the safety of others.
- **Alienation.** As your attitude and personality change from the effects of substance abuse, you may hurt those who are close to you.
- **Addiction.** Whether it's alcohol, tobacco, or another substance, addiction can lead people to take desperate measures to get what they want.
- **Financial difficulties.** Taking drugs is a very expensive habit, and drug abusers often spend their money on drugs instead of paying their bills. Drug use on the job can lead to being fired.
- **Increase in crime.** Many crimes happen because of drugs. Users may steal to get money for drugs or even kill someone to get what they need. Drug-related crimes destroy families, neighborhoods, and lives.

PORTFOLIO DEVELOPMENT

Contents

In the search for more and better techniques to measure student performance in the classroom, the portfolio has come to the forefront. Your students may already be developing portfolios, but a fresh look could give you new ideas for implementation.

WHAT IS A PORTFOLIO?

A portfolio is a collection of samples of a person's work, carefully selected and refined in order to show skills and knowledge. The samples are assembled in a binder, folder, or other container that allows for simple, attractive presentation.

Portfolios are presented to potential employers to increase chances of being chosen for a job. Some people also submit portfolios to the admissions office when trying to gain entry into education and training programs. In any case, a portfolio is designed to reflect relevant skills and knowledge.

A TOOL FOR STUDENTS & TEACHERS

Portfolios are tools for students. Teachers recognize that students who know how to put a portfolio together have a better chance in the competitive job market. As students develop portfolios, they see more clearly how the work they do in school impacts them in the world of work. They discover that the skills and knowledge they gain are valued and usable on the job. For child care students, in particular, the link is a strong one. Students who develop effective portfolios have a tool that may be used to help them land a job or further their education.

Portfolios are also a tool for teachers. Portfolios can be used during conferences with parents and students as tangible evidence of accomplishment. As demonstrators of performance and progress, portfolios are a useful assessment tool. Testing alone is an insufficient means of evaluation. As educators expand their list of alternative methods of assessment, the portfolio is often included as one option.

THE PROCESS

Portfolio development need not be intimidating—for the student or teacher. If you decide to use portfolios in your classroom, you might want to take a simple approach, especially at the start. That way you can proceed at a reasonable pace to learn what works, without excessive demands on your workload.

Not every teacher handles portfolio development in exactly the same way. Subject matter makes a difference. So does the amount of time available to spend with individual students. What follows is a general plan for managing portfolio development. You may think of ways to put your own personal touch to the plan.

Basically, the process for development is simple. Throughout the course students collect assignments in a working folder or file. Periodically, they evaluate and refine their work. Near the end of the course, students choose several items that represent their best work to keep in their final portfolio. These may need one last refinement. To complete the portfolio, students learn how to prepare it for presentation to others.

Getting Started

To start the portfolio development process in your classes, begin by introducing students to the concept. The reproducible handout, "Developing a Portfolio," page 119 of this instructor guide, provides additional information for students.

(Continued on next page)

Explain to students what items, called work samples, you want them to place in their portfolios. Items like tests and quizzes are probably not needed. Point out that portfolio ideas are included at the end of each chapter in the text. Encourage students to think about the kinds of projects that would help them "sell" their skills to an employer. Students might have their own ideas about what they would like to include in addition to the work samples you require.

If possible, plan ahead, having in mind a number of work samples that are suitable for a portfolio. Remember, work samples need not be large. A variety in size and content is a good idea. You may want to prepare a master list for students to use in the course, requiring certain ones and asking them to consider additional ones on their own. Use the reproducible handout "What Could Go in a Career Portfolio?" on page 121 to get students thinking about what they might include.

Developing the Portfolio

To develop a portfolio, each student needs a large, expandable folder, or one with pockets. Some projects may not fit into the folder. In such instances, alternative arrangements can be made. Photographs and explanations of projects may be placed in the folder, with the actual components kept elsewhere. A bulletin board design, for example, could be photographed and described.

Sometimes students store their portfolios themselves. Help them think of ways to do so with care. Have them mark portfolios clearly with identification and choose a consistent, safe place to keep them throughout the course.

To prevent loss of portfolios, you might want to keep them in the classroom. Portfolios for a large number of students, however, can be space-consuming. Security is also an issue. If a safe location is available, using it to store portfolios is probably a good idea. Allow individual pieces from portfolios to be taken from the classroom, but not whole portfolios.

As work samples are completed, have students place them in their working portfolios. Each item should be dated and marked with identification.

Periodically, have students evaluate their work. The date on each item should help them analyze their progress. Ask students to compare past and current work. Would they do anything differently? Have they gained knowledge that could make their work better? Are they learning to use more criteria in evaluating their work?

At certain intervals, confer with students individually. During these conversations, you can help students identify answers to the questions just mentioned. As you check on portfolio progress, date and initial a sheet placed in the front of each one. If you check portfolios before talking with students, make note of specific points you want to cover with them in person.

Peer conferences are also useful. The "Peer Portfolio Evaluation" on page 122 can be used by students as they analyze each other's portfolios. You might place students together in small groups or ask them to trade portfolios for evaluation and input to each other.

Completing the Portfolio

At some point in time, students need to choose their best work for the completed portfolio. What are their plans for work or further education in the child care field? Can they gear the portfolio toward actual use after high school? Your input will be helpful to students as they make selections, but the final decisions should be their own. Students should take one last opportunity to refine the items they want to submit in the final portfolio.

The number of items to include is up to you and your students. A portfolio would probably look incomplete without at least four sections. If projects are small, more may be necessary. Extra items can be included if students want to keep track of a number of strong work samples that they might use in the future.

(Continued on next page)

Child & Adult Care Professionals Instructor Resource Guide
Copyright © Glencoe/McGraw-Hill

Remind students that when they actually submit a portfolio to a potential employer, several projects of superior quality are much better than a packed portfolio of mediocre work. Employers do not have time to peruse extensive materials, so a few outstanding items are more likely to make a positive impression.

When each item is placed in the final portfolio, an introduction should accompany it. A "Work Sample Summary" form for this purpose is supplied on page 124. In the summary, students explain what the work sample shows, what was done to create it, and what skills were gained from the effort. It may also include self-evaluation. A sample of a completed work sample summary is on page 123. You should sign each form to indicate that the work sample has been approved for entry in the final portfolio.

To complete their portfolios, have students create a title page that includes their name, a table of contents, and a preface. The preface describes the portfolio and explains its significance. A "Sample Preface" is provided on page 125.

As you monitor student portfolio development, you can keep track of their progress with the "Teacher's Record Sheet" on page 126. There is room to check off conferences with students as well as completed work samples. The blank columns on the right may be used to record the completion of the table of contents, preface, and the entire portfolio.

A CAREER PACKAGE

Some teachers combine portfolio development with career education. In other words, students learn how to put the portfolio together with other components needed in order to prepare for a job search. Letters of application, letters of recommendation, and résumés could all be studied and prepared for inclusion in the portfolio or to go along with it as part of a portfolio package. See the "Career" tab in this book for ideas on career exploration.

ASSESSING PORTFOLIOS

Before you use portfolios for assessment, think through your approach. What will be graded and what will not be graded? Will you use a point system or letter grades?

Because most students expect credit for the work they do in class, you will probably want to work out a system of evaluation and reward. If you use grades or a point system, establish the criteria ahead of time to guide the evaluation process, and make these known to students.

The "Work Sample Evaluation" form on page 127 can be used to assess individual work samples. You will need to list criteria for each specific project. For example, an evaluation of an original song with lyrics might have the following criteria:

- Original creation
- Pitch range appropriate for instrument or voice
- Notation correctly used
- Rhythmic pulse perceivable
- Has musical form
- Has unity and variety in form of repetition and contrast
- Expressive
- Uses variations in pitch and silence
- Conveys a message
- Music and lyrics work together

To evaluate the song, points could be awarded for each criteria. The total might be accumulated points or a grade designation, depending on your preference. Some teachers set up a rubric that uses numbers or letters to indicate performance level, with standards from poor to outstanding described.

Involving students in the evaluation process is essential. Some teachers set up a schedule for meeting with individual students to discuss progress. Teachers and students should work closely together to analyze and refine the samples that are kept in the working portfolio. Through collaboration, students discover what you see as

(Continued on next page)

specific requirements for improvement. Their own ability to recognize what can be done better improves. You may wish to keep examples of outstanding portfolios from previous years to show what can be done.

Help students see that they have much to gain from refining their work. They receive more credit for work that measures up better against the criteria. They gain a sense of personal pride in good work. Work samples that are well done contribute to a strong portfolio. An effective portfolio may be useful later when students present their skills to others.

Once a portfolio has been completed, an overall grade or points can be awarded. Again, a clear set of criteria gives students something to aim for and helps you evaluate the students' final efforts. The "Portfolio Evaluation" form on page 128 can be used to assess portfolios. It contains a set of criteria to which you could add others. These criteria, which are ranked according to three performance levels, are explained in the "Rubric for Portfolio Evaluation" on page 129.

PORTFOLIO PRESENTATION

In some classrooms, presentation of portfolios is required. Each student presents his or her portfolio to others. The method for doing this is arbitrary. Students could present to a small group of peers, or they could present to the whole class or just the instructor. If desired, you could even form a special panel to hear the presentations. This might be comprised of selected instructors, parents, administrators, advisory board members, school board members, professionals, and/or community members.

In any case, the student has the opportunity to display and describe work done. For those who have put forth a commendable effort, the opportunity to share the results brings pride. It also provides practice for portfolio presentation in the actual work world.

MOTIVATING STUDENTS

For some students anything that sounds like work is something to be avoided. For this reason, motivating students to take an interest in developing portfolios is a first step to success.

Some students may have trouble visualizing what a portfolio really is. Spark their interest by creating a bulletin board display of one portfolio. As an alternative, have a portfolio day, with several outstanding portfolios available to see. You could even plan a display for open house or plan a whole-school event that focuses on portfolios created in different subject areas.

The school-to-work connection is significant. Older students, especially, should be impressed by the long-term usefulness of a portfolio. Bring the reality of this home to them. For example, invite former students who have made practical use of their portfolios back to class to give their testimony. A current employer could also speak to students about the value of portfolios. You might even invite professionals or college students who have developed portfolios in early childhood care or older adult day care to come and show them. Some parents might be willing to do this.

Whatever you do, make portfolio development a goal to be eagerly sought. If you have enthusiasm, your students will too.

What does "putting your best foot forward" mean? It means that when others will be evaluating you for some reason, you make every effort to give a positive impression. That is what has to happen when you look for a job. If it does not happen, you may be overlooked.

One of the tools you can use when you go job hunting is a portfolio. When you apply for a job, you are likely to be one of many. Competition is part of almost any job search. To increase your chances of success, an effective portfolio can make a difference in your ability to compete.

WHAT IS A PORTFOLIO?

A portfolio contains samples of your best work, carefully selected and refined in order to show your skills and knowledge. The work samples are assembled in a binder, folder, or other container that allows for simple, attractive presentation.

You can take your portfolio to a job interview. You can also submit it to an admissions office to help you gain entry into an education or training program.

The skills and knowledge you acquire in school are useful and valuable in the work world. A portfolio is a good way to show others how well prepared you are for a particular job.

WHAT'S INSIDE?

What would a photographer put in a portfolio? Photographs, of course, but there might be more. A magazine layout might show photos taken by the photographer. A written explanation might describe how school yearbook pictures were taken in an orderly, timesaving manner.

What would a computer consultant put in a portfolio? Printouts of original programs might be included. A letter of appreciation from a client for a job well done is another possibility.

Anything that shows skills and knowledge in a positive way can go into a portfolio. If an item is too large, you can enter a description and photographs of your work instead.

As you proceed in this course, you will discover many portfolio content ideas. They are in your text and in your thinking, if you put your mind to it.

THE PROCESS

In this course your instructor will guide your portfolio development. You will be asked to save some or all assignments. Put these in a folder or binder. This is your working portfolio.

With your instructor's help, evaluate each assignment and look for ways to improve it. Assignments may be graded or have points awarded along the way. You might think of additional items you would like to put in your portfolio. Talk to you instructor about adding them.

When the course nears a close, you will be asked to choose several of your best work samples to put in your final portfolio. Choose a variety that shows the range of your skills and knowledge.

THE FINAL TOUCHES

A portfolio is more than just the work samples inside. A few additional components complete it.

Introduce each work sample with a brief description of the project and what you did to complete it. Tell what skills you gained and give an evaluation of your effort.

(Continued on next page)

In addition, begin the portfolio with a title page, a table of contents, and a preface. The preface briefly describes your portfolio and its significance to you.

Preparing your portfolio for use in a job search means adding other items to the package. A résumé, letters of recommendation, and a letter of application can go in the portfolio or accompany it.

When your portfolio is complete, you will have a tool that can be used after graduation as you look for a job or seek more education or training. Your instructor may award a grade or points for your overall effort and results.

A HIGH STANDARD

To help you rather than hurt you, a portfolio should be of the highest standard. A neat, clean presentation is fundamental. The binder and everything in it should be in good condition. Type or print materials if you can. Legibility is important.

Do not settle for less than a high standard. Remember that people who do not know you will be forming a picture of you. If your portfolio is neat, they will decide that you do neat work. If your portfolio shows accuracy, they will conclude that you pay attention to details. If your portfolio is interesting and has unique approaches to situations, they are likely to see you as creative.

One young man learned this lesson the hard way. While working on his portfolio, he decided quantity was better than quality. He put all his papers and projects, including the less effective ones, into two binders and submitted them during a job interview. The interviewer took one quick look at the contents and did not open the binders again. Needless to say, the young man did not get the job.

Employers are usually very busy people. They seldom have time to pore over lengthy materials, especially those that are poorly prepared. A few outstanding examples, however, can be impressive and easy to review.

STORING YOUR PORTFOLIO

One time an artist left her portfolio in a cab as she was on her way to an interview. The lost portfolio was never found. It represented hundreds of hours of work, including original pieces that could not be replaced.

Think about this as you develop and store your portfolio. Do you need to make copies of anything? Are you keeping your portfolio in a safe place? Do you carry it around unnecessarily? A little forethought can save you the hurt that the artist experienced over her loss.

A PORTFOLIO IS FOREVER

A portfolio is something you can maintain for life. Since people usually have many jobs over the years, a portfolio can be saved and reworked when necessary.

Try to become portfolio conscious. In other words, all through your working life, remember to save examples of the best work that you do. Over time, you may replace some items with new ones. Often the best work you do is the most recent. That's because you have learned more and discovered how to apply your knowledge.

If you have set aside examples of your best work, you will have the resources you need when it comes time to revise your portfolio. After all, you never know when you might want to update and improve your portfolio because a new job has become part of your career plan.

What Could Go in a Career Portfolio?

Work Samples

- Activity ideas
- Adaptations of materials for children or older adults with special needs
- Bibliography of books read in subject area
- Bibliography of children's literature or literature for older adults
- Bulletin board ideas
- Child care center designs
- Facility designs for older adult care centers
- Field trip ideas, plans, and implementation
- Finger plays
- Flannel board story and materials
- Games for young and old
- Glossary of early childhood vocabulary
- Glossary of gerontology or geriatric vocabulary
- Instructor evaluation
- Interaction with children or older adults, demonstrated on video
- Learning center designs for children; recreational area designs for older adults
- Lesson plans; activity plans
- Menus for children or older adults
- Music for children or older adults
- Music ideas for use in an early childhood setting, older adult care setting, or intergenerational setting
- Music reviews
- Musical instruments
- Newspaper articles
- Objective writing sample
- Observation tools for children and older adults
- Observations of children or older adults
- Personal philosophy on working with children or older adults
- Play, theatrical, for children and older adults
- Poems for children or older adults
- Posters for children or older adults
- Prop box ideas for children
- Puppets for children or intergenerational use
- Recipes to use with children or older adults
- Research report on children or older adults
- Resource lists for working with children or older adults
- Reviews of books for children or older adults
- Safety checklist
- Self-evaluation
- Songs to use with children or older adults
- Stories for children or older adults
- Storytelling skills on tape
- Themes or projects, ideas for implementing
- Transition ideas

Formats

- Actual materials
- Charts
- Computer printouts
- Demonstrations
- Designs
- Diagrams
- Drawings
- Floor plans
- Graphs
- Lists
- Photographs
- Tapes
- Videos
- Written materials

Career Materials

- Letter of application
- Letters of recommendation
- Résumé

Documents

- Achievements
- Awards
- Certificates
- Community service examples

Peer Portfolio Evaluation

Directions: Have a team member evaluate your portfolio using the information that follows:

Name of Evaluator: _____ **Date:** _____

Owner of Portfolio Evaluated: _____ **Class:** _____

1. Is the portfolio up-to-date? Explain. _____

_____

_____

2. Which work sample shows your peer's best efforts? Why? _____

_____

_____

_____

_____

3. Choose one work sample and suggest ideas for improvement. _____

_____

_____

_____

4. Analyze the portfolio in each of the following areas, suggesting ideas for improvement:

   Creativity: _____

   Use of Language: _____

   Clarity: _____

   Thoroughness: _____

   Organization: _____

   Knowledge of Subject: _____

   Appearance: _____

5. What is your overall impression of this portfolio? _____

_____

_____

Child & Adult Care Professionals Instructor Resource Guide
Copyright © Glencoe/McGraw-Hill

Work Sample Summary Form (Completed)

Name: _Elena Smith_   **Date:** _11-30_

Title of Work Sample: _Poetry in Motion_

Directions—Part 1: In the space provided below, describe your work sample.

This work sample contains the materials I developed and used to bring poetry to life in activities for preschoolers. First, I decided to work with the children's poem, "Willie's Way," because it has always been one of my favorites. I then thought of creative movements that preschoolers could do while I read the poem to them.

Because this was successful as well as enjoyable, I wrote two poems of my own, also devising motions to go along with them. As my poetry project evolved, I found music to play in the background during the poetry readings. All three poems, along with the creative movement ideas, are included in this work sample. I have also included a video that shows my interaction with the children as I presented my poetry activity.

This project shows my ability to work creatively with children. I think my love of children was apparent as I used early childhood skills to encourage the preschoolers and guide them. Not only did I display my writing skills, but I also showed that I could put my ideas into action.

Through the poetry project, I learned something new. I now know firsthand that managing a group of preschoolers can be a challenge. Two of the children in the group needed special handling to keep them in control. I used some of the techniques I learned in class, and they worked. By the end of my time with the children, I felt that everything was going very smoothly. My increasing ability to manage a group of children will be very useful when I am eventually employed as a preschool teacher.

Directions—Part 2: Identify the skills practiced and improved during the completion of this project by placing a check mark in the appropriate boxes. List additional skills in the space provided on the right.

- ☑ Communication
- ☐ Interpersonal
- ☐ Personal
- ☐ Problem solving
- ☑ Professional

- ☑ _Writing_
- ☑ _Guiding behavior_
- ☐ _____
- ☐ _____
- ☐ _____

Directions—Part 3: Have your instructor approve your work sample description with his or her signature in the space provided.

Instructor Signature: _Mrs. Johnson_   **Date:** _11-30_

Work Sample Summary Form

Name: _____ **Date:** _____

Title of Work Sample: _____

Directions—Part 1: In the space provided below, describe your work sample.

_____

_____

_____

_____

_____

_____

_____

_____

_____

_____

_____

Directions—Part 2: Identify the skills practiced and improved during the completion of this project by placing a check mark in the appropriate boxes. List additional skills in the space provided on the right.

❑ Communication ❑ _____

❑ Interpersonal ❑ _____

❑ Personal ❑ _____

❑ Problem solving ❑ _____

❑ Professional ❑ _____

Directions—Part 3: Have your instructor approve your work sample description with his or her signature in the space provided.

Instructor Signature: _____ **Date:** _____

Child & Adult Care Professionals Instructor Resource Guide

Sample Preface

The sample that follows summarizes the portfolio experience for an occupational student in older adult care. Note that a preface should be included in any portfolio, whether your focus is in early childhood care and education, older adult day care, or intergenerational care.

PREFACE

As a high school senior, I am nearing graduation. One of my goals this year has been to plan the direction my life will take next year. My occupational coursework in older adult care has helped give me focus.

Through classes in adult development and professional older adult care, my interest in older adults has grown. I now know that someday I want to pursue work in gerontology or geriatrics that involves older adults. Further education and part-time employment will be my first steps toward becoming a director at an older adult day care facility.

This portfolio represents my growth and strengths in the older adult care field. It contains examples of the work that best conveys my skills. My creativity shows through in my plans for recreational activities. The video included demonstrates my ability to interact well with older adults.

Choosing what to include in my portfolio was not easy. When you put a lot of effort into every project, they all become personally important. In the end, I looked for a combination that shows varied skills.

Now that my portfolio is done, I like to browse through it. It brings back memories of moments with special older adults, of times when I struggled, and of times when the light dawned for me. Putting this portfolio together has been an interesting experience for me. I hope that reviewing it will be an interesting one for you.

Instructor _____ Course _____ Date _____

Instructor's Record Sheet

Students \ Due Dates →	Conferences				Completed Work Samples											

Work Sample Evaluation

Portfolio
P-9

Work Sample Title: _____

Criteria	Comments	Assessment	
		Total	

Name_____ Course _____ Date _____

Portfolio Evaluation

Criteria	Comments	Performance Level		
		1	2	3
Contains required content				
Well-organized				
Clearly written				
Free of grammar problems				
Content accurate				
Content thorough				
Contains original work				
Shows creativity				
Demonstrates knowledge				
Shows skill development				
Neatly presented				
Overall Rating				

Child & Adult Care Professionals Instructor Resource Guide
Copyright © Glencoe/McGraw-Hill

Rubric for Portfolio Evaluation

Portfolio
P-11

Criteria	Performance Level		
	1	2	3
Contains required content	Missing many parts or significant ones.	Nearly all parts included; may have small omissions.	Contains all required content; may contain more than required.
Well-organized	No sense of order apparent; random arrangement.	Minor problems with arrangement; may lack logical progression.	Order follows table of contents in logical pattern.
Clearly written	Written material lacks complete sentences; meaning hard to follow.	Points made are understandable although not polished.	Writing is clear and thoughtful, with outstanding vocabulary and phrasing.
Free of grammar problems	Written material contains many grammar problems; hampers readability.	Some grammar mistakes are present; not evidence of a serious problem.	Few, if any, grammar problems; attention given to detail.
Content accurate	Questionable material in terms of accuracy; may not have used resources.	Effort made to make sure information is accurate; may be some questions.	Evident that reliable resources were used; ideas carefully stated.
Content thorough	Skimpy work; items lack complete coverage; missing information.	Topics covered adequately but not in depth.	Topics covered well; provides extra coverage that adds information and interest.
Contains original work	Little attempt to do any original thinking; may have copied ideas from resources and peers.	Effort made to come up with original ideas and materials.	Highly successful in coming up with own ideas and materials evident throughout; strong reliance on own skills.
Shows creativity	Little or no attempt at presenting work in interesting, creative manner.	Effort made to take a creative approach on most projects.	Demonstrates highly creative approach; ideas and materials are distinctive and presented in interesting way.

(Continued on next page)

Child & Adult Care Professionals Instructor Resource Guide
Copyright © Glencoe/McGraw-Hill

Criteria	Performance Level		
	1	2	3
Shows skill development	Few, if any, work samples show skills the student has practiced and improved.	Work samples show several skills the student has practiced and improved.	Skills are amply depicted in work samples; clearly shows how student has advanced and acquired skills.
Neatly presented	Poor appearance: rumpled, dirty papers; material not typed; lacks margins, headers, etc.	Acceptable appearance, but could use some improvement.	Outstanding appearance; clean and neat; may have added design elements that add to presentation.

Child & Adult Care Professionals Instructor Resource Guide
Copyright © Glencoe/McGraw-Hill

EMPLOYABILITY SKILLS

Contents

Today's workplace offers challenges that earlier generations of workers did not face. First of all, the job market changes quickly. Tracking employment trends is one way to prepare for the future. What else can you do?

The average American has had at least seven jobs before reaching age 30. People can expect to change employers several—perhaps many—more times before they retire. This means that your career and your job security are in your own hands.

Keeping Up

Many companies invest heavily in employee education and training. Make use of all opportunities to keep your skills and knowledge up-to-date. In other words, become a lifelong learner. When new technology appears in your workplace, get involved right away. Volunteer for tasks that will give you hands-on training.

Growing in Your Job

Continuing to update and improve your skills and knowledge will make you valuable to your employer. It may also help you earn a promotion. People who earn promotions are those who have shown that they can handle additional responsibility. What qualities and behaviors do employers look for?

- **Knowledge and competence.** Employers want workers who know how to do their jobs, even if a new job requires different skills. Employers also look for workers who go a step beyond—workers who excel.

- **Willingness to learn.** Employers promote workers who show they want to increase their knowledge and skills.

- **Initiative.** You'll probably advance in your career if you take initiative on the job by solving problems, proposing new ideas, and taking leadership opportunities as they arise.

- **Perseverance.** Perseverance is the quality of finishing what you start. Employers want to know that you will see a job through to completion.

- **Cooperation.** Employers want people who can get along well with others.

- **Thinking skills.** When considering who should be promoted, employers look for people who can think through situations and solve problems.

- **Adaptability.** Employers want workers who can adapt to new situations.

- **Education and training.** Employers promote people who have the needed skills and education to do the job.

Handling Your New Responsibilities

Getting a promotion may change your work life in many ways. Often it means you will become a supervisor. Then you will be responsible for both your own work and the work of others.

Be aware that as a supervisor your relationships with your former coworkers will change. You will be the boss. You must oversee their work and give directions. You will review their performance.

Child & Adult Care Professionals Instructor Resource Guide

Effectiveness on the job does not happen by accident. Excellence and efficiency take communication, teamwork, respect, responsibility, good humor, honesty, and a willingness to learn.

Communicating with Others

❏ Working as part of a team requires you to listen and speak well. Without listening, you may not know what is expected. Ask for help when you need it. If you do not clearly explain information, everyone on the team may fail. To work well together, you need to show coworkers that you are interested in them. Notice what makes your coworkers unique. Try to see things from their point of view.

Teamwork

❏ You, your coworkers, supervisors, and the owners are all in business together. You are a team working toward a common goal. To show team loyalty, do not speak negatively about your employer or a supervisor when talking with others. Be positive and focus on finding solutions as a team rather than looking for others to blame. When there is a crisis, do your part to help the team get through it.

Respecting Others

❏ Without respect for one another, there can be little cooperation. The more respect you give others, the more you will receive in return. Two attitudes that prevent respect are a message of "I'm better than you" and jealousy. It is important to remember that each employee has something to contribute. Jealous workers view others as rivals and make cooperation difficult, if not impossible.

Taking on Responsibility

❏ Employers want employees to do what needs to be done without being told to do it and to take responsibility for their actions. The responsible employee is willing to accept a situation or problem and take charge of responding to what is needed. Some ways to focus on responsibility include:

• Identifying ways to become more efficient by examining your past and current work habits and performance.

• Asking coworkers and supervisors for feedback on how well you are doing your job.

Willingness to Learn

❏ Every company has its own ways of doing things. You need to learn the system. Be willing to learn any job, no matter how small. This information will help you do your job better and possibly prepare you for a promotion. Take advantage of opportunities to attend training programs, workshops, or other chances to learn more.

Keeping a Sense of Humor

❏ A sense of humor can get you and your coworkers through stressful times. It can help unite the team and make all members feel better about themselves. Rather than being a comedian, just try to see the light side of a situation.

Being Honest

❏ Employers expect their employees to be honest. One lie can destroy your reputation and not only threaten your current job, but future opportunities as well.

Finding and keeping a good job requires you to work well with other people and show that you are reliable. Here are the personal characteristics that will help you be successful on the job.

Communication

❏ Employees need to be able to speak, read, and write the language that is used on the job. It is equally important to listen well, to ask questions, and to explain things clearly. You will need to communicate with supervisors, customers, and coworkers.

Teamwork

❏ Even if your workplace is not organized into teams, you still need teamwork skills. One of the main reasons workers lose their jobs is because they cannot get along with coworkers. An employer expects employees to work cooperatively, plan and make decisions together, respect differing opinions, realize there is "give and take" in order to achieve group results, and encourage and support fellow team members.

Dependability

❏ What one person does, or does not do, affects others. If somebody does not show up for work on time or leaves early without permission, the other employees may not be able to finish their work. Your employer will not tolerate it, and your fellow employees will resent it if they cannot count on you.

Responsibility

❏ Employers want their employees to accept responsibility for their actions. It can be hard to take responsibility, especially when things go wrong, but it's important to be truthful. Explain what happened, but do not try to blame someone else or make excuses.

Initiative

❏ Taking initiative means doing what needs to be done without being told to do it. Employers value workers who are willing to go the "extra mile" and who look for opportunities to do more than just what they were hired to do.

Willingness to Learn

❏ Employers want people who can follow directions and do their jobs well. Listen carefully to instructions. If you are unsure about how to do something, ask questions. Be willing to learn any job, no matter how small. Learn all you can about your job and about the company. This information will help you do your job better and will prepare you for a possible promotion.

Positive Attitude

❏ Your attitude toward your job is a very important factor in your success. You have a choice: you can act positively or negatively. If you have a positive attitude toward your boss and coworkers, chances are that they will respond positively toward you.

Acceptance of Constructive Criticism

❏ Constructive criticism is part of a boss's job. He or she needs to let employees know how they are doing. If your boss tells you that you've done something incorrectly, consider it an opportunity to learn. Ask how you could improve, and follow through on your boss's suggestions.

Honesty

❏ Employers expect their employees to be honest. One dishonest act can destroy your reputation.

Workplace Skills Checklist

The following checklists identify skills people need to be successful in the workplace. Check the skills that you currently have. Those skills that remain unchecked are those you will need to develop to be successful on the job.

Seeking & Applying for Employment Opportunities

- ❏ Locate employment opportunities.
- ❏ Identify job requirements.
- ❏ Identify conditions for employment.
- ❏ Evaluate job opportunities.
- ❏ Prepare a résumé.
- ❏ Write job application letter.
- ❏ Complete job application form.
- ❏ Prepare for job interview.
- ❏ Send follow-up letter.

Accepting Employment

- ❏ Complete state and federal tax forms.
- ❏ Complete withholding allowance certificate form (W-4).

Communicating on the Job

- ❏ Communicate clearly with others.
- ❏ Ask questions about a task.
- ❏ Read and follow written directions.
- ❏ Prepare written communication.
- ❏ Interpret the use of body language.
- ❏ Use good telephone etiquette.
- ❏ Listen to directions and follow them.
- ❏ Use appropriate e-mail etiquette.

Demonstrating Teamwork

- ❏ Match team member's skills to group activities.
- ❏ Encourage shared participation.
- ❏ Provide support to team members.
- ❏ Build and maintain trust.
- ❏ Complete team tasks.
- ❏ Evaluate outcomes.

Maintaining Professionalism

- ❏ Treat people with respect.
- ❏ Exhibit positive behavior.
- ❏ Comply with organizational expectations.
- ❏ Use job-related terminology.
- ❏ Participate in meetings in a positive and constructive manner.

Maintaining a Safe & Healthy Environment

- ❏ Follow environmental practices and policies.
- ❏ Comply with safety procedures.
- ❏ Use and maintain proper tools and equipment.
- ❏ Maintain work area.
- ❏ Act appropriately during emergencies.

Demonstrating Work Ethics & Behavior

- ❏ Follow rules, regulations, and policies.
- ❏ Implement job responsibilities.
- ❏ Maintain regular attendance.
- ❏ Assume responsibility for decisions and actions.
- ❏ Demonstrate willingness to learn.
- ❏ Practice time management.
- ❏ Practice cost effectiveness.
- ❏ Display initiative.
- ❏ Exhibit pride in your work.

Using Resources

- ❏ Avoid waste and breakage.
- ❏ Divide your time to accomplish tasks.
- ❏ Make a list of supplies and materials needed to do a task.
- ❏ Follow a budget for projects.

(Continued on next page)

Using Interpersonal Skills

❑ Teach others how to perform a task.

❑ Assist customers with problems.

❑ Work well with people from different ethnic or cultural backgrounds.

❑ Respond to praise or criticism.

❑ Provide constructive criticism.

❑ Channel and control emotional reactions.

❑ Help resolve conflicts.

❑ Display a positive attitude.

❑ Report sexual harassment.

Using Information

❑ Read instructions and understand how it affects your job.

❑ Check supplies or products received against an invoice or packing slip.

❑ Find and evaluate information.

❑ Use a telephone directory.

Using Systems

❑ Understand how your department fits within the whole operation. Find out what work is done in each department and how it fits into the operation.

Demonstrating Technology Literacy

❑ Operate and maintain tools and equipment.

❑ Enter data into a computer system.

❑ Use word processing software.

❑ Use the computer to locate information via the Internet.

Interpreting the Economics of Work

❑ Describe responsibilities of employees.

❑ Describe responsibilities of employers.

Solving Problems

❑ Identify the problem.

❑ Use reasoning skills.

❑ Assess employer and employee responsibility in solving a problem.

❑ Identify solutions to the problem.

❑ Select and implement solutions.

❑ Evaluate options.

❑ Estimate results of implemented options.

Adapting/Coping with Change

❑ Exhibit ability to handle stress.

❑ Recognize need to change or quit a job.

❑ Write a letter of resignation.

Developing a Strong Work Ethic

Directions: Read through the entire activity. Follow the directions for Steps 1 and 2 and the Follow-Up.

Step 1: Holding work as an important value in life is the definition of a strong work ethic. Commitment and dedication to the job are indicators of a strong work ethic. Review the following traits and determine if you think they are indicators of a strong work ethic. Rate each of the possible indicators with a **YES** or **NO** response in the space provided to the left of each number.

Step 2: Choose the three traits you believe are the **BEST** indicators of a strong work ethic.

Possible Work Ethic Indicators

_____ 1. Showing up for work 20 minutes early so you are ready to work when the day begins.

_____ 2. Offering to help train new workers.

_____ 3. Using sick leave every time you have a cold or are tired.

_____ 4. Reading professional journals in your field to remain current.

_____ 5. Setting personal goals to improve your work performance.

_____ 6. Willingness to stay after work to complete an important assignment on time.

_____ 7. Dressing in a more professional manner than your coworkers.

_____ 8. Offering to help busy coworkers complete their assignments when your work is done.

_____ 9. Informing the boss about coworkers who are lax in the performance of their jobs.

_____ 10. Taking additional courses and seminars to improve your skills.

_____ 11. Doing everything you can to earn a promotion.

_____ 12. Admitting to your boss when you make a mistake.

_____ 13. Admitting to your coworkers when you make a mistake.

_____ 14. Complimenting others who have a strong work ethic.

_____ 15. Never misusing equipment on the job.

Follow-Up

- Write an essay of at least 150 words to convince an employer in early childhood or older adult care that you have a strong work ethic. Feel free to use real life examples to support your case.
- Create a collage of newspaper and magazine pictures that show people demonstrating a strong work ethic in early childhood or older adult care.

Name _____ Course _____ Date _____

Mapping Your Education & Training Options

Directions: To review different education and training options and help you identify the location of schools in your immediate area, follow the steps below.

Step 1: Use print, electronic, or Internet resources to identify schools and colleges in your area that offer preparation for careers in early childhood education and care and older adult day care. On a separate sheet of paper, make a list of at least three schools in your area.

Step 2: Use print or Internet resources to identify names, addresses, and telephone numbers for one school under each of the following four headings:

Career and Technology Center   Community or Technical College
Trade or Technical School   Four-Year College or University

Step 3: Contact the schools you listed in step two. Compare the following information:

	Career and Technology Center	Trade or Technical School	Community or Technical College	Four-Year College or University
Annual Tuition Costs				
Average Class Size				
Housing Available				
Scholarships Available				
Modern Facilities				
Up-to-Date Equipment				

Follow-Up

What conclusions can you draw about your educational options based on your comparison?

_____

_____

_____

Networking & Personal Contacts

Employability
E-7

Background Information

Did you ever hear the old saying that "people get jobs through people they know"? Well there appears to be some truth in it. Most people can name others who made them aware of job openings or served as personal references. Many people often credit these individuals with helping them get a job or just encouraging them to explore career opportunities in a given area. Family members, friends, and even mere acquaintances can be great sources of information regarding employment opportunities. They may be able to answer your questions or at least put you in contact with someone who can.

There are several reasons why personal connections are so helpful. Word of mouth information is often the best source of job openings. Employers want to know that others can vouch for a candidate's skills, experience, and positive attitude towards work before offering the position. Employers also want additional information to confirm what they learn during an interview.

The process of making friends and sharing information about jobs is called networking. Networking begins when you talk to people. Preparation for networking starts by making a list of people to whom you can talk. Anyone you feel comfortable talking to is a potential contact that can lead you to hundreds of others. The goals of networking are to increase your visibility with others and gain career information.

Most people are willing to help others if it only takes a few minutes. To network effectively, you will need to develop short statements that tell others who you are, what your goals are, and the type of assistance you need to reach your goals. These brief statements should be used when making new contacts.

Directions—Part 1: Complete the following four assignments to foster your networking efforts.

- **Assignment 1:** Write a short statement (75 words or less) that tells others who you are.

- **Assignment 2:** Write a short statement (75 words or less) that explains your career goals.

- **Assignment 3:** Write a short statement (75 words or less) that explains the information you need to reach your career goals. For example, "I need to know how to make contacts in the early childhood or older adult care field."

- **Assignment 4:** Complete the following network contact chart:

(Continued on next page)

Directions—Part 2: Most people have access to more contacts than they realize. Fill in the names of at least five people in each of the columns listed below. Can you name ten people in each column?

Family	Friends	Fellow Students	Neighbors	Others

Child & Adult Care Professionals Instructor Resource Guide

Name_____ Course_____ Date_____

Using the Occupational Outlook Handbook

Directions: Select a job in the early childhood or older adult care field that is described in the *Occupational Outlook Handbook (OOH)* and the *Occupational Outlook Quarterly Update to the OOH*. Then respond to the questions or statements that follow.

Early Childhood Occupation: _____

Older Adult Care Occupation:_____

1. Under what general career heading, or cluster, is this occupation in the table of contents?

_____

2. Under what subheading (a group of specific occupations), if any, is this occupation found?

_____

3. Briefly describe two facts about the nature of work in this occupation.

_____

_____

_____

_____

_____

4. Describe two characteristics of the working conditions in this occupation.

_____

_____

_____

_____

_____

5. Relate a fact concerning employment in this occupation.

_____

_____

_____

(Continued on next page)

6. What education or training is needed for this occupation?

_____

_____

_____

_____

7. What personal qualities are helpful for this occupation?

_____

_____

_____

_____

8. How would you describe the opportunities for advancement in this occupation?

_____

_____

_____

_____

9. Is the job outlook for this occupation promising? Explain.

_____

_____

_____

_____

10. According to the _OOH_, how much might a typical worker in this occupation earn?

_____

_____

11. List two sources of additional information about this occupation.

_____

_____

Child & Adult Care Professionals Instructor Resource Guide
Copyright © Glencoe/McGraw-Hill

Preparing a Résumé

As you think about getting a job in early childhood or older adult care, one of the first challenges you will face is developing a résumé. You may be wondering how to begin. As with many tasks, preparation is essential. The following hints can help you start preparing your résumé.

The Parts of a Résumé

Most parts of a résumé are essential because they provide information that employers need or want. Other parts are not as necessary, but give additional information to enhance your desirability as a job candidate.

Personal Information

Employers need to know who you are and where they may contact you. Use the following guidelines in providing this information:

- **Name:** Give your full first name, middle initial, and last name. Do not use nicknames. To avoid discrimination, do not use titles such as Ms. or Mr. before your name.
- **Address:** Use your street address (including any apartment letter or number) or your post office box number. Spell out the name of the city, but use the official abbreviation for your state. Be sure to include your zip code.
- **Telephone:** Give your home telephone number (including area code) or a telephone number where someone responsible can take a message for you.

Employment Objective

Your employment objective should clearly state what type of employment you are seeking. It should be short and to the point. A well-written objective might be "To obtain a teacher's aide position in a preschool program" or "Seeking employment as an adult day care director."

Special Skills

Special skills include any abilities and qualities you have that will make you a desirable job candidate. When seeking a position in early childhood care or older adult care, think about your skills or experience in the following areas.

- **Knowledge of Children or Older Adults:** What knowledge do you have related to child development or adult development? Are you experienced in observing and recording behavior?
- **Management:** What skills do you have that would help you to plan and administer a program, work with parents or family members, or supervise employees?
- **Aspects of Care:** Which of your qualities make you especially suited for caring for infants, toddlers, preschoolers, children with disabilities, older adults, and older adults with disabilities; for identifying and attending to the needs of children or older adults; and for guiding the behavior of children and older adults?
- **Preparation:** Can you set up a classroom, plan and prepare materials for learning activities and/or recreational activities, and prepare meals for children or older adults?
- **Activities:** What skills have you demonstrated in directing activities in an early childhood curriculum or older adult activity programs?
- **Maintenance:** What experience do you have in caring for facility materials, activity areas, and equipment?
- **Nutrition, Health, and Safety:** Can you plan nutritious meals and snacks, identify and eliminate safety hazards, administer first aid, or teach health and safety?

(Continued on next page)

After developing your list of special skills, you can choose those items most relevant to your employment objective. Concisely incorporate these into your résumé.

Educational Background

Potential employers need to know about your educational background and experience. List the schools you've attended (and years of attendance) in reverse chronological order, with the most recent listed first. Also include any additional programs or courses you have taken related to your employment objective. Any special honors you have received also enhance your image with employers.

Work Experience

Your work experience will be of key importance to your potential employer. List any former employers—including their complete addresses and your dates of employment, job titles, duties, and special achievements—in reverse chronological order.

If your work experience is limited, look for other ways to emphasize your skills and qualities. Any volunteer work that relates to the job you are seeking is especially helpful.

Preparing References

Most employers will ask for a list of references before hiring a job candidate. Select people who know you well, such as a coach, that can provide favorable information about your qualifications, character, and work habits. Be sure to request permission from these individuals so that they can be prepared with relevant details for your potential employer. Avoid using relatives as references, since employers may view them as biased.

Generally you should supply references only when an employer requests them. On your résumé, you may want to include a statement, such as "References available on request." Prepare your references list ahead of time, including complete names, addresses, and telephone numbers. Identify each person's relationship to you. Use a word processing program on your computer and print your references list. Keep several copies on hand.

Creating Your Résumé

Once you have gathered the information you would like to include on your résumé, the next step is to write a rough draft. Many different styles and formats are acceptable for a résumé. Check out resources in your school or community library for résumé examples.

Read through your rough draft with a critical eye. Is it concise, but complete? Does it show you in a positive light? If you were an employer, would you be favorably impressed when reading it? Consider asking an adult who knows you well to read your résumé and offer suggestions for improvement.

Use a computer or word processor to create the final version of your résumé. If you are unsure of your keyboarding skills, ask someone with these skills to do this for you.

Carefully proofread your résumé for any errors in spelling, punctuation, or grammar. Your résumé may be the first and last chance you have to make a good impression on an employer, so it should be free from errors. After making corrections, ask at least one other person to proofread the résumé again.

When you are satisfied that your résumé is accurate, neat, and error-free, make copies of your final version. You may wish to use the services of a reputable printer for professional-looking copies. The printer can also recommend appropriate paper choices for your résumé and references list.

Circulating Your Résumé

To circulate your résumé, consider networking. Making contact with people who can help you find a job may prove invaluable in getting your foot in the door for a job interview. Along with a well-prepared résumé, networking often makes the difference in a successful job search. Distribute copies of your résumé among friends, teachers, employers, and others you know.

Name _____ Course _____ Date _____

Résumé Fact Sheet

Directions: The first step in writing a résumé is to gather the information you would like to include. Complete this activity by filling in the information requested. You may wish to refer to the completed fact sheet when preparing your résumé and your references list.

1. **Personal Information.**

   Your name: _____

   Street address or P.O. Box: _____

   City, state, zip code: _____

   Telephone number (including area code): _____

   E-mail address (optional): _____

2. **Employment Objective.** List four positions for which you might be interested in applying (either early childhood care or older adult care).

   _____

   _____

   _____

   _____

3. **Special Skills.** Place a check mark next to each skill listed below that you have. If you identify other relevant skills, write them on a separate sheet of paper.

Knowledge of Development

_____ Knowledge of child development; knowledge of adult development

_____ Experience observing and recording behavior

Management

_____ Planning a program or administering a program

_____ Working with parents; working with family members of older adults

_____ Supervising Employees

Aspects of Care

_____ Identifying children's needs; identifying older adults' needs

_____ Attending to children's needs; attending to older adults' needs

_____ Guiding children's behavior; guiding older adults' behavior

_____ Caring for infants, toddlers, and preschoolers

_____ Caring for children with special needs

_____ Caring for older adults with special needs

(Continued on next page)

Child & Adult Care Professionals Instructor Resource Guide
Copyright © Glencoe/McGraw-Hill

Preparation

_____ Setting up classroom or activity areas

_____ Planning learning activities for children

_____ Planning recreational activities for older adults

_____ Preparing materials for use

_____ Preparing meals for children

_____ Preparing meals for older adults

Activities (Directing)

_____ Art activities

_____ Language activities

_____ Drama/dramatic play activities

_____ Social studies/social skills activities

_____ Music activities

_____ Science and math activities

_____ Active play or fitness activities

Maintenance

_____ Classroom or facility

_____ Play areas or recreational areas

_____ Materials and equipment

Nutrition, Health, and Safety

_____ Planning nutritious meals and snacks

_____ Identifying and eliminating safety hazards

_____ Administering first aid

_____ Teaching health and safety

_____ Certification in CPR

Miscellaneous Skills

_____ Operating a copier or fax machine

_____ Using a computer and word processing program; navigating e-mail and the Internet

_____ Answering telephones

_____ Driving a van

_____ Keeping records/books

_____ Typing (_____WPM)

Other Skills

_____

_____

_____

_____

4. **Educational Background.** Supply information about your education and training, giving the most recent first, on a separate sheet of paper and attach it to this activity.

5. **Work Experience.** List your work experience starting with the most recent job first. Remember to include volunteer work and paid employment. Write your list on a separate sheet of paper and attach it to this activity.

6. **Activities and Interests.** List your personal interests and leisure activities, especially those that might relate to the job(s) you are seeking. Write your list on a separate sheet of paper and attach it to this activity.

7. **References.** After receiving permission from at least three individuals, record the following information: name; relationship; position and place of employment; city, state, zip code; and telephone number. List your references on a separate sheet of paper and attach it to this activity.

Child & Adult Care Professionals Instructor Resource Guide

Writing a Letter of Application

By the time you get ready to write a letter of application, you may have already invested a great deal of time and effort in your job search. If you are serious about finding a job, you will also take the time to write a thoughtfully worded letter of application. A well-crafted letter and résumé help you stand out from the crowd in a positive way, convincing a potential employer that you deserve an interview.

Opening Sentences

The first sentences in a letter of application should inform the reader of its purpose. State that you would like to be considered for a particular position and tell how you learned about the job. For example:

- "I am writing to apply for the child care aide position advertised in the Tribune on April 10th."

- "My résumé is enclosed in response to your advertisement in the Gazette for a program director for Sunny Dale Adult Day Care."

If you would like to work in a certain program, but do not know if there is a position available, it may be worthwhile to send a letter of application just in case. Your initial paragraph might read:

- "I am writing in regard to possible employment with your program. I have the training and credentials required of a child care aide and would like to work for a company such as yours. Please consider me as an applicant if a position opens up."

- "Kindly enter this letter of application into your files for possible employment as an adult care aide. In the event that you have an opening, please consider me as a candidate."

Middle Section

The middle section of your letter should emphasize the qualifications detailed in your résumé. Show how you are qualified to fill the job vacancy. If you do not have much education or experience, emphasize your training. If all three areas—education, experience, and training—are impressive, mention them in this section. Here are several examples:

- "As my résumé states, I have received my training at Hills School. I have completed the Child Care Aide Program, and I am well prepared to work as a teacher's aide."

- "I recently completed my education and training in physical therapy with a focus in geriatrics. I have acquired the skills needed to effectively work with older adults in maintaining fitness and in rehabilitation. My training also included a supervised internship. I believe this practical work experience has prepared me for immediate employment in the field."

Closing Paragraph

In the final paragraph, ask for a response. Give your telephone number and request that you be contacted to make an appointment for an interview. This section might read:

- "If you would like more information concerning my qualifications, I would be glad to answer any questions that you may have. May I do so in a personal interview? I can be reached at the above address or by telephone at (555) 555-1234. I look forward to hearing from you."

- "I look forward to talking with you. I will contact your office on May 11th to see when an interview will be convenient."

Be sure to close your letter with a sentence thanking the prospective employer for his or her time and consideration. Finally, remember that, as with your résumé, the letter you send to a potential employer represents you. It should be neat and error-free.

Letter of Application Worksheet

Directions: Imagine that you are preparing to write a letter of application for a position in either the early childhood field or older adult care field. You may wish to choose a specific opening that you have seen advertised. Compose a draft of the body of your letter by responding to the statements that follow:

1. In one or two sentences, explain the position for which you are applying and how you learned about the availability of this position.

   _____

   _____

   _____

2. In the second paragraph, tell the prospective employer why you are a good candidate for the position. Emphasize your most important qualifications. Refer the employer to your résumé for more information.

   _____

   _____

   _____

   _____

   _____

   _____

   _____

3. In the third paragraph, ask for an interview and tell the employer how to contact you.

   _____

   _____

   _____

4. Close your letter with a sentence thanking the prospective employer.

   _____

   _____

Leadership in the Workplace

Are some people "born" leaders? Do leaders create themselves? In truth, everyone has skills and qualities to lead in his or her own way. Sharpening those skills and knowing how to use them is often what distinguishes a good leader from a potential one.

Leadership at Work

A person need not be appointed, win an election, or become a boss to be a leader. You probably have been a leader at various times and situations in your life. Maybe you took the lead in planning a family picnic or coordinating a campus-wide recycling drive. Likewise, a good deal of leadership in the workplace comes from people with no title at all. They assume leadership in informal ways, such as influencing and motivating others, promoting teamwork, and serving as role models.

What makes a good leader? Do you have what it takes? Certain factors are associated with good leadership. These factors are discussed as follows with examples of how you can develop and practice leadership skills in everyday life.

Skills and Qualities

Some people believe that technical ability and experience are the most important traits of good leaders. Certainly you cannot lead others if you do not know the way yourself. Knowledge and experience, however, are only part of the picture.

Good communication skills—speaking, listening, writing, and reading—are vital to good leadership in the workplace and elsewhere. This makes sense, for leaders by nature must deal with people. How can leaders direct others if they lack verbal skills to express themselves clearly?

Good leaders are also good listeners. They realize that the feelings behind the words are as important as the message itself.

Writing skills are especially valuable for leaders in the workplace, who write memos and reports describing their ideas and plans to coworkers and others involved in the business. Similarly, reading skills allow leaders to understand the written communication of others. This includes feedback from coworkers as well as information on new developments in their line of work. In this way, good leaders are also good learners.

Of course, there can be no leaders without followers. Good leaders have personal qualities that make others *want* to follow them. Most leaders are intelligent and energetic. They are able to make quick and accurate decisions. Good leaders are honest, creative, and enthusiastic. They know how to promote unity among group members. They are aware that a group becomes strong when individual members feel special and wanted.

Maintaining a good image is important to gaining the support of others. If coworkers see you as honest, intelligent, respected by others, and able to get things done, they will be more likely to trust your judgment, providing you with opportunities for leadership.

A positive self-concept helps create a positive image among others. Feeling good about yourself and your abilities can help give you confidence to take on a leadership role.

Styles of Leadership

People lead in different ways, depending on their style of leadership. In all organizations, there are people who have been given the title and authority to tell others what to do. They are leaders by position.

(Continued on next page)

People who may have the specific knowledge to make the best decisions are leaders by expertise. They know what needs to be done and know how to do it. Sometimes people follow others because they do their jobs well.

Some people are direct leaders and like to be involved in every part of a project. Others are indirect leaders that may delegate authority, staying in the background until they are needed. You may have observed people who lead by example rather than words. You may also know leaders who are very vocal and motivate others with frequent words of encouragement.

No single style of leadership is the best. Rather, one style may work best in a certain type of situation. Good leaders are familiar with the different styles and with the individuals with whom they work. They know that what works for one person in one situation may not work for another person in different circumstances.

Take the Lead

How can you develop your own leadership qualities? You might begin by observing others who model leadership skills at work, at school, and at home. A coworker who shows a new employee how to do a particular job demonstrates good communication skills. Identify the types of leadership used by different teachers at school. Determine why each style is effective.

Opportunities for practicing leadership, formally or informally, are all around you. You might encourage a sibling or classmate to try out for a sports team. You can join various organizations, such as FCCLA, National Honor Society, SkillsUSA-Vica, or scouting groups. These are just a few of the organizations that call for leadership among their members. If you lack confidence in your leadership abilities, choose an activity and a situation in which you do well. Developing self-confidence is a goal not only for leadership, but also for life.

Entrepreneurship

Entrepreneurs start, develop, and then run their own businesses. They may start their business ventures in one of four ways:

1. **Starting a new business.** Some entrepreneurs start their businesses from scratch. They see a need and start a business to meet that need. There are many challenges to starting a new business. The entrepreneur must find a location, buy or build a facility, purchase equipment, hire employees, and find ways to attract and keep customers. They must obtain financing and develop a business plan. A business plan identifies the goods or services that will be offered, tells where it will be located, outlines the owners' goals, describes customers, and identifies the type of marketing that will be done. The advantage of starting a new business is that the owner can decide just how the business will be developed and run.

2. **Buying an existing business.** People who buy an existing business get the facility, equipment, and even the employees in some cases. However, it is important to find answers to the following questions before buying a business. Why is the business being sold? Was it making a profit? Does it have a good reputation? Are the current employees skilled and motivated? What is the condition of the building, the equipment, and the inventory?

3. **Taking over the family business.** Entrepreneurs who take over a family business usually have the advantage of years of experience with the business. However, they must consider the same issues as those who are buying an existing business. In addition, they need to consider possible concerns and conflicts with other family members.

4. **Buying a franchise.** Many businesses are franchises. The entrepreneur who buys a franchise obtains the right to sell a company's products or services within a given area, or territory. The company provides the location, management training, and help with advertising and employee recruiting. In return, the franchise operator pays the company a share of the sales, in addition to the initial purchase price, and agrees to operate the business according to the company's stated policies.

Characteristics of an Entrepreneur

It takes a special kind of person to be a successful entrepreneur. Listed as follows are the most common characteristics:

- **Persistent.** Entrepreneurs work hard! They work until the job is done, no matter what the job. They know their livelihoods depend on getting the job done and reaching the goals they have set for themselves.

- **Risk-taking.** A good entrepreneur does a lot of research and planning before starting a business. Still, in the final analysis, the entrepreneur must put his or her money and reputation on the line.

- **Responsible.** Successful entrepreneurs take responsibility for their actions. They know they are accountable to their customers, employees, and investors. They keep their promises and treat people honestly and fairly.

- **Creative.** Entrepreneurs recognize opportunities and are always looking for ways to improve their businesses. They may develop new products or services or find new markets for their products or services.

(Continued on next page)

- **Self-confident.** If you do not believe in yourself, how can you expect your investors, customers, and employees to believe in you? Entrepreneurs must be confident in their business actions.

- **Independent.** Entrepreneurs make their own decisions. They run their businesses the way they believe is best. They will ask for advice, but they make the final decisions.

- **Goal-oriented.** Entrepreneurs set goals and then "go for it." They know what they want and work hard to achieve it. They are "driven" to reach their goals.

- **Competitive.** Entrepreneurs are always looking for ways to make their products or services better than the competition's. They learn as much as possible about things that might affect their businesses.

- **Demanding.** Entrepreneurs expect a lot from their employees, but they expect even more from themselves. Entrepreneurs need to focus on all areas of their business. In order to do that, they expect a great deal from everyone involved in the business.

Could You Be an Entrepreneur?

Read each statement on the chart that follows. If a statement strongly describes you, rate it a #5. If it does not describe you at all, rate it a #1. If the statement partly describes you, rate it as a #2, #3, or #4. Total your answers and divide by 10. The closer your total score is to 5, the more likely it is that you would enjoy being an entrepreneur.

Rate Your Entrepreneurship Qualities					
Qualities	1	2	3	4	5
I am creative.					
I take responsibility for my actions.					
I am independent and like to make my own decisions.					
I am persistent and finish a task, despite difficulties.					
I set goals and try to reach them.					
I like to work at my own pace.					
I believe in myself and what I am doing.					
I like challenges and am willing to take risks.					
I set high standards for myself.					
I am willing to learn in order to make wise decisions.					

Total Score: _____ ÷ 10 = _____

Child & Adult Care Professionals Instructor Resource Guide
Copyright © Glencoe/McGraw-Hill

How to Leave a Job

Employability
E-15

Every job has a beginning and an end. Sometimes employers choose to end a job when a worker's performance is poor or the employer no longer needs the service of an employee. More frequently, however, employees choose to leave their jobs. Some people may leave to return to school or begin a new job, while others stop working. While it is important to emphasize techniques for getting and keeping a job, it is equally important to use appropriate strategies when leaving a job. For example, "do not burn your bridges" is always sound advice. When leaving a job, you should be careful not to offend your supervisors or coworkers. By leaving on a positive note, you will leave a network in place that may become a lifesaver down the road. The following chart provides suggestions for leaving on a positive note.

Actions to Take Before You Leave	Workplace Behavior While You Are Still on the Job	Actions to Take as You Are Leaving
Tell your immediate supervisor first of your decision to leave the job. He or she needs to hear it directly from you.	Do not slack off or reduce your commitment to your current job during your last days. People tend to remember others by the last experience they have with them.	Leave your job in good shape. Finish all major projects. Leave details about projects for those who follow.
If you are leaving to advance your career, honestly state your reasons to your employer.	Continue to treat others with respect regardless of how you may be treated by others.	Be sure to turn in your keys, tools, or company uniforms when you leave.
Identify a specific date that you want to leave your job and provide your employer with at least two weeks notice.	Ask your supervisor if he or she would be willing to serve as an employment reference in the future.	Avoid making negative comments about your current job.
Thank your supervisor for the assistance and training you have received.		Submit a letter of resignation to your employer mentioning appropriate information from the previous suggestions.

Directions: Read through the suggestions above and complete the following activities.

1. Interview at least two people you know who have experiences leaving a job by choice. Were their experiences positive or negative? Why? Write an essay explaining how the suggestions above helped them leave their jobs. For the sake of privacy, do not include real names. Attach your essay to this activity.

2. Imagine that you have received and accepted a job offer for a position that better suits your needs and your career goals in early childhood or older adult care. However, in order to accept the offer, you must tell your current employer that you will be leaving. Write a letter of resignation to your employer that follows the suggestions given in the chart above. Attach your letter to this activity.

Preparing for Competitions

Participation in competitions is a good way for students to move forward along their career pathways in early childhood or older adult care. As the instructor, you must be committed to the goals of competition. Working with your students as they prepare for various early childhood or adult care competitions is a time-consuming process. However, your reward is watching your students increase their work skills while developing leadership and teamwork skills.

Preparing Yourself

After committing the time to prepare students for competitions, you will need to prepare yourself by:

- Attending advisor workshops or meetings about various competitions.
- Talking with other advisors who have had students compete.
- Obtaining copies of competition requirements from the various sponsoring organizations, such as FCCLA or SkillsUSA. (See pages 155 to 156.)
- Concentrating on just a few competition categories.
- Attending competitions to see firsthand what happens during each competition.
- Talking with administrators, students, and parents about competitive events.
- Locating resources for students to use for their competition events.

Your preparation will also include assisting at the competitions. For competitions to be successful, all advisors need to help organize and carry out the competitions. Your help will be needed to get rooms set up for competitions; find runners, room consultants, and judges; and tally score sheets.

Preparing Your Students

Talk with your students about the goals of the competitions and how they can benefit from competing. Explain the commitment involved in preparing for competitions.

Offer students choices in competitive events. Help them determine their strengths and select a competition which they will enjoy and benefit from. In addition, review the competition requirements, problems students will need to solve, and the evaluation processes for various competitions.

Practicing for the Competitions

To help your students practice, demonstrate an event or show a video of students competing. Discuss the steps students go through at competitions, the equipment and supplies needed, and the procedures to follow. You may also show samples of past projects prepared by former students.

Have students prepare and practice their events over and over. After students become comfortable with their events, have them actually perform for their classmates. Have "judges" evaluate and help students fine-tune their projects.

As a final step for competition, proofread all paperwork for proper spelling and grammar. Have students prepare a checklist for items they will need to take to the competition. You will need to help students register for the events and get to their assigned locations.

After the Competition

Discuss students' experiences following the competitions. Encourage students to continue to participate in competitions. Make recommendations for improvements and listen to their concerns about competing.

Family, Career and Community Leaders of America, Inc. (FCCLA) is a nonprofit national vocational student organization for young men and women in family and consumer sciences courses. Involvement in FCCLA offers members the opportunity to expand their leadership potential, explore careers, and develop skills for life.

Through FCCLA, students can participate in a number of programs and competitions to strengthen their skills and leadership abilities.

STAR Events

STAR Events are competitive events in which FCCLA members are recognized for proficiency and achievement in chapter and individual projects, leadership skills, and occupational preparation.

Depending upon specific event rules and procedures, projects may be carried out by individuals or teams. National *STAR Events* participants are selected by state-established procedures before moving on to nationals. Some event areas include:

- Occupational Child Care.
- Entrepreneurship.
- Focus on Children.
- Interpersonal Communications.

Career Connection

Through individual, cooperative, and competitive events, members discover their strengths, target career goals, and initiate a plan for living their chosen way of life. The activity areas offered in the *Career Connection* program include:

- Plug In to Careers.
- Sign On to the Career Connection.
- Program Career Steps.

- Link Up to Jobs.
- Access Skills for Career Success.
- Integrate Work and Life.

Leaders at Work

Leaders at Work is a national program that recognizes FCCLA members who create projects to strengthen their leadership goals on the job. The main program goals include recognizing career-oriented FCCLA members and encouraging leadership development.

Leaders at Work emphasizes leadership on the job and helps students identify skills they need to strengthen to become effective leaders. Leadership skill areas include:

- Communication.
- Interpersonal.
- Management.
- Entrepreneurship.

The program is open to any FCCLA member who has a paid, in school job or ongoing volunteer job related to one of the *Leaders at Work* career areas. The career area related to early childhood competitions includes:

- Early Childhood Education and Services.

Leaders at Work helps students prove they have the skills employers want and provides them with examples to use in job interviews and on college applications. Program participants can also apply to be recognized as an *Outstanding Leader* in the targeted career area related to their jobs. Through this program, students may also receive scholarships.

For Information:
http://www.fcclainc.org/

CHAMPIONSHIPS

The national SkillsUSA Championships are held annually in June. Thousands of students compete in more than 70 occupational and leadership skill areas. Competing against the clock and each other, the participants prove their expertise in early childhood-related skills. There are also competitions in leadership skills, such as extemporaneous speaking and parliamentary procedure. Students benefit from competition no matter how they place in the finals. They learn more about their skills and often make future job contacts.

Technical committees made up of industry representatives of labor and management plan the championships. The national technical committees are assisted by local representatives of education and industry. Along with technical skills, safety practices and procedures are also judged.

Early childhood care and education students may participate in the SkillsUSA Championships in the "Preschool Teaching Assistant" contest. The contest will evaluate the students' ability to plan and present appropriate activities for preschool-age children relating to a specific theme. The students must also demonstrate a general knowledge of quality child care.

Contact Information:

For a full listing of *all* SkillsUSA Championships competitions, go to:

http://www.skillsusa.org

INSTRUCTIONAL PLANS

Contents

INSTRUCTIONAL PLAN ════════════════════════════════

Understanding Child Development

FOCUS & PLANNING

Section Objectives

❑ Describe the areas of child development.

❑ Explain three of the theories about child development.

❑ Identify the general principles of child development.

❑ Explain how children progress through developmental stages.

Instruction & Student Practice

❑ **Reading.** Have students read *Section 1-1* on text pages 27-37. Assign the *Section 1-1 Knowledge Check* and *Mini Lab*.

❑ **Brain Models.** Have students work in cooperative teams. Provide various materials, such as dough, clay, string, dried beans, plastic, eggs, bristle blocks, and art supplies. Have the groups create models showing how the brain works. Have a team reporter explain the team's model to the class.

❑ **Writing.** Have students research and write an information guide showing new parents how to foster brain development in young children. These guides may be published using a computer-assisted program and distributed at a doctor's office or health agency.

❑ **Lab Manual.** Assign *Lab Activity 1* on page 9 and *Lab Activity 2* on page 11 of the Lab Manual.

❑ **Child & Adult Care Study Guides.** Assign *Study Guide 1-1* from the Student Motivation Kit.

❑ **Child & Adult Care Applications.** Assign *Activity 1* from the Student Motivation Kit.

❑ **Child & Adult Care Observations.** Assign *Observation 44* from the Student Motivation Kit.

❑ **Child & Adult Care Career Profiles.** Assign *Career Profiles* as desired from the Student Motivation Kit.

Review & Student Performance

❑ **PowerPoint® Slides.** Use the *Section 1-1 PowerPoint®* slides on the Effective Instruction CD-ROM.

❑ **Section 1-1 Test.** Have students complete the *Section 1-1 Test* on pages 301-302 of this guide. Or, create your own test by using the **Exam***View*® Test Generator found on the ***Child & Adult Care Professionals*** Effective Instruction CD-ROM.

KEY TERMS

- cognitive
- sensorimotor
- sensory
- temperament
- environment
- heredity
- neurons
- synapses

CARE PROVIDER TIP

Students learn best in courses in which they feel ownership. Have each student create a K, W, L (know, want to know, learned) chart for his or her journal. Adapt the curriculum to include the topics that students want to learn. Update the chart periodically for the students to record what they have learned and to set new goals.

(Continued on next page)

Answers to Section 1-1 Knowledge Check

1. Social, emotional, intellectual, physical.
2. Binet believed one test score could represent a person's overall intelligence. Gardner disagreed. He believes there are multiple intelligences and learning styles that cannot be reflected by a score on one test.
3. Sensory-motor; repeated and related experiences, developmentally appropriate.

(**MINI LAB**)— *Reports will vary*.

Answers to Section 1-1 Test

Matching:

1.	A	5.	B
2.	E	6.	C
3.	F	7.	D
4.	H	8.	G

Short Answers:

9. Hold up their heads and later creep and crawl.
10. Concepts are developed as children gather information through their five senses.
11. To help them understand consequences of their actions.
12. By showing them love, respect, and support.
13. The child will feel alone and unworthy.
14. Listening and taking turns.
15. A child's synapse activity is more than two times faster than an adult's.

(**WORKPLACE CHALLENGE**)—Binet believed that a single test (IQ test) can prove a person's intelligence. However, Gardner believes that many kinds of intelligence exist and that the IQ test focuses on only a few. Gardner proposed the multiple intelligences theory.

INSTRUCTIONAL PLAN ━━━━━━━━━━━━━━━━━

Influences on Development

FOCUS & PLANNING

Section Objectives

☐ Differentiate between heredity and environment in child development.

☐ Identify other important factors that affect proper child development.

☐ Describe potential characteristics of children at risk.

☐ Explain how prevention and intervention services help at-risk children and their families.

Instruction & Student Practice

☐ **Reading.** Have students read *Section 1-2* of on text pages 38-45. Assign the *Section 1-2 Knowledge Check* and *Mini Lab.*

☐ **Journal Entry.** Have each student write a one-page essay describing the impact of heredity and environment on his or her personal development.

☐ **Internet Search.** Assign each student a topic, such as miscarriage, amniocentesis, Rh factor, or other birth defects to research on the Internet. Have students give a brief report to the class on their findings.

☐ **Explore a Web Site.** Assign each student a topic such as miscarriage, amniocentesis, or Rh factor to research on the March of Dimes web site. After the student studies the information, she/he should make a brief report to the class.

☐ **Lab Manual.** Assign *Lab Activity 3* on page 12 of the Lab Manual.

☐ **Child & Adult Care Study Guides.** Assign *Study Guide 1-2* from the Student Motivation Kit.

☐ **Child & Adult Care Applications.** Assign *Application Activity 4* from the Student Motivation Kit.

☐ **Child & Adult Care Career Profiles.** Assign *Career Profiles* as desired from the Student Motivation Kit.

Review & Student Performance

☐ **PowerPoint® Slides.** Use the Section 1-2 PowerPoint® slides on the Effective Instruction CD-ROM.

☐ **Section 1-2 Test.** Have students complete the Section 1-2 Test on pages 303-304 of this guide. Or, create your own test by using the **Exam***View*® Test Generator found on the ***Child & Adult Care Professionals*** Effective Instruction CD-ROM.

KEY TERMS

• **at risk**
• **prenatal**
• **cesarean birth**
• **intervention services**
• **referral**

CARE PROVIDER TIP

Good nutrition is one of the most important factors in a healthy pregnancy. Since the diets of many teenage females are deficient in nutrients, such as calcium, iron, and folic acid, it is important that high school students learn what eating habits need to be changed for a healthy pregnancy.

(Continued on next page)

Answers to Section 1-2 Knowledge Check

1. Heredity and environment, maternal health prior to delivery, prenatal drug use, birth process, health, nutrition, care & nurturing, economic resources.

2. Drug exposure prior to birth; premature birth; low birth weight; physical, mental, or emotional disability; malnutrition; poverty; neglect or abuse; exposure to violence.

3. Intervention services, parent education, support services, hospitals, health departments, schools, social service agencies.

MINI LAB —*Answers will vary.*

Answers to Chapter 1 Review & Activities

1. *Intellectual:* how children gather and process information; *emotional:* ability to identify and control one's emotions; *physical:* growth pattern of body; *social:* ability to interact with others.

2. *Any four:* Jean Piaget, Lawrence Kohlberg, Eric Erikson, Alfred Binet, Urie Bronfrenbrenner, Benjamin Bloom, Lev Vygotsky, Abraham Maslow, B.F. Skinner, Sigmund Freud, Bruce Perry, Howard Gardner, Stella Chess & Alexander Thomas. See pages 32–33 for their influence on the study of child development.

3. The brain coordinates development: development rate is individual; development is sequential; development is interrelated. Examples will vary.

4. Synapses.

5. They reinforce connections and synapses along neural (learning) pathways.

6. Critical times of development during which specific types of experiences are most beneficial and necessary for learning.

7. Drug exposure prior to birth; premature birth; low birth weight; physical, mental, or emotional disability; malnutrition; poverty; neglect or abuse; exposure to violence.

8. Poverty can result in malnutrition or poor health care. Lack of necessary daily resources negatively affects sound development.

9. Avoid drug abuse, acquire parent education, provide good nutrition and health care.

10. Books, videos, lending libraries, hospitals, child care and health care personnel.

Answers to Section 1-2 Test

Matching:

1. A
2. D
3. B
4. C
5. E

Short Answer:

6. Heredity and environment.

7. Hair and eye color, adult height, body shape, and physical, intellectual, emotional, and social strengths and weaknesses.

8. Problems before birth or during delivery and injury or illness during the earliest years of life.

9. Whole grains, proteins, and fresh fruits and vegetables.

10. Exhibit warm facial expressions and speak calmly.

11. Unique experiences, ethnicity, homeland, and religion.

12. Poor brain development and lower energy level for play; also taxes the child's stamina for learning.

13. Poor social development.

14. Time management, basic first aid, childhood nutrition, and positive ways of guiding children's behavior.

15. YWCA and Cooperative Extension Service.

WORKPLACE CHALLENGE —A stable environment for a child, provided by parents and care providers, should include good nutrition and health care, responsive care and nurturing, and an engaging play environment.

INSTRUCTIONAL PLAN ━━━━━━━━━━━━━━━━━━━━━━━━━━━━━

Aging & Adult Development

Section **2-1**

FOCUS & PLANNING

Section Objectives

❑ Identify myths and stereotypes about aging.

❑ Describe three principles of aging.

❑ Compare the researchers' strategies of adult development.

❑ Discuss two aging issues linked to the increasing older adult population.

Instruction & Student Practice

❑ **Reading.** Have students read *Section 2-1* on text pages 26-47. Assign the *Section 2-1 Knowledge Check* and *Mini Lab*.

❑ **Interview.** Have students develop interview questions relating to life experiences. Assign each student to interview a grandparent or other older adult and report the responses to the class.

❑ **Analyze Film Clips.** Show film clips from TV programs or movies that include older adults. Discuss if the older adults are depicted realistically or if myths or stereotypes are promoted.

❑ **Research services.** Using the Internet, phone books, and community service directories, have students list and categorize local services that are available for older adults. Have them report their findings to the class.

❑ **Lab Manual.** Assign *Lab Activity 4* on page 13 and *Lab Activity 5* on page 17 of the Lab Manual.

❑ **Child & Adult Care Study Guides.** Assign *Study Guide 2-1* from the Student Motivation Kit.

❑ **Child & Adult Care Applications.** Assign *Activities 28, 29, 31, 32, 73 to 79*, and *87 to 91* as desired from the Student Motivation Kit.

❑ **Child & Adult Care Observations.** Assign *Observations OA-1 to OA-22* as desired from the Student Motivation Kit.

❑ **Child & Adult Care Career Profiles.** Assign *Career Profiles* as desired from the Student Motivation Kit.

Review & Student Performance

❑ **PowerPoint® Slides.** Use the *Section 2-1 PowerPoint®* slides on the Effective Instruction CD-ROM.

❑ **Section 2-1 Test.** Have students complete the *Section 2-1 Test* on pages 305-306 of this guide. Or, create your own test by using the **Exam***View*® Test Generator found on the ***Child & Adult Care Professionals*** Effective Instruction CD-ROM.

(Continued on next page)

KEY TERMS

- gerontology
- sociology
- geriatrics
- longevity
- generativity
- elder
- baby boomers

CARE PROVIDER TIP

Since many older adults and their families may not be familiar with community resources and services, it is important that care providers be knowledgeable about the available resources and services and prepared to assist the adult in accessing the services.

Answers to Section 2-1 Knowledge Check

1. Those 85 years and older.

2. Both Levinson and Gould studied adult development, but neither one addressed adults beyond 65 years of age. Both theories described life's structure that build and change throughout adulthood. Both scholars believe that as people age they become stable.

3. Change must occur in order to meet the demands of the growing aging adult population. The greatest demand will be of the society's social, political, and economic institutions. Age-related issues will have a significant impact on every area of the health-care industry.

MINI LAB —*Answers will vary*.

Answers to Section 2-1 Test

Matching:

1. D   4. B
2. E   5. A
3. C

Short Answers:

6. Memory, learning, intelligence, and personality.

7. To help older people and their families meet their long-term care needs, which involves helping with money management, family or individual therapy, and decisions on that will supervise their overall care.

8. Positive end is love; negative end is being alone and isolated.

9. People become depressed or preoccupied with death.

10. Midlife transition (ages 40 to 45).

11. Middle adulthood (ages 45 to 60).

12. Change is constant in adulthood, and it is not a time of stable emotions and motivation.

13. Living within a multicultural society and the growth of a large percentage of Americans who will soon enter late adulthood.

14. 82 years of age.

15. This population shift will greatly expand career options in gerontology and geriatrics.

WORKPLACE CHALLENGE —1.) As people age, their brains must be challenged for them to continue to learn. Some older adults experience intellectual decline, although not severe enough to interfere with daily living. 2.) As people age, many tend to experience some memory loss for various reasons. 3.) Older adults tend to have happier moods than do younger adults. 4.) Older adults contribute greatly to society by volunteering in their communities and helping family members. 5.) Older adults appreciate others showing respect. If they receive respectful treatment, they will return it.

Child & Adult Care Professionals Instructor Resource Guide

INSTRUCTIONAL PLAN ━━━━━━━━━━━━━━━━━━━━━━

Basic Needs of Older Adults

Section **2-2**

FOCUS & PLANNING

Section Objectives

❑ List the kinds of basic needs of older adults.

❑ Compare the types of independent living arrangements available to older adults.

❑ Identify the stages of death and dying.

Instruction & Student Practice

❑ **Reading.** Have students read *Section 2-2* on text pages 59-69. Assign the *Section 2-2 Knowledge Check* and *Mini Lab*.

❑ **Service Learning.** Have students plan an activity such as a holiday celebration or game party for the participants of an older adult day care center. Students should then take the class to the adult facility and lead the activity.

❑ **Speaker.** Have an administrator from a retirement community speak to the class about the different levels of adult care available and the factors that determine when an individual moves from one level to another.

❑ **Research Health Problems.** Using print and Internet resources, students should research common health problems of older adults. Have the students describe the healthy habits that can help people possibly avoid or delay these health problems.

❑ **Lab Manual.** Assign *Lab Activity 6* on page 20 and *Lab Activity 7* on page 21 of the Lab Manual.

❑ **Child & Adult Care Study Guides.** Assign *Study Guide 2-2* from the Student Motivation Kit.

❑ **Child & Adult Care Applications.** Assign *Activities 29, 31, 32, 73 to 79,* and *87* to *91* as desired from the Student Motivation Kit.

❑ **Child & Adult Care Observations.** Assign *Observations OA-1 to OA-22* as desired from the Student Motivation Kit.

❑ **Child & Adult Care Career Profiles.** Assign *Career Profiles* as desired from the Student Motivation Kit.

Review & Student Performance

❑ **PowerPoint® Slides.** Use the *Section 2-2 PowerPoint®* slides on the Effective Instruction CD-ROM.

❑ **Section 2-2 Test.** Have students complete the *Section 2-2 Test* on pages 307-308 of this guide. Or, create your own test by using the **Exam**View® Test Generator found on the **Child & Adult Care Professionals** Effective Instruction CD-ROM.

(Continued on next page)

> ## KEY TERMS
>
> • **discretionary income**
> • **family care manager**
> • **self-perception**
> • **hospice**

> ### CARE PROVIDER TIP
>
> Service learning is an important component of instruction. Consider developing a point system and requiring students to earn a certain number of service points. Allow students to schedule the service learning experiences to fit into their academic, extra curricular, and work schedules. Since service-learning projects are often completed after school hours, such learning experiences may become FFCLA or SkillsUSA-VICA activities.

Answers to Section 2-2 Knowledge Check

1. The seven kinds of basic needs of older adults include social interaction and support, financial security, living arrangements, transportation, health care, support during death of a loved one, and emotional security.

2. The basic types of independent living arrangements for older adults include apartments for older adults, congregate housing, public housing, subsidized housing, Section 8 vouchers, adult communities, naturally occurring retirement communities, and shared housing.

3. Kübler-Ross's five stages of death and dying include denial, anger, bargaining, depression, and acceptance.

MINI LAB —*Answers will vary.*

Answers to Chapter 2 Review & Activities

1. Gerontology is the study of the aging process. Geriatrics is a field of medicine that focuses on preventing or managing common diseases for older adults.

2. Young people benefit from studying aging because it will help them to know if they are interested in a career in caring for older adults. It also teaches young people facts about aging, so they avoid stereotyping older adults.

3. *Any four:* Aging happens to everyone; aging is a normal process; aging varies; older adults do continue to learn; older adults can and do adjust to change; and older adults want to continue to make decisions about their lives.

4. It provides you with background knowledge about aging that can help you develop a healthy attitude about the aging process.

5. The greatest demand will be on society's social, political, and economic institutions.

6. *Social Security*: Retirement money received by older adults who have paid into the Social Security fund; *Medicare*: Health insurance provided through Social Security funds to retired persons; *Federal Insurance Contributions Act (FICA)*: Funds that support Medicare; *Medicaid*: Medical assistance for low-income people paid through Social Security funding.

7. Basic needs include social interaction and support, financial security, living arrangements, transportation, health care, and emotional security.

8. Financial difficulties may occur due to poor or low Social Security benefits; some older adults must work to continue earning a living wage.

9. The basic needs of a dying person are food, clothing, shelter, rest, and warmth.

Answers to Section 2-2 Test

Matching:

1. E
2. A
3. B
4. D
5. C

Short Answer:

6. Volunteers and part-time employees.
7. Financial, home maintenance, and safety.
8. Area Agency on Aging (AAA).
9. His or her home.
10. Thirty percent.
11. Familiarize them with the key colors and familiar locations on a bus or subway route map.
12. Emotional needs.
13. They still want to contribute to family decision making and maintain relationships with health-care professionals they know.
14. After moving through the grief process, a person has a healthy acceptance of the changes that the loved one's death has created.
15. Denial and isolation.

WORKPLACE CHALLENGE —*Any five:* Personal insights; what other people have told them; how they think others view them; their standing in their community; loss of a spouse; development of a disability.

Child & Adult Care Professionals Instructor Resource Guide
Copyright © Glencoe/McGraw-Hill

INSTRUCTIONAL PLAN ━━━━━━━━━━━━━━━━━━━━

Caring for Children

Section 3-1

FOCUS & PLANNING

Section Objectives

❑ Identify three factors that contribute to an increasing demand for early childhood providers.

❑ Describe ten characteristics of a successful early childhood professional.

❑ Identify places to work and positions in early childhood care and education.

❑ Summarize three major legal responsibilities of early childhood professionals.

Instruction & Student Practice

❑ **Reading.** Have students read *Section 3-1* on text pages 73-83. Assign the *Section 3-1 Knowledge Check* and *Mini Lab*.

❑ **Career Ladders.** Have students develop a career ladder illustrating a path for a career working with young children. Each level should represent a higher level of education, training, or experience.

❑ **Shadow a Preschool Teacher.** The class develops interview questions and/or an observation guide. Students should shadow a teacher and report the teacher's traits and their observations.

❑ **Lab Manual.** Assign *Lab Activity 8* on page 23, *Lab Activity 9* on page 26, *Lab Activity 10* on page 27, *Lab Activity 11* on page 29, and *Lab Activity 12* on page 33 of the Lab Manual.

❑ **Child & Adult Care Study Guides.** Assign *Study Guide 3-1* from the Student Motivation Kit.

❑ **Child & Adult Care Applications.** Assign *Activities 30, 34, 95,* and *96* as desired from the Student Motivation Kit.

❑ **Child & Adult Care Observations.** Assign *Observations C-44 to C-45* and *OA-1* as desired from the Student Motivation Kit.

❑ **Child & Adult Care Career Profiles.** Assign *Career Profiles* as desired from the Student Motivation Kit.

Review & Student Performance

❑ **PowerPoint® Slides.** Use the *Section 3-1 PowerPoint®* slides on the Effective Instruction CD-ROM.

❑ **Section 3-1 Test.** Have students complete the *Section 3-1 Test* on pages 309-310 of this guide. Or, create your own test by using the **Exam***View®* Test Generator found on the ***Child & Adult Care Professionals*** Effective Instruction CD-ROM.

KEY TERMS

• **trend**
• **entrepreneur**
• **Child Development Associate (CDA)**
• **mandated**

CARE PROVIDER TIP

Reliability, teamwork, patience, and a love of people are essential traits for success on the job as a care provider for children and adults.

(Continued on next page)

Answers to Section 3-1 Knowledge Check

1. Both parents employed outside the home, single parents, greater respect for the affect of early education on development.

2. Success in a particular career position requires specific talents. Varying levels of employment have different requirements for education; higher-level positions usually require more years of specific education and experience.

3. Criminal background checks, privacy and confidentiality, mandated reporting of suspected child abuse and/or neglect.

MINI LAB—*Answers will vary.*

Answers to Section 3-1 Test

Matching:

1. D
2. B
3. A
4. C

Short Answer:

5. Set educational goals.
6. Positive impact on some children's social and psychological development.
7. Increasing number of dual-career families and single parents.
8. Recent shifts in economic and job security plus the expenses children require.
9. Center-based child care, family child care homes, or part-day nursery or preschools.
10. Serve as a volunteer or a teacher's aide.
11. Americans with Disabilities Act (ADA).
12. Discipline, meal service, and toilet training.
13. Colds, flu, and chicken pox.
14. The ability to think quickly and react promptly.
15. An associate's degree (two-year college degree).

WORKPLACE CHALLENGE—*Any five:* Do I have the necessary experience and knowledge of child development, child care, or education? If not, what education and experience must I have before I open my business? From what sources will I obtain the financial backing I need to start my business? Have I saved enough money to pay for at least six months of personal living expenses? Am I willing to research the laws in my city and state related to operating a business, such as taxes, safety regulations, and zoning? Am I willing to research the licensing requirements for my type of business? Am I willing to research the need for my business in the area and the prices that customers will pay? Do I have the time and energy to start a business and maintain it daily? Am I mature enough to accept ultimate responsibility for a business? Do I have the patience and commitment to see a business through problems and slow periods? How might my business affect my family and personal life?

INSTRUCTIONAL PLAN ━━━━━━━━━━━━━━━━━━━━━━━━━

Caring for Older Adults

Section
3-2

FOCUS & PLANNING

Section Objectives

❑ Differentiate Medicare from Medicaid.

❑ Describe the characteristics of a successful care professional of older adults.

❑ Describe the traditional models for adult day care and intergenerational care programs.

❑ Identify places to work and positions in older adult care.

❑ Identify issues related to balancing work and home responsibilities.

Instruction & Student Practice

❑ **Reading.** Have students read *Section 3-2* on text pages 84-95. Assign the *Section 3-2 Knowledge Check* and *Mini Lab*.

❑ **Article Review.** Have students read and review, either orally or in writing, an article that reflects the positives of life as an older adult or the challenges that older adults face. A publication such as AARP's *Modern Maturity* is a good source of articles.

❑ **Lab Manual.** Assign *Lab Activity 9* on page 26 and *Lab Activity 12* on page 33 of the Lab Manual.

❑ **Child & Adult Care Study Guides.** Assign *Study Guide 3-2* from the Student Motivation Kit.

❑ **Child & Adult Care Applications.** Assign *Activities 30, 34, 95,* and *96* as desired from the Student Motivation Kit.

❑ **Child & Adult Care Observations.** Assign *Observations C-44* to *C-45* and *OA-1* as desired from the Student Motivation Kit.

❑ **Activity Cards for Children.** Assign *Activity Cards C-1* to *C-96* as desired from the Student Motivation Kit.

❑ **Activity Cards for Older Adults.** Assign *Activity Cards OA-1* to *OA-47* as desired from the Student Motivation Kit.

❑ **Child & Adult Care Career Profiles.** Assign *Career Profiles* as desired from the Student Motivation Kit.

Review & Student Performance

❑ **PowerPoint® Slides.** Use the *Section 3-2 PowerPoint®* slides on the Effective Instruction CD-ROM.

❑ **Section 3-2 Test.** Have students complete the *Section 3-2 Test* on pages 311-312 of this guide. Or, create your own test by using the **Exam***View®* Test Generator found on the **Child & Adult Care Professionals** Effective Instruction CD-ROM.

(Continued on next page)

KEY TERMS

- **Medicare**
- **Medicaid**
- **ageism**
- **intergenerational programs**
- **multidisciplinary**
- **burnout**

CARE PROVIDER TIP

Since many older adults have visual impairments, it is important to have "a place for everything and everything in its place." Adults feel more independent if they can take care of their personal items, and they can do this more easily if they have a logical, easy-to-access place for their belongings.

Answers to Section 3-2 Knowledge Check

1. *Medicare:* Health insurance program for older adults; *Medicaid:* Health insurance program for low-income people.

2. Traditional adult day care is based on one of three models: activity model, medical model, and social-medical model; interaction between generations is not emphasized. Intergenerational care encourages interaction between two or more generations.

3. You may become so involved in your work that you may neglect your family or suffer burnout.

(**MINI LAB**)—*Answers will vary.*

Answers to Chapter 3 Review & Activities

1. Dual career marriages, increase in single parenting, increase in divorce.

2. Create inclusive, diverse, family-friendly environments.

3. Maintain nutrition, exercise regularly, set realistic expectations, master time management, learn to say "no," set goals and prioritize, share home and work responsibilities, maintain friendships, enjoy a hobby, seek help when needed.

4. High energy, health, positive attitude, sense of humor, dedication, respect for diversity, appreciation of children and their development, patience, ability to understand a child's and parent's point of view, self-starter, good communicator, stable mood, consistency in work, flexibility, ability to complete tasks, cooperative, punctual.

5. Protects personal and educational records.

6. Report and document any suspected case of child abuse and/or neglect, become trained in spotting symptoms of child abuse or neglect.

7. Care providers in intergenerational programs develop activities to encourage interactions between two or more generations.

8. Gerontology is a multidisciplinary field; geriatrics is a health-related field.

9. Medical records are the most important document of a person's life and must be handled with confidentiality.

10. Employees are better able to balance their work and home life and are absent less from work when they create their own schedules.

Answers to Section 3-2 Test

Matching:

1. E   3. B   5. D
2. A   4. C   6. F

Short Answer:

7. They will serve as tour companions, geriatric fitness trainers, and personal secretaries or shoppers.

8. Area Agency on Aging, American Association of Retired Persons (AARP), and other profit and nonprofit organizations.

9. Social model.

10. Child care centers in long-term care facilities.

11. An understanding of later life development, skills in communication, and empathy for older adults.

12. By the adult's preferred name.

13. Balance the responsibilities of work and home as stress-free as possible.

14. A friendly smile and tone of voice and a good sense of humor; demonstrates an interest in others.

15. To investigate possible abuse and neglect.

(**WORKPLACE CHALLENGE**)—Hear, listen, understand, and respect what an older adult says; make certain you repeat what you heard, which confirms that you were listening; help older adults stick to the topic by asking a question; take into account the speaker's views and preferences; use "I" statements to help older adults understand what you are saying.

INSTRUCTIONAL PLAN ━━━━━━━━━━━━━━━━━━━━━━━━━━━━━ *Section*

Preparing for Employment   **4-1**

FOCUS & PLANNING

Section Objectives

❑ Describe the basic employability skills that applicants for positions in early childhood care and older adult care need.

❑ Identify effective verbal, nonverbal, written, and electronic communication skills.

❑ Identify the traits and behaviors of a worker with a positive work ethic.

❑ Compare the types of resources care professionals use in their careers.

Instruction & Student Practice

❑ **Reading.** Have students read *Section 4-1* on text pages 99-108. Assign the *Section 4-1 Knowledge Check* and *Mini Lab.*

❑ **Write a Memo.** Give the students a job-related situation and have them write a business memo, peer edit the memos, and publish them.

❑ **Argument Cards.** Write qualities of a strong work ethic and effective leadership on 3- by 5-inch cards. Have each student draw a card, think through the importance of the quality, and develop an argument stating why a worker should possess the quality.

❑ **Child & Adult Care Study Guides.** Assign *Study Guide 4-1* from the Student Motivation Kit.

❑ **Child & Adult Care Applications.** Assign *Activities 30, 34, 35, 36, 93, 95,* and *96* as desired from the Student Motivation Kit.

❑ **Child & Adult Care Observations.** Assign *Observations C-44* to *C-45* and *OA-1* as desired from the Student Motivation Kit.

❑ **Activity Cards for Children.** Assign *Activity Cards C-1* to *C-96* as desired from the Student Motivation Kit.

❑ **Activity Cards for Older Adults.** Assign *Activity Cards OA-1* to *OA-47* as desired from the Student Motivation Kit.

❑ **Child & Adult Care Career Profiles.** Assign *Career Profiles* as desired from the Student Motivation Kit.

Review & Student Performance

❑ **PowerPoint® Slides.** Use the *Section 4-1 PowerPoint®* slides on the Effective Instruction CD-ROM.

❑ **Section 4-1 Test.** Have students complete the *Section 4-1 Test* on pages 313-314 of this guide. Or, create your own test by using the **Exam***View®* Test Generator found on the ***Child & Adult Care Professionals*** Effective Instruction CD-ROM.

(Continued on next page)

KEY TERMS

- **active listening**
- **body language**
- **work ethic**
- **flexibility**
- **prioritize**

CARE PROVIDER TIP

Many students seldom use formal English conversationally and do not realize that the way they speak at home and with peers is not appropriate in an interview or on the job. Provide classroom opportunities to practice speaking using formal English.

Answers to Section 4-1 Knowledge Check

1. Basic skills you will need to practice on the job include verbal and written communication; math that involves adding, subtracting, multiplying, and dividing; and thinking skills that involve critical thinking, decision making, problem solving, responsibility, teamwork, reliability, flexibility, commitment, and honesty.

2. Honesty, responsibility, teamwork, reliability, flexibility, and commitment.

3. Care professionals will need people, information, technology, time, energy, money, equipment, and supplies to perform their jobs effectively.

MINI LAB —*Answers will vary.*

Answers to Section 4-1 Test

Matching:

1. E   4. C
2. A   5. D
3. B   6. F

Short Answer:

7. They will serve as tour companions, geriatric fitness trainers, and personal secretaries or shoppers.
8. Area Agency on Aging, American Association of Retired Persons (AARP), and other profit and non-profit organizations.
9. Social model.
10. Child care centers in long-term care facilities.
11. An understanding of later life development, skills in communication, and empathy for older adults.
12. By the adult's preferred name.
13. Balance the responsibilities of work and home as stress-free as possible.
14. A friendly smile and tone of voice and a good sense of humor; demonstrates an interest in others.
15. To investigate possible abuse and neglect.

WORKPLACE CHALLENGE —Hear, listen, understand, and respect what an older adult says; make certain you repeat what you heard, which confirms that you were listening; help older adults stick to the topic by asking a question; take into account the speaker's views and preferences; use "I" statements to help older adults understand what you are saying.

Child & Adult Care Professionals Instructor Resource Guide

INSTRUCTIONAL PLAN ━━━━━━━━━━━━━━━━━━━━━━ *Section*

Seeking Employment *4-2*

FOCUS & PLANNING

Section Objectives

❏ Describe four resources for job leads.

❏ Contrast employment agencies and temporary employment agencies.

❏ Prepare a résumé and cover letter.

❏ Practice skills needed for job interviewing.

Instruction & Student Practice

❏ **Reading.** Have students read *Section 4-2* on text pages 109-119. Assign the *Section 4-2 Knowledge Check* and *Mini Lab.*

❏ **Explore a Web Site.** Using Internet resources, have students investigate one of the child or adult care professional organizations listed in the text. Have them report about the job opportunities listed on the Web site and identify the education/training needed for each.

❏ **Write a Résumé.** Have students write a résumé for an entry-level job in child care or gerontology.

❏ **Write a Cover Letter.** Have students write a cover letter to accompany a résumé that is to be sent to a potential employer.

❏ **Lab Manual.** Assign *Lab Activity 13* on page 37, *Lab Activity 14* on page 39, *Lab Activity 15* on page 42, *Lab Activity 16* on page 43, and *Lab Activity 17* on page 44 of the Lab Manual.

❏ **Child & Adult Care Study Guides.** Assign *Study Guide 4-2* from the Student Motivation Kit.

❏ **Child & Adult Care Applications.** Assign *Activities 30, 34, 35, 36, 93, 95,* and *96* as desired from the Student Motivation Kit.

❏ **Child & Adult Care Observations.** Assign *Observations C-44* to *C-45* and *OA-1* as desired from the Student Motivation Kit.

❏ **Child & Adult Care Career Profiles.** Assign *Career Profiles* as desired from the Student Motivation Kit.

Review & Student Performance

❏ **PowerPoint® Slides.** Use the *Section 4-2 PowerPoint®* slides on the Effective Instruction CD-ROM.

❏ **Section 4-2 Test.** Have students complete the *Section 4-2 Test* on pages 315-318 of this guide. Or, create your own test by using the **Exam***View*® Test Generator found on the ***Child & Adult Care Professionals*** Effective Instruction CD-ROM.

KEY TERMS

- **networking**
- **referral**
- **trade publications**
- **résumé**
- **service learning**
- **keywords**

CARE PROVIDER TIP

Invite members of your advisory committee or a local business or vocational college to assist with the interviews as described in the Interview Practice section of the text.

(Continued on next page)

Answers to Section 4-2 Knowledge Check

1. *Answers will vary, but may include*: Networking, referrals, the Internet, professional organizations, trade publications, and employment agencies.

2. The key elements of a résumé include contact information, career objective, relevant work experience, key skills, education, training, and references.

3. *Before the interview:* Find out information about your prospective employer, choose appropriate clothing, and write down the date, time, and place of your interview, so you can be prompt; *during the interview:* Shake hands at introduction, make eye contact throughout the interview, speak clearly, use good manners, answer questions thoughtfully and completely, ask questions, leave gracefully; *after the interview:* Send a thank-you letter the day after the interview, follow up with the employer at the appointed time if you've been asked to do so.

MINI LAB —*Answers will vary.*

Answers to Section 4-2 Test

Matching:

1. B   4. E
2. C   5. D
3. F   6. A

Short Answer:

7. Treat it with respect, follow up with the employer responsibly, return phone calls, be on time for interviews, always present yourself in a professional manner.

8. Review job postings, network with other people, contact professional organizations, read online versions of professional publications, register with online employment agencies.

9. Job listings, job placement services, scholarships, workshops, conferences.

10. Chance to see what the child care field or the older adult care field is like without committing to an employer.

11. Write down everything you are told to do and the name of person with whom you talked.

12. Brief summary of your education, experience, and job qualifications.

13. You should be bathed with hair and nails well trimmed; clothing should be appropriate for a business meeting; clothes should fit properly, be clean, pressed, and in good condition; shoes should be polished and appropriate to your outfit.

14. Introduce yourself in return; offer your hand for a firm, confident handshake; remain standing until the interviewer asks you to take a seat.

15. What is the nature of the job? What are my responsibilities? What are the working environment conditions?

16. After waiting the specified time, telephone the employer and politely request information about the status of your application.

17. Simply say in your response, "Thank you for considering me, but I am not interested in taking the position."

18. Be polite and respectful.

19. It shows that you are listening and are interested in what the interviewer is saying.

20. Job Search Journal.

WORKPLACE CHALLENGE —*Any five:* Print neatly, using blue or black ink; use cursive handwriting for your signature only; read the instructions for completing each section before responding and try not to make errors; if you must correct something, draw a line through it; carry important information with you, including your Social Security number; driver's license number; the names, addresses, and phone numbers of previous employers; and the dates of your employment; carry your list of references with you including the complete names, addresses, and telephone numbers of your references; make sure you have their permission to use them as a reference; do not leave any part of the application form blank unless you are asked to do so—if a question does not apply, write NA, which means "not applicable," in the space provided; always tell the truth; submitting false information is illegal.

INSTRUCTIONAL PLAN ━━━━━━━━━━━━━━━━━━━━━━━━━━━━━━

On the Job *Section* **4-3**

FOCUS & PLANNING

Section Objectives

❏ Summarize the rights and responsibilities of employees and employers.
❏ Perform calculations related to wages and benefits.
❏ Describe fair labor practices.
❏ Identify effective methods to maintain and terminate employment.

Instruction & Student Practice

❏ **Reading.** Have students read *Section 4-3* on text pages 120-127. Assign the *Section 4-3 Knowledge Check* and *Mini Lab*.

❏ **Observation.** Have students visit a child or adult care facility and complete an observation guide recording the job responsibilities for staff.

❏ **Employer costs.** Have students survey local care providers and determine a range of employer costs for employee benefits, including the cost of wages, social security, pension, and benefits, such as sick and vacation days, insurance, and staff development.

❏ **Examine Evaluation Forms.** Collect staff evaluations from several child and adult care facilities. Have students identify common qualities employers expect.

❏ **Child & Adult Care Study Guides.** Assign *Study Guide 4-3* from the Student Motivation Kit.

❏ **Child & Adult Care Applications.** Assign *Activities 34, 35, 36, 93, 95,* and *96* as desired from the Student Motivation Kit.

❏ **Child & Adult Care Observations.** Assign *Observations C-44* to *C-45* and *OA-1* as desired from the Student Motivation Kit.

❏ **Activity Cards for Children.** Assign *Activity Cards C-1* to *C-96* as desired from the Student Motivation Kit.

❏ **Activity Cards for Older Adults.** Assign *Activity Cards OA-1* to *OA-47* as desired from the Student Motivation Kit.

❏ **Child & Adult Care Career Profiles.** Assign *Career Profiles* as desired from the Student Motivation Kit.

Review & Student Performance

❏ **PowerPoint® Slides.** Use the *Section 4-3 PowerPoint®* slides on the Effective Instruction CD-ROM.

❏ **Section 4-3 Test.** Have students complete the *Section 4-3 Test* on pages 319-320 of this guide. Or, create your own test by using the **Exam***View*® Test Generator found on the **Child & Adult Care Professionals** Effective Instruction CD-ROM.

(Continued on next page)

KEY TERMS

- empathy
- workers' compensation
- minimum wage
- compensatory time
- labor union
- collective bargaining
- discrimination
- sexual harassment
- probation
- ethics

CARE PROVIDER TIP

Gossip in the workplace is a leading cause of low morale among employees. Focus on your job responsibilities, and if you have legitimate complaints, learn to work through the proper channels to solve problems.

Child & Adult Care Professionals Instructor Resource Guide
Copyright © Glencoe/McGraw-Hill

Answers to Section 4-3 Knowledge Check

1. *Answers include:* Complete each assigned task, respect the employer's priority, use time responsibly, respect the rules and others, work safely, maintain confidentiality, work as a team, keep a positive attitude, and work at resolving conflicts.

2. *Answers include:* Clearly outlining work responsibilities and expectations, providing safe working conditions, protecting employees from unfair treatment on the job, and providing feedback on job performance.

3. With a salary, the employer pays you a set amount of money regardless of the hours worked. With an hourly wage, you are paid for each hour you work. Pay varies with the number of hours worked during a pay period.

MINI LAB —*Answers will vary.*

Answers to Chapter 4 Review & Activities

1. Activity listening is a skill that requires you to pay attention and interact with the speaker.

2. *See list on page 103.*

3. *Any four:* Responsibility, teamwork, reliability, flexibility, commitment, quality, excellence, and honesty.

4. *Answers include:* Motivating others to accomplish goals, showing a high level of commitment to goals, desiring to reach the highest standards of quality, and self-improvment.

5. People, information, technology, time, energy, money, and equipment and supplies.

6. It involves making use of all of personal and professional contacts to further career goals.

7. Because they offer fast placement.

8. Prepare for an interview by learning about your prospective employer, choosing appropriate clothing for a good first impression, and being prompt and courteous for the interview. In following up after an interview, send a thank-you letter, respond at the time appointed if you have been asked to do so, telephone the employer and politely request information on the status of your application if time passes, keep a record of all events and comments in a job search journal.

9. *Any two employee responsibilities:* Earn your pay, use time responsibly, respect the rules, work safely, maintain confidentially, practice good teamwork, keep a positive attitude, and show respect and appreciation for others; *any two employer responsibilities:* Clearly identify your responsibilities and expectations, provide safe working conditions, demonstrate fair labor practices, provide regular performance evaluations and fair wages.

10. *See list on page 126.*

Answers to Section 4-3 Test

Matching:

1.	E	3.	I	5.	H	7.	D	9.	F
2.	M	4.	C	6.	A	8.	J	10.	K

Short Answer:

11. Your level of skills and experience, the difficulty of the work, and the number of people competing for the same job.

12. Accept responsibility for your own actions, learn from your mistakes, and take care of your appearance.

13. Be on time for work, return promptly from designated breaks and meal periods, don't waste time chatting with coworkers and ignoring those in your care, never use work time or resources for personal business.

14. Job knowledge and how the employee applies that knowledge, willingness to work cooperatively as a team member, ability to communicate effectively on the job, positive attitude and workplace ethic.

15. Give the required advance notice to your employer that you are terminating your employment and work as hard as you always have until you leave your place of employment.

WORKPLACE CHALLENGE —Provide equipment and materials necessary to do the job safely; eliminate any recognized health and safety hazards; inform employees when conditions or materials pose dangers to health and safety; maintain records of job-related illnesses and injuries; comply with environmental protection policies for safely disposing of waste materials.

INSTRUCTIONAL PLAN ━━━━━━━━━━━━━━━━━━━━━━━━

Professional Communication

Section **5-1**

FOCUS & PLANNING

Section Objectives

❏ Explain the barriers to effective communication.

❏ Identify ways communication is used in the workplace.

❏ Identify effective ways to minimize and resolve conflict.

❏ Describe ways to use documentation in the workplace.

Instruction & Student Practice

❏ **Reading.** Have students read *Section 5-1* on text pages 131-139. Assign the *Section 5-1 Knowledge Check* and *Mini Lab.*

❏ **Newsletter Articles.** Have students write a monthly newsletter article featuring program information, care tips, and special events. Be certain that the newsletter exhibits good writing skills. If your facility does not have an on-site lab, have students submit the articles to the programs of their job sites.

❏ **Role-playing.** Act out situations that reflect work-related conflicts. Have students practice using mediation skills to resolve the conflicts.

❏ **Lab Manual.** Assign *Lab Activity 18* on page 45 and *Lab Activity 19* on page 48 of the Lab Manual.

❏ **Child & Adult Care Study Guides.** Assign *Study Guide 5-1* from the Student Motivation Kit.

❏ **Child & Adult Care Applications.** Assign *Activities 34, 36, 95,* and *96* as desired from the Student Motivation Kit.

❏ **Child & Adult Care Observations.** Assign *Observations C-1* to *C-45* and *OA-1* to *OA-22* as desired from the Student Motivation Kit.

❏ **Activity Cards for Children.** Assign *Activity Cards C-1* to *C-96* as desired from the Student Motivation Kit.

❏ **Activity Cards for Older Adults.** Assign *Activity Cards OA-1* to *OA-47* as desired from the Student Motivation Kit.

❏ **Child & Adult Care Career Profiles.** Assign *Career Profiles* as desired from the Student Motivation Kit.

Review & Student Performance

❏ **PowerPoint® Slides.** Use the *Section 5-1 PowerPoint®* slides on the Effective Instruction CD-ROM.

❏ **Section 5-1 Test.** Have students complete the *Section 5-1 Test* on pages 321-322 of this guide. Or, create your own test by using the **Exam***View*® Test Generator found on the ***Child & Adult Care Professionals*** Effective Instruction CD-ROM.

(Continued on next page)

KEY TERMS

• communication
• barriers
• public relations

CARE PROVIDER TIP

When care providers point out problems during a conference, family members want to hear positive suggestions for solutions. If there is a problem to report, be prepared to suggest a plan of action to help the care providers and the family work together to solve the problem.

Answers to Section 5-1 Knowledge Check

1. *Cultural and language differences:* Take time to establish a trusting relationship. *Medical factors:* Learn how to help a client manage an aid device, such as a hearing aid. *Social factors:* Use humor or music, ask open-ended questions.
2. Respectful discussion, cooperative planning, and minimizing conflict.
3. Recording concerns, individualized services, and referrals.

MINI LAB —*Answers will vary.*

Answers to Section 5-1 Test

Matching:

1. B   4. D
2. E   5. A
3. C

Short Answer:

6. Vision or hearing loss, medical illnesses, and medication use.
7. Age, education, family, friends, and contact with care providers.
8. Take the time to get to know children and older adults in your care.
9. How will physical, social, and emotional needs be met? How are meals served? How are menus developed? How are special dietary needs met?
10. Appropriate dress, a well-prepared presentation, good audiovisuals.
11. It is cost-efficient; it is an effective way to communicate a variety of information to a wide audience; and it is helpful for people who cannot contact a program during its hours of operation.
12. Avoid making negative comments and discussing confidential matters where others may overhear.
13. Informal conversations, staff meetings, and written and technological communication.
14. If asked for feedback, offer helpful suggestions; express thoughts and feelings in a positive, non-judgmental way; avoid demeaning or attacking a person if you disagree; compliment a coworker when he or she does an especially good job.
15. Be tactful; ask for input on why the problem exists and how it might be solved; address issues with a cooperative, rather than judgmental, tone.

WORKPLACE CHALLENGE —Keep lines of communication open; resolve small differences right away, before they grow into major conflicts; keep discussions positive; address issues, not personalities; do not jump to conclusions; give people a chance to explain their side of the story.

INSTRUCTIONAL PLAN

Professional Ethics

FOCUS & PLANNING

Section Objectives

❏ Define professional ethnics.

❏ Explain the importance of professional ethics.

❏ Describe the ethical responsibilities of human-service professionals.

Instruction & Student Practice

❏ **Reading.** Have students read *Section 5-2* on text pages 140-149. Assign the *Section 5-2 Knowledge Check* and *Mini Lab*.

❏ **Posters.** After studying NAEYC Code of Ethics and/or Ethical standards for Human Service Professionals, students should create posters that illustrate workplace ethics.

❏ **Service Project.** Have students plan and conduct a family night or afternoon at a child care center or older adult day care center. Have students plan intergenerational activities for the children or adults to do with family members.

❏ **Observation.** Have students develop a diversity checklist and observe at a child or older adult care facility to note how diversity is respected.

❏ **Lab Manual.** Assign *Lab Activity 19* on page 48 and *Lab Activity 20* on page 49 of the Lab Manual.

❏ **Child & Adult Care Study Guides.** Assign *Study Guide 5-2* from the Student Motivation Kit.

❏ **Child & Adult Care Applications.** Assign *Activities 34* and *95* as desired from the Student Motivation Kit.

❏ **Child & Adult Care Observations.** Assign *Observations C-1 to C-45* and *OA-1 to OA-22* as desired from the Student Motivation Kit.

❏ **Activity Cards for Children.** Assign *Activity Cards C-1 to C-96* as desired from the Student Motivation Kit.

❏ **Activity Cards for Older Adults.** Assign *Activity Cards OA-1 to OA-47* as desired from the Student Motivation Kit.

❏ **Child & Adult Care Career Profiles.** Assign *Career Profiles* as desired from the Student Motivation Kit.

Review & Student Performance

❏ **PowerPoint® Slides.** Use the *Section 5-2 PowerPoint®* slides on the Effective Instruction CD-ROM.

❏ **Section 5-2 Test.** Have students complete the *Section 5-2 Test* on pages 323-324 of this guide. Or, create your own test by using the **Exam***View*® Test Generator found on the **Child & Adult Care Professionals** Effective Instruction CD-ROM.

(Continued on next page)

KEY TERMS

• **professional ethics**
• **confidentiality**
• **dress code**
• **continuing education**
• **conferences**

CARE PROVIDER TIP

When selecting a technical school, community college, or university for a training program, encourage students to investigate whether the program is accredited and whether the credits transfer to other institutions. It is a good idea to inquire about the percentage of program completers who have been successfully placed in jobs.

Answers to Section 5-2 Knowledge Check

1. Both ethics and professional ethics are standards that guide a person's actions. In general, ethics are principles or morals that guide one's personal actions. Professional ethics are standards of right and wrong that apply to a person's behavior on the job.

2. Individual family information and staff member and program information should be kept private.

3. The ethical responsibilities program staff members have to children and older adults include ensuring a safe environment and maintaining confidential information, unless they have written permission to release the information in writing. Responsibilities to families include having family members involved in program services and decisions, such as partnership in caring, information sharing, open-door policies, and cooperative care. Responsibilities to coworkers are to demonstrate respect and courtesy, keep ongoing communication, and participate in cooperative planning. Responsibilities to community and society include compliance with laws related to child and older adult care, cooperation with other professionals, and community outreach.

MINI LAB —*Answers will vary.*

Answers to Section 5-2 Test

Matching:

1. F
2. E
3. D
4. B
5. C

Short Answer:

6. Honesty, dependability, and trustworthiness.

7. Avoid those with inappropriate pictures or slogans.

8. Join organizations in the professional field and subscribe to their periodicals.

9. National Association for the Education of Young Children (NAEYC).

10. You can measure your own skills and knowledge against a national standard and get feedback from peers and authorities in the field.

11. Nursing, gerontology, geriatrics, social work, or counseling.

12. Medical and environmental precautions.

13. Program brochures, policy handbooks, newsletters, reports on daily activities, and monthly family meetings.

14. Participating in family events and special daytime celebrations and volunteering time or special talents.

15. Coworkers can put their unique strengths and talents to good use.

WORKPLACE CHALLENGE —Keep individual family information private; keep individual staff member information private; keep sensitive information private; share information only when family members give written permission; follow a program's specific written guidelines concerning confidentiality and providing information.

INSTRUCTIONAL PLAN ━━━━━━━━━━━━━━━

Advocacy

Section **5-3**

FOCUS & PLANNING

Section Objectives

❏ Describe a human service professional's advocacy responsibilities.
❏ Explain how individual rights are protected.
❏ Describe advocacy issues and the levels of advocacy involvement.
❏ Summarize how to contact legislators.

Instruction & Student Practice

❏ **Reading.** Have students read *Section 5-3* on text pages 150-155. Assign the *Section 5-3 Knowledge Check* and *Mini Lab*.

❏ **Report on Care Issues.** Using print or Internet resources, have students find an article about a child care issue or an older adult care issue and briefly report to the class.

❏ **Service Project.** Have students collect gently used children's books and deliver them to schools, day cares, or shelters.

❏ **Write a Legislator.** Have students select a controversial child or adult care issue, become knowledgeable about the issue, and write a letter to a legislator stating his or her position on the issue.

❏ **Lab Manual.** Assign *Lab Activity 21* on page 51 of the Lab Manual.

❏ **Child & Adult Care Study Guides.** Assign *Study Guide 5-3* from the Student Motivation Kit.

❏ **Child & Adult Care Applications.** Assign *Activities 1, 2, 3, 4, 12, 26, 29,* and *32* as desired from the Student Motivation Kit.

❏ **Child & Adult Care Observations.** Assign *Observations C-1 to C-45* and *OA-1 to OA-22* as desired from the Student Motivation Kit.

❏ **Activity Cards for Children.** Assign *Activity Cards C-1 to C-96* as desired from the Student Motivation Kit.

❏ **Activity Cards for Older Adults.** Assign *Activity Cards OA-1 to OA-47* as desired from the Student Motivation Kit.

❏ **Child & Adult Care Career Profiles.** Assign *Career Profiles* as desired from the Student Motivation Kit.

Review & Student Performance

❏ **PowerPoint® Slides.** Use the *Section 5-3 PowerPoint®* slides on the Effective Instruction CD-ROM.

❏ **Section 5-3 Test.** Have students complete the *Section 5-3 Test* on pages 325-326 of this guide. Or, create your own test by using the **Exam***View*® Test Generator found on the **Child & Adult Care Professionals** Effective Instruction CD-ROM.

KEY TERMS

- **advocacy**
- **advocates**
- **constituents**

CARE PROVIDER TIP

The Week of the Young Child is the second week in April and the Week of the Family is the fourth week of November every year. These are appropriate times to plan special activities for the children or older adults in your care.

(Continued on next page)

Answers to Section 5-3 Knowledge Check

1. To inform others to influence change for the best interests of clients and the profession.
2. *Low level:* Monthly participation, including keeping informed via news reports, newsletters, mailing lists of advocacy groups, journals, and by talking with others; *medium level:* Weekly participation, including maintaining memberships in professional organizations and contacting a legislator or local agency about clients' needs; *high level:* Make viewpoints known to fellow voters.
3. Schedule a personal visit, write letters, make telephone calls.

(**MINI LAB**)—*Answers will vary.*

Answers to Chapter 5 Review & Activities

1. Workplace communication, public relations, family communications.
2. Cultural and language differences, health condition, physical and mental abilities, age, and education.
3. Telephone, brochures and advertisements, public presentations, and Web sites.
4. To aid staff in providing high quality care. Records include concerns, specific behavior incidents, lesson and activity plans, and referrals.
5. Establishes a trusting relationship regardless of background; accommodates medical and social needs; practices respectful communication; plans cooperatively; minimizes conflict; records concerns, services, and referrals; maintains confidentiality, and follows laws.
6. Attend college classes, learn first aid and CPR, attend weekend workshops, attend professional conferences, and visit other programs.
7. Include foods, activities, and cultural practices related to all clients and provide bilingual services to translate information.
8. Lose the trust of clients and fellow staff, termination of employment, violation of confidentiality laws.
9. So they can follow laws, provide high-quality care, and advocate for laws that are in their clients' best interests.
10. News reports, agency newsletters, professional organizations, journals of professional organizations, and experts.

Answers to Section 5-3 Test

Matching:
1. A   2. B   3. C

Short Answer:
4. The privilege to make your opinions known to those who create laws.
5. Research all of the facts related to the issue.
6. Call his or her office to make an appointment.
7. The Internet.
8. The Honorable.
9. One.
10. Request for a direct response regarding the legislator's stand on the issue.
11. The telephone call helps confirm your stand on the issue.
12. Thank the legislator for his or her time and consideration of the matter.
13. High school students visit homebound older adults and learn about 20th century events from those who lived through them.
14. Emotional support for abused children, tutoring for children with learning difficulties, mentors for troubled teens, care for children who are disabled or severely ill.
15. Visit frail older adults. During their visits, students and older adults may read/write letters, go for walks, watch movies, run errands, do chores, play games, and more.

(**WORKPLACE CHALLENGE**)—*Any five:* Abuse and Neglect Act; Americans with Disabilities Act; Individuals with Disabilities Education Act; Family Educational Rights and Privacy Acts; Harassment Act; Social Security Administration (Fraud) Act 1997.

INSTRUCTIONAL PLAN ━━━━━━━━━━━━━━━━━━━━━

Health & Safety for Children

Section **6-1**

FOCUS & PLANNING

Section Objectives

❑ Describe a healthy environment in a child care setting.
❑ Explain the practices used to check for illnesses.
❑ Identify children's special health conditions.
❑ Explain how to eliminate safety hazards.
❑ List the supplies in a first aid kit.

Instruction & Student Practice

❑ **Reading.** Have students read *Section 6-1* on text pages 159-172. Assign the *Section 6-1 Knowledge Check* and *Mini Lab.*

❑ **Sanitizing Solutions.** Have students mix bleach water in strengths recommended for cleaning tables, diaper-changing surfaces, and body fluid spills. Have students check the strength of the solutions using chlorine test strips available from restaurant suppliers.

❑ **Health Screening Checklist.** Have students develop a brief healthy child checklist for a teacher to use as the children arrive at the center. Discuss why and how experienced preschool teachers learn to visually screen the children.

❑ **Toy Safety.** Using Internet resources, have students investigate toy safety and develop brochures to give out in the community.

❑ **Lab Manual.** Assign *Lab Activity 22* on page 53 and *Lab Activity 23* on page 55 of the Lab Manual.

❑ **Child & Adult Care Study Guides.** Assign *Study Guide 6-1* from the Student Motivation Kit.

❑ **Child & Adult Care Applications.** Assign *Activities 5, 6, 18, 24, 41, 104,* and *105* as desired from the Student Motivation Kit.

❑ **Child & Adult Care Observations.** Assign *Observations C-16* and *C-17* as desired from the Student Motivation Kit.

❑ **Child & Adult Care Career Profiles.** Assign *Career Profiles* as desired from the Student Motivation Kit.

Review & Student Performance

❑ **PowerPoint® Slides.** Use the *Section 6-1 PowerPoint®* slides on the Effective Instruction CD-ROM.

❑ **Section 6-1 Test.** Have students complete the *Section 6-1 Test* on pages 327-328 of this guide. Or, create your own test by using the **Exam***View®* Test Generator found on the *Child & Adult Care Professionals* Effective Instruction CD-ROM.

KEY TERMS

- **pathogens**
- **immunization**
- **universal precautions**
- **biohazardous**
- **hypothermia**
- **frostbite**
- **heat exhaustion**
- **screenings**
- **safety policy**
- **risk-management plan**

CARE PROVIDER TIP

In child care centers that have multi-age and/or inclusion programs, toys need to be available for children at different developmental stages. Toys that may pose a safety hazard for younger children or children with special needs should be available to children only when extra supervision is available.

(Continued on next page)

Answers to Section 6-1 Knowledge Check

1. Turn on water, wet hands and forearms. Apply liquid soap and lather. Rub hands for 20 seconds. Rinse well. Dry hands with paper towel. Turn off faucet with paper towel.

2. Protect staff from contagious disease and prevent it from spreading. Whenever handling bodily fluids, such as diapering, cleaning up vomit, or coming into contact with blood while providing first aid.

3. Injury, suspected abuse, releasing children, and emergency treatment.

MINI LAB—*Newsletters will vary.*

Answers to Section 6-1 Test

Matching:

1. F   3. J   5. D   7. C   9. H
2. E   4. A   6. B   8. I   10. G

Short Answer:

11. Chicken pox and strep throat.

12. Doctor's report of good health; negative tuberculosis test; information about known conditions, diseases, or other problems; and an immunization record.

13. Whenever you might come into contact with bodily fluids, such as during diapering, toileting, or treating an injury.

14. Double-bag the material, securely tie the bag, and label each bag as biohazardous waste.

15. Do not allow children to play outdoors for long periods in hot weather; play in shaded areas, if possible, have children to drink water frequently.

16. The public health department.

17. The teacher should stay with the child and administer any appropriate first aid, while someone else calls for emergency assistance.

18. Coughing, wheezing, and whistling breathing.

19. Keep children from trigger substances and maintain cleanliness standards.

20. With their custodial parent or legal guardian; however, parents may sign a waiver giving release permission to someone else.

WORKPLACE CHALLENGE—1) Turn on the water and wet your hands and forearms. Warm water at 110°F is recommended. 2) Apply liquid soap and build up a good lather. 3) Rub your soaped hands for 20 seconds. Wash the backs of hands, wrists, between fingers, and under fingernails. Clean fingernails with a brush. 4) Rinse well. 5) Dry hands with a paper towel. 6) Turn off the water faucet using a paper towel, not your clean hands. *Any two:* Upon arrival; before and after preparing or eating meals and snacks; after handling pets; after coughing, sneezing, and toileting; before and after diapering; and after messy activities.

INSTRUCTIONAL PLAN ━━━━━━━━━━━━━━━━━━━━━━━━ *Section*

Health & Safety for Older Adults   *6-2*

FOCUS & PLANNING

Section Objectives

❑ Identify ways to promote and maintain good health and wellness practices for older adults.

❑ Determine how stress can trigger illness during older years.

❑ Identify safety practices for older adults in adult day centers.

Instruction & Student Practice

❑ **Reading.** Have students read *Section 6-2* on text pages 173-181. Assign the *Section 6-2 Knowledge Check* and *Mini Lab.*

❑ **Journal Entry.** Have students brainstorm causes of stress among older adults. Students should write suggestions for caregiver to help relieve the stress, thus improving the quality of life.

❑ **Home Safety.** Have students devise a home safety checklist to distribute to families of older adults at a local older adult activity or day care center.

❑ **Service Project.** Have students make first aid kits for older adults and distribute them at a neighborhood center that services low-income adults. Have students contact local businesses to donate or reduce the cost of supplies.

❑ **Lab Manual.** Assign *Lab Activity 24* on page 57 and *Lab Activity 25* on page 59 of the Lab Manual.

❑ **Child & Adult Care Study Guides.** Assign *Study Guide 6-2* from the Student Motivation Kit.

❑ **Child & Adult Care Applications.** Assign *Activities 28, 71, 74, 75, 77,* and *78* as desired from the Student Motivation Kit.

❑ **Child & Adult Care Observations.** Assign *Observations OA-4 to OA-22* as desired from the Student Motivation Kit.

❑ **Activity Cards for Older Adults.** Assign *Activity Cards OA-1 to OA-47* as desired from the Student Motivation Kit.

❑ **Child & Adult Care Career Profiles.** Assign *Career Profiles* as desired from the Student Motivation Kit.

Review & Student Performance

❑ **PowerPoint® Slides.** Use the *Section 6-2 PowerPoint®* slides on the Effective Instruction CD-ROM.

❑ **Section 6-2 Test.** Have students complete the *Section 6-2 Test* on pages 329-330 of this guide. Or, create your own test by using the **Exam***View®* Test Generator found on the *Child & Adult Care Professionals* Effective Instruction CD-ROM.

KEY TERMS

- **pediatrician**
- **geriatrican**
- **disparities**
- **polypharmacy**
- **stress**
- **cardiopulmonary resuscitation (CPR)**

CARE PROVIDER TIP

Since many older adults have much time to think, they tend to dwell upon disasters and negative world events, such as the events of September 11, 2001. Encourage student care providers to help older adults by patiently listening to their concerns and redirecting their attention to the people who are helping. Help them relate their concerns to similar situations from history.

(Continued on next page)

Answers to Section 6-2 Knowledge Check

1. Maintaining a wellness plan helps older adults stay in good health because it outlines specific activities that include nutrition awareness, stress management, physical fitness, being aware of the surrounding environment, safety, and getting regular medical screenings.

2. Older adults experience stress due to living alone, having financial worries or having too much or too little leisure time, lacking transportation, or caring for a spouse with an illness or disability.

3. Clear a walking path by moving furniture and stray electrical and telephone cords; check for fixtures that allow for extra support, such as grab bars in bathrooms and rails on stairways and in halls; place frequently used items in easily reachable places in cabinets; secure loose rugs on the floors.

(**MINI LAB**)—*Courses will vary.*

Answers to Section 6-2 Test

Matching:

1.	D	3.	B	5.	F
2.	C	4.	E	6.	A

Short Answer:

7. *Goal 1.* Increase the quality and years of healthy life. *Goal 2.* Eliminate health disparities.
8. Illness, depression, and other serious problems.
9. Universal precautions, proper sanitation, regular immunizations, and proper use of medications.
10. Difficulty with daily living skills and a lower, fixed income.
11. Good nutrition, regular exercise and activities, and social interaction.
12. Bathing, cooking, and climbing stairs.
13. Falls.
14. Immediate action.
15. Maintain a healthful lifestyle, maintain self-reliance, and maintain independence.

(**WORKPLACE CHALLENGE**)—*Any five:* Clear walking paths of all furniture, electrical cords, and telephone cords; make sure lighting is adequate; provide grab bars in bathrooms and along stairways and halls; place frequently used items in cabinets within easy reach to avoid the use of stools or ladders; secure loose rugs with double-sided sticky tape or remove them; place non-slip mats in tubs and showers; monitor older adults who take medications for drowsiness or dizziness; encourage older adults to get regular eye exams and regular exercise to improve balance; help older adults choose low-heeled, well-fitting shoes without slick soles.

Child & Adult Care Professionals Instructor Resource Guide

INSTRUCTIONAL PLAN ━━━━━━━━━━━━━━━━━━━━━

Health & Safety for Staff

FOCUS & PLANNING

Section Objectives

❑ Describe procedures to maintain the health and safety of all staff members.

❑ Identify procedures to limit the health and safety risks to staff members.

❑ Summarize the emergency skills training needed by staff members.

Instruction & Student Practice

❑ **Reading.** Have students read *Section 6-3* on text pages 182-187. Assign the *Section 6-3 Knowledge Check* and *Mini Lab.*

❑ **Examine OSHA Standards.** Have students examine OSHA standards using either the Internet or government materials. Have students discuss why such standards are important to protect employees and determine the proper procedure for issuing a complaint if the standards are not being followed.

❑ **CPR and First Aid Training.** Have a certified trainer from the American Heart Association or the American Red Cross visit the class and train students in CPR, Heimlich, and first aid for procedures for handling common injuries, seizures, and poisonings.

❑ **Lab Manual.** Assign *Lab Activity 26* on page 60, *Lab Activity 27* on page 61, and *Lab Activity 28* on page 62 of the Lab Manual.

❑ **Child & Adult Care Study Guides.** Assign *Study Guide 6-3* from the Student Motivation Kit.

❑ **Child & Adult Care Applications.** Assign *Activities 5, 6, 7, 8, 9, 10, 18, 24, 25, 44, 60,* and *104* as desired from the Student Motivation Kit.

❑ **Child & Adult Care Observations.** Assign *Observations C-1* to *C-45* as desired from the Student Motivation Kit.

❑ **Activity Cards for Children.** Assign *Activity Cards C-1* to *C-96* as desired from the Student Motivation Kit.

❑ **Child & Adult Care Career Profiles.** Assign *Career Profiles* as desired from the Student Motivation Kit.

Review & Student Performance

❑ **PowerPoint® Slides.** Use the *Section 6-3 PowerPoint®* slides on the Effective Instruction CD-ROM.

❑ **Section 6-3 Test.** Have students complete the *Section 6-3 Test* on pages 331-332 of this guide. Or, create your own test by using the **Exam***View®* Test Generator found on the ***Child & Adult Care Professionals*** Effective Instruction CD-ROM.

KEY TERMS

• **foodservice sanitation certificate**
• **toxins**
• **Heimlich maneuver**
• **automated external defibrillation (AED)**

CARE PROVIDER TIP

Even though he or she knows better, it is easy for a care provider to get distracted and leave a container of soap or sanitizing solution within the reach of a child. Establish a convenient, safe place to always store such products and train care providers to automatically put products in that place.

(Continued on next page)

Answers to Section 6-3 Knowledge Check

1. Illness policies, food service sanitation, immunizations and vaccinations, first aid, and CPR.

2. Lifting procedures include the following: stand properly, keep your balance, know your limits, lift with your legs, use your whole body as a unit, and work as a team.

3. Choking, injury, accidental poisoning, heart failure, and inability to breathe.

MINI LAB — *Courses will vary.*

Answers to Chapter 6 Review & Activities

1. Proper hand washing, regular cleaning and regular disinfection of toys and surfaces, restricting attendance of ill clients and staff, ongoing health checks, and immunizations.

2. A daily fresh solution of 1 tablespoon of bleach per gallon of water is good for sanitizing. Wear disposable gloves when using a strong sanitizing solution of ¾-cup bleach to one-gallon water for blood and body fluid spills.

3. *Answers include:* Tetanus, polio, chicken pox, hepatitis, diphtheria, tetanus, pertussis, meningitis, pneumonia, infections (Hemophilus influenza type b), measles, mumps, and rubella.

4. Colds, flu, pink eye, asthma, allergies, giardia, head lice, epilepsy, diabetes, sickle-cell anemia, drug-exposed clients, and HIV.

5. Written emergency procedures staff must follow, such as procedures in case of fire, severe weather, earthquake, or civil defense.

6. *Answers include:* Promotion of a healthful lifestyle, self-reliance and independent living, regular health screenings, and immunizations at the right times.

7. Medications can react with each other and cause bigger health problems.

8. Sick leave policies, proper lifting procedures, and emergency-skills training.

9. Both methods are used to assist victims in emergencies cases. Rescue breathing is used when a person stops breathing but has a heartbeat. CPR is used to keep a person alive until emergency medical professional arrive. CPR is administrated when no heartbeat or pulse is detected for 10-12 seconds. Used for suffocation, drug overdose, electrical shock, choking, drowning, and heat failure victims.

10. *Signs include:* Burns around or in the mouth and throat; vomiting from swallowing poisons; burns or rash on the skin from direct contact with poisons or chemicals; burning or irritation of the eyes or blindness caused by poisons or chemicals coming in contact with the eyes; choking, coughing, headache, nausea, or dizziness from inhaling fumes, sprays, or poisonous gases.

Answers to Section 6-3 Test

Matching:

1. E   5. C
2. H   6. A
3. G   7. B
4. F

Short Answer:

8. First aid certificate and a CPR certificate.

9. Twelve weeks.

10. The supervisor.

11. The local health department foodservice unit.

12. Hot foods should be served at 140° F or above, cold foods at 41° F or below.

13. The person is unable to speak and his or her face becomes red, pale, or somewhat bluish in color.

14. Back blows and chest compressions.

15. Put all infants into one evacuation crib that is on wheels to speed evacuation.

WORKPLACE CHALLENGE —Tilt the victim's head back; lift the chin; pinch the nose shut; seals mouth over the victim's; gives a breath about every five seconds.

INSTRUCTIONAL PLAN

Observing Children

FOCUS & PLANNING

Section Objectives

❏ Explain why care providers observe and record children's behavior.
❏ Identify specific types of observation.
❏ Summarize behaviors that show children's development.
❏ Describe items to include in a child's portfolio that will reflect development.

Instruction & Student Practice

❏ **Reading.** Have students read *Section 7-1* on text pages 191-200. Assign the *Section 7-1 Knowledge Check* and *Mini Lab.*

❏ **Summary Interpretations.** After observing using an anecdotal record, have students interpret the observation(s) by writing a summary paragraph. Have students pair, share, and compare observations.

❏ **Child Poster or Portfolio.** Assign each student a preschool child to observe with permission from the child's parent(s). After completing a series of observations over time, taking photographs of the child at play, and collecting samples of the child's artwork, each student should make a poster or portfolio showing the child's development.

❏ **Lab Manual.** Assign *Lab Activity 29* on page 63, *Lab Activity 31* on page 67, and *Lab Activity 32* on page 68 of the Lab Manual.

❏ **Child & Adult Care Study Guides.** Assign *Study Guide 7-1* from the Student Motivation Kit.

❏ **Child & Adult Care Applications.** Assign *Activities 1* to *27, 33* to *66,* and *93* to *119* as desired from the Student Motivation Kit.

❏ **Child & Adult Care Observations.** Assign *Observations C-1* to *C-45* as desired from the Student Motivation Kit.

❏ **Activity Cards for Children.** Assign *Activity Cards C-1* to *C-96* as desired from the Student Motivation Kit.

❏ **Child & Adult Care Career Profiles.** Assign *Career Profiles* as desired from the Student Motivation Kit.

Review & Student Performance

❏ **PowerPoint® Slides.** Use the *Section 7-1 PowerPoint®* slides on the Effective Instruction CD-ROM.

❏ **Section 7-1 Test.** Have students complete the *Section 7-1 Test* on pages 333-334 of this guide. Or, create your own test by using the **Exam***View®* Test Generator found on the ***Child & Adult Care Professionals*** Effective Instruction CD-ROM.

(Continued on next page)

KEY TERMS

- **objective observation**
- **subjective description**
- **naturalistic observation**
- **participant observer**
- **anecdotal record**
- **running record**
- **frequency count**
- **checklist**
- **rating scale**

CARE PROVIDER TIP

Since children develop at different rates and have different interests, emphasize the development of the total child. For instance, some children may develop socially and cognitively and show less interest in physical skills for a period of time. Growth often occurs in spurts, and a child works on one skill at a time. It is important not to jump to conclusions about developmental delays.

Answers to Section 7-1 Knowledge Check

1. Know individual children better; identify special needs; address specific problems; guide curriculum development; document progress and assess skill development; evaluate program; learn about child development.

2. Name of observer; date and beginning and ending time; list of children involved and their ages; list of adults involved; identification and description of setting; behaviors and events in order they happened.

3. By recording specifically what they see occur, not their opinions or impressions or secondhand information.

MINI LAB —*Observations and answers will vary.*

Answers to Section 7-1 Test

Matching:

1. F
4. G
7. B
2. K
5. A
8. I
3. E
6. C
9. J

Short Answer:

10. Be quiet, courteous, and respectful to children and staff.

11. Say, "I am writing down how children play, so I can remember it later."

12. Consider using false names or initials to identify children who have been observed.

13. They look for patterns and try to draw conclusions about the causes and meaning of behavior.

14. Consult with the child's family.

15. Take care to stay in the background as much as possible.

16. Your purpose for observing.

17. They can give parents a picture of how their child is developing.

18. Concentration and a long attention span.

19. A custodial parent or legal guardian.

20. A rating scale.

WORKPLACE CHALLENGE —*Any five:* Sit in a low chair; position yourself at the side of the room but where you can still observe easily; wear simple, appropriate clothing; do not start a conversation with children or maintain prolonged eye contact; if a child asks what you are doing, give a brief but honest answer; do not interfere in what is going on unless a child is in immediate danger and no other adult is available.

INSTRUCTIONAL PLAN ━━━━━━━━━━━━━━━━

Observing Older Adults

FOCUS & PLANNING

Section Objectives

❏ Identify reasons why older adults need to be observed in an adult day center.

❏ Determine ways to observe older adults in adult day centers.

❏ Outline procedures for observing older adults in day centers.

Instruction & Student Practice

❏ **Reading.** Have students read *Section 7-2* on text pages 201-209. Assign the *Section 7-2 Knowledge Check* and *Mini Lab*.

❏ **Observations.** Have students practice observing older adults by viewing a videotape of an activity at an adult day care center. Students should pair together to compare their observations.

❏ **Observation Guides.** Have students complete a series of different guides while observing the same older adult. Have students write an objective summary of the individual's skills, activities, and interests.

❏ **Listening Skills.** Have each student attempt to build a rapport with an older adult that he or she has been observing. The student should actively listen to the adult by forming eye contact and should engage the adult in conversation by asking open-ended questions. After each visit, the student should record journal recollections.

❏ **Lab Manual.** Assign *Lab Activity 30* on page 65 of the Lab Manual.

❏ **Child & Adult Care Study Guides.** Assign *Study Guide 7-2* from the Student Motivation Kit.

❏ **Child & Adult Care Applications.** Assign *Activities 67* to *92* as desired from the Student Motivation Kit.

❏ **Child & Adult Care Observations.** Assign *Observations OA-1* to *OA-22* from the Student Motivation Kit.

❏ **Activity Cards for Older Adults.** Assign *Activity Cards OA-1* to *OA-47* as desired from the Student Motivation Kit.

❏ **Child & Adult Care Career Profiles.** Assign *Career Profiles* as desired from the Student Motivation Kit.

Review & Student Performance

❏ **PowerPoint® Slides.** Use the *Section 7-2 PowerPoint®* slides on the Effective Instruction CD-ROM.

❏ **Section 7-2 Test.** Have students complete the *Section 7-2 Test* on pages 335-336 of this guide. Or, create your own test by using the **Exam***View*® Test Generator found on the **Child & Adult Care Professionals** Effective Instruction CD-ROM.

(Continued on next page)

KEY TERMS

- **subjective reporting**
- **objective reporting**
- **agitated**
- **Activity of Daily Living (ADL)**
- **radial pulse**

CARE PROVIDER TIP

When relating stories, older adults sometimes ramble and confuse memories. If the listener corrects the adult, a communication barrier may be formed. It is better to listen and attempt to stimulate the story-teller's memory by asking questions.

Answers to Section 7-2 Knowledge Check

1. Effective communication helps you to avoid confusion. "I" statements help to communicate sensitively.

2. Frequency counts are important when observing older adults because it helps the care provider verify the number of times medication is given.

3. Objective reporting requires that the observer leave any personal judgment out of the observation. Subjective reporting allows the observer to make a judgment during an observation.

MINI LAB —*Answers will vary*.

Answers to Chapter 7 Review & Activities

1. Know individual children better; identify special needs; address specific problems; guide curriculum development; document progress and assess skill development; evaluate program; learn about child development.

2. Observers record children in their everyday setting and record their natural behaviors as they occur.

3. Advantages: natural setting, typical behaviors, can be done while working. Disadvantages: can distract observer from his or her job, makes it harder to be objective, observer becomes part of the setting and observation.

4. So the observer doesn't interfere with the events or distract those being observed.

5. For children: Name of observer; date and beginning and ending time; list of children involved and their ages; list of adults involved; identification and description of setting; behaviors and events in order they happened. For older adults: time and amount of medications taken.

6. For children: the number of times a particular behavior occurs. For older adults: the number of times a medication is taken or a medical procedure conducted.

7. A checklist is a list of specific items, such as skills or behaviors, to observe. A rating scale provides a verbal or numerical evaluation of the skills or behaviors observed.

8. Interpreting is making sense of what is observed. Interpreting helps observers draw conclusions about what they've observed and determine reasons for behaviors or incidents.

9. Watching and listening are important skills to have when observing older adults because you can see their reactions and hear their conservations as a way of learning more about them.

Answers to Section 7-2 Test

Matching:

1. H
2. F
3. B
4. A
5. G

Short Answer:

6. To determine the types of activities to offer.

7. Watching, listening, and using body language that shows you are listening.

8. So you can stay focused on the topic.

9. Ask them to repeat what they heard and give you the opportunity to confirm your intention.

10. Use "I" statements, such as "I think," "I feel," and "I want."

11. Checklists.

12. It helps staff to make an evaluation based on vital sign readings at particular times during the day.

13. Daily task records.

14. It gives a clear picture of the intervals, frequency, and results of the screenings over a period of time.

15. Strong emotions, exercise, body temperature, and pain.

WORKPLACE CHALLENGE —Record the details immediately after an activity; write it in story form; write in chronological order by activity; include details about the older adult's physical condition and level of involvement; draw brief conclusions about what you observe.

INSTRUCTIONAL PLAN ━━━━━━━━━━━━━━━━━━━━━━━

Child Abuse & Neglect

FOCUS & PLANNING

Section Objectives

❏ Identify the types of child abuse and neglect.

❏ Describe the symptoms and signs of child abuse and neglect.

❏ Identify documenting and reporting responsibilities of early childhood staff.

❏ Explain the methods of preventing child abuse and neglect.

❏ Describe the ways of building resilience in children.

Instruction & Student Practice

❏ **Reading.** Have students read *Section 8-1* on text pages 213-219. Assign the *Section 8-1 Knowledge Check* and *Mini Lab*.

❏ **Incidence of Abuse.** Have students log on to Web sites for local social service agencies such as Prevention of Child Abuse and Child Protective Services and gather information about the incidence of abuse and reporting procedures. Have them report their findings to the class.

❏ **Lab Manual.** Assign *Lab Activity 34* on page 71 and *Lab Activity 36* on page 74 of the Lab Manual.

❏ **Child & Adult Care Study Guides.** Assign *Study Guide 8-1* from the Student Motivation Kit.

❏ **Child & Adult Care Applications.** Assign *Activities 5, 6, 8, 9, 10,* and *104* as desired from the Student Motivation Kit.

❏ **Child & Adult Care Observations.** Assign *Observation C-20* from the Student Motivation Kit.

❏ **Activity Cards for Children.** Assign *Activity Cards C-1* to *C-96* as desired from the Student Motivation Kit.

❏ **Child & Adult Care Career Profiles.** Assign *Career Profiles* as desired from the Student Motivation Kit.

Review & Student Performance

❏ **PowerPoint® Slides.** Use the *Section 8-1 PowerPoint®* slides on the Effective Instruction CD-ROM.

❏ **Section 8-1 Test.** Have students complete the *Section 8-1 Test* on pages 337-338 of this guide. Or, create your own test by using the **Exam***View®* Test Generator found on the ***Child & Adult Care Professionals*** Effective Instruction CD-ROM.

KEY TERMS

- child neglect
- child abuse
- documenting
- crisis nursery
- resilience

CARE PROVIDER TIP

Since many child abusers were abused as children, they may not recognize their behavior as being abusive or may not have learned the skills to guide children in appropriate ways. There is often confusion between parental rights to punish a child and abusive behavior. It is the job of the child care professional to educate parents about child abuse.

(Continued on next page)

Answers to Section 8-1 Knowledge Check

1. *Physical abuse:* Unexplained injuries, such as bumps, bruises, welts, and burns. *Emotional abuse:* Low self-esteem, depression, lack of confidence, uncontrollable aggression and outbursts; anxiety and fear; trouble sleeping; change in appetite; isolation and withdrawal. *Sexual abuse:* Unusual knowledge of sex acts for child's age; soreness or injury in genital regions; very low self-esteem; drawings with sexual themes; advanced sexual play with peers or dolls.

2. Symptoms observed should be recorded in writing and reported to the appropriate state agency. All documentation and records should be maintained in the child's confidential file. Supervisors should be notified of any suspicions of abuse or neglect.

3. The ability to cope with and eventually recover from trauma, abuse, or neglect.

(MINI LAB)—*Observations and answers will vary.*

Answers to Section 8-1 Test

Matching:

1. B   4. D
2. C   5. G
3. E

Short Answer:

6. On bony areas such as the knees, shins, and forehead.
7. Ridicule, torment, and unmerciful teasing.
8. Intimidation and fear.
9. Low self-esteem.
10. Offer evening workshops to deal with these issues.
11. Classroom routines promote a sense of security and stability.
12. Conduct a criminal background check before hiring.
13. Hormones prevent the brain from transferring information along the central nervous system.
14. Older adults who stay in touch with friends and who participate in groups and functions outside their homes.
15. Keep belongings orderly.

(WORKPLACE CHALLENGE)—*Any five:* Give children individualized attention; spend quality time with children to build sense of self-worth; respond warmly to children to help them relax; talk with children and listen to them closely; give children some decision-making power and control over their daytime experiences; provide children with a consistent daily routine.

INSTRUCTIONAL PLAN

Elder Abuse & Neglect

FOCUS & PLANNING

Section Objectives

❑ Determine why older adults are vulnerable to abuse and neglect.

❑ Identify the signs of abuse among older adults.

❑ Identify the agencies that assist older adults who experience abuse.

❑ Describe a procedure to report abuse and neglect of older adults.

Instruction & Student Practice

❑ **Reading.** Have students read *Section 8-2* on text pages 220-227. Assign the *Section 8-2 Knowledge Check* and *Mini Lab*.

❑ **Speaker.** Invite a gerontologist to speak to the class about signs of elder abuse and services available to counsel victims of abuse.

❑ **Research.** Have students investigate your state's laws for reporting elder abuse. Have them report differences between cases that require mandatory reporting and those that require voluntary reporting.

❑ **Journal Entry.** Have students respond to the following in a written paragraph. If an older adult who visits the adult day care center where you work confides in you that a family member is mistreating him or her, what would you say to encourage the person to report the abuse?

❑ **Lab Manual.** Assign *Lab Activity 34* on page 71 and *Lab Activity 36* on page 74 of the Lab Manual.

❑ **Child & Adult Care Study Guides.** Assign *Study Guide 8-2* from the Student Motivation Kit.

❑ **Child & Adult Care Applications.** Assign *Activity 28* from the Student Motivation Kit.

❑ **Child & Adult Care Observations.** Assign *Observation OA-20* from the Student Motivation Kit.

❑ **Activity Cards for Older Adults.** Assign *Activity Cards OA-1* to *OA-47* as desired from the Student Motivation Kit.

❑ **Child & Adult Care Career Profiles.** Assign *Career Profiles* as desired from the Student Motivation Kit.

Review & Student Performance

❑ **PowerPoint® Slides.** Use the *Section 8-2 PowerPoint®* slides Effective Instruction CD-ROM.

❑ **Section 8-2 Test.** Have students complete the *Section 8-2 Test* on pages 339-340 of this guide. Or, create your own test by using the **Exam***View®* Test Generator found on the ***Child & Adult Care Professionals*** Effective Instruction CD-ROM.

KEY TERMS

- **vulnerable**
- **elder abuse**
- **financial abuse**
- **fraud**
- **con artist**
- **quackery**
- **adult protective services**

CARE PROVIDER TIP

Since many baby boomers are in denial of the aging process, they may seldom visit older family members who are placed in residential adult care centers. The center's employees then take the place of the absent family members in the resident's daily life.

(Continued on next page)

Answers to Section 8-2 Knowledge Check

1. Being frail, isolated, unable to defend against acts of unkindness or mistreatment.
2. *Any five: See the chart on page 224 of the text.*
3. Agencies include The Administration on Aging (AoA), U.S. Department of Health and Human Services, National Center on Elder Abuse, Adult Protective Services, Eldercare Locator, National Organization for Victim Assistance, and AARP—Criminal Justice Services.

MINI LAB —*Answers will vary.*

Answers to Chapter 8 Review & Activities

1. *Child abuse:* Intentional injured, whether physically, emotionally, or sexually. *Child neglect:* Failure to provide child with basic necessities of life, including food, clothing, shelter, or medical care.
2. *Physical abuse:* Unexplained injuries, such as bumps, bruises, welts, and burns. *Emotional abuse:* Low self-esteem, depression, lack of confidence, uncontrollable aggression and outbursts; anxiety and fear; trouble sleeping; change in appetite; isolation and withdrawal. *Sexual abuse:* Unusual knowledge of sex acts for child's age; soreness or injury in genital regions; very low self-esteem; drawings with sexual themes; advanced sexual play with peers or dolls.
3. Those who are required by law to report suspicions of child abuse and/or neglect.
4. *Any three:* Give individual attention; spend quality time to build self-worth; respond warmly; encourage relaxation; model a positive attitude; listen to children's fears and thoughts; give chances for control and decision making; provide consistent daily routine.
5. *See list on page 217.*
6. To prevent the hiring of those who have committed past crimes against children or older adults. To protect the rights and welfare of children, families, and staff.
7. Isolation and frailty make abuse easier to commit and more difficult to notice.
8. Physical abuse, sexual abuse, emotional abuse, neglect, and financial abuse. *See chart on page 224 for examples.*
9. The Administration on Aging (AoA), U.S. Department of Health and Human Services, National Center on Elder Abuse.
10. *Voluntary reporting:* Reporters do not have to provide their name. You also have legal protection, and no one can file lawsuits against you. *Mandatory reporting:* Care providers are mandated to report suspected abuse.

Answers to Section 8-2 Test

Matching:

1.	J	3.	F	5.	B	7.	A
2.	C	4.	G	6.	H		

Short Answer:

8. Isolation from close family members and friends.
9. Slapping, bruising, molesting, or restraining.
10. They want power and control.
11. They tend to trust strangers, trust those who offer miracle cures for their medical problems, and are most likely to be home alone and willing to talk with callers or people who come to their door.
12. Depression caused by grief.
13. The Older Americans Act.
14. Call your local Area Agency on Aging.
15. *Any three:* Fear of retaliation; fear of being put in an institution; shame that a family member mistreats them; belief that the police and social agencies can not really help them or believe them; unsure of whom to call; fear of getting involved.

WORKPLACE CHALLENGE —*Any five:* Let older adults know you support and care for them; let victims know you want to listen to their fears; listen but don't question them about the abuse or give opinions; offer to take victims to the doctor, police, or victim services; tell them about available services, such as counseling; help the older adult with chores, such as shopping or preparing meals.

Child & Adult Care Professionals Instructor Resource Guide

INSTRUCTIONAL PLAN

Schedules & Routines for Children

Section
9-1

FOCUS & PLANNING

Section Objectives

❑ Explain what a schedule is and how one is developed.

❑ Describe common routines incorporated into a daily schedule.

❑ Explain why and how transitions are used.

❑ Identify the need for safety checks as part of the care provider's regular routine.

Instruction & Student Practice

❑ **Reading.** Have students read *Section 9-1* on text pages 231-238. Assign the *Section 9-1 Knowledge Check* and *Mini Lab*.

❑ **Simulation.** Change the classroom routine by randomly changing the seating arrangement, changing the order of the lesson, and eliminating the usual structure. Have students write a journal entry reacting to the lack of routine.

❑ **Compare Schedules.** Have students contrast the daily schedules of several program types, such as a half-day preschool verses a full-day day care center or a toddler room verses a four-year old room.

❑ **Use a Transition Technique.** Assign the students to use several transition techniques with the children where they work. Have them report to the class which techniques were successful.

❑ **Lab Manual.** Assign *Lab Activity 37* on page 75, *Lab Activity 38* on page 79, and *Lab Activity 39* on 83 of the Lab Manual.

❑ **Child & Adult Care Study Guides.** Assign *Study Guide 9-1* from the Student Motivation Kit.

❑ **Child & Adult Care Observations.** Assign *Observation C-18* from the Student Motivation Kit.

❑ **Activity Cards for Children.** Assign *Activity Cards C-1* to *C-96* as desired from the Student Motivation Kit.

❑ **Child & Adult Care Career Profiles.** Assign *Career Profiles* as desired from the Student Motivation Kit.

Review & Student Performance

❑ **PowerPoint® Slides.** Use the *Section 9-1 PowerPoint®* slides on the Effective Instruction CD-ROM.

❑ **Section 9-1 Test.** Have students complete the *Section 9-1 Test* on pages 341-342 of this guide. Or, create your own test by using the **Exam***View®* Test Generator found on the **Child & Adult Care Professionals** Effective Instruction CD-ROM.

(Continued on next page)

KEY TERMS

• schedule
• self-directed
• routine
• transition
• transition techniques
• chore board
• job jar
• choice time

CARE PROVIDER TIP

Routine is so important to young children that they often become over-stimulated when the routine is changed. Preparing children for a change in routine helps minimize the problems that result when children become over-excited.

Answers to Section 9-1 Knowledge Check

1. Helps children make the adjustment from home to school; predictable and warm arrival routines helps everyone start off with a positive attitude and helps the whole day go more smoothly.

2. Daily schedule: greeting, snacks, individual and small group activities and play time; morning meeting/project work/activity time; music time; lunch; rest or quiet time; outdoor play time. Daily routines: hand washing; picking up toys; health checks; toileting; transitions; departure routine.

3. Transition techniques: song or music to cue clean-up time; flicker lights to signal children to move to the circle for story time; movement activities to help children focus while traveling from area to area.

MINI LAB —*Observations and answers will vary.*

Answers to Section 9-1 Test

Matching:

1. I	5. H
2. J	6. B
3. F	7. D
4. G	8. A

Short Answer:

9. Gradual wake-up, toileting and hand washing, snack, and self-directed play.

10. Play with and read or sing to children.

11. Allows children to develop large and small muscle control.

12. Provides orderliness and discourages conflict.

13. Children can help by setting tables and using utensils and lunch kits.

14. Care providers and children gather in a group to discuss the upcoming day's activities.

15. Prevents crowding and keeps the classroom atmosphere relaxed and orderly.

WORKPLACE CHALLENGE —*Any five:* Sing a simple tune when it is time to pick up toys; jingle chimes to gather the group in a circle for music; flicker the lights off and on to signal story time; play a recording to a drumbeat to lead children to outdoor play; ask children to move like gorillas, rabbits, or robots as they go to wash hands; use puppets, fingerplays, or props to focus children's interest during group discussion; add a surprise to capture curiosity; play thinking games.

INSTRUCTIONAL PLAN ━━━━━━━━━━━━━━━━━━━━━━━━━━ *Section* 9-2

Schedules & Routines for Older Adults

FOCUS & PLANNING

Section Objectives

❑ Determine how staffing needs impact schedules in an older adult day care program.

❑ Describe how program needs impact schedules in older adult day care programs.

❑ Identify typical routines in older adult day care programs.

Instruction & Student Practice

❑ **Reading.** Have students read *Section 9-2* on text pages 239-245. Assign the *Section 9-2 Knowledge Check* and *Mini Lab*.

❑ **Plan a Schedule.** Have students plan a sample daily schedule for an adult day care center. Students should consider the hours of operation, services offered, and the needs of the participants.

❑ **Assist an Older Adult.** Have students practice skills and schedule a time to assist older adults at their work sites with an ADL or IADL.

❑ **Service Project.** Have students plan and lead an intergenerational group social activity for the adults at an adult activity center. Have students schedule the event with the activity coordinator and evaluate the response of the older adults.

❑ **Lab Manual.** Assign *Lab Activity 40* on page 86 of the Lab Manual.

❑ **Child & Adult Care Study Guides.** Assign *Study Guide 9-2* from the Student Motivation Kit.

❑ **Child & Adult Care Observations.** Assign *Observations OA-2, OA-5, OA-6,* and *OA-20* from the Student Motivation Kit.

❑ **Activity Cards for Older Adults.** Assign *Activity Cards OA-1 to OA-47* as desired from the Student Motivation Kit.

❑ **Child & Adult Care Career Profiles.** Assign *Career Profiles* as desired from the Student Motivation Kit.

Review & Student Performance

❑ **PowerPoint® Slides.** Use the *Section 9-2 PowerPoint®* slides on the Effective Instruction CD-ROM.

❑ **Section 9-2 Test.** Have students complete the *Section 9-2 Test* on pages 343-344 of this guide. Or, create your own test by using the **Exam***View*® Test Generator found on the **Child & Adult Care Professionals** Effective Instruction CD-ROM.

KEY TERMS

• schedule
• routines
• full-time employee (FTE)
• geriatric care manager
• instrumental activities of daily living (IADL)

CARE PROVIDER TIP

Older adults like the security of a routine. When the routine is disrupted with a new activity, the adult may become disgruntled and be reluctant to participate. Caregivers may need to encourage the adults to participate and allow themselves to enjoy the activity.

(Continued on next page)

Answers to Section 9-2 Knowledge Check

1. Maintaining a schedule and routine help guide daily routines and encourage older adults to participate in center programs. They also help staff members understand their daily responsibilities.

2. Eating, toileting, dressing, bathing, walking, getting in and out of bed or chair, and getting outside.

3. Staff responsibilities include helping with arrival tasks, such as signing in at the center; accessing meal participation; touring the facility; arranging for special needs; and taking vital signs; helping with activities, such as preparing areas for activities; assisting older adults to specific areas; providing personal care; and arranging for transportation for medical treatment; helping with mealtimes, such as preparing meals; assisting those who need help eating; conducting nutritional tips at each meal; and assisting with departure, such as checking for belongings and assisting those who need transportation.

MINI LAB—*Answers will vary*.

Answers to Chapter 9 Review & Activities

1. A schedule is a plan that shows task assignments for each staff member and activities for participants. It helps to make the services run smoothly.

2. Developmental areas; active and quiet play; small-group and individual play and attention; indoor and outdoor play; large- and small-group activities.

3. Regular, expected procedure that is followed to accomplish something.

4. An activity or technique to guide children from one activity, routine, or event to another.

5. *Signals:* Lights flickered, drumbeats or piano keys tickled can signal clean-up time. *Music:* Songs can be sung to bring group together for greeting or good-byes. *Chore boards:* Used to organize daily duties such as watering plants or setting snack tables; *Job jars:* Used to add a surprise element to clean-up time at closing time; *Choice time:* Helps distribute children throughout the whole classroom.

6. Activities of daily living are tasks that people need to perform to maintain a quality of life. Instrumental activities of daily living are home-management activities that older adults perform on a regular basis to live independently.

7. Preparing meals, shopping for personal items, managing money, using the telephone, doing heavy and light housework.

8. *Social worker:* Providing social services activities; making referrals for other needed services; *nutritionist:* Providing nutritious mid-morning snack, lunch, and afternoon snack; *nurse:* Offering nursing care for vital signs and medication monitoring; *nurse's aid:* Assisting with activities of daily living; *activity coordinator:* Conducting appropriate physical activities; providing opportunities to develop peer relationships and friendships; providing social, recreational, and entertainment activities.

9. A document that serves as a road map to achieve program goals.

Answers to Section 9-2 Test

Matching:

1. F   2. E   3. B   4. D   5. A

Short Answer:

6. Program requirements.

7. Listing activities helps identify the number of staff members needed to carry out the activities and the need for full- or part-time staff members.

8. Center director.

9. Six.

10. Family life educator.

11. So the director can develop programs and activities and make staff assignments.

12. The plan serves as a road map for care providers to achieve their goals.

13. It affects the safety of the participants.

14. Children may be fearful of spending one-on-one time with older adults.

15. There is always a chance that the activity may not interest the participants.

WORKPLACE CHALLENGE—Privacy and confidentiality; personal dignity; social, emotional, and physical health and well-being; activity choices and opportunities to participate and maintain independence; respect for culture beliefs.

INSTRUCTIONAL PLAN ━━━━━━━━━━━━━━━━━━━━━━━━

Child Nutrition

Section **10-1**

FOCUS & PLANNING

Section Objectives

❑ Explain the impact of nutrition on early childhood development.

❑ Identify nutrients required for good nutrition.

❑ Plan balanced menus for young children.

❑ Describe proper food safety and sanitation practices.

❑ Identify meal-service guidelines.

Instruction & Student Practice

❑ **Reading.** Have students read *Section 10-1* on text pages 249-259. Assign the *Section 10-1 Knowledge Check* and *Mini Lab.*

❑ **Analyze Labels.** Have students collect and analyze the nutrient labels from fruit juices and drinks. Have them conclude why it is recommended to serve only citrus juices or fortified fruit juices to children.

❑ **Color Snacks.** Have students plan snacks using foods that are the "color of the day." For instance, on red day students might serve cherry tomatoes, strawberries, or red apples.

❑ **Serving Sizes.** Have students use measuring cups and serving scoops to measure food servings for children of various ages. Dry beans may be used to measure fruits and vegetables.

❑ **Lab Manual.** Assign *Lab Activities 41* to *45* on pages 87 to 94 of the Lab Manual.

❑ **Child & Adult Care Study Guides.** Assign *Study Guide 10-1* from the Student Motivation Kit.

❑ **Child & Adult Care Observations.** Assign *Observations C-16, C-17,* and *C-19* from the Student Motivation Kit.

❑ **Activity Cards for Children.** Assign *Activity Cards C-87* and *OA-12* as desired from the Student Motivation Kit.

❑ **Activity Cards for Older Adults.** Assign *Activity Cards OA-14* to *OA 20* as desired from the Student Motivation Kit.

❑ **Child & Adult Care Career Profiles.** Assign *Career Profiles* as desired from the Student Motivation Kit.

Review & Student Performance

❑ **PowerPoint® Slides.** Use the *Section 10-1 PowerPoint®* slides on the Effective Instruction CD-ROM.

❑ **Section 10-1 Test.** Have students complete the *Section 10-1 Test* on pages 345-348 of this guide. Or, create your own test by using the **Exam***View*® Test Generator found on the **Child & Adult Care Professionals** Effective Instruction CD-ROM.

(Continued on next page)

KEY TERMS

- **nutrients**
- **nutrition**
- **fiber**
- **amino acids**
- **complete protein**
- **incomplete protein**
- **deficiency**
- **Food Guide Pyramid**
- **perishable**
- **health department inspector**

CARE PROVIDER TIP

Children eat best when offered a variety of nutritious foods. Offer child-sized portions of a well-balanced meal. Allow children to eat what they wish and remember not to give up on new foods. It often takes many exposures to a new food before a child will try it.

Answers to Section 10-1 Knowledge Check

1. Carbohydrates, proteins, fats, vitamins, minerals, water.
2. Children prefer a colorful variety of foods. Younger children especially enjoy food that can be eaten with the fingers. Foods that cause choking should be avoided. Basic nutrition must be provided.
3. Store, serve, and maintain food at proper temperatures. Thaw foods appropriately. Cook foods thoroughly. All food preparation surfaces and utensils, as well as meal service areas and utensils should be clean and sanitized. Hand-washing should be frequent; latex gloves used when necessary.

MINI LAB —*Activities and answers will vary.*

Answers to Section 10-1 Test

Matching:

1.	J	6.	I
2.	K	7.	E
3.	F	8.	G
4.	B	9.	L
5.	D	10.	H

Short Answer:

11. It provides the foundation for children's normal physical growth.
12. In the first two years of life.
13. Vegetables, breads and cereals, rice, and pasta.
14. Meat, poultry, fish, eggs, and dairy products.
15. It helps the body eliminate waste.
16. Meat, vegetable oils, whole dairy products, egg yolks, nuts, margarine, mayonnaise, and salad dressing.
17. They help keep the body working properly and help other nutrients do their jobs.
18. Calcium and phosphorus.
19. They help regulate body processes, and they become parts of the body's bones, tissues, and fluids.
20. Rickets.
21. Fats, oils, and sweets.
22. One tablespoon of each food choice per year of child's age.
23. At least 2 cups.
24. Children's taste buds are sensitive.
25. Child and Adult Care Food Program (CACFP).
26. Allergies, other medical problems, and religious beliefs.
27. Valuable nutrients can be lost during cooking.
28. United States Department of Agriculture (USDA) and the Food and Drug Administration (FDA).
29. 155°F; 165°F.
30. One tablespoon of ultra bleach per gallon of water.

WORKPLACE CHALLENGE —*Any four:* Food is fuel for the body, it helps people grow, and it gives them energy; people should eat a variety of foods every day to remain healthy; people need to drink eight glasses of water every day; food comes from plants and animals; people eat different parts of plants, including stems, roots, leaves, and seeds; most food is grown on the farm and then taken to a supermarket; people can grow their own food in gardens; people from different parts of the world eat different foods; food can be cooked in many different ways; when preparing food, hands must be clean before and during cooking. *Any one:* Simple cooking activities; link other activities, such as reading books or taking field trips, to nutrition and food preparation; teach parents about good nutrition.

INSTRUCTIONAL PLAN ━━━━━━━━━━━

Nutrition for Older Adults

Section 10-2

FOCUS & PLANNING

Section Objectives

❏ Identify the nutritional needs of older adults.

❏ Summarize the guidelines for effective meal planning for older adults.

❏ Explain how to effectively make food purchases, label food properly, and handle food safely.

❏ Describe how illness and medications impact nutrition for older adults.

❏ Summarize the key components of food assistance programs.

Instruction & Student Practice

❏ **Reading.** Have students read *Section 10-2* on text pages 260-273. Assign the *Section 10-2 Knowledge Check* and *Mini Lab*.

❏ **Service Learning.** Have students eat a meal at an adult day care center with the older adults. When they return to class, have them write a journal entry relating their impressions of the dining room's atmosphere and the adult's enjoyment of the dining experience.

❏ **Field Trip.** Take the students to a commercial kitchen where food is prepared for children or older adults. Have students observe the sanitation standards and food preparation practices.

❏ **Lab Manual.** Assign *Lab Activities 41* to *45* on pages 87 to 94 of the Lab Manual.

❏ **Child & Adult Care Study Guides.** Assign *Study Guide 10-2* from the Student Motivation Kit.

❏ **Child & Adult Care Applications.** Assign *Activities 71* and *76* from the Student Motivation Kit.

❏ **Child & Adult Care Observations.** Assign *Observation OA-15* from the Student Motivation Kit.

❏ **Activity Cards for Older Adults.** Assign *Activity Cards OA-11 to OA-20* and *OA-31* as desired from the Student Motivation Kit.

❏ **Child & Adult Care Career Profiles.** Assign *Career Profiles* as desired from the Student Motivation Kit.

Review & Student Performance

❏ **PowerPoint® Slides.** Use the *Section 10-2 PowerPoint®* slides on the Effective Instruction CD-ROM.

❏ **Section 10-2 Test.** Have students complete the *Section 10-2 Test* on pages 349-350 of this guide. Or, create your own test by using the **Exam**View® Test Generator found on the **Child & Adult Care Professionals** Effective Instruction CD-ROM.

(Continued on next page)

KEY TERMS

- antioxidants
- anemia
- nutrient dense
- osteoporosis
- shelf life
- Elderly Nutrition Program (ENP)
- Meals on Wheels
- congregate meals

CARE PROVIDER TIP

Older adults have developed food habits and preferences over a lifetime. Since those habits are not readily changed, adults generally eat better if they are given menu choices or are involved in menu planning.

Answers to Section 10-2 Knowledge Check

1. Factor that impact nutrition for older adults include not being able to see, smell, or taste foods; reduction in gastrointestinal motility; decline in lean body mass; changes in kidney and bladder control; decline in bone density; illness; and dental problems.

2. Older adults are at greater risk of becoming seriously ill from eating tainted food because of limited sight, smell, and taste.

3. *Elderly Nutrition Program (ENP):* Program that provides nutrient-dense meals, nutrition counseling, and links to support and health services; *Meals on Wheels:* Program that provides home-delivered meals to older adults; *Congregate meals:* Program that provides meals to people with disabilities who reside in housing facilities.

MINI LAB —*Activities and answers will vary.*

Answers to Chapter 10 Review & Activities

1. Bread, cereal, rice, and pasta group; vegetable group; fruit group; milk, yogurt, and cheese group; meat, poultry, fish, dry beans, eggs, and nut group; fats and sweets.

2. To welcome and show respect to all clients, to illustrate a variety of styles of food preparation, to encourage all children to get adequate nutrition.

3. Grapes, peanuts, popcorn, hotdogs.

4. So bacteria doesn't grow that can cause illness.

5. Carbohydrates: main source of body energy.

6. Proteins: Help body build, maintain, and repair body cells.

7. The Food Guide Pyramid for older adults encourages eating a well-balanced diet of at least the minimum number of servings from each food group; eating foods with added vitamin B_{12}, calcium, and vitamin D; and drinking eight full glasses of water a day. This is very important due to the medication that older adults take.

8. Assist them with eating, if necessary, and refer them to the Elderly Nutrition Programs and Meals on Wheels.

9. Wash hands properly, wear latex gloves to cover wounds, and clean and sanitize all utensils and cooking surfaces.

10. Vitamins, minerals, and calcium.

Answers to Section 10-2 Test

Matching:

1. A	3. G	5. E	7. D
2. H	4. I	6. F	

Short Answer:

8. 55 to 60 percent.

9. Interference with healing, inability to fight off illness, and a reduction in strength of body muscles.

10. Vitamins C, E, and A.

11. 30 percent.

12. Milk-based soups and puddings.

13. Vitamin B_{12} and folic acid.

14. Calcium, iron, and zinc.

15. Fights infection and builds and repairs body tissues.

16. Decrease in food intake or a disinterest in food that older adults once enjoyed.

17. Some cereals and soft-textured foods such as soft-cooked eggs, chopped meats, potatoes, and other soft vegetables and fruits.

18. Exchange lists, or groups of foods that have similar food values.

19. Some older adults have heart disease or gallbladder disease and should avoid high-fat foods.

20. Administration on Aging (AoA).

WORKPLACE CHALLENGE —*Any five:* Follow dietary needs outlined in older adults' enrollment records; use standardized recipes that require little fat, cholesterol, sodium, or sugar; use low-fat cooking methods, such as broiling, baking, and steaming instead of frying; use standard recipes that provide a consistent, nutritious product with every use; choose healthful, ready-prepared food products that meet specific nutrition needs; prepare tasty menu items with good visual appeal and fragrant aromas.

INSTRUCTIONAL PLAN ━━━━━━━━━━━━━━━━━━━━━━━━━━━━

Building Social Skills

FOCUS & PLANNING

Section Objectives

❏ Describe social competence.

❏ Identify effective social skills.

❏ Describe ways to foster social development.

❏ Explain how communication skills and parenting styles affect social development.

❏ Explain how culture may influence social skills.

Instruction & Student Practice

❏ **Reading.** Have students read *Section 11-1* on text pages 277-280. Assign the *Section 11-1 Knowledge Check* and *Mini Lab.*

❏ **Use Library Books.** Have students select books that encourage children to practice positive social skills. Assign students to read the stories to the children and discuss the social skills.

❏ **Teamwork.** Have teams of students plan a lesson activity that requires the children to work in teams. Have students observe the groups for teamwork skills, such as working as a leader, idea contributor, worker, or encourager.

❏ **Lab Manual.** Assign *Lab Activity 46* on page 95 of the Lab Manual.

❏ **Child & Adult Care Study Guides.** Assign *Study Guide 11-1* from the Student Motivation Kit.

❏ **Child & Adult Care Applications.** Assign *Activities 1* to *10, 13* to *15, 20, 21, 27, 39, 42, 99,* and *106* from the Student Motivation Kit.

❏ **Child & Adult Care Observations.** Assign *Observations C-1 to C-12, C-21, C-22, C-23* and *C-27* from the Student Motivation Kit.

❏ **Activity Cards for Children.** Assign *Activity Cards C-1 to C-96* as desired from the Student Motivation Kit.

❏ **Child & Adult Care Career Profiles.** Assign *Career Profiles* as desired from the Student Motivation Kit.

Review & Student Performance

❏ **PowerPoint® Slides.** Use the *Section 11-1 PowerPoint®* slides Effective Instruction CD-ROM.

❏ **Section 11-1 Test.** Have students complete the *Section 11-1 Test* on pages 351-352 of this guide. Or, create your own test by using the **Exam***View®* Test Generator found on the ***Child & Adult Care Professionals*** Effective Instruction CD-ROM.

KEY TERMS

- **social competence**
- **empathy**
- **compassion**

CARE PROVIDER TIP

Children who are in preschool or day care programs usually learn social skills, such as sharing, taking turns, teamwork, and cooperation, at an earlier age than do those who are home with a parent or babysitter. Most children who have not had the opportunity to play with others quickly learn the give and take of social skills in kindergarten and first grade.

(Continued on next page)

Answers to Section 11-1 Knowledge Check

1. A person's ability to get along with others in an acceptable and appropriate manner.

2. Model respect, acceptance, and positive social skills; encourage empathy and compassion; encourage cooperation and teamwork; require self-control.

3. Communication styles and practices vary among cultures. Knowing how specific cultures prefer to communicate increases understanding between care providers and clients.

MINI LAB —*Answers will vary.*

Answers to Section 11-1 Test

Matching:

1. D
2. B
3. A

Short Answer:

4. Kindness, courtesy, adapting to peers, and respect for others.
5. Respect for self and others.
6. The child will develop socially acceptable ways of behaving throughout life.
7. Explain situations, discuss feelings, and display empathy.
8. Group projects such as gardening, building with blocks, and creating art murals.
9. Anger, disappointment, frustration, and jealousy.
10. Card and board games, sandbox play, and group storytelling.
11. Listening to and speaking with infants and using short sentences and exaggerated facial expressions.
12. Active listening.
13. Permissive.
14. Child is given much love and attention, which provides a sense of security and belonging.
15. Behavior expectations, consequences for misbehavior, and who has final say in behavior guidance.

WORKPLACE CHALLENGE —*Any five:* Brain development and thinking strategies are nurtured; mental abilities are stretched; children learn to better understand someone else's point of view; language skills develop; negotiation and compromise are learned; children expand their thinking by building on their play partners' ideas; they learn more about how the world works and how to productively participate in it.

Child & Adult Care Professionals Instructor Resource Guide

INSTRUCTIONAL PLAN ━━━━━━━━━━━━━━━━━

Guiding Children

FOCUS & PLANNING

Section Objectives

❏ Identify the guidance goals of the early childhood classroom.

❏ Describe effective techniques for communicating with young children.

❏ Explain how planning the schedule and environment limits guidance problems.

❏ Distinguish between effective and ineffective guidance techniques.

❏ Define an I-message and explain its use.

❏ Summarize ways to approach behavior challenges.

Instruction & Student Practice

❏ **Reading.** Have students read *Section 11-2* on text pages 281-289. Assign the *Section 11-2 Knowledge Check* and *Mini Lab.*

❏ **Transition Activities.** Have students write transition activities to try on 3- by 5-inch cards as they work with children. Students should practice each transition activity until they are comfortable using the activity without the prompt of the card.

❏ **Behavior Interventions.** As a class, list examples of misbehaviors and analyze why children may exhibit them. Have students develop strategies for handling the inappropriate behaviors. Have them practice the interventions as they work with children.

❏ **Lab Manual.** Assign *Lab Activity 47* on page 97 of the Lab Manual.

❏ **Child & Adult Care Study Guides.** Assign *Study Guide 11-2* from the Student Motivation Kit.

❏ **Child & Adult Care Applications.** Assign *Activities 83, 86,* and *91* from the Student Motivation Kit.

❏ **Child & Adult Care Observations.** Assign *Observations OA-2, OA-4, OA-13,* and *OA-20* from the Student Motivation Kit.

❏ **Activity Cards for Older Adults.** Assign *Activity Cards OA-1 to OA-47* as desired from the Student Motivation Kit.

❏ **Child & Adult Care Career Profiles.** Assign *Career Profiles* as desired from the Student Motivation Kit.

Review & Student Performance

❏ **PowerPoint® Slides.** Use the *Section 11-2 PowerPoint®* slides on the Effective Instruction CD-ROM.

❏ **Section 11-2 Test.** Have students complete the *Section 11-2 Test* on pages 353-356 of this guide. Or, create your own test by using the **Exam***View*® Test Generator found on the *Child & Adult Care Professionals* Effective Instruction CD-ROM.

(Continued on next page)

KEY TERMS

- **self-discipline**
- **I-messages**
- **redirection**
- **consequences**
- **positive reinforcement**
- **cool-down moments**

CARE PROVIDER TIP

When working with children with special needs, teaching is a more powerful behavior management tool than punishing. Often a child behaves inappropriately because he or she does not have the language skills to express needs, wants, and feelings. The child needs to be taught to use those skills. For instance, if a child is running out of the room in order to escape, teach the child to ask to leave the room. The child will no longer need to run out of the room, because he or she will have a new appropriate behavior that allows him or her to meet his needs.

Answers to Section 11-2 Knowledge Check

1. Offer choices; teach ways to resolve conflict; teach problem-solving skills; model sharing, trading, and negotiating; coach positive social behaviors; use positive discipline.

2. Effective guidance builds independence skills and helps children learn how to control their own behavior. Effective guidance—with clear expectations and consequences for behavior—builds self-confidence and self-esteem. Ineffective guidance frightens and punishes children, is inconsistent, and leaves children confused about expectations and limits.

3. *Children fighting over toys*: Provide enough toys for sharing. *Child tearing a book page*: Have child help tape the page back together.

MINI LAB —*Observations and answers will vary.*

Answers to Section 11-2 Test

Matching:

1.	H	5.	F
2.	C	6.	I
3.	G	7.	B
4.	A			

Short Answer:

8. Expectations must be simple, clear, and understandable and age-appropriate.

9. Agree on basic general rules and set up guidelines that will assist children with routine activities and learning areas.

10. Tells children what they can do instead of what they cannot do.

11. Display them on a poster in each learning center.

12. Through careful planning, which results in a structured schedule and environment that minimizes boredom, frustration, and conflict.

13. Give a comforting hug and kind words.

14. Children might become frustrated and resort to aggressive behavior.

15. Children will play more cooperatively, and conflict is reduced.

16. It prevents children from misbehaving to get a care provider's attention.

17. Provide children with a positive example to follow, obey classroom rules just as children are expected to, and model desirable social skills as you interact with children and adults.

18. I-messages do not attack the child's character; instead, they help the child see why the behavior is a problem and give the child an opportunity to independently choose a more respectful behavior.

19. Boredom, frustration, hunger, fatigue, illness, or problems at home.

20. Discourage the misbehavior without discouraging the child.

21. Prevents needless power struggles with care providers.

22. Motivation, initiative, and assertiveness.

23. Use distraction techniques.

24. Natural consequences should be used only if they do not endanger the child or others.

25. So the child understands the consequences are in response to a particular misbehavior.

26. No longer than three to five minutes.

27. The same provider who took the child to the cool-down area.

28. Communication, negotiation, cooperation, and the ability to stand up for your own rights while respecting the rights of others.

29. Determine if there is a pattern or specific cause for a problem by making frequent, objective observations. Schedule a parent conference to address the unresolved behavior problems.

30. Record the incident and the circumstances under which it occurred and then inform both families of the incident. Seek input from the parents of the child who bites and ask if this occurs at home and, if so, how it is handled.

WORKPLACE CHALLENGE —*Any five:* Plan a balanced schedule; follow a consistent schedule with smooth transitions and routines; plan a wide variety and choice of interesting activities; plan activities appropriate for abilities; provide enough equipment; arrange the physical environment to promote children's success; provide individual attention; consider each child's special circumstances.

Child & Adult Care Professionals Instructor Resource Guide

INSTRUCTIONAL PLAN ━━━━━━━━━━━━━━━━━━━━━━━━━━

Section

Guiding Older Adults **11-3**

FOCUS & PLANNING

Section Objectives

❑ Describe the process of talking with older adults.

❑ Describe how healthy development and well-being impact behavior.

❑ Identify the principles of conflict management.

❑ Determine an action plan for positive guidance.

Instruction & Student Practice

❑ **Reading.** Have students read *Section 11-3* on text pages 290-297. Assign the *Section 11-3 Knowledge Check* and *Mini Lab*.

❑ **Discuss the Effects of Stress.** Have students read an article about emotional problems caused by stress in the life of an older adult. Discuss why the "golden years" may be the most stressful in the life cycle.

❑ **Role Play Conflict Management Skills.** After students write scenarios describing conflicts that older adults might have with family members, caregivers, or peers, have them role play the situations with a student acting as a mediator. The mediator should demonstrate the use of I-messages.

❑ **Practice Listening Skills.** As they work with older adults, assign students to consciously practice the listening skills described in the text. Have them report on the success of using listening skills.

❑ **Lab Manual.** Assign *Lab Activity 48* on page 99 of the Lab Manual.

❑ **Child & Adult Care Study Guides.** Assign *Study Guide 11-3* from the Student Motivation Kit.

❑ **Child & Adult Care Applications.** Assign *Activities 83, 86,* and *91* from the Student Motivation Kit.

❑ **Child & Adult Care Observations.** Assign *Observations OA-2, OA-4, OA-13,* and *OA-20* from the Student Motivation Kit.

❑ **Child & Adult Care Career Profiles.** Assign *Career Profiles* as desired from the Student Motivation Kit.

Review & Student Performance

❑ **PowerPoint® Slides.** Use the *Section 11-3 PowerPoint®* slides on the Effective Instruction CD-ROM.

❑ **Section 11-3 Test.** Have students complete the *Section 11-3 Test* on pages 353-356 of this guide. Or, create your own test by using the **Exam***View®* Test Generator found on the *Child & Adult Care Professionals* Effective Instruction CD-ROM.

KEY TERMS

- **small talk**
- **search talk**
- **fight talk**
- **spite talk**
- **conflict-management plan**
- **action plan**

CARE PROVIDER TIP

Positive behavior management techniques are emphasized for caregivers of young children, but positive behavior management is just as important when working with older adults. Adults have positive self-esteem when they have a balance of activities that stimulate the mind and body. Offer adults choices of stimulating activities and encourage their participation.

(Continued on next page)

Child & Adult Care Professionals Instructor Resource Guide
Copyright © Glencoe/McGraw-Hill

Answers to Section 11-3 Knowledge Check

1. Small talk is light, casual conservation that is used when chatting, whereas fight talk is used as a defensive way of talking.

2. Effective verbal communication includes speaking clearly, using proper language and "I" statements, and speaking at a moderate pace. Effective nonverbal communication includes direct eye contact and standing or sitting facing the person. Make certain that your verbal and nonverbal messages match. The tone of voice, facial expressions, and gestures should say the same thing.

3. Older adults that are receiving good health care interacts positively with others; those who receive poor or no health care tend not to feel well and act gruff with others.

MINI LAB —*Answers will vary.*

Answers to Chapter 11 Review & Activities

1. Children learn how to make decisions and learn to be accountable for their behavior.

2. Children's self-esteem can be lowered and they can learn to expect less from themselves. Children will learn to behave according to how they are labeled.

3. Be clear, simple, and specific. Tell children what to do rather than what not to do. Rules should be age appropriate and understandable to children.

4. They will better understand the reasons for rules and will be more committed to following them.

5. It encourages a behavior to be repeated.

6. Children will know what to expect and will stop testing rules.

7. Use active listening, help initiate problem-solving process, model appropriate behavior, initiate a cool-down moment, offer choices, coach appropriate behavior, redirect behavior.

8. Older adults might use small talk, which is light, casual conversation, or search talk, which is used when a person is trying to find words to generate a conversation.

9. *Any three:* Use direct eye contact; use facial expressions to convey emotion; stand or sit facing the older adult to whom you are talking; make sure your verbal and nonverbal messages match.

10. Identify the problem; design a fair conflict-resolution plan; anticipate what could go wrong during negotiations; work together in a positive manner; set ground rules for mutual respect and trust; focus only on one issue at a time; avoid imposing a solution to rush to solve the resolution; allow enough time to solve the problem effectively and evaluate the process.

Answers to Section 11-3 Test

Matching:

1. H
2. G
3. F
4. I
5. E
6. D
7. A

Short Answer:

8. Communicate effectively by using active listening, speaking clearly, and being aware of nonverbal language.

9. Healthy development and well-being.

10. Medication noncompliance.

11. Love, friendship, understanding, and dignity.

12. Hurt feelings.

13. Chronic physical problems, cognitive impairments, and significant emotional losses.

14. Retirement or change in income, death of a loved one, injury or illness, or a change in living conditions or residence.

15. Positive thinking.

16. Take care of themselves physically and mentally.

17. Food, shelter, and security.

18. Gather information about the problem and suggest ways to solve it.

19. Finger pointing, shaking the finger, frowning.

20. Allow people to give constructive feedback.

WORKPLACE CHALLENGE —*Any four:* Help older adults identify needs and goals regarding conflict; involve everyone in developing the plan; avoid rushing to a solution to avoid frustration; after developing a plan, everyone must agree to it; expect to modify the plan as new conflicts occur.

Instructor _____ Course _____ Date _____

INSTRUCTIONAL PLAN ━━━━━━━━━━━━━━━━━━━━━━

Sensory-Appropriate Indoor Environments

Section 12-1

FOCUS & PLANNING

Section Objectives

❑ Identify licensing regulation and accreditation criteria that apply to early childhood and older adult facilities.

❑ Identify how environments can respond to all areas and levels of child and adult development.

❑ Explain how facilities can be arranged to accommodate children and adults with special needs.

❑ Describe the variety and purpose of learning centers and activity areas.

❑ Evaluate environments for safety and developmental appropriateness.

❑ Describe adult day program facility standards.

Instruction & Student Practice

❑ **Reading.** Have students read *Section 12-1* on text pages 301-313. Assign the *Section 12-1 Knowledge Check* and *Mini Lab*.

❑ **Investigate State Licensing Laws.** Have students study state licensing requirements for day care facility requirements and then plan a classroom for a specified group of children.

❑ **Lab Manual.** Assign *Lab Activity 49* on page 101 and *Lab Activity 50* on page 103 of the Lab Manual.

❑ **Child & Adult Care Study Guides.** Assign *Study Guide 12-1* from the Student Motivation Kit.

❑ **Child & Adult Care Applications.** Assign *Activities 45, 54, 56, 57, 58, 60, 61, 63, 66, 92,* and *103* from the Student Motivation Kit.

❑ **Child & Adult Care Observations.** Assign *Observations C-13, C-14, C-15, C-16,* and *OA-2* from the Student Motivation Kit.

❑ **Activity Cards for Children.** Assign *Activity Cards C-1 to C-96* as desired from the Student Motivation Kit.

❑ **Activity Cards for Older Adults.** Assign *Activity Cards OA-1 to OA-47* as desired from the Student Motivation Kit.

❑ **Child & Adult Care Career Profiles.** Assign *Career Profiles* as desired from the Student Motivation Kit.

Review & Student Performance

❑ **PowerPoint® Slides.** Use the *Section 12-1 PowerPoint®* slides on the Effective Instruction CD-ROM.

❑ **Section 12-1 Test.** Have students complete the *Section 12-1 Test* on pages 359-362 of this guide. Or, create your own test by using the **Exam***View*® Test Generator found on the *Child & Adult Care Professionals* Effective Instruction CD-ROM.

(Continued on next page)

KEY TERMS

- **accreditation criteria**
- **isolation room**
- **toxic**
- **sensory**
- **traffic pattern**
- **learning centers**
- **functional furniture**

CARE PROVIDER TIP

There is never enough storage in early childhood classrooms. If you ever design or renovate an on-site child or adult day care center, plan for plenty of storage space. Not only does each participant need personal storage, but also equipment, supplies, and partially completed projects require adequate storage. Staff and volunteers need a place for their personal items as well as for materials they will be using with the children or adults. It is also a good idea to assign to staff members to inventory and clean storage areas on a regular basis.

Child & Adult Care Professionals Instructor Resource Guide
Copyright © Glencoe/McGraw-Hill

211

Answers to Section 12-1 Knowledge Check

1. Environments for each should have functional furniture and equipment that meets the needs of all age groups.

2. There should be opportunities for privacy as well as small-group and large-group activities. Sensory details, such as color, sound, lighting, pattern, texture and shape enhance the space for all.

3. Centers should be well defined and organized around a particular curriculum topic or theme, and they should allow children to see where to get and return materials to promote independence and encourage decision making.

(**MINI LAB**)—*Newsletters will vary.*

Answers to Section 12-1 Test

Matching:
1. A   5. J
2. G   6. I
3. F   7. E
4. C

Short Answer:
8. Program services.

9. Looking at the classroom from a child's level.

10. Napping, toileting, hand washing, eating, and tooth brushing.

11. High morale and positive attitudes toward the children.

12. To make them convenient and to encourage children to be responsible for their possessions.

13. Space for parents to sign children in and out on a daily attendance sheet and a display space for posting various items.

14. A balance room arrangement with appealing items that are easily changed.

15. They promote relaxation.

16. Fatigue and eye strain.

17. Art, language arts, dramatic play, music, science, math, blocks, and active play.

18. Have at least two routes, one located near a door or stairway with an unobstructed path to the outside of the building.

19. Sofa, chairs, end tables, lamps, bookcases, and a television.

20. Six.

21. A library, game room, music room, and social activity areas.

22. Brings people together and encourages sharing.

23. Separate space for children and older adults, along with a common area for intergenerational interaction; furnishings and other materials that meet the needs of all participants; sounds that promote well-being; sensory activities that have a significant purpose.

24. The director can view who enters and leaves the center.

25. Three.

26. Books, puppets, and puzzles.

27. To help older adults use their sight effectively.

28. These colors tend to be blinding.

29. Pattern designs.

30. Four.

(**WORKPLACE CHALLENGE**)—*Any five early childhood facility requirements:* Child-size, with sinks low enough for children to reach; low, with child-size chairs; hard surfaced, using material such as tile or wood; diapering areas for infant/toddler programs, proper warmth; separate areas for napping for infants, toddlers, and preschoolers. *Any five older adult facility requirements:* 35 square feet of space for each adult; space of large and small group activities; secure storage for participant's belongings; locked storage for medications; at least one toilet for every 12 people; a room for resting; at least one room for health exams; and office area for confidential discussions; at least two exits; floors with nonslip surfaces; freedom from hazards; posted fire safety procedures; visible/accessible first aid kits.

INSTRUCTIONAL PLAN ━━━━━━━━━━━━━━━━━━━━━━━━━━ *Section*

Sensory-Appropriate Outdoor Environments **12-2**

FOCUS & PLANNING

Section Objectives

❏ Identify licensing laws and accreditation criteria that apply to play yards and recreational areas.

❏ Explain how outdoor areas can be designed to meet the developmental needs and abilities of young children and older adults, including those with disabilities.

❏ Describe the role outdoor design plays in health, recreation, and overall learning for children and older adults.

❏ Describe the variety and purpose of play areas recommended for an outdoor environment.

❏ Identify outdoor sensory experiences that benefit children and older adults.

❏ Evaluate an outdoor environment for safety for children and older adults.

Instruction & Student Practice

❏ **Reading.** Have students read *Section 12-2* on text pages 314-321. Assign the *Section 12-2 Knowledge Check* and *Mini Lab.*

❏ **Lab Manual.** Assign *Lab Activity 51* on page 105, *Lab Activity 52* on page 107, and *Lab Activity 53* on page 108 of the Lab Manual.

❏ **Child & Adult Care Study Guides.** Assign *Study Guide 12-2* from the Student Motivation Kit.

❏ **Child & Adult Care Applications.** Assign *Activities 45, 54, 56, 57, 58, 60, 61, 63, 66, 92,* and *103* from the Student Motivation Kit.

❏ **Child & Adult Care Observations.** Assign *Observations C-13, C-14, C-15, C-16,* and *OA-2* from the Student Motivation Kit.

❏ **Child & Adult Care Career Profiles.** Assign *Career Profiles* as desired from the Student Motivation Kit.

Review & Student Performance

❏ **PowerPoint® Slides.** Use the *Section 12-2 PowerPoint®* slides on the Effective Instruction CD-ROM.

❏ **Section 12-2 Test.** Have students complete the *Section 12-2 Test* on pages 363-364 of this guide. Or, create your own test by using the **Exam***View®* Test Generator found on the **Child & Adult Care Professionals** Effective Instruction CD-ROM.

KEY TERMS

- **fall zones**
- **nontoxic**
- **therapeutic**
- **dehydrated**

CARE PROVIDER TIP

Since being outdoors for long periods of time is often a challenge for adults or children with disabilities, bringing the outdoors inside creates a pleasant environment and allows them to enjoy nature. You can easily accomplish this by placing bird and squirrel feeders outside windows and planting flowers in atrium windows or window boxes.

(Continued on next page)

Answers to Section 12-2 Knowledge Check

1. The area should provide sounds that promote well-being, opportunities for water play, raised tables, a separate play yard built for their size and limited mobility, color, texture, aroma, trees, shrubs, nontoxic plants, birdhouses, hanging wind chimes.

2. Outdoor areas that accommodate children and older adults include individualized walking paths, gardening spaces, and art areas created on concrete walkway.

3. By checking equipment and surface materials for breakage, splintering, rusting, or jagged edges.

MINI LAB —*Plans and answers will vary.*

Answers to Chapter 12 Review & Activities

1. Licensing laws, accreditation criteria, developmental needs, staff and storage needs, and safety concerns; goals, philosophy and hours of operation; ages, abilities and overall developmental characteristics and needs; diversity and special needs of enrolled children; staff job responsibilities and desirable work conditions; parent involvement and family support services.

2. Elements of design can be included such as color, texture, pattern, lighting, sound, and aroma.

3. Soft furniture, such as couches or bean bags, for seating, greenery like hanging plants or floor plants, terrariums and an aquarium.

4. To help prevent the spread of illness. Ill people remain in an isolation room to remain comfortable awaiting pickup.

5. So they are better able to perform their duties and have desirable work conditions.

6. To observe child development and hear children's discussions without interrupting activities.

7. *Any five:* Art, language arts, dramatic play, music, science, math, blocks, active play, woodworking, computer stations. Learning centers direct children to activities, allow children to learn by doing, provide opportunities for independent and small-group play, distribute children throughout the classroom, and minimize conflicts and noise.

8. *Infant and toddler:* Proper ventilation and easy access to diaper disposal areas; hand-washing sinks close by to limit the spread of diseases; low windows for toddlers to see outside; separate areas for napping, playing, and eating. *School-age:* Areas for group board and card games; designated space of their own to have privacy or pursue hobbies; homework area; relaxing areas to read books, listen to music, or chat with friends; private storage area for belongings; play yard for older children's size and abilities.

9. Circular design brings people together; spaces where activities, such as gardening and cooking, can be done by all age groups; comfortable seating and activity tables for all age groups; common areas where table games can take place.

10. All equipment routinely checked for breakage, splintering, rusting, or jagged edges that could cause injury; only nontoxic plants used or displayed; cleaning equipment safely locked away; appropriately sized furniture prevents falls.

Answers to Section 12-2 Test

Matching:

1. B   4. G
2. D   5. A
3. E

Short Answer:

6. By including trees, shrubs and other types of nontoxic plants.
7. Pines and lilacs, herbs, and flowers.
8. Americans with Disabilities Act (ADA).
9. Ground level and elevated.
10. Ramps, landings, and transfer points.
11. Minimum clear width of 36 inches, 12-inch maximum rise, and a slope of 1 inch for every foot of ramp run.
12. 20-28 inches above ramp surface.
13. A curb is required along both edges.
14. Development of children's small and large motor skills.
15. It can help with heart and circulatory problems, tight joints, and emotional health.

WORKPLACE CHALLENGE —Accessible routes, ramps, landings, wheelchair accessible platforms, transfer systems, and accessible play opportunities.

INSTRUCTIONAL PLAN ━━━━━━━━━━━━━━

Early Childhood Equipment & Supplies

Section **13-1**

FOCUS & PLANNING

Section Objectives

- ❑ Explain how equipment and supplies support program goals.
- ❑ List items that meet children's basic needs.
- ❑ Identify criteria for supplying and equipping early childhood environments.
- ❑ Describe well-equipped learning centers.
- ❑ Evaluate equipment, materials, and toys.

Instruction & Student Practice

- ❑ **Reading.** Have students read *Section 13-1* on text pages 325-331. Assign the *Section 13-1 Knowledge Check* and *Mini Lab.*
- ❑ **Evaluate Toys.** Have students analyze a variety of toys by classifying them according to appropriate age and evaluating how playing with the toys fosters physical, emotional-social, and cognitive development in children. Have students determine which toys would be good selections for a childcare center.
- ❑ **Cultural Materials Analysis.** Have students observe at a center for the integration of cultural materials. Have them write a journal entry describing what cultural materials are available and giving suggestions for improvements.
- ❑ **Lab Manual.** Assign *Lab Activity 54* on page 109 of the Lab Manual.
- ❑ **Child & Adult Care Study Guides.** Assign *Study Guide 13-1* from the Student Motivation Kit.
- ❑ **Child & Adult Care Applications.** Assign *Activities 45, 54, 56, 57, 58, 60, 61, 63, 66,* and *103* from the Student Motivation Kit.
- ❑ **Child & Adult Care Observations.** Assign *Observations OA-1, OA-2, OA-19,* and *OA-22* from the Student Motivation Kit.
- ❑ **Activity Cards for Children.** Assign *Activity Cards C-1* to *C-96* as desired from the Student Motivation Kit.
- ❑ **Child & Adult Care Career Profiles.** Assign *Career Profiles* as desired from the Student Motivation Kit.

Review & Student Performance

- ❑ **PowerPoint® Slides.** Use the *Section 13-1 PowerPoint®* slides on the Effective Instruction CD-ROM.
- ❑ **Section 13-1 Test.** Have students complete the *Section 13-1 Test* on pages 365-366 of this guide. Or, create your own test by using the **Exam***View*® Test Generator found on the ***Child & Adult Care Professionals*** Effective Instruction CD-ROM.

(Continued on next page)

KEY TERMS

- • **developmentally appropriate**
- • **nontoxic**
- • **sanitized**

CARE PROVIDER TIP

Dress up is a favorite game for many children. Children enjoy dressing up in party clothes, uniforms, and accessories, such as scarves, ties, hats, and stoles or capes. Second-hand shops and garage sales are good places to buy such items. Look for clothing that can be washed and that is sized to fit up to 10 to 12 year olds.

Answers to Section 13-1 Knowledge Check

1. Provide toys and equipment that match the children's age and developmental level.
2. Storage for belongings; napping equipment; meal service, first aid, and emergency supplies.
3. Include cultural foods in meal service, include cultural dress-up clothing, play cultural music, and sing multi-cultural songs.

(MINI LAB)—*Answers will vary*.

Answers to Section 13-1 Test

Matching:

1. A   2. C   3. D

Short Answer:

4. So children can be successful during learning and play.
5. Balls and balance beams.
6. Frustrated.
7. Tape a family photo inside the child's cubby.
8. Flashlight, battery-operated radio, and a fire extinguisher.
9. Poor choices can create safety hazards and increase behavior problems.
10. Children learn they are not dependent on costly items to have fun.
11. Puzzles with knobbed pieces.
12. Children are frustrated and the stage is set for fights.
13. A computer and printer, computer table, computer games, VCR and videotapes, tape recorder and blank cassette tapes, and a handheld camcorder.

14. Separate play areas protect the safety of each age group and prevent conflicts between children of varying abilities.
15. It should be fenced, accessible to all, have a drinking fountain, and offer some shade.

(WORKPLACE CHALLENGE)—*Any five: Climbers*—Ramps, slides, swinging bridge, and firefighter poles; *Swings*— Individual or porch-style; *Sand play equipment*—Sandbox or table with buckets, shovels, scoops, plastic dishes, molds, measuring cups, and plastic zoo, farm, or dinosaur animals; *Wheel toys*—Scooters, wagons, tricycles, push-pull toys, and large strollers for infants and toddlers; *Balls*—Rimball with basketballs, soccer balls, soft foam balls, T-balls, and other balls; *Garden toys*—Flower or vegetable garden space, water source, hose, watering cans, and gardening tools; *Dramatic play toys*—Play house, log cabin, tree house, teepees, tents and the equipment and supplies to go with each.

Child & Adult Care Professionals Instructor Resource Guide

INSTRUCTIONAL PLAN ━━━━━━━━━━━━━━━━━━━━━━━━━━ *Section*

Adult Care Center Equipment & Supplies *13-2*

FOCUS & PLANNING

Section Objectives

❑ Describe the equipment used in indoor and outdoor areas in an adult day center.

❑ List ethically appropriate activities for an adult day center.

❑ Describe how a daily cleaning procedure is conducted in an adult day center.

Instruction & Student Practice

❑ **Reading.** Have students read *Section 13-2* on text pages 332-337. Assign the *Section 13-2 Knowledge Check* and *Mini Lab.*

❑ **Service Project.** Have students collect items, such as used greeting cards, wallpaper books, and plastic containers for crafts, used books and books on tape for the library, and records, cassettes, and CDs for the music area at an adult care center.

❑ **Program Calendar.** Have students plan a monthly program calendar for an adult activity center. Students should consider the season of the year, include ethnically appropriate activities, and plan for a balance to meet the needs and interests of all participants.

❑ **Assist with Computer Skills.** Have students volunteer at an adult center to assist an older adult with his or her computer skills.

❑ **Lab Manual.** Assign *Lab Activity 55* on page 111 of the Lab Manual.

❑ **Child & Adult Care Study Guides.** Assign *Study Guide 13-2* from the Student Motivation Kit.

❑ **Child & Adult Care Applications.** Assign *Activities 34 to 36, 94,* and *95* as desired from the Student Motivation Kit.

❑ **Child & Adult Care Observations.** Assign *Observations OA-1, OA-2, OA-19,* and *OA-22* from the Student Motivation Kit.

❑ **Activity Cards for Older Adults.** Assign *Activity Cards OA-1 to OA-47* as desired from the Student Motivation Kit.

❑ **Child & Adult Care Career Profiles.** Assign *Career Profiles* as desired from the Student Motivation Kit.

Review & Student Performance

❑ **PowerPoint® Slides.** Use the *Section 13-2 PowerPoint®* slides on the Effective Instruction CD-ROM.

❑ **Section 13-2 Test.** Have students complete the *Section 13-2 Test* on pages 367-368 of this guide. Or, create your own test by using the **Exam***View*® Test Generator found on the ***Child & Adult Care Professionals*** Effective Instruction CD-ROM.

KEY TERMS

• **consumable supplies**
• **inventory**
• **lap pool**

CARE PROVIDER TIP

Videotape student activities with older adults in the adult care center. The older adults and their family members will enjoy watching the tapes. Students can use the tapes to document their work at the center. Students may wish to edit the tapes to develop a video portfolio recording several samples of their interactions with older adults.

(Continued on next page)

Child & Adult Care Professionals Instructor Resource Guide
Copyright © Glencoe/McGraw-Hill

Answers to Section 13-2 Knowledge Check

1. Computers, books, photo cameras, video cameras, musical instrumentals, and sound systems.
2. Cleaning should take place throughout the day as needed. A thorough cleaning should be done at the end of each day. Outdoor areas should be cleaned at least twice a week.
3. Nonporous surfaces are sanitized with a solution of one tablespoon of liquid ultra bleach to one gallon of water.

MINI LAB —*Activities will vary.*

Answers to Chapter 13 Review & Activities

1. Make certain the equipment and supplies are aligned with the program activities.
2. Promote the goals of the program.
3. *Any five:* Art, sensory play area, woodworking area, block center, cooking center, dramatic play and puppetry center, language and relaxation center, music center, media stations, manipulatives center, large movement center. Descriptions may vary.
4. *Any five:* Is the item safe? Is it able to withstand heavy or rough use? Can it be used by children of different ages? Does it encourage cooperative play? Can it be used by more than one child at a time? Do you have space for it? Does it encourage creativity? Does the item encourage active involvement? Will children learn basic concepts while playing with the toy? Will both girls and boys enjoy the toy? Will children have fun with the toy?
5. Climbers, swings, sand play equipment, wheeled toys, balls, garden toys, dramatic play toys.
6. Equipment and supplies that might be found in a social-medical adult day program include a bed or recliner, a first aid kit, a blood pressure device, and weight scales.
7. Computers, photo cameras and video cameras, and sound systems are examples of equipment found in the support areas of adult day facility.
8. A lap pool is a small pool designed for swimming in a small area. It has a stream of water that keeps the body forced back while a person swims as if swimming laps in a full-size pool.
9. The cleaning procedures for indoors and outdoors should be written and posted to ensure that the facility and equipment are free of clutter, soils, and spills. Indoor equipment should be cleaned at the end of each day; outdoor equipment should be cleaned at least twice a week, depending on the usage and seasons, which may require more frequent cleaning.

Answers to Section 13-2 Test

Matching:

1. B 2. D 3. E

Short Answer:

4. Computers, photo cameras and video cameras, and sound systems.
5. Exercise chairs, weights, and floor mats.
6. They should consult with their health-care specialists for approval.
7. The area should follow center standards and those of the Occupational Health and Safety administration (OSHA).
8. They should be posted visibly in the kitchen area.
9. They should be arranged to accommodate wheelchairs, scooters, and other personal modes of transportation.
10. The rest rooms should have handgrips on or near the toilets.
11. All storage areas should follow OSHA standards.
12. This area should be equipped with a bench, outdoor chairs, or swings.
13. They can partner with other groups, such as a local school, to provide a successful outdoor program.
14. By following the procedures, care providers ensure that the facility and equipment are tidy and free of clutter, soils, and spills.
15. Be sure to follow the manufacturer's instructions.

WORKPLACE CHALLENGE —There should be trails to provide a place for older adults to walk; there should be garden plants and flowers, and feeding areas for birds plus a supply of birdseed; benches and chairs should be supplied along walking paths so that older adults can sit and rest when they want; trails should be kept free of weeds, branches, and any other objects that will get in the way of older adults with walkers and wheelchairs.

INSTRUCTIONAL PLAN ━━━━━━━━━━━━━━

Program Types

Section **14-1**

FOCUS & PLANNING

Section Objectives

❑ Give examples of program philosophy statements and goals.

❑ Describe different types of early childhood programs.

❑ Explain licensing and registration requirements.

❑ Identify the benefits of accreditation.

Instruction & Student Practice

❑ **Reading.** Have students read *Section 14-1* on pages 341-349. Assign the *Section 14-1 Knowledge Check* and *Mini Lab*.

❑ **Child Care Program Tour.** Arrange for students to tour facilities of various programs. After the tour, discuss the advantages of each.

❑ **Develop a Rating Scale.** Have students develop a rating scale that parents might use to compare the programs and services of various child care centers. Students should publish the rating scale and distribute it to young parents.

❑ **Compare Standards.** Have students research and compare licensing standards with NAEYC accreditation standards.

❑ **Chart.** Have students create a chart that compares various types of programs available in the local community.

❑ **Lab Manual.** Assign *Lab Activity 56* on page 113 and *Lab Activity 57* on page 115 of the Lab Manual.

❑ **Child & Adult Care Study Guides.** Assign *Study Guide 14-1* from the Student Motivation Kit.

❑ **Child & Adult Care Applications.** Assign *Activities 34 to 36, 94,* and *95* as desired from the Student Motivation Kit.

❑ **Child & Adult Care Observations.** Assign *Observations C-14, C-44* and *C-45* as desired from the Student Motivation Kit.

❑ **Activity Cards for Children.** Assign *Activity Cards C-1 to C-96* as desired from the Student Motivation Kit.

❑ **Child & Adult Care Career Profiles.** Assign *Career Profiles* as desired from the Student Motivation Kit.

Review & Student Performance

❑ **PowerPoint® Slides.** Use the *Section 14-1 PowerPoint®* slides on the Effective Instruction CD-ROM.

❑ **Section 14-1 Test.** Have students complete the *Section 14-1 Test* on pages 369-370 of this guide. Or, create your own test by using the **Exam***View®* Test Generator found on the ***Child & Adult Care Professionals*** Effective Instruction CD-ROM.

(Continued on next page)

KEY TERMS

- **philosophy**
- **program goals**
- **for-profit**
- **nonprofit**
- **program sponsors**
- **nanny**
- **au pair**
- **license exempt**
- **registration**

CARE PROVIDER TIP

Before selecting a child care program, it is important for parents to take time to observe the program in action. Encourage parents to read the program information before the visit. When observing, determine if the staff practices the policies outlined in the literature, if the curriculum is developmentally appropriate, and if the values taught reflect your personal values.

Answers to Section 14-1 Knowledge Check

1. Parent involvement enhances children's overall development; children have different learning styles, rates of learning, and developmental levels.

2. Gain high self-esteem and a positive attitude; learn self-help skills and responsibility; develop positive social skills; develop large- and small-motor skills; improve communication skills; develop curiosity, creative thinking, and problem-solving ability; learn to respect, accept, and understand the rights and feelings of others.

3. Licensing is mandatory by law for child care services and is developed and enforced by the state government. Accreditation is a voluntary system of identifying programs that meet criteria for high-quality early childhood care and education.

MINI LAB — *Materials will vary.*

Answers to Section 14-1 Test

Matching:

1.	H	6.	E
2.	I	7.	A
3.	B	8.	D
4.	F	9.	K
5.	J		

Short Answer:

10. Its program philosophy.
11. To provide a safe and healthy learning environment for children.
12. Learning activities, meals, snacks, and naptime.
13. Three to eight children of varying ages.
14. Learning skills and social development.
15. To prepare children for success in elementary school and beyond.
16. They benefit from the older adults' care and wisdom.
17. Until a working parent can go back to the regular care provider.
18. To prepare economically disadvantaged preschoolers for school success.
19. Programs associated with a parochial school that is part of a place of worship and family child care homes that care for fewer than three children.
20. The National Academy of Early Childhood Programs.

WORKPLACE CHALLENGE —*Any four:* Health, safety, and child nutrition; maximum group size of clients by age; staff-to-client ratio; square footage of space per client for indoor and outdoor areas; minimum staff qualifications and in-service training requirements; minimum amount of equipment and supplies for each classroom.

INSTRUCTIONAL PLAN ━━━━━━━━━━━━━━━━━━━━━━━━━━

Managing Program Services

Section
14-2

FOCUS & PLANNING

Section Objectives

❑ Describe the role of the director in managing program services.

❑ Identify director management and supervision duties.

❑ Identify the qualification of early childhood staff members.

❑ Summarize the key factors of program governance.

❑ Explain financial management for early childhood care programs.

❑ Explain the ways directors conduct public relations.

Instruction & Student Practice

❑ **Reading.** Have students read *Section 14-2* on text pages 350-361. Assign the *Section 14-2 Knowledge Check* and *Mini Lab*.

❑ **Shadow a Director.** After having students shadow a child care director, assign them to write a job description including desired personal qualities, job responsibilities, and qualifications.

❑ **Compare Job Responsibilities.** Obtain job descriptions for staff from several area child care centers. Have students compare the responsibilities and qualifications of each position.

❑ **Lab Manual.** Assign *Lab Activity 58* on page 117 and *Lab Activity 59* on page 120 of the Lab Manual.

❑ **Child & Adult Care Study Guides.** Assign *Study Guide 14-2* from the Student Motivation Kit.

❑ **Child & Adult Care Applications.** Assign *Activities 34 to 36, 94,* and *95* as desired from the Student Motivation Kit.

❑ **Child & Adult Care Observations.** Assign *Observations C-14, C-44* and *C-45* as desired from the Student Motivation Kit.

❑ **Activity Cards for Children.** Assign *Activity Cards C-1 to C-96* as desired from the Student Motivation Kit.

❑ **Child & Adult Care Career Profiles.** Assign *Career Profiles* as desired from the Student Motivation Kit.

Review & Student Performance

❑ **PowerPoint® Slides.** Use the *Section 14-2 PowerPoint®* slides on the Effective Instruction CD-ROM.

❑ **Section 14-2 Test.** Have students complete the *Section 14-2 Test* on pages 371-372 of this guide. Or, create your own test by using the **Exam***View®* Test Generator found on the ***Child & Adult Care Professionals*** Effective Instruction CD-ROM.

(Continued on next page)

KEY TERMS

• **job descriptions**
• **organizational chart**
• **reference checks**
• **inventory record**
• **board**
• **program governance**
• **advisory board**
• **governing board**
• **financial management**
• **public relations**

CARE PROVIDER TIP

When students work in or visit a childcare facility, people observing the facility consider them staff. Therefore, students need to be professional in appearance and behavior.

Answers to Section 14-2 Knowledge Check

1. Director, assistant director, teaching staff and substitutes, foodservice staff, transportation staff, custodial and grounds crew, health care staff, family involvement coordinator, curriculum coordinator.

2. Building costs, utilities, facility upkeep, staff wages and training costs, vehicle purchase and care, equipment and supplies, printing, postage.

3. Sound organizational structure, good supervision of staff, adequate staffing, screened staff members who are well trained, continuing education for staff, compliance with licensing, and satisfaction of accreditation criteria.

MINI LAB —*Answers will vary.*

Answers to Chapter 14 Review & Activities

1. Beliefs, concepts, and attitudes of a program in regards to its services.

2. Children learn best by doing.

3. Basic skills, concepts, and attitudes to be developed by the program. Children will develop small- and large-motor skills.

4. Child care or preschool offered to students, employees, or community members at a college or university. These programs often serve as training sites for child development students.

5. To manage all program services.

6. Daily conversation, postings, newsletters, e-mail.

7. To promote a positive program image to the community.

8. Teacher/child interactions, curriculum, teacher/family relationships, staff qualifications and professional development, administration, staffing.

9. Philosophy/goals; staff knowledge of child development; proper guidance; basic health, safety, and nutrition; developmentally appropriate curriculum; organized daily schedule; family involvement; ongoing staff training.

Answers to Section 14-2 Test

Matching:

1. F	5. A
2. E	6. D
3. B	7. C
4. G	8. I

Short Answer:

9. Annually.

10. A program's purpose, services, and size.

11. By paying part of an employee's conference attendance expenses or the cost of a seminar or college course.

12. Direct, objective observation of an employee's performance.

13. In licensing laws and accreditation criteria.

14. The item, date of purchase, place of purchase, cost, and warranty date, if any.

15. Budget, finance, and fundraising decisions; enrollment policies; staff employment decisions; and decisions regarding fees for services.

16. The constitution and bylaws.

17. The director.

18. Conduct parent-teacher conferences, initiate parent communications, and invite family members to serve on advisory boards.

19. To confirm that quality is achieved.

20. Review the application to make sure candidate meets minimum requirements for state licensing laws and accreditation criteria. Review the applicant's work history, educational background, and résumé. Make reference checks with people who know the applicant. Conduct a criminal background check on the applicant.

WORKPLACE CHALLENGE —Write down the date, time, and location of the incident; write down the situation surrounding the violation; tell the program director about the violation; and if violation continues, notify an agent from the licensing office.

INSTRUCTIONAL PLAN ━━━━━━━━━━━━━━━━━━━━━━━━

Older Adult Activity Programs

Section **15-1**

FOCUS & PLANNING

Section Objectives

❏ Explain how philosophy and goals impact the quality of older adult activity programs.

❏ Summarize the types of quality activities offered at older adult activity programs.

❏ Describe three types of older adult activity facilities and how they are supplied and maintained.

❏ Explain how older adult activity programs are licensed, accredited, and staffed.

❏ Describe how older adult activity programs are operated and governed.

❏ Explain factors that influence the management of participant services and quality assurance.

Instruction & Student Practice

❏ **Reading.** Have students read *Section 15-1* on text pages 365-374. Assign the *Section 15-1 Knowledge Check* and *Mini Lab*.

❏ **Posters or Displays.** Have teams of students make seasonal posters or displays for the adult center to inform participants of events.

❏ **Lab Manual.** Assign *Lab Activity 60* on page 121 of the Lab Manual.

❏ **Child & Adult Care Study Guides.** Assign *Study Guide 15-1* from the Student Motivation Kit.

❏ **Child & Adult Care Applications.** Assign *Activities 28 to 32 and 67 to 92* as desired from the Student Motivation Kit.

❏ **Child & Adult Care Observations.** Assign *Observations OA-1 to OA-22* as desired from the Student Motivation Kit.

❏ **Activity Cards for Older Adults.** Assign *Activity Cards OA-1 to OA-47* as desired from the Student Motivation Kit.

❏ **Child & Adult Care Career Profiles.** Assign *Career Profiles* as desired from the Student Motivation Kit.

Review & Student Performance

❏ **PowerPoint® Slides.** Use the *Section 15-1 PowerPoint®* slides on the Effective Instruction CD-ROM.

❏ **Section 15-1 Test.** Have students complete the *Section 15-1 Test* on pages 373-374 of this guide. Or, create your own test by using the **Exam***View*® Test Generator found on the **Child & Adult Care Professionals** Effective Instruction CD-ROM.

(Continued on next page)

KEY TERMS

- **multipurpose senior center**
- **recreational programs**
- **Material Safety Data Sheets (MSDS)**
- **gerontology**
- **geriatrics**

CARE PROVIDER TIP

Many older adults enjoy sharing their life experiences and can offer high school students insights that can assist with decision making. High school students feel valued as they assist older adults with services. Since many high school students do not have the opportunity to spend time with their grandparents or great-grandparents, and many adults do not get to associate with youth, the partnering of the teen and older adult is often an enriching experience for both. Try to find ways for local high school students to work with the older adults in your care.

Answers to Section 15-1 Knowledge Check

1. The philosophy and goals determine the types of services offered.

2. All adult day centers must meet state standards for licensure to operate a center. Accreditation, which is optional, assures that center and programs meet high standards outlined by the accreditation agency.

3. The director is responsible for advertising and recruiting participants, oversees the facility operations, and makes sure the program meets states and accreditation standards.

(**MINI LAB**)— *Materials will vary.*

Answers to Section 15-1 Test

Matching:

1. D
2. G
3. C
4. B
5. A

Short Answer:

6. They help meet the needs of participants from many cultures and with different health concerns.

7. *Any one:* To provide counseling services and referrals to agencies that assist with financial planning, mental or emotional problems, workplace discrimination, or legal issues.

8. The program sponsor, such as business, community agencies, corporations, the general public, and grants from foundations that support projects related to aging issues.

9. Places of worship, parks and recreation centers, and social services agencies.

10. The funding organization's.

11. The board of directors and the executive director.

12. To make certain the programs are planned and carried out according to the program goals.

13. Must meet educational requirements, enjoy working with older adults, and have knowledge about aging.

14. Personnel policies, how the center handles sexual harassment, sick leave, and vacation time.

15. The program director.

(**WORKPLACE CHALLENGE**)—An advisory board usually includes a chairperson, treasurer, secretary, and at least three directors who make note of changes in laws and program governance and funding. The advisory board also supplies expertise and advice in various areas, such as fundraising and managing volunteers.

Child & Adult Care Professionals Instructor Resource Guide

INSTRUCTIONAL PLAN ────────────────────

Social-Medical & Medical Model Programs

Section 15-2

FOCUS & PLANNING

Section Objectives

❏ Identify the primary goal of social-medical and medical model adult day care programs.

❏ Describe the two adult day care programs models.

❏ Identify factors that indicate program quality.

❏ Determine the staff requirements for the social-medical and medical model adult day care programs.

❏ Determine the process of managing participant services in a medical model adult day center.

Instruction & Student Practice

❏ **Reading.** Have students read *Section 15-2* on text pages 375-385. Assign the *Section 15-2 Knowledge Check* and *Mini Lab*.

❏ **Speaker.** Invite a licensing consultant for adult day care programs to visit the class to explain the process of obtaining a license, licensing standards, and inspection procedures.

❏ **Service Project.** Partner with an adult day care center and have students plan monthly visits with preschoolers. Students should plan a craft activity with the children and adults during the visits.

❏ **Lab Manual.** Assign *Lab Activity 61* on page 125 and *Lab Activity 62* on page 125 of the Lab Manual.

❏ **Child & Adult Care Study Guides.** Assign *Study Guide 15-2* from the Student Motivation Kit.

❏ **Child & Adult Care Applications.** Assign *Activities 28* to *32* and *67* to *92* as desired from the Student Motivation Kit.

❏ **Child & Adult Care Observations.** Assign *Observations OA-1* to *OA-22* as desired from the Student Motivation Kit.

❏ **Activity Cards for Older Adults.** Assign *Activity Cards OA-1* to *OA-47* as desired from the Student Motivation Kit.

❏ **Child & Adult Care Career Profiles.** Assign *Career Profiles* as desired from the Student Motivation Kit.

Review & Student Performance

❏ **PowerPoint® Slides.** Use the *Section 15-2 PowerPoint®* slides on the Effective Instruction CD-ROM.

❏ **Section 15-2 Test.** Have students complete the *Section 15-2 Test* on pages 375-376 of this guide. Or, create your own test by using the **Exam***View*® Test Generator found on the **Child & Adult Care Professionals** Effective Instruction CD-ROM.

KEY TERMS

- respite care
- shareholders

CARE PROVIDER TIP

When taking young children to visit the adults at a care center, prepare them by talking about what they will see and how they will participate. Do not expect the children to "warm-up" to the adults on the first visit. After two or three visits, the children will overcome their fears and enjoy the interactions.

(Continued on next page)

Answers to Section 15-2 Knowledge Check

1. Medical supervision and health-related care, dispensing of medicine and monitoring of health conditions, therapy services (speech or physical).

2. Quality staff who provide a full range of services; an evaluation plan to determine the quality of the services; newsletters and reports that describe the services offered and the program performance.

3. *Nurse:* Oversees medication and health care plans; plans activities based on the care plan of the participant; *social worker:* Provides health, maintenance, and social day care services; conducts home assessments; coordinates admission process; counsels participants and family members; *registered dietitian:* Plans meals according to participant care plan; *physical, occupational, and speech therapists:* Design and carry out participant care plans.

MINI LAB —*Answers will vary.*

Answers to Chapter 15 Review & Activities

1. Volunteers often assist with activities, and their activity assignments are based on the personal interests, skills, and time availability.

2. To assure quality programs that meet the needs of the participants.

3. So staff can keep current in their work area.

4. To show that the program meets the high standards of the accrediting organization and to show that a center provides quality programs.

5. National Institute of Senior Centers; The Rehabilitation Accreditation Commission.

6. A staff ratio of 1 to 5 excluding the director. Typical staff includes a center director, secretary, assistant/aids, custodian, volunteers, nurse, nutritionist, recreation coordinator, transportation personnel, and therapists.

7. *Any five from lists on pages 367 and 376.*

8. Both model programs meet the health and support services needs of older adults and may be offered within the same center. Social-medical includes care for rehabilitative, physical, or mental needs, such as monitoring of health conditions, and medication management. The medical model program offers assistance with personal care, therapy, daily medical supervision and health-related care, dispensing of medicine, and monitoring medical conditions.

9. To work together to form a quality plan of care for the participant.

10. Responsibilities include managing participant services; maintaining adequate staff and activities; designing activities to meet the needs of participants; and ensuring participants' rights; confidentiality, and security of personnel files.

Answers to Section 15-2 Test

Short Answer:

1. Shareholders.

2. Respite care.

3. A variety of health, social, and support services in a protective environment during daytime hours.

4. Rapid growth of the aging population.

5. Health care, social and recreational services, and activities for persons who are physically frail.

6. Physical, emotional, and mental needs.

7. It increases strength, flexibility, and balance and improves mood.

8. Transportation, health screening or monitoring, meals and snacks, personal care, or educational activities.

9. Health, rehabilitative, and mental health needs.

10. Individuals who recently were discharged from a hospital.

11. In each state's standards for operation.

12. Hire an independent contractor to come as needed to perform the specific task.

13. At least twice a year.

14. Staff to participant ratio is 1 to 5.

15. A physician, geriatric social worker or geriatric family life specialist, center staff, and family care provider.

WORKPLACE CHALLENGE —*Any five from list under Procedures & Schedules on page 384.*

INSTRUCTIONAL PLAN ━━━━━━━━━━━━━━━━━━━━━━━━ *Section*

Intergenerational Care Program Basics *16-1*

FOCUS & PLANNING

Section Objectives

❑ Define intergenerational care.

❑ Identify goals and philosophy of intergenerational care programs.

❑ Summarize the benefits of intergenerational care for children and older adults.

❑ Identify intergenerational services.

Instruction & Student Practice

❑ **Reading.** Have students read *Section 16-1* on text pages 389-392. Assign the *Section 16-1 Knowledge Check* and *Mini Lab.*

❑ **Benefits of Intergenerational Activities.** Have students brainstorm a list of intergenerational activities. Have students determine the benefits of each activity for the children and for the older adults.

❑ **Service Project.** Have students plan a multi-generational activity, such as a patriotic picnic, for not only children and older adults, but also for their families, the children, and older adults.

❑ **Journal Entry.** Have students write a journal entry based on field trip to child care, adult care, and intergenerational centers. Which type of program would they prefer for a family member?

❑ **Lab Manual.** Assign *Lab Activity 63* on page 129 of the Lab Manual.

❑ **Child & Adult Care Study Guides.** Assign *Study Guide 16-1* from the Student Motivation Kit.

❑ **Child & Adult Care Observations.** Assign *Observations C-13, C-24, OA-8* from the Student Motivation Kit.

❑ **Activity Cards for Children.** Assign *Activity Cards C-27 to C-96* as desired from the Student Motivation Kit.

❑ **Activity Cards for Older Adults.** Assign *Activity Cards OA-1 to OA-47* as desired from the Student Motivation Kit.

❑ **Child & Adult Care Career Profiles.** Assign *Career Profiles* as desired from the Student Motivation Kit.

Review & Student Performance

❑ **PowerPoint® Slides.** Use the *Section 16-1 PowerPoint®* slides on the Effective Instruction CD-ROM.

❑ **Section 16-1 Test.** Have students complete the *Section 16-1 Test* on pages 377-378 of this guide. Or, create your own test by using the **Exam*View*®** Test Generator found on the ***Child & Adult Care Professionals*** Effective Instruction CD-ROM.

(Continued on next page)

KEY TERMS

• partnership
• integrated services
• support services

CARE PROVIDER TIP

Since both children and older adults often enjoy singing, teach the children songs that the older adults will probably know, such as "You Are My Sunshine" and "Bicycle Built for Two."

Answers to Section 16-1 Knowledge Check

1. Programs that simultaneously provide care for children and older adults.

2. Activities, and often facilities, include individuals throughout the lifespan, rather than segregating age groups into different activities or buildings.

3. Networking is different agencies cooperating on a common project. This avoids duplication of services. Support services are activities offered directly by programs to enhance the well-being of participants.

(**MINI LAB**)—*Answers will vary.*

Answers to Section 16-1 Test

Matching:
1. E
2. C
3. D

Short Answer:
4. *Any two:* Children and older adults deserve high quality, developmentally appropriate services; Lifespan developmental stages are important; family members should have active involvement in the program; generations benefit from being together; intergenerational activities address cultural, heritage, traditions, and personal histories; mixing of ages, rather than age separation, reflects real life; society benefits from strong relationships between young and old; intergenerational activities promote an inclusive sense of community.

5. *Any three:* Program sponsor's goals; program's purpose; facility design; frequency of intergenerational contact; or the nature of activities offered.

6. Activities may take place in either facility; each program has separate administration; skilled staff from each program work together to plan and conduct intergenerational activities.

7. These programs have one administration.

8. They should be accessible to all participants, regardless of age or ability level.

9. *Any two benefits for children:* A realistic view of the aging process; more attention, encouragement, and nurturing; improving social skills and behaviors; increasing in knowledge, skills, and guidance from older adults. *Any two benefits for older adults:* Chances to share time, talents, and culture; maintenance of old skills and development of new skills; motivation to remain actively engaged in life.

10. Older adults get a chance to talk to an interested audience and to revisit their past.

(**WORKPLACE CHALLENGE**)—*Answers will vary.*

Child & Adult Care Professionals Instructor Resource Guide

INSTRUCTIONAL PLAN

Managing Intergenerational Programs

FOCUS & PLANNING

Section Objectives

❑ Describe the staffing needs of intergenerational programs.

❑ Explain the qualifications and training guidelines for successful intergenerational staff.

❑ Describe an effective program schedule.

❑ Summarize how intergenerational activities are planned.

❑ List appropriate intergenerational activities.

Instruction & Student Practice

❑ **Reading.** Have students read *Section 16-2* on text pages 393-399. Assign the *Section 16-2 Knowledge Check* and *Mini Lab.*

❑ **Shared Staff.** After studying the staffing needs of child and adult care centers, have students determine the positions that could be shared.

❑ **Speaker.** Invite a representative from the state licensing agency or a community college to speak to the class about cross-training opportunities.

❑ **Role Play.** Have students write and act out scenarios depicting an older adult becoming impatient with a child. Include appropriate staff interventions.

❑ **Lab Manual.** Assign *Lab Activity 64* on page 131 of the Lab Manual.

❑ **Child & Adult Care Study Guides.** Assign *Study Guide 16-2* from the Student Motivation Kit.

❑ **Child & Adult Care Observations.** Assign *Observations C-13, C-24, OA-8* from the Student Motivation Kit.

❑ **Activity Cards for Children.** Assign *Activity Cards C-27 to C-96* as desired from the Student Motivation Kit.

❑ **Activity Cards for Older Adults.** Assign *Activity Cards OA-1 to OA-47* as desired from the Student Motivation Kit.

❑ **Child & Adult Care Career Profiles.** Assign *Career Profiles* as desired from the Student Motivation Kit.

Review & Student Performance

❑ **PowerPoint® Slides.** Use the *Section 16-2 PowerPoint®* slides on the Effective Instruction CD-ROM.

❑ **Section 16-2 Test.** Have students complete the *Section 16-2 Test* on pages 379-380 of this guide. Or, create your own test by using the **Exam**View® Test Generator found on the **Child & Adult Care Professionals** Effective Instruction CD-ROM.

KEY TERMS

- **intergenerational coordinator**
- **cross-training**
- **proactive**

CARE PROVIDER TIP

Sometimes young children become rambunctious when moving between locations. When conducting activities with young children and older adults, plan to move the children first and lead a transition activity while the older adults move at their comfortable pace.

(Continued on next page)

Answers to Section 16-2 Knowledge Check

1. Staff must be able to meet the needs of children and older adults, meet the requirements mandated by law, and understand specific ways to encourage relationships between children and adults.

2. The program must be prepared to accommodate all older adults, including those with mobility and special needs and health issues.

3. Knowledge of child and older adult development; skill in managing staff, effective communication and problem-solving skills, leadership skills, and decision-making skills.

MINI LAB—*Answers will vary.*

Answers to Chapter 16 Review & Activities

1. Programs that simultaneously provide care for children and older adults.

2. Increased self-esteem and self-worth, individual attention, accurate view of aging process, social attachments and friendships with elders.

3. Ability to share knowledge, skills, abilities, and values; increased memory; motivation to remain active; increased self-esteem and self-worth.

4. Staff is trained in the development and needs of both children and older adults.

5. Balance of activities, pacing, time for transitions, inclusion of daily routines, and opportunities for individual, small-group, and large-group activities.

6. Music, gardening, field trips, storytelling, meal service, reading, walks, show and tell, computer play, woodworking, sharing hobbies, puppetry.

7. Based on cleanliness, sanitation, quality of staff, adequate supervision, daily schedule, safety, written statement of goals and philosophy.

8. Someone trained to plan, coordinate, and implement activities for both young children and older adults.

9. Knowledge of children and older adult development and how to support brain development and function throughout the lifespan and skill in planning activities for all age groups.

Answers to Section 16-2 Test

Matching:

1. B   2. A   3. D

Short Answer:

4. Program type.

5. Individual state licensing laws.

6. Knowledge of both early childhood development and older adult development, knowledge of how to support brain development and function across the lifespan, and a strong knowledge of activity planning that encourages development and interactions across all age groups.

7. They must respond to all participants' developmental needs.

8. They should consider motor skills and capabilities, mobility equipment usage, special needs of children, special needs of older adults, and staff-to-client ratios.

9. *Any five:* Storytelling, show and tell, taking walks together, field trips, meals, naps and rest time, exercise, and medical or therapeutic treatment.

10. A program's philosophy and goals.

11. The Americans with Disabilities Act.

12. Free of trip hazards for those who use walkers or crutches; traffic pathways wide enough to accommodate wheelchairs; activity and meal tables that accommodate mobility equipment.

13. Participants' abilities, personal interests, and attention span.

14. Checklist, daily journal, random survey, and focus groups.

15. *Any two from the list on page 399.*

WORKPLACE CHALLENGE—*Any five:* Arrivals and departures should foster communication between families and staff; the pace of the day should be leisurely; transition times should be adequate for participants to move to other activities; participants should be able to choose to participate in activities, such as solitary, small-group, or large-group activities; daily routines should include time for group meetings, meal service, and naps or rest time; built-in flexibility for medication schedules and therapeutic appointments; time for formal and spontaneous interactions.

INSTRUCTIONAL PLAN ━━━━━━━━━━━━━━━

Services & Referrals

FOCUS & PLANNING

Section Objectives

- ❑ Explain how family involvement helps participants.
- ❑ Explain an open door policy.
- ❑ Identify needs and opportunities for parental or family involvement in the child or older adult care setting.
- ❑ Explain types of family referrals.
- ❑ Determine appropriate ways to make necessary and useful service referrals.

Instruction & Student Practice

- ❑ **Reading.** Have students read *Section 17-1* on text pages 403-409. Assign the *Section 17-1 Knowledge Check* and *Mini Lab*.
- ❑ **Directory of Agencies.** Have teams of students create a directory of referral agencies for needs of adults or children. Students should use the format described in the text. Have students distribute the directories at local adult or child care centers.
- ❑ **Family Activity Night.** Have students plan and lead a family activity night or afternoon in a child or adult care center. Students should plan events that include family volunteers.
- ❑ **Lab Manual.** Assign *Lab Activity 65* on page 129 and *Lab Activity 66* on page 134 of the Lab Manual.
- ❑ **Child & Adult Care Study Guides.** Assign *Study Guide 17-1* from the Student Motivation Kit.
- ❑ **Child & Adult Care Applications.** Assign *Activities 12, 22* and *95* from the Student Motivation Kit.
- ❑ **Activity Cards for Children.** Assign *Activity Cards C-27* to *C-96* as desired from the Student Motivation Kit.
- ❑ **Activity Cards for Older Adults.** Assign *Activity Cards OA-1* to *OA-47* as desired from the Student Motivation Kit.
- ❑ **Child & Adult Care Career Profiles.** Assign *Career Profiles* as desired from the Student Motivation Kit.

Review & Student Performance

- ❑ **PowerPoint® Slides.** Use the *Section 17-1 PowerPoint®* slides on the Effective Instruction CD-ROM.
- ❑ **Section 17-1 Test.** Have students complete the *Section 17-1 Test* on pages 381-382 of this guide. Or, create your own test by using the **Exam*View*®** Test Generator found on the **Child & Adult Care Professionals** Effective Instruction CD-ROM.

KEY TERMS

- **open door policy**
- **support groups**
- **referrals**
- **community service directory**

CARE PROVIDER TIP

Adults and children are proud of their families. Having family members visit the center and participate in activities boosts the individual's self-esteem. Include actual and surrogate family members in as many activities as possible.

(Continued on next page)

Answers to Section 17-1 Knowledge Check

1. When approved family members are allowed into a program at any time.
2. Conferences and scheduled meetings, chaperones on field trips, sibling and family member visits, family night and weekend family events, activity volunteers, advisory board involvement, committee involvement, support groups.
3. When families are sent to other agencies to receive needed services.

MINI LAB — *Materials will vary.*

Answers to Section 17-1 Test

Matching:
1. C
2. F
3. E
4. A

Short Answer:
5. Welcome them warmly.
6. Through effective communication care providers encourage family members to use their knowledge and skills in the program.
7. It encourages families to visit often, offers them the opportunity for many chances to be active in program activities, reassures them that programs have nothing to hide, and during visits, family members are better able to check on service quality.
8. Once or twice a year.
9. Visits build a sense of community for everyone.
10. They allow families to get to know one another and share their unique cultural foods.
11. Their help allows group activities to go more smoothly, and families get to see which types of activities are appropriate for their loved one's age and abilities.
12. Single-parent groups, grandparent groups, and groups for parents of children with special needs.
13. A physical therapist.
14. *Opportunities include:* Assist in planning and running daily activities; serve on an advisory committee or board for the program; sponsor specific events; or lead family support groups for family care providers.
15. *Any four:* Nutrition education, blood pressure follow-up treatment, hearing and vision screenings, legal advice, occupational therapy, and financial assistance.

WORKPLACE CHALLENGE —*Agency description:* full name of the agency and its specific services; *eligibility requirements:* those who may use the service are listed along with requirements, such as geographic area, age ranges, and income levels; *contact information and application procedure:* agency telephone number, e-mail address, and fax number are listed along with whom to contact; *location:* the specific address is listed; *cost for services:* directory lists an agency's current costs and information on how charges are made.

INSTRUCTIONAL PLAN ━━━━━━━━━━━━━━━━━━━━━━━

Section
17-2

Legal Issues

FOCUS & PLANNING

Section Objectives

❏ Identify family involvement in legal issues that apply to early childhood and adult care programs.

❏ Describe legal enrollment practices.

❏ Summarize the purpose of complying with laws and regulations.

❏ Explain how staff should respond to program violations that affect participants and their families.

❏ Identify legal concerns that many impaired children and older adults encounter.

❏ Identify the steps family members should take to assist children or older impaired adults.

Instruction & Student Practice

❏ **Reading.** Have students read *Section 17-2* on text pages 410-414. Assign the *Section 17-2 Knowledge Check* and *Mini Lab*.

❏ **Speaker.** Invite an attorney to explain legal issues that affect many older adults.

❏ **Inspections.** Obtain and have students examine the checklists used by state licensing inspectors, health department inspectors, and fire marshals. Discuss the importance of compliance with these standards.

❏ **Lab Manual.** Assign *Lab Activity 65* on page 129 and *Lab Activity 66* on page 134 of the Lab Manual.

❏ **Child & Adult Care Study Guides.** Assign *Study Guide 17-2* from the Student Motivation Kit.

❏ **Child & Adult Care Applications.** Assign *Activities 28* and *42* from the Student Motivation Kit.

❏ **Activity Cards for Older Adults.** Assign *Activity Cards OA-1* to *OA-47* as desired from the Student Motivation Kit.

❏ **Child & Adult Care Career Profiles.** Assign *Career Profiles* as desired from the Student Motivation Kit.

Review & Student Performance

❏ **PowerPoint® Slides.** Use the *Section 17-2 PowerPoint®* slides on the Effective Instruction CD-ROM.

❏ **Section 17-2 Test.** Have students complete the *Section 17-2 Test* on pages 383-384 of this guide. Or, create your own test by using the **Exam** *View*® Test Generator found on the **Child & Adult Care Professionals** Effective Instruction CD-ROM.

KEY TERMS

- **fee agreement contract**
- **durable power of attorney**
- **advanced directive**
- **living will**

CARE PROVIDER TIP

Abuse is a sensitive issue for some students because they or family members have been abused. Give students the opportunity to leave the classroom and talk to a counselor if the discussion of abuse triggers uncomfortable feelings. Provide an opportunity to discuss how abuse of children or older adults impacts care providers.

(Continued on next page)

Child & Adult Care Professionals Instructor Resource Guide
Copyright © Glencoe/McGraw-Hill

Answers to Section 17-2 Knowledge Check

1. Complying with laws, collecting information required by law, using nonbiased enrollment practices, ensuring privacy and confidentiality, reporting suspected child abuse and/or neglect.

2. Child name, birth date, age, home address, and contact information and custodial parent or legal guardian information, such as home and work addresses and telephone numbers.

3. Failure to maintain legal records; illegal financial practices; licensing and/or accreditation violations; health, safety, and fire code violations; suspected child abuse and/or neglect.

MINI LAB —*Answers will vary.*

Answers to Section 17-2 Test

Matching:

1. D
2. B
3. A
4. F
5. C

Short Answer:

6. *Any three:* Programs must offer enrollment services on an equal opportunity basis; those receiving government funds cannot reject a client for reasons of gender, religion, income, race or other protected statuses; ADA law ensure the enrollment rights of those with special needs; if enrollment ends, one week's notice with suitable documentation for discontinuing enrollment must be given.

7. Program must provide at least one week's notice and must document suitable reasons for discontinuing enrollment.

8. Specific supervising staff.

9. Written permission from a legal parent or guardian.

10. Make the adult child or family member a joint owner of the bank account.

11. Discuss his or her medical care desires with a doctor and attorney.

12. An understanding of the aging process and its challenges and an awareness of support systems.

13. Adult day care centers must follow state and certification standards to provide services and for cost reimbursement. Senior centers do not have these strict guidelines because they offer recreational and leisure activities and are operated mostly by volunteers.

14. Income, equipment, expenditures, and free services.

15. Fact sheet; medical, accident and illness, and attendance records; home situation and referral records.

WORKPLACE CHALLENGE — Medicare, Medicaid, and public aid; Medicare claims and appeals; Social Security and disability claims and appeals; supplemental and long-term health insurance issues; guardianship issues; probate, or establishing that a will is valid, in court; long-term care placements in nursing, housing, and life-care communities; elder abuse and fraud recovery; The Patient's Bill of Rights.

INSTRUCTIONAL PLAN

Family Care Management

FOCUS & PLANNING

Section Objectives

❑ Define family care management.

❑ Identify roles of a family care manager.

❑ Determine how roles are assigned when family members care for older adults.

Instruction & Student Practice

❑ **Reading.** Have students read *Section 17-3* on text pages 415-417. Assign the *Section 17-3 Knowledge Check* and *Mini Lab*.

❑ **Family Care Manager Job Description.** Have students use the Internet and print resources to research the occupation of family care manager and write a job description including the qualifications and desirable personal skills for a family care manager.

❑ **Conflict Resolution.** Have students role play situations that demonstrate common conflicts among family members related to the care and the use of resources of older adults. Then demonstrate how a skillful family care manager might resolve the conflicts.

❑ **Lab Manual.** Assign *Lab Activity 65* on page 129 and *Lab Activity 66* on page 134 of the Lab Manual.

❑ **Child & Adult Care Study Guides.** Assign *Study Guide 17-3* from the Student Motivation Kit.

❑ **Child & Adult Care Applications.** Assign *Activities 22, 30, 100,* and *101* from the Student Motivation Kit.

❑ **Activity Cards for Children.** Assign *Activity Cards C-27* to *C-96* as desired from the Student Motivation Kit.

❑ **Activity Cards for Older Adults.** Assign *Activity Cards OA-1* to *OA-47* as desired from the Student Motivation Kit.

❑ **Child & Adult Care Career Profiles.** Assign *Career Profiles* as desired from the Student Motivation Kit.

Review & Student Performance

❑ **PowerPoint® Slides.** Use the *Section 17-3 PowerPoint®* slides on the Effective Instruction CD-ROM.

❑ **Section 17-3 Test.** Have students complete the *Section 17-3 Test* on pages 385-386 of this guide. Or, create your own test by using the **Exam***View®* Test Generator found on the ***Child & Adult Care Professionals*** Effective Instruction CD-ROM.

KEY TERMS

- family care management
- family care manager
- daily care plan
- interpersonal relationships

CARE PROVIDER TIP

It is common for family members to have disagreements over the type of care and the use of resources to meet the care needs of older adults. It is difficult for many to keep the best interest of the adult in perspective when making these important decisions. Unless high school students have had family experiences with making such decisions, they might not understand the importance of having the family care manager on the decision-making team.

(Continued on next page)

Answers to Section 17-3 Knowledge Check

1. Family care management is the process through which family members and service providers work together as a team to manage the care of a dependent family member.

2. The roles of a care manager include identifying resources, activating existing resources, networking with other groups, and coordinating legal and financial affairs of a dependent family member.

3. Family members assign roles by conducting family meetings and scheduling regular tasks for family members.

MINI LAB —*Answers will vary.*

Answers to Chapter 17 Review & Activities

1. When approved family members are allowed into a program at any time.

2. Parent-teacher conferences, field trip chaperones, sibling visits, family nights, weekend family events, activity volunteers, advisory board member, committee member, support group.

3. Zoo, park, museum, festivals.

4. Nutrition education or medical referral.

5. Listing of local programs that can help meet family needs for assistance.

6. Agency description, eligibility requirements, contact information, application procedure, location, cost for services.

7. Enrollment practices, privacy and confidentiality, fee agreement.

8. Days and times of client attendance, cost for services, procedure for payment, and consequences for nonpayment.

9. In a living will, the person states what type of medical procedures he or she would like performed if unable to make those decisions; in a durable power of attorney, the person is naming someone else to make those decisions.

10. The roles of a family care manager include identifying resources that a dependent family needs for his or her activities of daily living or activates existing resources that have not been used, networking with other groups and organizations to obtain services that the family member needs, and coordinating his or her legal and financial affairs.

Answers to Section 17-3 Test

Matching:

1. A
2. B
3. D

Short Answer:

4. Doctors, dietitians, therapists, or social workers.

5. Make regular visits to the adult day program to gain and offer helpful information; identify resources; activate existing resources; network with other groups; and coordinate legal and financial affairs.

6. *Any two:* Activities of daily living, vision or hearing assistance, or mobility assistance.

7. Alzheimer's association and a dialysis clinic.

8. Wills, Social Security papers, deeds, and bank accounts.

9. Keep a clear list of duties for the care of dependent family members to reduce conflict.

10. Take time out from the care-providing situation.

11. Have each family member take a small role in caring for a loved one.

12. Have a family meeting to discuss the roles each family member can take.

13. Mowing the lawn and shoveling snow.

14. Give a copy of the list to all family members and the adult day program staff.

15. Friends of the family.

WORKPLACE CHALLENGE —*Any five:* Medical treatments; Meals on Wheels; home health services; monetary benefits, such as Social Security benefits or disability insurance; therapies, such as speech or physical therapy; equipment such as hearing devices, eye glasses, walkers, or wheelchairs.

INSTRUCTIONAL PLAN ━━━━━━━━━━━━━━━━━━━━━━━━━━━

Infant Development & Care

Section **18-1**

FOCUS & PLANNING

Section Objectives

❏ Summarize the stages, terms, and factors influencing prenatal development.

❏ Describe factors affecting the growth and development of infants.

❏ Identify and define infant reflexes.

❏ Identify the signs of infant physical, intellectual, emotional, and social development.

❏ Describe the sensorimotor period of development.

❏ Describe three types of temperament.

Instruction & Student Practice

❏ **Reading.** Have students read *Section 18-1* on text pages 421-430. Assign the *Section 18-1 Knowledge Check* and *Mini Lab*.

❏ **Developmental Timeline.** Have students research and list developmental milestones for infants. Place the milestones on a timeline using color-coded symbols. Have the students discuss why knowing these milestones is important for care providers.

❏ **Lab Manual.** Assign *Lab Activity 67* on page 135 of the Lab Manual.

❏ **Child & Adult Care Study Guides.** Assign *Study Guide 18-1* from the Student Motivation Kit.

❏ **Child & Adult Care Applications.** Assign *Activities 38, 45, 46, 111,* and *114* from the Student Motivation Kit.

❏ **Child & Adult Care Observations.** Assign *Observations C-1* and *C-2* from the Student Motivation Kit.

❏ **Activity Cards for Children.** Assign *Activity Cards C-27* to *C-96* as desired from the Student Motivation Kit.

❏ **Child & Adult Care Career Profiles.** Assign *Career Profiles* as desired from the Student Motivation Kit.

Review & Student Performance

❏ **PowerPoint® Slides.** Use the *Section 18-1 PowerPoint®* slides on the Effective Instruction CD-ROM.

❏ **Section 18-1 Test.** Have students complete the *Section 18-1 Test* on pages 387-388 of this guide. Or, create your own test by using the **Exam***View*® Test Generator found on the **Child & Adult Care Professionals** Effective Instruction CD-ROM.

KEY TERMS

- **reflexes**
- **perceptual motor skills**
- **eye-hand coordination**
- **sensorimotor period**
- **object permanence**
- **vocalizations**
- **attachment behavior**
- **temperament**
- **egocentric**
- **stranger anxiety**

CARE PROVIDER TIP

Since the infant with the easy temperament is not as demanding of care provider attention as the difficult and slow-to-warm-up infant, he or she often does not get the attention needed to stimulate development. Be certain that all infants have an interesting environment and receive one-on-one attention every day.

(Continued on next page)

Section 18-1 Continued

INSTRUCTIONAL PLAN *Continued*

Answers to Section 18-1 Knowledge Check

1. Zygote, embryo, fetus. Good maternal physical and nutritional condition, age of mother, maternal smoking or exposure to secondary smoke, drug use, maternal injury, mother's mental health.
2. Mother's physical and mental health, nutrition, temperament, attachment and bonding, appropriate stimulation.
3. Fear of new people.

MINI LAB — *Observations will vary.*

Answers to Section 18-1 Test

Matching:

1. H   6. L
2. F   7. A
3. C   8. K
4. I   9. B
5. E   10. J

Short Answer:

11. Good health services, sound nutrition, and loving care.
12. Good maternal nutritional and mental health.
13. In a secure environment.
14. Interesting and repeated experiences.
15. Up to 17 hours a day.
16. Provide brightly colored objects and patterns for infants to view; offer variety in textures for infants to feel.
17. When infants see a toy move, reach, and grasp for it.
18. Cause and effect.
19. It is necessary for good self-esteem.
20. Inherited traits and experiences with the environment.

WORKPLACE CHALLENGE —Tell young children and older adults in advance that another group will be joining them; tell children about the physical limitations of the older adults they will meet; remind older adults about the energy levels of small children.

Child & Adult Care Professionals Instructor Resource Guide
Copyright © Glencoe/McGraw-Hill

INSTRUCTIONAL PLAN ━━━━━━━━━━━━━━━━━━━

Managing Infant Programs

Section 18-2

FOCUS & PLANNING

Section Objectives

❏ Describe the responsibilities of infant care providers.
❏ Plan ways to respond to infant development.
❏ Identify components of infant programs.
❏ Suggest ways to communicate effectively with parents.

Instruction & Student Practice

❏ **Reading.** Have students read *Section 18-2* on text pages 431-437. Assign the *Section 18-2 Knowledge Check* and *Mini Lab*.

❏ **Responsibilities of Infant Care Providers.** Obtain daily schedules from day care centers that provide infant care. Have students outline a typical day for the infant care provider.

❏ **Plan Infant Activities.** Have students develop an individual activity schedule for an infant of a given age. Students should plan activities to stimulate all areas of development.

❏ **Chart the Costs.** Have students survey infant care programs to find the costs and services offered and analyze the results of the survey.

❏ **Lab Manual.** Assign *Lab Activity 68* on page 137 and *Lab Activity 69* on page 139 of the Lab Manual.

❏ **Child & Adult Care Study Guides.** Assign *Study Guide 18-2* from the Student Motivation Kit.

❏ **Child & Adult Care Applications.** Assign *Activities 38, 45, 46, 111, and 114* from the Student Motivation Kit.

❏ **Child & Adult Care Observations.** Assign *Observations C-1* and *C-2* from the Student Motivation Kit.

❏ **Activity Cards for Children.** Assign *Activity Cards C-27* to *C-96* as desired from the Student Motivation Kit.

❏ **Child & Adult Care Career Profiles.** Assign *Career Profiles* as desired from the Student Motivation Kit.

Review & Student Performance

❏ **PowerPoint® Slides.** Use the *Section 18-2 PowerPoint®* slides on the Effective Instruction CD-ROM.

❏ **Section 18-2 Test.** Have students complete the *Section 18-2 Test* on pages 389-390 of this guide. Or, create your own test by using the **Exam***View*® Test Generator found on the *Child & Adult Care Professionals* Effective Instruction CD-ROM.

KEY TERMS

• **staff turnover**
• **on demand**
• **care provider report form**
• **parent report form**

CARE PROVIDER TIP

Lap time is important for developing infants. To provide that lap time, care providers need to hold the infant not only while feeding, but also while singing, talking, and reading to the infant.

(Continued on next page)

Answers to Section 18-2 Knowledge Check

1. Paying attention to emerging skills, interpreting infant cues, observing and recording behavior, communicating with parents, maintaining records, maintaining appropriate and safe environment.

2. Use sounds in response to infant's vocalizations, use language frequently to describe actions, use facial expressions to convey meaning, look at pictures and books together, play with puppets and stuffed animals, sing, play games, provide engaging toys.

3. Share information daily. Complete and offer parents a care provider report form and ask parents to complete a parent report form each morning. Share photos of children at play. Invite parents to participate in the classroom.

MINI LAB—*Answers will vary.*

Answers to Chapter 18 Review & Activities

1. The first year of life.
2. *See the list on page 425.*
3. Children use their senses and motor abilities to learn about the world around them, through touching, tasting, smelling, and hearing.
4. Understanding that an object continues to exist even when out of sight. *Examples will vary.*
5. *Easy:* Flexible, social, adjusts quickly; *slow to warm up:* Needs more time to adjust to new situations and people; *difficult:* Harder time controlling emotions, easily over stimulated, high energy, resists change and transitions, experiences intense emotions.
6. Respond immediately; pick child up, rock, rub back, sing softly, determine if child needs feeding or diaper changed.
7. Play with puppets, describe pictures, talk during care routines, read books together, make meal times social events.
8. Staff turnover is the rate at which employees leave their jobs, creating the need for new employees to be hired. When staff turnover is high, infants don't have a chance to bond with one care provider. Infants need familiar and predictable care. Too much change is upsetting to them and can hinder their emotional and social development.
9. There is more staff to children in infant programs. Infants require more individualized care.
10. Involve them in the classroom, communicate often, show parents photos of their children at play, share parenting information from articles, videotapes, or books.

Answers to Section 18-2 Test

Matching:

1. F   2. D   3. B   4. E

Short Answer:

5. Because many families today are headed by single parents or dual-earner couples.
6. By understanding infant development.
7. Records of activities planned for and conducted with children; copies of communications with fellow staff, parents, or social service personnel; regular inspection records; and an inventory of equipment and supplies and their condition.
8. Specific staff members are assigned as primary providers of care for individual children.
9. Six to eight infants with two or three care providers.
10. One child to one primary care provider.
11. *See list in the left column on page 433.*
12. Get to know each infant, and if you feel an infant is lagging in an area of development, provide activities to help the child develop skills.
13. Muscle growth and coordination.
14. *Any three:* Respond to an infant's vocalizations with the same sounds; use language frequently; use three- or four-word sentences; use facial expressions and lively tone of voice; look at pictures and read books together; play with puppets and stuffed animals; sing to infants; carry infants around; play games; offer toys of different shapes, colors, and textures.
15. *Any two from the list on page 436.*

WORKPLACE CHALLENGE—*Any five as found on pages 435-436.*

INSTRUCTIONAL PLAN ━━━━━━━━━━━━━━━

Toddler Development & Care

Section **19-1**

FOCUS & PLANNING

Section Objectives

❏ Explain the signs of and influences on the physical, emotional, social, and intellectual development of toddlers.

❏ Identify the characteristics of the preoperational period.

❏ Describe an environment that promotes healthy emotional development.

❏ Summarize the impact of play on social development.

❏ Identify ways to promote responsibility in toddlers.

Instruction & Student Practice

❏ **Reading.** Have students read *Section 19-1* on text pages 441-448. Assign the *Section 19-1 Knowledge Check* and *Mini Lab.*

❏ **Timeline.** Have teams of students develop a timeline showing milestones of toddler development in all developmental areas.

❏ **Care Provider Guidelines.** Have students write guidelines for adults to encourage toddlers to use words to express wants and needs.

❏ **Library Books.** Have students visit a library and select books suitable for toddlers. Have them read the books to toddlers.

❏ **Lab Manual.** Assign *Lab Activity 70* on page 141 and *Lab Activity 72* on page 142 of the Lab Manual.

❏ **Child & Adult Care Study Guides.** Assign *Study Guide 19-1* from the Student Motivation Kit.

❏ **Child & Adult Care Applications.** Assign *Activities 8, 46, 47, 48, 54, 110,* and *112* from the Student Motivation Kit.

❏ **Child & Adult Care Observations.** Assign *Observations C-3* and *C-4* from the Student Motivation Kit.

❏ **Activity Cards for Children.** Assign *Activity Cards C-27* to *C-96* as desired from the Student Motivation Kit.

❏ **Child & Adult Care Career Profiles.** Assign *Career Profiles* as desired from the Student Motivation Kit.

Review & Student Performance

❏ **PowerPoint® Slides.** Use the *Section 19-1 PowerPoint®* slides on the Effective Instruction CD-ROM.

❏ **Section 19-1 Test.** Have students complete the *Section 19-1 Test* on pages 391-392 of this guide. Or, create your own test by using the **Exam***View*® Test Generator found on the ***Child & Adult Care Professionals*** Effective Instruction CD-ROM.

(Continued on next page)

KEY TERMS

- **self-help skills**
- **attention span**
- **symbolic thinking**
- **preoperational period**
- **concepts**
- **assimilation**
- **accommodation**
- **autonomy**
- **solitary play**
- **parallel play**

CARE PROVIDER TIP

Since toddlers are learning to be autonomous, it is best to allow them to explore as much as they wish, as long as the environment is safe. Have student care providers contrast the safety needs of toddlers and preschoolers.

Answers to Section 19-1 Knowledge Check

1. Motor development and coordination progresses quickly. New physical abilities, especially motor abilities such as walking, climbing, and using wheeled toys, increase. Fine motor skills are refined allowing children to string beads and build with blocks.

2. Children understand that one thing can stand for something else. They learn to use images, art, and language as symbols to represent objects, events, and concepts.

3. Toddlers are usually calmed when a care provider is close at hand. Children overcome fears when reassuring care providers are patient. It often helps to talk with children about fears. Gradually introduce children to experiences that scare them.

MINI LAB —*Answers will vary.*

Answers to Section 19-1 Test

Matching:

1. J   6. B
2. C   7. A
3. L   8. D
4. I   9. K
5. E   10. H

Short Answer:

11. *Any three:* Growth in height and weight slows; less fuel is needed for growth, so appetite decreases; teeth come in rapidly between 18 and 24 months; body proportions gradually change to more mature proportions.

12. Small motor skills, which require use of muscles in the fingers, wrists, and ankles.

13. Getting dressed, washing hands, eating with utensils, brushing teeth, and putting away toys.

14. Discovery through many hands-on experiences; learning by doing; freedom and time to explore a safe environment to satisfy curiosity; care provider responses to multiple questions; trial and error, repetition, and imitation.

15. Increasing memory, or the ability to recall images and information, leads to learning.

16. They use images, art, and language as symbols to represent objects, events, and concepts.

17. With assimilation, children take in new information and try to make it fit with what they already know and understand; with accommodation, children change their thinking to make the new information fit.

18. Saying "no"; resisting routines; showing sensitivity to being shown, helped, or directed; and doing the opposite of what a care provider wants.

19. From lack of experience, misconceptions, or learning them from other children and adults.

20. By modeling appropriate behavior; promoting the use of self-help skills; setting limits and rules that primarily relate to safety.

WORKPLACE CHALLENGE —Dress the child in elastic-waist, pull-down pants for easy removal; be alert for signs that children need to use the toilet, such as tugging at their pants; remind children of feelings that signal it is time to use the toilet; take children to the toilet as frequently as needed; if a child does not urinate or have a bowel movement within five minutes of sitting on the toilet, allow the child to resume play; always use sanitary procedures when toileting or diapering.

INSTRUCTIONAL PLAN ━━━━━━━━━━━━━━━━━━━━━━

Managing Toddler Programs

Section **19-2**

FOCUS & PLANNING

Section Objectives

❑ Identify key features of toddler programs.

❑ Plan a safe, healthy, and developmentally appropriate environment for toddlers.

❑ Describe how to nurture toddlers' overall development.

❑ Suggest ways to handle common challenges of the toddler years.

Instruction & Student Practice

❑ **Reading.** Have students read *Section 19-2* on text pages 449-455. Assign the *Section 19-2 Knowledge Check* and *Mini Lab.*

❑ **Develop Guidelines.** Have students develop five rules for a toddler classroom. The rules must be stated in positive language.

❑ **Demonstration.** Have students demonstrate care provider behaviors that help toddlers face emotional and social challenges.

❑ **Lesson Activity.** Have students plan an open-ended art activity suitable for a toddler classroom. They could either use the activity at the work site or demonstrate its use in a classroom presentation.

❑ **Lab Manual.** Assign *Lab Activity 72* on page 143 and *Lab Activity 73* on page 145 of the Lab Manual.

❑ **Child & Adult Care Study Guides.** Assign *Study Guide 19-2* from the Student Motivation Kit.

❑ **Child & Adult Care Applications.** Assign *Activities 8, 46, 47, 48, 54, 110,* and *112* from the Student Motivation Kit.

❑ **Child & Adult Care Observations.** Assign *Observations C-3* and *C-4* from the Student Motivation Kit.

❑ **Activity Cards for Children.** Assign *Activity Cards C-27* to *C-96* as desired from the Student Motivation Kit.

❑ **Child & Adult Care Career Profiles.** Assign *Career Profiles* as desired from the Student Motivation Kit.

Review & Student Performance

❑ **PowerPoint® Slides.** Use the *Section 19-2 PowerPoint®* slides on the Effective Instruction CD-ROM.

❑ **Section 19-2 Test.** Have students complete the *Section 19-2 Test* on pages 393-394 of this guide. Or, create your own test by using the **Exam**View® Test Generator found on the *Child & Adult Care Professionals* Effective Instruction CD-ROM.

KEY TERMS

• receptive language
• productive language
• separation anxiety
• negativism
• temper tantrum

CARE PROVIDER TIP

Since toddlers have a strong need for security, it is best not to change care providers during naptime.

(Continued on next page)

Answers to Section 19-2 Knowledge Check

1. Toddler programs are designed to help toddlers develop their new abilities and gain independence by using age-appropriate furniture and toys, providing security items, and supplying learning centers with items that encourage physical, intellectual, emotional, and social development.
2. Dressing, tooth brushing, hand washing, toileting, feeding.
3. It shows a child has a strong bond and attachment to parents and primary care providers.

MINI LAB —*Activities will vary.*

Answers to Chapter 19 Review & Activities

1. Toward the end of the toddler stage of development.
2. Ability to focus on a specific activity for a period of time.
3. *Assimilation* is when children incorporate new knowledge into existing concepts. For instance, very young children may believe all animals with four legs are called dogs. *Accommodation* is when children change mental concepts to make sense of new information. When a child learns that different four-legged animals have different names, he or she is accommodating.
4. Sense of independence. They want to make decisions and enjoy developing self-help skills.
5. Predictable routines, secure attachment to stable care providers.
6. Eight care providers, one for every four children.
7. Toddler equipment allows for greater independence and increased use of abilities.
8. Eating, toileting, sleeping habits and routines; large- and small-motor development and abilities; health status.
9. Small wheel toys and wagons, low swings and climbers, obstacle courses, and tunnels (or large boxes) to crawl through. Toddlers also enjoy balls that they can safely kick, roll, and toss.
10. Skills build on each other. Each child goes through stages at his or her own individual rate. Practice and repeated activities help skills develop and become refined.

Answers to Section 19-2 Test

Matching:

1.	E	4.	A
2.	D	5.	G
3.	F		

Short Answer:

6. Helps toddlers feel secure.
7. Information helps the program provide individualized care and activities that nurture all areas of development.
8. Scribbling, finger painting, painting with brushes, cutting with scissors, and molding dough.
9. He or she may simply be gathering new information about the world before participating.
10. Show empathy and understanding.
11. Give toddlers plenty of opportunities to make choices and practice self-help skills.
12. Provide age-appropriate activities, so toddlers can experience success; offer reasonable choices; and let toddlers do as much as possible for themselves.
13. Notify parents at the end of the day, ask how tantrums are handled at home, and allow parents to give you input on how to effectively deal with tantrums.
14. Groups of two or three.
15. They can distract or redirect the child or divert the child's attention.

WORKPLACE CHALLENGE —*Any five:* Lock up all toxic substance, such as medicines and cleaning agents; lock the classroom refrigerator; continue to keep small objects that could cause choking out of toddlers' reach; choose toys with safety in mind and check them daily for loose or broken parts; use safety caps on electrical outlets; use nonslip rugs; secure shelves, so they will not fall over on children.

INSTRUCTIONAL PLAN ━━━━━━━━━━━━━━━━━━━━━━━━

Preschooler Development & Care

Section **20·1**

FOCUS & PLANNING

Section Objectives

❑ Explain the influences and signs of the physical, emotional, social, and intellectual development of preschoolers.

❑ Describe the key points of children's understanding in Piaget's pre-operational period.

❑ Explain Vygotsky's sociocultural theory.

Instruction & Student Practice

❑ **Reading.** Have students read *Section 20-1* on text pages 459-466. Assign the *Section 20-1 Knowledge Check* and *Mini Lab.*

❑ **Helper Charts.** Have students identify ways preschoolers can help in the classroom and develop charts to rotate the helpers.

❑ **Large Motor Activity.** Have students set up an obstacle course for preschoolers using equipment such as a balance beam, tunnel, tumbling mats, tricycles, etc. Students should observe and assess each child's motor skills.

❑ **Lab Manual.** Assign *Lab Activity 74* on page 147, *Lab Activity 75* on page 149, and *Lab Activity 76* on page 150 of the Lab Manual.

❑ **Child & Adult Care Study Guides.** Assign *Study Guide 20-1* from the Student Motivation Kit.

❑ **Child & Adult Care Applications.** Assign *Activities 6, 7, 37, 54, 55, 56,* and *57* from the Student Motivation Kit.

❑ **Child & Adult Care Observations.** Assign *Observations C-6, C-7, C-8, C-13, C-22, C-27, C-31,* or *C-35* from the Student Motivation Kit.

❑ **Activity Cards for Children.** Assign *Activity Cards C-27* to *C-96* as desired from the Student Motivation Kit.

❑ **Child & Adult Care Career Profiles.** Assign *Career Profiles* as desired from the Student Motivation Kit.

Review & Student Performance

❑ **PowerPoint® Slides.** Use the *Section 20-1 PowerPoint®* slides on the Effective Instruction CD-ROM.

❑ **Section 20-1 Test.** Have students complete the *Section 20-1 Test* on pages 395-396 of this guide. Or, create your own test by using the **Exam***View®* Test Generator found on the ***Child & Adult Care Professionals*** Effective Instruction CD-ROM.

KEY TERMS

• **centration**
• **seriation**
• **rote counting**
• **one-to-one correspondence**
• **rational counting**
• **conservation**
• **native language**
• **bilingual**
• **cooperative play**
• **sociocultural theory**

CARE PROVIDER TIP

Many preschoolers quickly develop pre-reading skills, such as recognizing letters, articulating sounds, and writing with invented spelling. Children learn such skills quickly through a language-rich environment and developmentally appropriate play activities.

(Continued on next page)

Answers to Section 20-1 Knowledge Check

1. Physical growth during the preschool years is gradual. As preschoolers grow, their bodies appear less babylike. Body fat is reduced, and most growth occurs in the muscles and bones. Their posture becomes erect, the neck lengthens, the shoulders widen and flatten, the stomach flattens, and the legs become proportionally longer.

2. Ask parents of non-English-speaking children to complete a home language survey, which provides translations and phonetic spellings of common native language words and phrases. Include parents in the classroom as often as possible; encourage them to share native customs, children's books, cultural toys, songs, and traditional recipes; and encourage them to form friendships with other parents who use the program, and arrange weekend play dates for their child by inviting other program children to their home or neighborhood park. Use native as well as non-native language when creating signs.

3. Vygotsky's sociocultural theory states that children learn their culture's beliefs, customs, and skills through social interactions with skilled peers and adults. By talking and playing with others, children gradually master language and thinking and problem-solving skills and learn to behave according to their culture's specific rules.

(**MINI LAB**)—*Observations and answers will vary.*

Answers to Section 20-1 Test

Matching:

1.	C	6.	D
2.	K	7.	F
3.	J	8.	B
4.	G	9.	E
5.	I	10.	L

Short Answer:

11. A three-year-old can throw a ball; a five-year-old can catch a ball.

12. Climbing.

13. They can understand the difference between "now" and "later" but not the passage of time according to a clock or calendar.

14. Talk and read to them daily.

15. Their thinking ability exceeds their speaking ability.

16. Loneliness, disappointment, anticipation, and sympathy.

17. They recognize and understand the feelings of others, learn to regret actions that hurt others and begin to help others without expecting a reward.

18. Dress themselves, eat neatly, and use good manners.

19. Age 5.

20. Firmly tell the child that name-calling is not allowed because it hurts people's feelings.

(**WORKPLACE CHALLENGE**)—*Any five:* Use names correctly; use cultural greeting songs; label learning centers in English and the children's native languages; use both languages at snack time; play ethnic music at nap time; use native language at departure time.

INSTRUCTIONAL PLAN ━━━━━━━━━━━━━━━━━━━━━

Managing Preschool Programs

Section **20-2**

FOCUS & PLANNING

Section Objectives

❑ Identify features of preschool programs.

❑ Describe how to broaden preschoolers' skills.

❑ Explain how preschoolers develop literacy.

❑ Cite ways to encourage cooperative learning.

❑ Suggest ways to introduce children to community participation.

Instruction & Student Practice

❑ **Reading.** Have students read *Section 20-2* on text pages 467-471. Assign the *Section 20-2 Knowledge Check* and *Mini Lab.*

❑ **Plan for the First Day.** Have students develop a lesson plan for the first day of preschool. Be sure that students include activities that teach the rules, routines, and names.

❑ **Classroom Labels.** Have students make labels for the centers and parts of the classroom. The labels should include pictures and the words in more than one language. Laminate the labels and have students use them at their work sites.

❑ **Lab Manual.** Assign *Lab Activity 77* on page 151 of the Lab Manual.

❑ **Child & Adult Care Study Guides.** Assign *Study Guide 20-2* from the Student Motivation Kit.

❑ **Child & Adult Care Applications.** Assign *Activities 6, 7, 37, 54, 55, 56,* and *57* from the Student Motivation Kit.

❑ **Child & Adult Care Observations.** Assign *Observations C-6, C-7, C-8, C-13, C-22, C-27, C-31,* or *C-35* from the Student Motivation Kit.

❑ **Activity Cards for Children.** Assign *Activity Cards C-27* to *C-96* as desired from the Student Motivation Kit.

❑ **Child & Adult Care Career Profiles.** Assign *Career Profiles* as desired from the Student Motivation Kit.

Review & Student Performance

❑ **PowerPoint® Slides.** Use the *Section 20-2 PowerPoint®* slides on the Effective Instruction CD-ROM.

❑ **Section 20-2 Test.** Have students complete the *Section 20-2 Test* on pages 397-398 of this guide. Or, create your own test by using the **Exam***View®* Test Generator found on the ***Child & Adult Care Professionals*** Effective Instruction CD-ROM.

KEY TERMS

• literacy
• cooperative learning

CARE PROVIDER TIP

Preschoolers are very dependent upon routines. When a special activity, such as a field trip or guest, disrupts the routine, prepare the children ahead of time by explaining to them what to expect.

(Continued on next page)

Answers to Section 20-2 Knowledge Check

1. Arrival; meals, including breakfast, morning snack, lunch, afternoon snack, supper, evening snack; personal hygiene, such as hand washing; morning group meetings to plan the day's events; large-group experiences, such as story time; activity times for individual and small-group learning; free play time for self-chosen activities; field trips related to curriculum; toy clean up; outdoor play; nap or rest time; end of day group activity; departure.

2. *See list on page 468.*

3. Create learning centers that encourage group play. Include more toys that require cooperative play, such as board games. Plan projects that require teamwork, such as making murals or cardboard cities. Conduct activities that allow children to plan together and make decisions, such as creating and putting on a play.

MINI LAB—*Answers will vary.*

Answers to Chapter 20 Review & Activities

1. Classification, centration, seriation, rote counting, one-to-one correspondence, beginning rational counting, inability to conserve.

2. Focus on content rather than on grammar or speech mechanics. Model the correct language.

3. They may leave long pauses between words or repeat a sound or word many times before continuing a sentence. It is the natural result when thinking ability exceeds speaking ability.

4. Recognize and understand feelings of others.

5. Feelings of independence, self-confidence, and ability to start and complete activities. According to Erikson, accomplishing tasks gives children good feelings; to increase these good feelings, children contribute in groups or help others.

6. Increased self-esteem results when children achieve goals and challenges.

7. Playing together, agreeing on play activities and themes.

8. *Answers will vary, but may include:* Offering field trips to introduce children to their community's diversity; using community resources to expand on curriculum learning; including children in community service projects, such as picking up litter or donating toys; drawing children's attention to basic rules and laws communities set for behavior to protect all community members' safety and well-being.

9. Books, magazines, paper, crayons, markers, items for making books.

10. *Answers will vary, but may include:* Using recipes during cooking activities, including menus in a pretend restaurant, using traffic signs and toy cars in block center, placing a telephone book in a pretend home.

Answers to Section 20-2 Test

Short Answer:

1. The ability to read and write language.

2. A way to investigate a specific topic of interest.

3. More freedom to make independent choices during play and learning times.

4. Preschoolers now enjoy a wider variety of games and physical activities.

5. Small muscles, such as coordination of fingers.

6. Ability to handle a pencil for writing.

7. Intellectual development.

8. More complex thinking skills.

9. Read books to groups of children and individuals several times a day and let children look at books or listen to books on tape alone.

10. Reading a recipe during cooking or reading directions to put together a new toy.

11. Greater language mastery.

12. Jealousy, sense of loss, and sorrow.

13. Give them many opportunities to express their emotions and ideas.

14. Coach them through the positive steps for problem solving and conflict resolution.

15. They see how they can participate in communities when they become adults.

WORKPLACE CHALLENGE—Post boldly labeled escape directions near every entrance and exit; identify clear evacuation pathways for each type of emergency; color-code pathways for different emergencies; post primary and secondary escape routes for fire emergencies; laminate the evacuation sheets, so they remain in good, readable condition; update evacuation directions as necessary.

Child & Adult Care Professionals Instructor Resource Guide
Copyright © Glencoe/McGraw-Hill

INSTRUCTIONAL PLAN ━━━━━━━━━━━━━━━━━━━━━━━━━━ *Section*

School-Ager Development & Care *21-1*

FOCUS & PLANNING

Section Objectives

❑ Describe the overall development of school-age children.

❑ Explain how improved motor and perceptual motor skills influence school-age children's activities.

❑ Analyze the impact of puberty, self-esteem, competition, fear, stress, and rules on school-age children.

❑ Contrast friendship among preschoolers to that of school-age children.

Instruction & Student Practice

❑ **Reading.** Have students read *Section 21-1* on text pages 475-482. Assign the *Section 21-1 Knowledge Check* and *Mini Lab.*

❑ **Chart.** Have students chart the physical development of children ages 6 to 12. They should make suggestions for age groupings for children in school-age programs based upon development.

❑ **Debate.** Divide the class into teams. Have students debate the advantages and disadvantages of competitive activities for school-age children.

❑ **Lab Manual.** Assign *Lab Activity 78* on page 153 of the Lab Manual.

❑ **Child & Adult Care Study Guides.** Assign *Study Guide 21-1* from the Student Motivation Kit.

❑ **Child & Adult Care Applications.** Assign *Activities 7, 41, and 57* from the Student Motivation Kit.

❑ **Child & Adult Care Observations.** Assign *Observations C-10, C-11, or C-12* from the Student Motivation Kit.

❑ **Activity Cards for Children.** Assign *Activity Cards C-27 to C-96* as desired from the Student Motivation Kit.

❑ **Child & Adult Care Career Profiles.** Assign *Career Profiles* as desired from the Student Motivation Kit.

Review & Student Performance

❑ **PowerPoint® Slides.** Use the *Section 21-1 PowerPoint®* slides on the Effective Instruction CD-ROM.

❑ **Section 21-1 Test.** Have students complete the *Section 21-1 Test* on pages 399-400 of this guide. Or, create your own test by using the **Exam**View® Test Generator found on the **Child & Adult Care Professionals** Effective Instruction CD-ROM.

KEY TERMS

- **growth plateau**
- **puberty**
- **hormones**
- **depth perception**
- **concrete operations period**
- **industry**
- **inferiority**
- **egocentric**
- **diversity**

CARE PROVIDER TIP

After a busy day of school, children need the opportunity to let off steam and pursue activities of personal interest. Provide an environment structured enough for the children to learn behavior expectations and offer them choices of interesting activities.

(Continued on next page)

Answers to Section 21-1 Knowledge Check

1. Around age 12, children undergo a surge of growth. Hormones cause girls to menstruate, usually between ages 10 and 14; girls' body fat increases, so they may weigh slightly more than boys; girls may pass up boys in height; once boys are well into puberty, their height and weight surpass girls'; boys develop more muscle tissue, which adds weight; facial hair appears; male hormone production causes boys' voices to gradually lower; the high level of hormone production can cause mood swings in both boys and girls.

2. Ages 6–7 years: learns to print capital and small letters, reads simple books alone, recognizes simple word endings; ages 8–9 years: learns script handwriting, reads aloud fluently, writes simple stories alone, begins to use a dictionary; ages 10 years and older: reads for information and writes simple reports; uses indexes, appendices, and footnotes; learns to use prefixes and suffixes.

3. Hours of energy needed to develop new intellectual and physical skills; new fears or excessive emphasis on competition; rejection by peers; less relaxation and leisure time at home with family and friends; family and personal problems or changes, such as new siblings or parents divorce.

(**MINI LAB**)—*Answers will vary.*

Answers to Section 21-1 Test

Matching:

1.	F	5.	I	8.	L
2.	K	6.	J	9.	C
3.	B	7.	D	10.	G
4.	A				

Short Answer:

11. Ages five or six.
12. Usually six months to a year earlier.
13. Because girls' body fat increases.
14. Galloping and leaping.
15. Hockey, dodge ball, and baseball.
16. They can remember the past, consider the present, and anticipate and plan for the future.
17. Children can better recognize, understand, and sympathize with the feelings of others.
18. Successful experiences with peers—through games, sports activities, and group projects.
19. They sincerely appreciate the characteristics of another person.
20. They continue to obey rules to earn rewards and avoid punishment; they also begin to see that rules are needed for people to live together peacefully.

(**WORKPLACE CHALLENGE**)—*Any five:* Regularly take time to listen to school-age children; express trust in children's ability to make good independent decisions; guide children to anticipate positive and negative consequences for behavior; help children to value friends who do not pressure them to engage in questionable activities; build self-esteem so children are not desperate to find love and attention from others; maintain a calm environment where children feel safe and loved; remind children that some secrets are too dangerous to keep.

INSTRUCTIONAL PLAN ────────────────────

Managing School-Age Programs

FOCUS & PLANNING

Section Objectives

❑ Explain the need for school-age child care programs.

❑ Describe an appropriate environment for school-age children.

❑ Discuss considerations in planning schedules, routines, and activities for school-age children.

❑ Identify ways to nurture overall development of school-age children.

Instruction & Student Practice

❑ **Reading.** Have students read *Section 21-2* on text pages 483-491. Assign the *Section 21-2 Knowledge Check* and *Mini Lab.*

❑ **Service Project.** Have students volunteer to assist children enrolled in a school-age program with their homework.

❑ **Plan Activities.** Have students plan a rotation of activities for groups of children in a school-age program.

❑ **Develop a Schedule.** Have students schedule a typical day for a school-age child who is in care before and after school. Have them identify the developmental needs of the child that should be met.

❑ **Lab Manual.** Assign *Lab Activity 79* on page 155 and *Lab Activity 80* on page 157 of the Lab Manual.

❑ **Child & Adult Care Study Guides.** Assign *Study Guide 21-2* from the Student Motivation Kit.

❑ **Child & Adult Care Applications.** Assign *Activities 7, 41, and 57* from the Student Motivation Kit.

❑ **Child & Adult Care Observations.** Assign *Observations C-10, C-11, or C-12* from the Student Motivation Kit.

❑ **Activity Cards for Children.** Assign *Activity Cards C-27 to C-96* as desired from the Student Motivation Kit.

❑ **Child & Adult Care Career Profiles.** Assign *Career Profiles* as desired from the Student Motivation Kit.

Review & Student Performance

❑ **PowerPoint® Slides.** Use the *Section 21-2 PowerPoint®* slides on the Effective Instruction CD-ROM.

❑ **Section 21-2 Test.** Have students complete the *Section 21-2 Test* on pages 401-402 of this guide. Or, create your own test by using the **Exam***View®* Test Generator found on the **Child & Adult Care Professionals** Effective Instruction CD-ROM.

KEY TERMS

- latchkey children
- special activities

CARE PROVIDER TIP

Some older school-age children can become helpers with the younger children. Provide opportunities for the older age grouping to volunteer to assist the younger children with such activities as computer skills, games, and crafts.

(Continued on next page)

Answers to Section 21-2 Knowledge Check

1. Children who stay home alone before and after school.

2. A relaxed, casual and comfortable atmosphere with learning centers and private areas; furnishings — soft sofas or beanbag chairs, tables, or desks for doing homework; learning centers have age-appropriate materials; and outdoor areas; on-site programs usually have access to the school gymnasium, playing fields, and sports equipment.

3. Clubs for children may include creative writing, photography, collecting trading cards, drama, or art.

MINI LAB —*Answers will vary.*

Answers to Chapter 21 Review & Activities

1. By age 10, all types of large-motor movement are possible. Children enjoy tag and other active games, hold relay races, or play team sports, such as T-ball, or snow skiing; enjoy jumping rope, skating, using outdoor play equipment, and creative movement. Small-motor skills and eye-hand coordination are strengthened through handwriting or playing a musical instrument.

2. Erikson believed school-age children strive to develop a sense of industry, or a desire to perform skills, succeed at tasks, and make social contributions. He claimed that if school-age children don't feel productive, they will develop a sense of inferiority, a feeling of not having met expected standards, which damages self-esteem.

3. *Positive:* Competition can motivate children to do their best, refine skills and talents, and increase cooperation. *Negative:* Emphasis on competition can damage self-esteem, cause children to focus on their weaknesses not their strengths, and cause them to avoid activities.

4. School-age children are fearful of not belonging to a group and of being teased and criticized. They may imagine that others are talking about them behind their back. Many school-age children fear failure; fear disappointing parents, teachers, and other respected adults; and worry more about world events.

5. Children are left unsupervised at home and become bored and aimless. In the event of an accident or emergency, they confront danger.

6. 20, with one teacher for every 10 children.

7. They should offer a wider variety of materials for advanced abilities and interests.

8. See the *How To...* feature on page 480.

Answers to Section 21-2 Test

Short Answer:

1. Children who stay home alone before or after school.

2. *Any two:* Gymnastics, swimming lessons, or organized sports.

3. They can become bored and aimless. In an accident or emergency, they may confront real danger.

4. A safe place for children until they go home; parental peace of mind knowing children are safe.

5. Between ages 6 and 10.

6. From 6:00 a.m. to 9:00 a.m. and after school, from 2:00 p.m. to 6:00 p.m.

7. Organizing groups of younger and older children, creating mixed-age groupings, and providing experiences that interest younger and older children.

8. They stimulate interest and offer new experiences.

9. *See physical development on page 487.*

10. Needlework, pottery, basket weaving, woodworking, and model building.

11. *Any three:* Experimenting with art materials; building new block structures; writing; and performing a puppet show, using a script they write themselves and puppets they make.

12. Through drama activities and other creative activities; keeping a diary, and supplying good books dealing with school-age emotions.

13. Increased self-esteem.

14. *Any three:* Working together to paint a mural, construct a large papier-mâché dinosaur, or prepare a meal and go on field trips.

15. They are more likely to follow rules.

WORKPLACE CHALLENGE —*Any five:* Arrival and departure time, both morning and afternoon; arrival routine—greeting and health check; a planning time, for activities; meals, including breakfast and an afternoon snack; rest time; time for grooming and hygiene.

INSTRUCTIONAL PLAN ━━━━━━━━━━━━━━━━━━━━━━━━━

Section
22-1

Development & Care of Children with Special Needs

FOCUS & PLANNING

Section Objectives

❑ Explain the meaning of special needs.

❑ Identify the laws that impact the care and education of children with special needs.

❑ Describe some specific needs of children with disabilities and gifted children.

❑ Explain the ways to respond to a child's unique special needs.

Instruction & Student Practice

❑ **Reading.** Have students read *Section 22-1* on text pages 495-501. Assign the *Section 22-1 Knowledge Check* and *Mini Lab*.

❑ **Plan Classroom Adaptations.** Have students assess a preschool classroom and plan adaptations for a child with vision impairment.

❑ **Guest Speaker.** Invite a school psychologist to show how they use assessment tools to diagnose cognitive delays in preschool children.

❑ **Evaluate a Lesson Activity Plan.** Have students analyze a lesson activity they have completed with young children and predict how a gifted child would approach the activity.

❑ **Lab Manual.** Assign *Lab Activity 81* on page 159 of the Lab Manual.

❑ **Child & Adult Care Study Guides.** Assign *Study Guide 22-1* from the Student Motivation Kit.

❑ **Child & Adult Care Applications.** Assign *Activities 6 to 10, 19, 20, 21,* and *27* from the Student Motivation Kit.

❑ **Child & Adult Care Observations.** Assign *Observations C-21* and *C-25* from the Student Motivation Kit.

❑ **Activity Cards for Children.** Assign *Activity Cards C-27 to C-96* as desired from the Student Motivation Kit.

❑ **Child & Adult Care Career Profiles.** Assign *Career Profiles* as desired from the Student Motivation Kit.

Review & Student Performance

❑ **PowerPoint® Slides.** Use the *Section 22-1 PowerPoint®* slides on the Effective Instruction CD-ROM.

❑ **Section 22-1 Test.** Have students complete the *Section 22-1 Test* on pages 403-404 of this guide. Or, create your own test by using the **Exam***View®* Test Generator found on the ***Child & Adult Care Professionals*** Effective Instruction CD-ROM.

KEY TERMS

- **special needs**
- **accommodations**
- **learning disability**
- **aphasia**
- **dyslexia**
- **dyscalcula**
- **learning specialists**
- **attention deficit hyperactivity disorder (ADHD)**
- **autism**

CARE PROVIDER TIP

Young children are very accepting of others with developmental differences. Sometimes parents may fear that children with special needs take teacher time away from their children. The teacher must reassure parents that all children receive appropriate attention.

(Continued on next page)

Answers to Section 22-1 Knowledge Check

1. Individuals with Disabilities Act (IDEA), Americans with Disabilities Act (ADA), Rehabilitation Act, Section 504.

2. Hearing impairment or visual, physical and motor impairment, mental impairment, learning disabilities, behavior and emotional disabilities, health conditions.

3. Advanced vocabulary and language skills, developmental skills acquired earlier than most peers, walking and talking earlier than usual in infancy, creativity in inventing and problem solving, intense curiosity, advanced attention span, ability to concentrate on and persist in complex tasks, unusual attention to detail, perfectionism, good memory, preference for company of adults and older playmates, good sense of humor, ease in grasping new concepts and ideas, talent for making plans and organizing tasks.

MINI LAB —*Answers will vary*.

Answers to Section 22-1 Test

Matching:

1. K	4. C	7. J
2. A	5. H	8. D
3. I	6. G	9. E

Short Answer:

10. Individuals with Disabilities Education Act (IDEA).

11. Props, pictures, and hands-on experiences.

12. Ensure that the building is accessible.

13. Learn more slowly; shorter-than-average attention span; affected motor skills and eye-hand coordination; and less emotional control and fewer social skills than other children.

14. Errors in fetal brain development, mother's alcohol and drug use during pregnancy, problems during birth, and environmental toxins.

15. They may lose interest and not bother to do their best.

WORKPLACE CHALLENGE —*Any two:* Plan enrichment activities that explore concepts in more depth; plan group projects and involve gifted children in the planning and organizing processes; include field trips and special visitors to help satisfy a gifted child's intellect and stimulate and motivate other children as well.

INSTRUCTIONAL PLAN ━━━━━━━━━━━━━━━━━━━━━━━━━━

Managing Inclusive Programs

Section **22-2**

FOCUS & PLANNING

Section Objectives

❑ Explain the meaning of inclusion and why it is practiced.

❑ Discuss how to encourage a classroom atmosphere of acceptance and respect for individual abilities.

❑ Outline ways to adapt a child care program to meet special needs.

Instruction & Student Practice

❑ **Reading.** Have students read *Section 22-2* on text pages 502-507. Assign the *Section 22-2 Knowledge Check* and *Mini Lab*.

❑ **Article Review.** Have students read about inclusion in *Young Children* or a similar professional publication and write a review or give a report summarizing the content.

❑ **Guest Speaker.** Invite a preschool special education teacher to speak regarding classroom adaptations.

❑ **Review IEP Goals.** Have students review a sample Individualized Educational Plan and write classroom adaptations.

❑ **Lab Manual.** Assign *Lab Activity 82* on page 161 and *Lab Activity 83* on page 165 of the Lab Manual.

❑ **Child & Adult Care Study Guides.** Assign *Study Guide 22-2* from the Student Motivation Kit.

❑ **Child & Adult Care Applications.** Assign *Activities 6 to 10, 19, 20, 21,* and *27* from the Student Motivation Kit.

❑ **Child & Adult Care Observations.** Assign *Observations C-21* and *C-25* from the Student Motivation Kit.

❑ **Activity Cards for Children.** Assign *Activity Cards C-27* to *C-96* as desired from the Student Motivation Kit.

❑ **Child & Adult Care Career Profiles.** Assign *Career Profiles* as desired from the Student Motivation Kit.

Review & Student Performance

❑ **PowerPoint® Slides.** Use the *Section 22-2 PowerPoint®* slides on the Effective Instruction CD-ROM.

❑ **Section 22-2 Test.** Have students complete the *Section 22-2 Test* on pages 405-406 of this guide. Or, create your own test by using the **Exam***View*® Test Generator found on the **Child & Adult Care Professionals** Effective Instruction CD-ROM.

KEY TERMS

- inclusion
- primary care provider
- early intervention programs
- Individualized Family Service Plan (IFSP)
- Individualized Education Program (IEP)
- accessible

CARE PROVIDER TIP

Preschool children are very curious about wheelchairs and other types of assistive equipment that a child with special needs might use. If a child with a wheelchair or other special equipment is included in the preschool classroom, take some time to explain to the children the purpose of the equipment and allow them to examine the equipment under your supervision. Then tell the children that the special equipment belongs to a certain child and is not for others to use for play.

(Continued on next page)

Answers to Section 22-2 Knowledge Check

1. Combining children with average abilities and children with special needs in the same classroom as much as possible.

2. Inclusion encourages all children to value diversity; teaches them to be compassionate, respectful, and appreciative of those different from themselves; helps children be more comfortable and less fearful of disabilities. Children with special needs learn to function in the real world and provides them with enriching experiences they might otherwise miss.

3. The environment can be easily used by those with disabilities.

MINI LAB *—Answers will vary*.

Answers to Chapter 22 Review & Activities

1. Early intervention programs.

2. The same as other children as much as possible. Each child should be expected to work and learn to the best of their individual ability.

3. Make sure pathways are wide and clear and include ramps for use along with stairs.

4. To assist a child with attention or help during basic care routines or curriculum activities.

5. Help teachers understand their child's specific needs by explaining past and current development; share ways to help their child respond. Teachers can refer parents to helpful support organizations and include them in their child's program.

6. Current level of the child's abilities, annual goals for the child's development, short-term educational goals, educational services to be provided, degree to which the child will be included in a regular classroom, the procedure for determining whether the plan's goals are being met.

7. Learning and teaching with all senses. Keep classroom furniture arrangement the same or give tours when furniture is moved, offer written text that is in large print or written in Braille, seat children closer to the teacher for better visibility.

8. This federal law states that children who have disabilities must be educated with children who are not disabled whenever possible.

9. A learning disability relates to problems a child has with processing information—concepts can still be learned but in different ways than typical. In mental impairment, the extent of thinking and learning ability is diminished.

10. They should be given more time because they often enjoy detailed projects and fully investigate activities.

Answers to Section 22-2 Test

Matching:

1. E
2. H
3. D
4. G
5. F
6. A

Short Answer:

7. In the natural environment, in which they can learn from positive role models.

8. The Easter Seals organization. Volunteers, training programs, and special funding also may be available through community resources.

9. Positive attitudes among care providers.

10. They should be treated like any other child.

11. Public school administrators, parents, teachers, and specialists.

12. *Any three from list on page 506.*

13. Avoid planning separate activities for children with special needs whenever possible. Plan activities in which all children can participate.

14. Allow for extra time when planning the schedule.

15. Request specific written instructions from parents to meet these needs.

WORKPLACE CHALLENGE *—Call 911 immediately; gently guide the child safely to the floor until emergency help arrives; a qualified staff person should administer needed first aid until emergency staff arrives; so treatment can be quickly and safely provided, keep multiple copies of a child's vital information in a handy file and give medical personnel a copy of the sheet; provide a parent-signed emergency medical treatment waiver, in case the child is transported to a hospital for further care.*

Child & Adult Care Professionals Instructor Resource Guide
Copyright © Glencoe/McGraw-Hill

INSTRUCTIONAL PLAN ━━━━━━━━━━━━━━━━━━━━━━━

Physical Care of Older Adults

FOCUS & PLANNING

Section Objectives

❏ Identify changes in older adults that may lead to the need for care.

❏ Explain chronic health conditions and how these impact activities of daily living.

❏ Summarize the role of older-adult care providers in meeting the physical needs of older adults.

Instruction & Student Practice

❏ **Reading.** Have students read *Section 23-1* on text pages 511-518. Assign the *Section 23-1 Knowledge Check* and *Mini Lab.*

❏ **Assess a Film Clip.** After viewing a movie that has an older adult main character, such as *Driving Miss Daisy*, have students assess the increased physical care needed by the older adults.

❏ **Journal Entry.** Have students respond to the issue of an older adult's need for assistance versus independence by answering the question, "How much help is too much help?"

❏ **Lab Manual.** Assign *Lab Activity 84* on page 167 and *Lab Activity 85* on page 169 of the Lab Manual.

❏ **Child & Adult Care Study Guides.** Assign *Study Guide 23-1* from the Student Motivation Kit.

❏ **Child & Adult Care Applications.** Assign *Activities 67, 69, 78, 79, 80,* and *83* to *89* as desired from the Student Motivation Kit.

❏ **Child & Adult Care Observations.** Assign *Observations OA-2, OA-3, OA-14,* and *OA-16* to *OA-19* as desired from the Student Motivation Kit.

❏ **Activity Cards for Older Adults.** Assign *Activity Cards OA-40* to *OA-47* as desired from the Student Motivation Kit.

❏ **Child & Adult Care Career Profiles.** Assign *Career Profiles* as desired from the Student Motivation Kit.

Review & Student Performance

❏ **PowerPoint® Slides.** Use the *Section 23-1 PowerPoint®* slides on the Effective Instruction CD-ROM.

❏ **Section 23-1 Test.** Have students complete the *Section 23-1 Test* on pages 407-408 of this guide. Or, create your own test by using the **Exam** *View®* Test Generator found on the ***Child & Adult Care Professionals*** Effective Instruction CD-ROM.

KEY TERMS

- **chronic**
- **functional ability**
- **functionally dependent**
- **learned helplessness**

CARE PROVIDER TIP

An older adult's physical needs are interrelated with health issues and socio-emotional needs. Healthy older adults who remain physically and socially active may need little physical care.

(Continued on next page)

Answers to Section 23-1 Knowledge Check

1. Characteristics include gradual reductions in functions of internal organs, gradual decrease in muscle mass, and a decrease in bone density.
2. *Any two:* High blood pressure, obesity, high cholesterol, arthritis, heart disease, or hearing problems.
3. The ability of older adults to take care of themselves and manage their environments.

(**MINI LAB**)—*Answers will vary.*

Answers to Section 23-1 Test

Matching:
1. B   3. D
2. C   4. F

Short Answer:
5. One in five.
6. Cardiovascular disease.
7. They have reduced immune functioning.
8. A blood clot restricts blood flow in the heart.
9. The 140 represents the systolic blood pressure—the pressure when the heart muscle contracts. The 90 represents the diastolic blood pressure—the pressure when the heart muscles relax.
10. Heart disease, a broken hip, and loss of vision.
11. Activities of daily living, or ADLs.
12. Increased social isolation and loss of balance, which increases the risk of falling.
13. The type of assistance required and how the assistance should be offered.
14. Understand what people want and are able to do themselves, offer encouragement, and offer grooming assistance when asked for by older adults.
15. Ask if the person would like to take your arm, let the person know where your arm is, walk at the person's pace, and give verbal instructions as you walk.

(**WORKPLACE CHALLENGE**)—Whether the chronic illness affects a person's ability to function independently; whether the older adult is able to manage his or her daily tasks alone; whether the older adult requires some assistance; if the older adult needs assistance, how much and what type of help he or she needs; what kind of help the older adult needs to manage activities of daily living.

INSTRUCTIONAL PLAN ───────────────────────────────

Social, Emotional & Cognitive Care of Older Adults

Section **23-2**

FOCUS & PLANNING

Section Objectives

❑ Describe the social, emotional, mental, and cognitive care needs of older adults.

❑ Summarize theories associated with the social changes of aging.

❑ Identify ways to meet the social needs of older adults.

❑ Identify special emotional needs of older adults.

❑ Utilize care provider techniques promoting positive emotional health of older adults.

❑ Determine the impact of family support on the emotional well-being of older adults.

Instruction & Student Practice

❑ **Reading.** Have students read *Section 23-2* on text pages 519-529. Assign the *Section 23-2 Knowledge Check* and *Mini Lab*.

❑ **Service Learning.** Plan a game afternoon for an adult day care center. Have pairs of students play games with the older adults. Serve simple refreshments, such as lemonade and popcorn.

❑ **Lab Manual.** Assign *Lab Activity 86* on page 170 of the Lab Manual.

❑ **Child & Adult Care Study Guides.** Assign *Study Guide 23-2* from the Student Motivation Kit.

❑ **Child & Adult Care Applications.** Assign *Activities 28* to *32* and 67 to *91* as desired from the Student Motivation Kit.

❑ **Child & Adult Care Observations.** Assign *Observations OA-2* to *OA-22* as desired from the Student Motivation Kit.

❑ **Activity Cards for Older Adults.** Assign *Activity Cards OA-1* to *OA-10* and *OA-31* to *OA-39* as desired from the Student Motivation Kit.

❑ **Child & Adult Care Career Profiles.** Assign *Career Profiles* as desired from the Student Motivation Kit.

Review & Student Performance

❑ **PowerPoint® Slides.** Use the *Section 23-2 PowerPoint®* slides on the Effective Instruction CD-ROM.

❑ **Section 23-2 Test.** Have students complete the *Section 23-2 Test* on pages 409-410 of this guide. Or, create your own test by using the **Exam**View® Test Generator found on the **Child & Adult Care Professionals** Effective Instruction CD-ROM.

KEY TERMS

- **continuity theory**
- **engagement**
- **formal support**
- **informal support**
- **intergenerational support**
- **cognitive ability**
- **depression**
- **anxiety**
- **grief**
- **assessment**
- **consumer-directed care**

CARE PROVIDER TIP

Many older adults are too proud to ask for help. Family members and care providers need to carefully balance allowing adults to help themselves and giving the help needed to maintain quality of life. This balance allows the adult to feel independent and in control of his or her life.

(Continued on next page)

INSTRUCTIONAL PLAN *Continued*

Answers to Section 23-2 Knowledge Check

1. Individualized support, interaction with others, support of friends and family, and social activities.

2. Cognitive impairment; difficulty performing complex tasks, such as managing finances; eventual difficulty performing simple tasks, such as eating.

3. Having feelings of sadness, hopelessness, helplessness, and worthlessness over a period of time. Symptoms include feeling and acting sad or blue, loss of interest in activities, sleeping too much or too little, overeating, feelings of guilt and worthlessness, agitation or extreme lack of emotion, inability to concentrate, thoughts of suicide.

MINI LAB —*Activities and answers will vary.*

Answers to Chapter 23 Review & Activities

1. *Activities of daily living:* Tasks related to self-care, such as bathing, dressing, toileting, and eating; *instrumental activities of daily living:* Tasks related to home care, such as shopping, doing light housework, managing money, and using the phone.

2. Increased risk of disease and a decrease in functions of internal organs, bone density, muscle mass, and strength.

3. Emotional needs: the need for family support and the support of friends to decrease loneliness and depression; social needs: interacting with others and engaging in social activities.

4. They help older adults with daily tasks, participate in activities with older adults, and help older adults deal with loss of a loved one.

5. As people age, specific health concerns arise, such as diabetes, high blood pressure, and osteoporosis.

6. Arthritis, cancer, diabetes, high blood pressure, and osteoporosis.

7. Older adults prefer to remain independent and maintain their dignity, so care providers need to understand what tasks older adults can perform and allow them to do as much on their own as possible.

8. Sensory impairment, such as hearing and vision loss, can affect older adults' functional ability and social interaction.

9. Maintain the balance between helping too much and not helping enough.

10. A decrease in the ability to think, problem solve, reason, and learn. Older adults might fear what were otherwise normal activities, such as shopping, managing finances, and interacting with others.

Answers to Section 23-2 Test

Matching:

1. D	6. C
2. F	7. B
3. G	8. E
4. I	9. A
5. J	10. H

Short Answer:

11. Assessment.

12. Social, emotional, mental, and cognitive needs.

13. Would you like a little time to yourself? What would you like to do this afternoon? You seem unusually quiet. Is anything wrong?

14. Reassure older adults that they enjoy their work and the time they spend with them.

15. Offer valuable social and emotional support, as well as physical support.

16. Dancing, yoga, and tai chi chuan.

17. Older adults can maintain memory and concentration and build friendships.

18. Cognitive impairment—such as Alzheimer's disease, depression, and anxiety.

19. Provide an opportunity to talk about the loss.

20. Helps keep the mind sharp.

WORKPLACE CHALLENGE —Tell them you know they are trying; simplify things; when appropriate, keep important items where they can be found easily; use routines; make lists.

Child & Adult Care Professionals Instructor Resource Guide
Copyright © Glencoe/McGraw-Hill

INSTRUCTIONAL PLAN ═══════════════════════════

Teaching Children

FOCUS & PLANNING

Section Objectives

- ❏ Describe principles related to how children learn.
- ❏ Explain the role of play in children's learning.
- ❏ Describe the characteristics of different learning styles.
- ❏ Summarize the concept of multiple intelligences.
- ❏ Explain how grouping of children affects teaching.

Instruction & Student Practice

- ❏ **Reading.** Have students read *Section 24-1* on text pages 533-539. Assign the *Section 24-1 Knowledge Check* and *Mini Lab*.

- ❏ **Evaluate Learning.** Assign teams of students a toy and have them, using the principles listed in the text, evaluate how a child could learn by playing with the toy.

- ❏ **Debate Groupings.** Have student teams research and debate the pros and cons of same-age, developmental, and multi-age groupings.

- ❏ **Lab Manual.** Assign *Lab Activity 87* on page 171 and *Lab Activity 88* on page 173 of the Lab Manual.

- ❏ **Child & Adult Care Study Guides.** Assign *Study Guide 24-1* from the Student Motivation Kit.

- ❏ **Child & Adult Care Applications.** Assign *Activities 19, 23, 37, 49, 50, 51, 52, 53, 100, 101, 102,* and *108* from the Student Motivation Kit.

- ❏ **Child & Adult Care Observations.** Assign *Observations C-14, C-15, C-22, C-23,* and *C-25* from the Student Motivation Kit.

- ❏ **Activity Cards for Children.** Assign *Activity Cards C-27 to C-96* as desired from the Student Motivation Kit.

- ❏ **Child & Adult Care Career Profiles.** Assign *Career Profiles* as desired from the Student Motivation Kit.

Review & Student Performance

- ❏ **PowerPoint® Slides.** Use the *Section 24-1 PowerPoint®* slides on the Effective Instruction CD-ROM.

- ❏ **Section 24-1 Test.** Have students complete the *Section 24-1 Test* on pages 411-412 of this guide. Or, create your own test by using the **Exam***View*® Test Generator found on the *Child & Adult Care Professionals* Effective Instruction CD-ROM.

KEY TERMS

- manipulatives
- intelligence quotient
- multiple intelligences
- facilitate
- teachable moments
- open-ended materials
- close-ended materials

CARE PROVIDER TIP

Inexperienced teachers of young children often try to teach as they are taught as adults. The experienced teacher understands that children learn only when they are involved in the process and the teacher assumes the role of the facilitator.

(Continued on next page)

Answers to Section 24-1 Knowledge Check

1. Intelligence quotient operates on the premise that one number from a test can represent overall intelligence. Multiple intelligences' premise is that different people have different types of intelligences that cannot be presented by results of one test.

2. Some children are more expressive, others more quiet. Some children are visual learners, such as by watching others, looking at pictures in a book, or seeing a video. Others learn more naturally through listening and language activities. Some children like to jump in and experiment in a new activity, while others wait for step-by-step instruction. Individual and small-group learning is best for some children; however, other children bloom in larger groups. They enjoy performing and participating with others.

3. Paints and dough and other art materials, water and sand toys, blocks.

MINI LAB —*Observations and answers will vary.*

Answers to Section 24-1 Test

Matching:

1. G   5. J
2. F   6. I
3. H   7. A
4. D

Short Answer:

8. Because at birth, only about 25 percent of the brain's learning pathways are developed.

9. *Any four:* Children learn best by doing; children learn best when using their senses; children often learn through trial and error; children learn best when all areas of development are nurtured; children learn through positive reinforcement; children acquire and experiment with new behaviors through imitation and role modeling.

10. He believes that people vary in terms of intelligence and learning strength and that individual intelligence varies just as learning styles do.

11. Same-age grouping, developmental grouping, and mixed-age grouping.

12. The amount of personal attention an activity requires.

13. Groups should be small enough to prevent overcrowding.

14. This approach gives children a chance to be creative and independent.

15. Open-ended materials allow children to creatively develop independence, language skills, decision-making and problem-solving skills, and imagination. In contrast, close-ended materials help children learn how to follow directions and help develop sensory perception and motor skills.

WORKPLACE CHALLENGE —*Answers will vary.*

Child & Adult Care Professionals Instructor Resource Guide
Copyright © Glencoe/McGraw-Hill

INSTRUCTIONAL PLAN ═══════════════════════════════

Curriculum Planning for Children

Section **24-2**

FOCUS & PLANNING

Section Objectives

❑ Describe the qualities of a strong curriculum.
❑ Create a lesson plan.
❑ Describe approaches to teaching.
❑ Explain the impact of teaching style on learning.

Instruction & Student Practice

❑ **Reading.** Have students read *Section 24-2* on text pages 540-548. Assign the *Section 24-2 Knowledge Check* and *Mini Lab.*

❑ **Write Objectives.** Have students practice writing objectives for activities by connecting what the child will do with the area of development.

❑ **Project Plan.** Have teams of students plan curriculum using the project approach. Students should be certain to select a project that is of interest to a variety of children, involve the children in the planning process, and consider all points listed in the text.

❑ **Theme Unit Plan.** Have students plan a weekly unit around a theme. Have them contrast the theme and project approaches.

❑ **Lab Manual.** Assign *Lab Activity 89* on page 175 and *Lab Activity 90* on page 176 of the Lab Manual.

❑ **Child & Adult Care Study Guides.** Assign *Study Guide 24-2* from the Student Motivation Kit.

❑ **Child & Adult Care Applications.** Assign *Activities 19, 23, 37, 49, 50, 51, 52, 53, 100, 101,* and *102* from the Student Motivation Kit.

❑ **Child & Adult Care Observations.** Assign *Observations C-13, C-14, C-15, C-22,* and *C-23* from the Student Motivation Kit.

❑ **Activity Cards for Children.** Assign *Activity Cards C-27 to C-96* as desired from the Student Motivation Kit.

❑ **Child & Adult Care Career Profiles.** Assign *Career Profiles* as desired from the Student Motivation Kit.

Review & Student Performance

❑ **PowerPoint® Slides.** Use the *Section 24-2 PowerPoint®* slides on the Effective Instruction CD-ROM.

❑ **Section 24-2 Test.** Have students complete the *Section 24-2 Test* on pages 413-414 of this guide. Or, create your own test by using the **Exam***View®* Test Generator found on the **Child & Adult Care Professionals** Effective Instruction CD-ROM.

KEY TERMS

- **curriculum**
- **developmentally appropriate curriculum**
- **objectives**
- **Bloom's Taxonomy**
- **project approach**
- **Reggio Emilia Approach**
- **theme**
- **lesson plan**
- **open-ended questions**

CARE PROVIDER TIP

In order to learn and to improve skills for teaching young children, it is important to evaluate approaches and activities. The best time to evaluate is immediately after an activity is used while the results are fresh in the mind. When evaluating, answer such questions as these: "Did I meet my objectives?" "Was the activity developmentally appropriate?" "What would I do differently next time?"

(Continued on next page)

Answers to Section 24-2 Knowledge Check

1. Developmentally appropriate curriculum refers to activities that are geared to children's individual stage and rate of development and their unique abilities.
2. Project approach, Reggio Approach, theme approach.
3. It impacts on how lesson plans are presented to children. Teaching styles of teachers can vary according to children's stage of development or unique personality.

MINI LAB —*Answers will vary*.

Answers to Section 24-2 Test

Matching:

1. B	4. A	7. K
2. C	5. I	8. F
3. G	6. J	9. H

Short Answer:

10. Well-planned activities.
11. Goals that relate to all areas of development.
12. Interdependent relationships.
13. The program director.
14. Grouping children; project goals; use of resources; field trips; gathering, organizing, and representing information; assessing the project.
15. The theme is selected by the care provider, rather than based on children's interest.
16. Encourage children's basic learning skills.
17. Art construction, drawing, modeling with clay, building with blocks, dictating stories, making books, and putting on plays and puppet shows.
18. Major learning theories.
19. A care provider often plans activities that fit with his or her teaching style.
20. Children have chances to learn in different ways, adapt to varied situations, and respect diversity.

WORKPLACE CHALLENGE —Look at books on the topic of pets; allow children's pets to visit the classroom with parents; bring in resources that relate to the topic, such as photos of children's pets; invite a special visitor, such as a veterinarian, into the classroom to explain pet care; include a trip to a pet store, the animal humane society, or a pet breeder.

INSTRUCTIONAL PLAN

Teaching Older Adults

FOCUS & PLANNING

Section Objectives

- ❑ Describe older adult learners.
- ❑ Identify learning styles of older adults.
- ❑ Determine ways to treat adult learners.

Instruction & Student Practice

- ❑ **Reading.** Have students read *Section 24-3* on text pages 549-553. Assign the *Section 24-3 Knowledge Check* and *Mini Lab.*

- ❑ **Learning Styles.** Have teams of students select a topic that would be of interest to many older adults and describe how to teach the concepts using all learning styles.

- ❑ **Motivating Adults.** Have students examine the motivational ideas that stimulate interest among the participants at their work site and report to the class.

- ❑ **Program Assessment.** Have students devise a four- to five-question interview form to use informally with older adults who have participated in a program. Have students use the information to assess the retention and transfer of learning.

- ❑ **Lab Manual.** Assign *Lab Activity 91* on page 177 of the Lab Manual.

- ❑ **Child & Adult Care Study Guides.** Assign *Study Guide 24-3* from the Student Motivation Kit.

- ❑ **Child & Adult Care Applications.** Assign *Activities 31, 81, 82,* and *83* from the Student Motivation Kit.

- ❑ **Child & Adult Care Observations.** Assign *Observations OA-2, OA-4, OA-5,* and *OA-6* as desired from the Student Motivation Kit.

- ❑ **Activity Cards for Older Adults.** Assign *Activity Cards OA-1* to *OA-10* as desired from the Student Motivation Kit.

- ❑ **Child & Adult Care Career Profiles.** Assign *Career Profiles* as desired from the Student Motivation Kit.

Review & Student Performance

- ❑ **PowerPoint® Slides.** Use the *Section 24-3 PowerPoint®* slides on the Effective Instruction CD-ROM.

- ❑ **Section 24-3 Test.** Have students complete the *Section 24-3 Test* on pages 415-416 of this guide. Or, create your own test by using the **Exam***View®* Test Generator found on the **Child & Adult Care Professionals** Effective Instruction CD-ROM.

KEY TERMS

- **reinforcement**
- **retention**
- **transfer learning**

CARE PROVIDER TIP

Older adults may participate in educational programs more for the socialization than for the information. Serving refreshments, allowing time for discussion, and building on past experiences are ideas to provide the socialization.

(Continued on next page)

Answers to Section 24-3 Knowledge Check

1. Environmental learners, auditory learners, visual learners, and kinesthetic learners.
2. Factors that motivate adults to learn include social relationships, authoritarian expectations, social welfare, personal advancement, ability to change routine, and cognitive interest.
3. Older adults should be treated with dignity and respect. Whenever possible, care providers should provide opportunities for them to share their viewpoints and knowledge.

MINI LAB—*Answers will vary.*

Answers to Section 24-3 Test

Matching:
1. D
2. E
3. F

Short Answer:
4. Problem solving.
5. The interests of the older adults and the cultural differences of the participants.
6. Their experience, skills, and knowledge.
7. Self-directed learning, goal-oriented learning, applicable learning, practical learning.
8. *Any two:* Care providers should give detailed information about learning topics; tailor activities to the culture, age, and gender of older adults; present information in a way that older adults can process easily; use hands-on materials and visuals.
9. *Any three:* Social relationships, authoritarian expectations, social welfare, personal advancement, ability to change routines, cognitive interest.
10. Hands-on materials.
11. Enough time to learn and practice new skills; limited environmental distractions.
12. Retention depends on how much they originally learned.
13. Provide training, practice, and support.
14. When older adults relate new information to something they already know.
15. Skills and information that is useful to them.

WORKPLACE CHALLENGE—*Answers will vary.*

INSTRUCTIONAL PLAN

Program Planning for Older Adults

Section **24-4**

FOCUS & PLANNING

Section Objectives

❏ Identify the characteristics of developmentally appropriate programs for older adults.

❏ Identify various types of activities for older adults, including intergenerational activities.

❏ Determine the characteristics of effective program planning.

❏ Describe the use of facilitation with older adult learners.

Instruction & Student Practice

❏ **Reading.** Have students read *Section 24-4* on text pages 554-559. Assign the *Section 24-4 Knowledge Check* and *Mini Lab.*

❏ **Program Planning.** Have students search the Internet for topics that may be of interest to older adults. Students should find local resources related to the topics and report to the class potential program ideas.

❏ **Lesson Activity.** Have students plan and lead a lesson activity for a group of older adults at an adult center. Have students evaluate the lesson in their journals.

❏ **Lab Manual.** Assign *Lab Activity 92* on page 178 of the Lab Manual.

❏ **Child & Adult Care Study Guides.** Assign *Study Guide 24-4* from the Student Motivation Kit.

❏ **Child & Adult Care Applications.** Assign *Activities 31, 81, 82, 83,* and *90* from the Student Motivation Kit.

❏ **Child & Adult Care Observations.** Assign *Observations OA-2, OA-4,* and *OA-13* as desired from the Student Motivation Kit.

❏ **Activity Cards for Older Adults.** Assign *Activity Cards OA-1* to *OA-10* as desired from the Student Motivation Kit.

❏ **Child & Adult Care Career Profiles.** Assign *Career Profiles* as desired from the Student Motivation Kit.

Review & Student Performance

❏ **PowerPoint® Slides.** Use the *Section 24-4 PowerPoint®* slides on the Effective Instruction CD-ROM.

❏ **Section 24-4 Test.** Have students complete the *Section 24-4 Test* on pages 417-418 of this guide. Or, create your own test by using the **Exam***View®* Test Generator found on the ***Child & Adult Care Professionals*** Effective Instruction CD-ROM.

KEY TERMS

• **activity plan**
• **facilitation**

CARE PROVIDER TIP

The care provider's voice and presentation style may contribute as much to the older adults' enjoyment of programs as the content. Since many older adults have difficulty hearing, they appreciate a care provider who speaks slowly in a low voice. They also like care providers who relate the information to their many life experiences.

(Continued on next page)

Answers to Section 24-4 Knowledge Check

1. Increase self-esteem, create opportunities for learning at every stage of development, promote physical and mental health, and foster mutual respect for all ethnic groups.

2. Games, clubs, and cards; arts and crafts; fitness and exercise.

3. Direct instruction tells learners new knowledge as they listen and provides all content to the learner. Facilitation allows learners to discover new knowledge through questioning, probing, and hands-on experiences.

MINI LAB — *Observations and answers will vary.*

Answers to Chapter 24 Review & Activities

1. Children learn best by doing and using their senses, through trial and error and positive reinforcement, and when all developmental areas are nurtured and they can experiment with new behaviors.

2. Intelligence quotient is the ratio between mental age and chronological to represent overall intelligence. Multiple intelligences states that different people have different types of intelligences that cannot be represented by one test.

3. *Any three:* Stimulating, varied, not repetitive, captures children's interest, balanced to include activities for all areas of development and subjects.

4. For young children, learning is play.

5. A project refers to an in-depth investigation of a specific topic. The project topic is decided on by both children and teachers and stems from children's interests and questions. A theme is one central topic selected by the teacher. Teachers think of, plan, gather resources, and conduct activities.

6. Age group, activity title, objectives, procedures, materials required, evaluation.

7. *Open-ended* materials are items that can be used in a variety of ways, with no single "correct" outcome expected. Examples include paints and dough. *Close-ended* materials are used in primarily one way, with an expected result. Examples: puzzles, matching games, snap beads.

8. Visual learners learn best by visual illustrations or demonstrations. Kinesthetic learners learn best when they can touch and feel materials.

9. *See Fig. 24-27 on page 558.*

10. Direct instruction tells learners new knowledge as they listen and provides all the content to the learner. Facilitation allows learners to discover new knowledge through questioning, probing, and hands-on experiences.

Answers to Section 24-4 Test

Short Answer:

1. *Any four from the list on page 554.*

2. *Any two:* Observe, note any changes in the older adults during activities; respond to changes to ensure learning continues; be flexible and make changes if an activity is not working; offer activity choices.

3. Planning and presenting the activities.

4. The information that older adults want to know and how they best learn.

5. When they help to create and select activities.

6. Making activities pleasurable and satisfying and addressing cultural and personal interests.

7. *Any five from the list on page 557.*

8. Learning opportunities; time; resources; learners; learning experiences; and content outline.

9. Gardening activities build motivation, stimulate cognitive thinking, help manage stress, and create a positive environment for older adults.

10. They promote learning and meet the needs of youth, older adults, and communities.

11. *See list on page 557.*

12. Gather together a group of older adults, which represents the ages of all program participants. The group does some brainstorming, and the coordinator then guides the group in planning the activities.

13. Humor helps learners relax, and it helps build relationships among older adults.

14. Encourage older adults to work in groups.

15. By being involved.

WORKPLACE CHALLENGE —Document what occurred during the activity; reflect on and write about the activity; were objectives met; did the activity support the overall program goal; encourage older adults to write a news release about the event.

INSTRUCTIONAL PLAN

Developing Language Skills

Section 25-1

FOCUS & PLANNING

Section Objectives

- ❏ Explain how the early childhood environment can promote development of language skills.
- ❏ Plan a language arts learning center for preschoolers.
- ❏ Assess the suitability of specific books for children.
- ❏ Demonstrate the ability to read a story effectively to preschoolers.
- ❏ Explain how to prepare children for reading and writing.
- ❏ Plan and lead language arts activities.

Instruction & Student Practice

- ❏ **Reading.** Have students read *Section 25-1* on text pages 563-570. Assign the *Section 25-1 Knowledge Check* and *Mini Lab*.
- ❏ **Write Dictated Stories.** Have students write stories that children dictate to them. Students should ask the children to illustrate their stories and include the stories in the children's portfolios.
- ❏ **Reading to Children.** After students have practiced story-reading skills, videotape them reading to a group of children. Have each student watch the tape to evaluate his or her skills.
- ❏ **Lab Manual.** Assign *Lab Activity 93* on page 179 of the Lab Manual.
- ❏ **Child & Adult Care Study Guides.** Assign *Study Guide 25-1* from the Student Motivation Kit.
- ❏ **Child & Adult Care Applications.** Assign *Activities 14, 20, 21, 54, 55, 56, 57, 58,* and *59* from the Student Motivation Kit.
- ❏ **Child & Adult Care Observations.** Assign *Observations C-14, C-31,* and *C-32* from the Student Motivation Kit.
- ❏ **Activity Cards for Children.** Assign *Activity Cards C-41* to *C-49* as desired from the Student Motivation Kit.
- ❏ **Child & Adult Care Career Profiles.** Assign *Career Profiles* as desired from the Student Motivation Kit.

Review & Student Performance

- ❏ **PowerPoint® Slides.** Use the *Section 25-1 PowerPoint®* slides on the Effective Instruction CD-ROM.
- ❏ **Section 25-1 Test.** Have students complete the *Section 25-1 Test* on pages 419-420 of this guide. Or, create your own test by using the **Exam***View*® Test Generator found on the ***Child & Adult Care Professionals*** Effective Instruction CD-ROM.

KEY TERMS

- language arts
- bilingual children
- emergent literacy
- print-rich environment
- whole language
- auditory discrimination
- finger plays
- visual discrimination
- invented spelling

CARE PROVIDER TIP

When reading to a group of children, it is best not to ask questions until the end of the story. If the reader pauses to ask questions during the story, all children will want to contribute and the continuity of the story will be lost.

(Continued on next page)

Answers to Section 25-1 Knowledge Check

1. Listening, speaking, reading, and writing.

2. A setting that uses printed materials throughout the classroom in meaningful ways.

3. They have large, often full-page illustrations; each page has anything from no words to a few sentences; the plot is simple, so it can be told in pictures; the words and pictures are matched carefully.

MINI LAB *—Activities and answers will vary.*

Answers to Section 25-1 Test

Matching:

1. G	4. H	7. E
2. C	5. K	8. J
3. D	6. B	9. F

Short Answer:

10. Encourage children's interest, instill confidence in them, and help them develop coordination and small motor skills.

11. *Any three:* Use language during mealtimes to describe food, practice good manners, and talk about the day's activities; involve children in a letter-writing activity; place toy telephones in the dramatic play center to encourage conversation; tell stories and read books aloud; explain procedures to children; observe and listen to children and then expand their language by asking questions; encourage children to ask their own questions.

12. *Answers will vary, but may include:* When playing restaurant, a print-rich environment would include a telephone book and menus; the science center may include nature books.

13. The library corner, storytelling area, and writing area.

14. *Infants and toddlers:* Books that emphasize words they know, stories about others their own age, animal and vehicle books, and books that have rhythm, rhyme, and repetition; *Preschoolers:* Books about familiar characters and experiences—other children, family, and community workers, make-believe books about talking animals, and books with funny situations, surprises, and exaggeration; *School-agers:* Books vary according to interests, books about nature, science, community life, fantasy and humorous books.

15. *Any three:* Sound-matching games; finger plays, nursery rhymes, and songs; sharing time; puppetry and dramatic play; flannel board play.

16. Small motor skills impact the strength of thumb and fingers that in turn control the writing tool.

17. Printing their names on paintings, name tags, and cubbies.

18. *Any two:* Playing with dough or clay, playing with manipulative toys, using safety scissors, crayons, markers, and paintbrushes.

19. Stringing beads and working puzzles.

20. Be patient with the child; ask the child to read it to you.

WORKPLACE CHALLENGE *—Any five:* Prepare by selecting an appropriate book and reading it aloud several times to yourself; as children seat themselves, do a simple hand game, chant, or sing songs until they settle; be certain that all children can see the book; introduce the story with an interesting technique or prop to capture interest; show children the jacket cover and ask them if they can guess what the story will be about; read the book title and the name of the author and illustrator before beginning to read; hold the book open beside you, facing the children as you read; read with expression and enthusiasm and use different voices for story characters; whisper, talk louder, or include a child's name in the story to keep the group's attention; occasionally move back and forth from the book to children to maintain eye contact.

INSTRUCTIONAL PLAN ━━━━━━━━━━━━━━━━━━━━

Developing Social Responsibility

Section **25-2**

FOCUS & PLANNING

Section Objectives

❑ Identify goals of a social studies curriculum.

❑ Describe areas of study in a social studies curriculum.

❑ Explain how preschoolers can learn about diversity, aging, and environmental issues.

❑ Identify methods of helping children become socially responsible citizens.

❑ Plan and lead social studies activities.

Instruction & Student Practice

❑ **Reading.** Have students read *Section 25-2* on text pages 571-576. Assign the *Section 25-2 Knowledge Check* and *Mini Lab*.

❑ **Parent Involvement.** Have students arrange for parents to visit their work-site center and share information about their occupation or family history. Encourage parents to use props or storybooks to stimulate interest.

❑ **Plan a Lesson.** Have students plan lessons with a cultural theme.

❑ **Lab Manual.** Assign Lab Activity 94 on page 181 of the Lab Manual.

❑ **Child & Adult Care Study Guides.** Assign *Study Guide 25-2* from the Student Motivation Kit.

❑ **Child & Adult Care Applications.** Assign *Activities 10, 14, 20, 39, 41, 42, 43, 98,* and *105* from the Student Motivation Kit.

❑ **Child & Adult Care Observations.** Assign *Observations C-5, C-7, C-21, C-27,* and *C-35* from the Student Motivation Kit.

❑ **Activity Cards for Children.** Assign *Activity Cards C-50* to *C-57* as desired from the Student Motivation Kit.

❑ **Child & Adult Care Career Profiles.** Assign *Career Profiles* as desired from the Student Motivation Kit.

Review & Student Performance

❑ **PowerPoint® Slides.** Use the *Section 25-2 PowerPoint®* slides on the Effective Instruction CD-ROM.

❑ **Section 25-2 Test.** Have students complete the *Section 25-2 Test* on pages 421-422 of this guide. Or, create your own test by using the **Exam**View® Test Generator found on the ***Child & Adult Care Professionals*** Effective Instruction CD-ROM.

KEY TERMS

- **social studies**
- **social responsibility**

CARE PROVIDER TIP

As children become aware of differences in race, they become conscious of skin colors. When questions are asked, care providers should acknowledge the differences and encourage children's acceptance of others.

(Continued on next page)

Answers to Section 25-2 Knowledge Check

1. Family members have different jobs and expectations according to their culture and individual family beliefs, families are the foundation of society, families take care of each other physically and emotionally, and families guide children as they grow into happy, responsible adults.

2. Children should learn to accept basic social skills and responsibilities, ranging from respecting property to voting in elections.

3. Expressing feelings; calmly discussing differing ideas; sharing, trading, or taking turns with toys; compromising and negotiating.

MINI LAB —*Activities and answers will vary.*

Answers to Section 25-2 Test

Short Answer:

1. It teaches children about themselves, their families, communities, and the world.

2. A practice in which people make a positive contribution to the community and obey community laws.

3. By building their self-esteem.

4. By planning activities in which children can succeed, acknowledge children's strengths and positive traits, and provide activities that explore children's likes, abilities, and interests.

5. Understanding and liking oneself.

6. Show respect and appreciation for children's heritage.

7. *Answers will vary, but may include any two:* Read books that include children from a variety of cultures and races; invite special visitors with different cultural backgrounds to visit the classroom; serve ethnic or traditional foods regularly as part of meals, snacks, and cooking activities; provide instruments from different cultures in the music center; play folk songs and other ethnic music; watch a videotape of cultural dances; and teach children simple cultural songs and dances.

8. *Any two:* Children learn about different types of families, such as nuclear and extended families; they learn that family types and roles vary among different cultures; children learn that strong families are the foundation of society; family members take care of each other physically and emotionally and guide children as they grow.

9. When children have little opportunity to interact with older adults.

10. Take a walk around your facility and ask questions about what is seen.

11. Reduce, reuse, and recycle.

12. Children should learn from an early age to accept basic social skills and responsibilities.

13. Include children in making classroom rules that protect individual safety as well as classroom property.

14. Allow children to choose which storybook they would like to hear or what song they would like to sing or choose a class mascot, a favorite video, or a preferred snack.

15. They can water plants, feed pets, and set tables for snack time.

WORKPLACE CHALLENGE —*Any five:* Provide opportunities for children to speak in the language of their choice; employ both male and female care providers who are qualified; include staff and volunteers of varying ages and different cultural backgrounds; include dolls of diverse gender and ethnicity in the dress-up area; give children various ethnic clothes for playing dress up; provide instruments from different cultures to play during music time; hang posters on walls that include children of varying abilities and backgrounds; read children's books that include characters of varying abilities and backgrounds; use recipes from different cultures for classroom cooking projects; in the dramatic play area, include a variety of cooking utensils, such as a wok or tortilla press, for pretend cooking; sing songs from different cultures; play lullabies from different cultures during nap time; make all classroom areas accessible to those with different abilities; participate in continuing education about different cultures and languages, learn about cultural resources in the community, and help support parents' use of two languages in the home.

INSTRUCTIONAL PLAN ━━━━━━━━━━━━━━━━━━━

Social Wellness for Older Adults

Section **25-3**

FOCUS & PLANNING

Section Objectives

❑ Define social well-being.

❑ Describe positive aging.

❑ Develop culturally diverse activities for older adults.

❑ Identify the care provider's role in assisting participants with social and language activities.

Instruction & Student Practice

❑ **Reading.** Have students read *Section 25-3* on text pages 577-581. Assign the *Section 25-3 Knowledge Check* and *Mini Lab.*

❑ **Chart Topics of Interest.** Have students record the favorite conversation topics for a group of older adults at their job site. Have students categorize topics using groupings, such as family, hobbies, current events, the future, the past, and health or financial problems.

❑ **Cooking Activity.** Have each student partner with an older adult from his or her job site, select a food that represents the adult's family history, prepare the food, and share it with other older adults.

❑ **Lab Manual.** Assign *Lab Activity 95* on page 183 of the Lab Manual.

❑ **Child & Adult Care Study Guides.** Assign *Study Guide 25-3* from the Student Motivation Kit.

❑ **Child & Adult Care Applications.** Assign *Activities 8, 82,* and *84* from the Student Motivation Kit.

❑ **Child & Adult Care Observations.** Assign *Observations OA-5, OA-6, OA-7,* and *OA-8* as desired from the Student Motivation Kit.

❑ **Activity Cards for Older Adults.** Assign *Activity Cards* as desired from the Student Motivation Kit.

❑ **Child & Adult Care Career Profiles.** Assign *Career Profiles* as desired from the Student Motivation Kit.

Review & Student Performance

❑ **PowerPoint® Slides.** Use the *Section 25-3 PowerPoint®* slides on the Effective Instruction CD-ROM.

❑ **Section 25-3 Test.** Have students complete the *Section 25-3 Test* on pages 423-424 of this guide. Or, create your own test by using the **Exam***View*® Test Generator found on the ***Child & Adult Care Professionals*** Effective Instruction CD-ROM.

KEY TERMS

• social well-being
• positive aging
• oral history

CARE PROVIDER TIP

Since many older adults may have limited experiences with diverse cultures, it is helpful for care providers hosting ethnic celebrations to relate the cultural food, dance, and traditions to the geography of the native country and history of the people.

(Continued on next page)

Answers to Section 25-3 Knowledge Check

1. Social well-being means having meaningful relationships and maintaining a network of supportive friends.

2. Spending time with friends and family; engaging in activities, such as taking walks, joining social clubs, or participating in fitness programs; eating healthful meals; planning ahead for the times when they may need more help; being allowed to make their own life decisions.

3. Engaging in a cooking project in which people of different cultures can converse about each culture's foods, sewing a quilt that illustrates different cultures, watching cultural movies or plays.

(**MINI LAB**)—*Activities and answers will vary.*

Answers to Section 25-3 Test

Matching:

1. E
2. D
3. B

Short Answer:

4. Experience life's ups and downs with enthusiasm and grace; allows people to maintain positive relationships with others when they experience difficult emotions.

5. Learn to balance daily activities; have compassion for others; dealing with issues of inner peace, and develop a strong sense of personal ethics.

6. Refer them to consumer financial counselors who will work with them to get them out of debt.

7. Design activities that promote healthful lifestyles, such as fitness activities or nutrition classes.

8. They have a sense of humor and the ability to understand their needs and how to meet them. They stay mentally and physically active and keep an optimistic attitude about the aging process.

9. Helps them interact with others in a variety of settings.

10. Children learn about history and interesting social behaviors of the past.

11. Conduct an interview with the older adult and record the historical event.

12. While cooking, they might share stories from their past, such as cooking with their parents or their children. As they sew together, they can share stories while they work or describe how cultural stories are sewn into the design of a quilt.

13. Have a sing-along session.

14. Encourage and make arrangements for older adults to go to movies, plays, and tours to explore various cultures.

15. Young children can learn to cook and sew by observing or participating in activities with older adults.

(**WORKPLACE CHALLENGE**)—Suggest they spend time with friends and family; encourage them to take walks; suggest they join a garden club project; encourage them to engage in an enjoyable fitness activity; encourage them to plan ahead for the times when they may need more help and let them make their own life decisions; suggest they eat healthful meals.

INSTRUCTIONAL PLAN ━━━━━━━━━━━━━━━━━━━━

Education & Technology for Older Adults

FOCUS & PLANNING

Section Objectives

- ❏ Describe how technology impacts older adults.
- ❏ Identify various types of assistive technology.
- ❏ Describe ways to incorporate assistive technology into social and language activities.
- ❏ Explain the care provider's role in helping older adults with assistive technology.

Instruction & Student Practice

- ❏ **Reading.** Have students read *Section 25-4* on text pages 582-587. Assign the *Section 25-4 Knowledge Check* and *Mini Lab*.
- ❏ **Role Plays.** Have students act out scenes in which care providers are teaching technology skills to older adults. Have them identify the differences between teaching and facilitating.
- ❏ **Guest Speaker.** Invite a physical or occupational therapist to demonstrate how simple devices can increase the independence of older adults in their homes.
- ❏ **Journal Entry.** Have students write an entry describing how the use of technology may increase the quality of life for older adults.
- ❏ **Child & Adult Care Study Guides.** Assign *Study Guide 25-4* from the Student Motivation Kit.
- ❏ **Child & Adult Care Applications.** Assign *Activities 69* to *77* from the Student Motivation Kit.
- ❏ **Child & Adult Care Observations.** Assign *Observations OA-3, OA-14,* and *OA-22* as desired from the Student Motivation Kit.
- ❏ **Activity Cards for Older Adults.** Assign *Activity Cards OA-31 to OA-39* as desired from the Student Motivation Kit.
- ❏ **Child & Adult Care Career Profiles.** Assign *Career Profiles* as desired from the Student Motivation Kit.

Review & Student Performance

- ❏ **PowerPoint® Slides.** Use the *Section 25-4 PowerPoint®* slides on the Effective Instruction CD-ROM.
- ❏ **Section 25-4 Test.** Have students complete the *Section 25-4 Test* on pages 425-426 of this guide. Or, create your own test by using the **Exam***View*® Test Generator found on the **Child & Adult Care Professionals** Effective Instruction CD-ROM.

KEY TERMS

- • **household automation**
- • **assistive technology**

CARE PROVIDER TIP

Older adults sometimes shy away from the use of assistive devices because they are too proud to admit that they have a disability or they lack confidence in their ability to use the device. It takes considerable patience and encouragement to teach some older adults to be proficient enough with the technology for them to recognize the personal benefits.

(Continued on next page)

Answers to Section 25-4 Knowledge Check

1. Automated teller machine, touch-tone telephone, remote-control and sensor lighting.
2. Equipment and services that allow older adults or people with limitations to continue to independently manage their lives.
3. FM systems, induction loop systems, infrared systems.

MINI LAB —*Activities and answers will vary.*

Answers to Chapter 25 Review & Activities

1. Exposure to daily language used in the home.
2. To communicate well with others through listening, speaking, reading, and writing.
3. *Answers will vary, but may include:* Library corner, storytelling area and writing area. *See pages 565-566 for details.*
4. Social studies teach children about themselves as well as their family, community, community diversity, the environment, and the world beyond home. *See page 571 for goals of social studies.*
5. It is most familiar and most relevant to children's daily lives. They learn best when studying things that are familiar and can be investigated.
6. *Any three:* Read books that include children from a variety of cultures and races; invite special visitors with different cultural backgrounds to the classroom; serve ethnic or traditional foods regularly as part of meals, snacks, and cooking activities; provide instruments from different cultures in the music center; teach children simple cultural songs and dances.
7. Social activity helps older adults with interaction skills and helps them to continue to grow.
8. *Any three*: Cultural foods and crafts, music activities, cultural movies, plays, tours, and outings.
9. Community involvement is a way for people to participate in community projects. It helps older adults to feel fully connected to the community.
10. Equipment and services that allow older adults with limitations to independently manage their lives. *Examples include:* Van conversions and lifts, large-print materials, wheelchair sensing systems, power doors, and full-spectrum lighting.

Answers to Section 25-4 Test

Short Answer:

1. Technology that controls functions in a home.
2. Equipment and services that allow older adults with limitations to manage their lives.

3. Older adults.
4. To communicate with their families and friends to avoid long-distance phone bills; to pay bills, make banking transactions, and purchase medications, groceries, or clothing; to conduct business on their own.
5. Customers can use it to withdraw or deposit money, 24 hours a day, without having to enter the bank.
6. A large-button touch-tone telephone.
7. They help older adults maintain their independence in their own homes, without lowering quality of life.
8. Explain different types of technology to them, reassure them, and instruct them in how to use a new device. Care providers may also need to make technology suggestions regarding appropriate devices to handle health problems.
9. Participating in recreational/leisure activities.
10. They sense when wheelchairs approach and activate lights and open doors.
11. Full-spectrum lighting.
12. Offer a full range of activities that include technology.
13. Provide large-print books, books on tape, and books on CDs and provide assistance to older adults in using the Internet.
14. Keep written instructions, in large print, next to each computer workstation.
15. Debit cards.

WORKPLACE CHALLENGE —Provide specially designed utensils and cutting boards for older adults with limited hand strength; lower cabinets to allow those in wheelchairs to participate; provide large-print calculators, timers and cookbooks to help older adults read and follow instructions; provide flashing devices as timers for older adults with hearing impairments; encourage older adults without special needs to search the Internet for special recipes.

Child & Adult Care Professionals Instructor Resource Guide

INSTRUCTIONAL PLAN ━━━━━━━━━━━━━━━━━━━━

Math Skills for Children

Section **26-1**

FOCUS & PLANNING

Section Objectives

❏ Discuss how math skills are used in children's daily lives.
❏ Describe the goals of math curricula.
❏ Explain how math activities benefit children.
❏ Identify math materials for preschoolers.
❏ Plan math activities.

Instruction & Student Practice

❏ **Reading.** Have students read *Section 26-1* on text pages 591-596. Assign the *Section 26-1 Knowledge Check* and *Mini Lab*.

❏ **Identify Mathematical Vocabulary.** Have students list mathematical vocabulary words. Have them use the vocabulary when facilitating math activities with the children.

❏ **Evaluate Math Materials.** Have students evaluate math materials, such as the ones listed in the text, by identifying the math skills that the materials will help children learn. Students should research the costs of the materials and report to the class.

❏ **Lab Manual.** Assign *Lab Activity 96* on page 185 of the Lab Manual.

❏ **Child & Adult Care Study Guides.** Assign *Study Guide 26-1* from the Student Motivation Kit.

❏ **Child & Adult Care Applications.** Assign *Activity 66* from the Student Motivation Kit.

❏ **Child & Adult Care Observations.** Assign *Observations C-39* and *C-40* as desired from the Student Motivation Kit.

❏ **Activity Cards for Children.** Assign *Activity Cards C-68* to *C-77* as desired from the Student Motivation Kit.

❏ **Child & Adult Care Career Profiles.** Assign *Career Profiles* as desired from the Student Motivation Kit.

Review & Student Performance

❏ **PowerPoint® Slides.** Use the *Section 26-1 PowerPoint®* slides on the Effective Instruction CD-ROM.

❏ **Section 26-1 Test.** Have students complete the *Section 26-1 Test* on pages 435-436 of this guide. Or, create your own test by using the **Exam***View®* Test Generator found on the *Child & Adult Care Professionals* Effective Instruction CD-ROM.

KEY TERMS

- mathematical vocabulary
- seriation
- rote counting
- rational counting
- numerals

CARE PROVIDER TIP

Math is everywhere! High school students think of math as algebra or geometry; however, math for children can be incorporated in art, music, dramatic play, motor development, and story time.

(Continued on next page)

Answers to Section 26-1 Knowledge Check

1. Words that represent numbers, shape, size, or quantities.

2. They teach children about shape and size and weight. Children can match, compare, sort, pattern, and seriate them.

3. Children can use a play cash register and money, weigh and count plastic food, and sort play clothes by color when pretending to do laundry.

MINI LAB —*Activities and answers will vary.*

Answers to Section 26-1 Test

Matching:

1. B
2. G
3. E
4. D
5. C

Short Answer:

6. Between ages five and seven.

7. To provide an environment that encourages the awareness and development of math skills.

8. Hands-on experience with real objects.

9. By observing children as they play, which helps care providers spot any learning problems children might have.

10. Give them colorful paper shapes to use in creating their own designs and patterns and provide shape-matching games, which also help children recognize shapes.

11. Fill a basket with small items and tell each child to pick out a different amount; make counting a physical activity by having children clap their hands, stomp their feet, or jump in place a certain number of times; and make a paper chain calendar, adding a link at the beginning of each day, and have the children count the number of links.

12. Count objects with the child as each object is touched, count steps as the class goes up or down them, and count graham crackers as the child places them on a tray at snack time.

13. Mark bushel baskets with a numeral and have children place the corresponding number of apples in each one; have children shape numerals from clay and then roll small bits of clay into the matching number of balls; take photographs of the children in groups of different sizes and then provide them with numeral cards and have them pair the cards with the pictures showing the same number of children; and when children build with blocks, talk about how many were used.

14. Use charts and bar graphs.

15. Paint numerals on toy cars and have the children race the cars, finishing in numerical order, and have children place leis, each with a different number of flowers, around each other's necks in sequential order.

WORKPLACE CHALLENGE —While at the supermarket, they can learn about shapes, sizes, color, and quantity of foods; back in the classroom, a care provider may help the children create a pretend supermarket in the dramatic play center, they can play with cash registers and pretend money; in the pretend supermarket, they also can weigh plastic vegetables on scales to determine weight and cost.

INSTRUCTIONAL PLAN ━━━━━━━━━━━━━━━━━━

Science Skills for Children

Section **26-2**

FOCUS & PLANNING

Section Objectives

❑ Explain how science activities benefit children.

❑ Describe the goals of science curriculum.

❑ Plan a science learning center for preschoolers.

❑ Explain the care provider's role in making science interesting and enjoyable for children.

❑ Plan and lead science activities.

Instruction & Student Practice

❑ **Reading.** Have students read *Section 26-2* on text pages 597-602. Assign the *Section 26-2 Knowledge Check* and *Mini Lab.*

❑ **Write Scientific Questions.** Have students write open-ended questions that encourage exploration. Have students make a visual posting the questions in the classroom and use the questions when facilitating science activities with children.

❑ **Sensory Activity.** Have students make a dough, clay, or squeezable material to use with children as a sensory activity. Color and scent the dough by adding unsweetened beverage mix.

❑ **Lab Manual.** Assign *Lab Activity 97* on page 187 of the Lab Manual.

❑ **Child & Adult Care Study Guides.** Assign *Study Guide 26-2* from the Student Motivation Kit.

❑ **Child & Adult Care Applications.** Assign *Activity 66* from the Student Motivation Kit.

❑ **Child & Adult Care Observations.** Assign *Observation C-41* as desired from the Student Motivation Kit.

❑ **Activity Cards for Children.** Assign *Activity Cards C-78* to *C-90* as desired from the Student Motivation Kit.

❑ **Child & Adult Care Career Profiles.** Assign *Career Profiles* as desired from the Student Motivation Kit.

Review & Student Performance

❑ **PowerPoint® Slides.** Use the *Section 26-2 PowerPoint®* slides on the Effective Instruction CD-ROM.

❑ **Section 26-2 Test.** Have students complete the Section 26-2 Test on pages 429-430 of this guide. Or, create your own test by using the **Exam** *View®* Test Generator found on the ***Child & Adult Care Professionals*** Effective Instruction CD-ROM.

KEY TERMS

- **sensory table**
- **light table**
- **rebus recipe**

CARE PROVIDER TIP

Safety must be a careful consideration when planning a science activity. Anticipate safety problems and plan to eliminate the potential hazards.

(Continued on next page)

Answers to Section 26-2 Knowledge Check

1. Curiosity and the need to explore.
2. A table with a boxlike, hollow top that can hold water, sand, beans, or other substances for children to explore.
3. Recipe contents and the chemical processes that occur during cooking and baking reflect science.

MINI LAB —*Activities and answers will vary.*

Answers to Section 26-2 Test

Matching:

1. D
2. A
3. C

Short Answer:

4. When care providers set the stage for safe exploration.
5. They guide learning by asking questions to encourage observation, analysis, and problem solving.
6. Open-ended questions.
7. The effect of temperature on objects, the effects of gravity, and how the sun and water help plants grow.
8. *Any three:* Fostering children's appreciation of nature and themselves; encouraging curiosity and providing chances to explore the world; allowing children to investigate the world using their senses; providing children with hands-on experiences that develop basic science concepts; increasing children's ability to observe, describe, classify, see relationships, and solve problems.
9. The care provider must find ways to make the concepts simple and understandable.
10. A hands-on approach.
11. The children's questions or experiences.
12. *Answers will vary, but may include any four:* Show children how to feel their pulse and heartbeat; watch popcorn popping; have children experiment with magnets of different strengths; make a rainbow by spraying water from a garden hose in the sunshine; experiment with foods in a birdfeeder outside the classroom window; make shadows in a darkened room with a flashlight; make static electricity by rubbing a balloon on a woolen cloth.
13. At the back of the room, away from the door and other learning centers.
14. *Answers will vary, but may include any five:* Leaves and twigs, nuts and seeds, shells, fossils, rock and mineral kits, ant farms, aquariums, terrariums, kaleidoscopes, prisms, and color paddles.
15. Test the recipe before having children prepare it.

WORKPLACE CHALLENGE —Using their senses to discover; questioning and thinking; noting relationships, such as cause and effect; noticing similarities and differences in objects, plants, and animals; using experimentation to test and retest scientific principles.

INSTRUCTIONAL PLAN ━━━━━━━━━━━━━━━━ *Section*
Nature & Gardening Activities **26-3**

FOCUS & PLANNING

Section Objectives

❑ Explain how the natural world can be used for nature education.

❑ Discuss what can be learned from studying the natural world.

❑ Plan nature and gardening activities for young children.

Instruction & Student Practice

❑ **Reading.** Have students read *Section 26-3* on text pages 603-608. Assign the *Section 26-3 Knowledge Check* and *Mini Lab.*

❑ **Nature Walk.** Take students on a nature walk at a park, pond, beach, or other appropriate place to gather materials for the children to examine at the nature table. (Note: Do not allow students to disturb habitats for wildlife.)

❑ **Indoor Gardening.** Have students test indoor gardening activities, such as those listed in the text, with groups of children and older adults. Create a display for visitors to view.

❑ **Lab Manual.** Assign *Lab Activity 98* on page 189 of the Lab Manual.

❑ **Child & Adult Care Study Guides.** Assign *Study Guide 26-3* from the Student Motivation Kit.

❑ **Child & Adult Care Applications.** Assign *Activities 49* and *82* from the Student Motivation Kit.

❑ **Child & Adult Care Observations.** Assign *Observations C-14* and *OA-8* as desired from the Student Motivation Kit.

❑ **Activity Cards for Children.** Assign *Activity Cards C-82* to *C-84* as desired from the Student Motivation Kit.

❑ **Activity Cards for Older Adults.** Assign *Activity Cards OA-11* to *OA-20* as desired from the Student Motivation Kit.

❑ **Child & Adult Care Career Profiles.** Assign *Career Profiles* as desired from the Student Motivation Kit.

Review & Student Performance

❑ **PowerPoint® Slides.** Use the *Section 26-3 PowerPoint®* slides on the Effective Instruction CD-ROM.

❑ **Section 26-3 Test.** Have students complete the *Section 26-3 Test* on pages 431-432 of this guide. Or, create your own test by using the **Exam***View*® Test Generator found on *the Child & Adult Care Professionals* Effective Instruction CD-ROM.

KEY TERMS

• **nature education**
• **field guide**
• **birding**

CARE PROVIDER TIP

Create a science table that is interesting and fun to explore. Line the table with nonskid shelving material so that magnifying glasses and other materials do not fall on the floor. Change the natural items frequently and encourage exploration by asking scientific questions.

(Continued on next page)

Answers to Section 26-3 Knowledge Check

1. A magnifying glass for looking closely at flowers, moss, or bird tracks; binoculars to bring wildlife closer; paper sacks, grocery bags, or backpacks to collect nature items for art projects; bug cages to observe insects or worms; a tape recorder to record nature sounds; sketch pad and some colored pencils for drawing nature sights; camera or a camcorder to record nature experiences; identification books to help name flowers, insects, birds, or trees.

2. Field trips, gardening, bird watching, walks, classroom pets.

3. Veterinarian certification of good health and confirmation that no one is allergic to the pet.

MINI LAB —*Activities and answers will vary.*

Answers to Section 26-3 Test

Matching:
1. D
2. C
3. A

Short Answer:

4. To be in tune with the life cycles of things on earth; experiences with natural elements are relaxing.

5. They build lasting memories; learn about forests and streams; develop map and compass reading skills; and learn about hiking and building campfires.

6. Gently touch nature items, such as satiny tree buds, fuzzy pussy willows, silky flower petals, mushy mud, and rough tree bark and talk about how the breeze feels on the skin and hair.

7. *Any three:* Observe the sun and shadows; notice how wind affects pinwheels, wind chimes, banners, kites, and windsocks; discuss types of clouds; watch the rain and its effects; and enjoy snow activities.

8. *Any five:* Magnifying glass; binoculars; paper bags, grocery bags, or backpacks; bug cages; tape recorder; sketch pads and colored pencils; cameras or a camcorder; a field guide; and a first aid kit.

9. Pets allow children to witness basic facts of the natural world up close.

10. They help children and older adults practice compassion and responsibility; having a pet depend on them helps people feel important and needed.

11. An older, well-trained dog.

12. Skills in concentration, observation, and reasoning.

13. Trees and shrubs, a birdbath, and food source.

14. Bees pollinate flowers as they feed; caterpillars feed on plants before turning into butterflies; birds eat flower seeds or carry them to new places; the plant flowers attract insects, on which birds can feed.

15. Reduced risk of cardiovascular disease and of falling, and improved ability to perform daily tasks.

WORKPLACE CHALLENGE —*Any five:* Growing houseplants, experimenting with celery, observing blooming buds, growing green-haired funny faces, creating a mini-greenhouse, making ivy sculptures, growing a pineapple, growing a sweet potato vine.

INSTRUCTIONAL PLAN ━━━━━━━━━━━━━━━━━━━━━━

Finances for Older Adults

Section **26-4**

FOCUS & PLANNING

Section Objectives

❏ Identify how to determine the financial needs of older adults.

❏ Analyze how geriatric care managers or providers can assist older adults with their finances.

❏ Explain the advantages and disadvantages of older adults using debit and credit cards.

❏ Determine ways family members can assist older adults with their finances.

Instruction & Student Practice

❏ **Reading.** Have students read *Section 26-4* on text pages 609-613. Assign the *Section 26-4 Knowledge Check* and *Mini Lab*.

❏ **Guest Speaker.** Have a banker or a daily money manager visit the class and present a simple financial management program suitable for older adults.

❏ **Service Learning.** Have students develop and present an educational program about avoiding fraud and financial abuse.

❏ **Lab Manual.** Assign *Lab Activity 99* on page 191 of the Lab Manual.

❏ **Child & Adult Care Study Guides.** Assign *Study Guide 26-4* from the Student Motivation Kit.

❏ **Child & Adult Care Applications.** Assign *Activity 28* from the Student Motivation Kit.

❏ **Child & Adult Care Observations.** Assign *Observations OA-9* and *OA-11* as desired from the Student Motivation Kit.

❏ **Child & Adult Care Career Profiles.** Assign *Career Profiles* as desired from the Student Motivation Kit.

Review & Student Performance

❏ **PowerPoint® Slides.** Use the *Section 26-4 PowerPoint®* slides on the Effective Instruction CD-ROM.

❏ **Section 26-4 Test.** Have students complete the *Section 26-4 Test* on pages 433-434 of this guide. Or, create your own test by using the **Exam***View*® Test Generator found on the *Child & Adult Care Professionals* Effective Instruction CD-ROM.

KEY TERMS

- daily money manager
- commercial exploitation

CARE PROVIDER TIP

With many older couples, one person manages the financial affairs. If that person dies or becomes disabled, it may be embarrassing for the spouse to ask for help.

(Continued on next page)

Child & Adult Care Professionals Instructor Resource Guide
Copyright © Glencoe/McGraw-Hill

Answers to Section 26-4 Knowledge Check

1. One form of retirement plan that is run by the government.

2. Conduct workshops at the adult day centers, write articles in monthly newsletters that alert family members about programs and activities that can help them with money management, and pay close attention to the spending habits of older adults.

3. Establishing budgets, keeping track of financial records, and balancing checkbooks.

(**MINI LAB**)—*Activities and answers will vary.*

Answers to Chapter 26 Review & Activities

1. *See the list on page 592.*

2. Recognizing shapes, matching, sorting, patterning, counting, creating charts and graphs.

3. Unit blocks, colored pattern chips, peg and pegboards, colored stringing beads of different shapes, interconnecting plastic blocks, colored 1-inch square table blocks, nesting toys, measuring spoons and cups, containers of different sizes, scales, height charts, tape measures and rulers, counters, counting and matching games, play cash register and play money, puzzles, clocks.

4. *See the list on the top of page 598.*

5. Using a variety of hands-on experiences, involving parents and other family members, engaging in cultural activities and using cultural materials.

6. To set the stage for safe exploration; guide children by asking questions that encourage observation, analysis, and problem solving; ask open-ended questions to help focus children's thinking; make the most of teachable moments to spark children's interest in science; and provide science materials and books to satisfy children's curiosity.

7. *Any two:* Teaches how animals live, eat, move, and communicate; shows how to care for animals; helps build compassion and responsibility.

8. They build physical and mental skills, provide opportunities for teamwork and cooperation, and encourage conversation.

9. Invite guest speakers to conduct programs for older adults, help maintain a record-keeping system, pay close attention to spending habits.

10. When older adults are unable to maintain finances.

Answers to Section 26-4 Test

Short Answer:

1. A person who offers financial services, such as budgeting and balancing checkbooks.

2. Because they watch a lot of television and can be overly influenced by advertisements.

3. Their income and their expenses.

4. Financial security and an improved quality of life.

5. Invite guest speakers to conduct programs that assist older adults in using their money wisely.

6. Care providers can create file folders that contain the older adult's financial records.

7. In a fire safe.

8. Knowing that a trusted family member will make decisions for them and carry out their wishes if they are ever unable to do so.

9. Conduct workshops and write articles about money management in monthly newsletters.

10. Pay close attention to older adults' spending habits; review checkbook, bank statements, and canceled checks to help determine the need for money management help.

11. Set up interviews of several candidates.

12. A debit card takes money out of a bank account, whereas a credit card charges the item, and the credit card company later sends a bill.

13. They seek out older adults who are home and then coerce them to make purchases.

14. Care providers can plan and implement programs to help older adults to be aware of schemes.

15. Suggest using color-coding to help older adults easily spot files and expandable files for those who have trouble with small motor skills.

(**WORKPLACE CHALLENGE**)— *Any two:* Have they worked and paid into a retirement plan? Have they worked long enough to receive Social Security income? Do they receive a spouse's Social Security income? Have they put money into a savings plan?

INSTRUCTIONAL PLAN ━━━━━━━━━━━━━━━━━━━━━━━━

Motor Development & Fitness

Section **27-1**

FOCUS & PLANNING

Section Objectives

- ☐ Identify the benefits of movement for children.
- ☐ Plan and lead creative movement activities.
- ☐ Describe the physical skills development for older adults and determine the benefits.
- ☐ Determine the effects of motor development and fitness on activities of daily living.

Instruction & Student Practice

- ☐ **Reading.** Have students read *Section 27-1* on text pages 617-623. Assign the *Section 27-1 Knowledge Check* and *Mini Lab*.
- ☐ **Skill Observation.** Arrange for students to observe the physical skills of preschool children in a mixed-age classroom. Have them compare and contrast the skill development.
- ☐ **Simulation.** Have students practice using a cane or other walking device and write a journal entry describing how the cane helped them physically and how they felt about using it.
- ☐ **Lab Manual.** Assign *Lab Activity 100* on page 193 of the Lab Manual.
- ☐ **Child & Adult Care Study Guides.** Assign *Study Guide 27-1* from the Student Motivation Kit.
- ☐ **Child & Adult Care Applications.** Assign *Activities 60, 61,* and *116* from the Student Motivation Kit.
- ☐ **Child & Adult Care Observations.** Assign *Observations C-42, C-70, OA-75, OA-76, and OA-80* as desired from the Student Motivation Kit.
- ☐ **Activity Cards for Children.** Assign *Activity Cards C-91 to C-96* as desired from the Student Motivation Kit.
- ☐ **Activity Cards for Older Adults.** Assign *Activity Cards OA-41 to OA-47* as desired from the Student Motivation Kit.
- ☐ **Child & Adult Care Career Profiles.** Assign *Career Profiles* as desired from the Student Motivation Kit.

Review & Student Performance

- ☐ **PowerPoint® Slides.** Use the *Section 27-1 PowerPoint®* slides on the Effective Instruction CD-ROM.
- ☐ **Section 27-1 Test.** Have students complete the *Section 27-1 Test* on pages 435-436 of this guide. Or, create your own test by using the **Exam***View®* Test Generator found on the **Child & Adult Care Professionals** Effective Instruction CD-ROM.

(Continued on next page)

KEY TERMS

- **creative movement**
- **gait**
- **locomotion compensation**
- **joint mobilization**

CARE PROVIDER TIP

The importance of movement activities for young children and older adults cannot be emphasized enough. One way for care providers to encourage physical activity during the day is to limit "screen-time." Using computers, playing videos, and watching television are all good examples of screen-time activities.

Answers to Section 27-1 Knowledge Check

1. Creative movement is responding to music or a mental image through physical movement.
2. To help children gradually achieve more advanced skills by providing appropriate experiences.
3. Three physical activities for older adults are stretching, walking, and pool exercise.

MINI LAB —*Activities and answers will vary.*

Answers to Section 27-1 Test

Matching:
1. A
2. C
3. E
4. D

Short Answer:
5. Physical fitness, good coordination, and body tone.
6. Movement activities.
7. Active participation.
8. These activities familiarize children with the parts of their bodies and their range of movement.
9. Vision problems, lack of balance, or other medical factors.
10. Gait and balance problems, visual impairments, and dizziness caused by medication.
11. Slippery surfaces, uneven floors, poor lighting, loose rugs, unstable furniture, and objects on floors.
12. A walking device, such as a cane or a walker.
13. Muscle-challenging activities, such as weight lifting.
14. Stretching in bed by pointing the toes, doing gentle side bends while watching television, and standing on the toes while talking on the telephone.
15. Increased strength, flexibility, and cardiovascular fitness.

WORKPLACE CHALLENGE —*Any two:* Play music with different tempos and have children move parts of their bodies to the beat; encourage expression and creativity in movement by having children dance with props, such as streamers, scarves, grass skirts, leis, boas, pom-poms, veils, and hats; have the children pretend to be sprouting seeds; verbally guide them into pretending to be saplings and then mature, leafy trees.

Child & Adult Care Professionals Instructor Resource Guide

INSTRUCTIONAL PLAN ━━━━━━━━━━━━━━━

Active Play & Recreation

FOCUS & PLANNING

Section Objectives

- ❏ Explain how active play benefits all areas of development.
- ❏ Plan active play learning centers (both indoor and outdoor) for pre-school children.
- ❏ List several ways of ensuring children's safety during active play.
- ❏ Identify some creative resources for active play.
- ❏ Plan and lead active play activities.

Instruction & Student Practice

- ❏ **Reading.** Have students read *Section 27-2* on text pages 624-631. Assign the *Section 27-2 Knowledge Check* and *Mini Lab*.
- ❏ **Field Day.** Have students implement an intergenerational field day for children and adults from centers. Be sure students select a location with plenty of shade and water fountains.
- ❏ **Service Learning.** Have students accompany older adults on a recreational outing sponsored by the adult care center.
- ❏ **Lab Manual.** Assign the *Lab Activity 101* on page 195 and *Lab Activity 102* on page 197 of the Lab Manual.
- ❏ **Child & Adult Care Study Guides.** Assign *Study Guide 27-2* from the Student Motivation Kit.
- ❏ **Child & Adult Care Applications.** Assign *Activities 60, 61,* and *116* from the Student Motivation Kit.
- ❏ **Child & Adult Care Observations.** Assign *Observations C-42, C-43,* and *OA-14* as desired from the Student Motivation Kit.
- ❏ **Activity Cards for Children.** Assign *Activity Cards C-91* to *C-96* as desired from the Student Motivation Kit.
- ❏ **Activity Cards for Older Adults.** Assign *Activity Cards OA-41 to OA-47* as desired from the Student Motivation Kit.
- ❏ **Child & Adult Care Career Profiles.** Assign *Career Profiles* as desired from the Student Motivation Kit.

Review & Student Performance

- ❏ **PowerPoint® Slides.** Use the *Section 27-2 PowerPoint®* slides on the Effective Instruction CD-ROM.
- ❏ **Section 27-2 Test.** Have students complete the *Section 27-2 Test* on pages 437-438 of this guide. Or, create your own test by using the **Exam***View*® Test Generator found on the ***Child & Adult Care Professionals*** Effective Instruction CD-ROM.

(Continued on next page)

KEY TERMS

- active play
- maze
- recreational therapy

CARE PROVIDER TIP

Since obesity among young children is increasing in our country and research shows that childhood obesity may lead to health problems later in life, care providers need to focus upon learning through active play.

Answers to Section 27-2 Knowledge Check

1. Activities that engage children in fun, physical participation.

2. *Physical development:* Muscles become stronger during active play; children develop greater control over their arms and legs and improve motor coordination and balance. *Intellectual development:* Following rules requires intellectual growth; games that require strategy and purposeful action develop children's problem-solving and goal-setting skills. *Emotional development:* Pride, self-confidence, and self-esteem grow; provides a constructive outlet for excess energy, which relieves tension and stress. *Social development:* Learn to work well with others and to abide by the rules; learn to cooperate with others to achieve common goals. Older children who play team sports learn positive character traits, such as fairness, honesty, and doing your best.

3. Fishing, camping, shuffleboard, yard darts, table tennis, walking, water aerobics, and dancing.

MINI LAB —*Activities and answers will vary.*

Answers to Section 27-2 Test

Matching:

1. C
2. A
3. F

Short Answer:

4. Games that require strategy and purposeful action.

5. Self-esteem and self-confidence grow.

6. Move classroom furniture to the edges of the room to make space for active play and use soft, flexible, active play props—such as sponge toys—to prevent damage to classroom materials.

7. Write rules simply and clearly in positive terms and focus on what children can do.

8. Materials should be fun and allow children to experience success alone or in a group.

9. Hopscotch, rim ball, and bowling.

10. Simon says, mirror game, color touch, and freeze tag or statue tag.

11. When they feel tired, short-winded, or are perspiring excessively.

12. They help older adults maintain good health while having fun.

13. Recreational therapy can help restore motor functions and cognitive skills.

14. Increased self-esteem, self-confidence, and independence.

15. Rugby, boxing, and football.

WORKPLACE CHALLENGE —*Any two:* Changes in older adults that result in vision, hearing, balance, coordination, and muscle deficiencies; chronic conditions and how they affect the ability of older adults to exercise safely; psychological and emotional factors and how they can impact an older adult's ability to perform activities; and medical and physical restrictions, such as cardiovascular or mobility problems.

INSTRUCTIONAL PLAN ━━━━━━━━━━━━━━━━━━━━

Self-Expression Through Drama

Section 27-3

FOCUS & PLANNING

Section Objectives

❑ Explain how dramatic play encourages growth and how care providers encourage it.

❑ Plan a dramatic play learning center and dramatic play activities for preschoolers.

❑ Choose items for a prop box.

❑ Explain how to make and use puppets and how children benefit from play with puppets.

❑ Describe intergenerational dramatic storytelling and guidelines for its implementation.

❑ Identify creative self-expression activities for older adults.

Instruction & Student Practice

❑ **Reading.** Have students read *Section 27-3* on text pages 632-637. Assign the *Section 27-3 Knowledge Check* and *Mini Lab*.

❑ **Puppet Workshop.** Have students make puppets that represent favorite storybook characters and use them for storytelling.

❑ **Lab Manual.** Assign the *Lab Activity 101* on page 195 and *Lab Activity 102* on page 197 of the Lab Manual.

❑ **Child & Adult Care Study Guides.** Assign *Study Guide 27-3* from the Student Motivation Kit.

❑ **Child & Adult Care Applications.** Assign *Activities 59* and *64* from the Student Motivation Kit.

❑ **Child & Adult Care Observations.** Assign *Observations C-33, C-34,* and *OA-5* as desired from the Student Motivation Kit.

❑ **Activity Cards for Children.** Assign *Activity Cards C-91* to *C-96* as desired from the Student Motivation Kit.

❑ **Activity Cards for Older Adults.** Assign *Activity Cards OA-41* to *OA-47* as desired from the Student Motivation Kit.

❑ **Child & Adult Care Career Profiles.** Assign *Career Profiles* as desired from the Student Motivation Kit.

Review & Student Performance

❑ **PowerPoint® Slides.** Use the *Section 27-3 PowerPoint®* slides on the Effective Instruction CD-ROM.

❑ **Section 27-3 Test.** Have students complete the *Section 27-3 Test* on pages 439-440 of this guide. Or, create your own test by using the **Exam***View®* Test Generator found on the **Child & Adult Care Professionals** Effective Instruction CD-ROM.

(Continued on next page)

KEY TERMS

• **dramatic play**
• **spontaneous dramatic play**
• **props**
• **prop box**

CARE PROVIDER TIP

Dramatic play is natural for young children as their imaginations develop. Storytelling is natural for older adults as they recall life experiences. Both are similar in that they give individuals the opportunity for self-expression.

Answers to Section 27-3 Knowledge Check

1. When children create realistic or fantasy situations and act them out.
2. *Any three:* Physical, intellectual, emotional, and social. *See page 633 for details.*
3. It stimulates cognitive and motor skills. Examples include charades, trivia games, and personality games.

MINI LAB *—Activities and answers will vary.*

Answers to Chapter 27 Review & Activities

1. Body awareness, force and time, space, loco-motion, weight, and moving in groups.
2. *Physical:* Small and large muscles become stronger; improved control over arms and legs; improved motor coordination and perceptual motor skills. *Intellectual:* Improved thinking, language skills, problem-solving and goal-setting skills. *Emotional:* Increased self-confidence and self-esteem; constructive outlet for excess. *Social:* Learn to work well with others and follow rules; develop a sense of unity and belonging.
3. Teeter totters, merry-go-rounds, high slides, or other unsafe equipment.
4. Keep free of items that could hurt children; check daily for such dangers as broken glass, splintered climbing equipment, and tacks on the floor; help children to follow rules to prevent injuries; state rules simply and clearly in positive terms; keep a close eye on children during active play and remind them of rules when needed. *See pages 625 and 626 for rules about using climbers, swings, and slides.*
5. *Any three: Physical:* Develop small-motor skills and large muscles. *Intellectual:* Use problem-solving skills, memory, and imagination. *Emotional:* Confront feelings and fears, try out all kinds of emotions, learn empathy. *Social:* Learn cooperation and compromising skills and assume social roles.
6. Dramatic play takes place in response to props or an area set aside for pretend play. Spontaneous dramatic play is when children engage in dramatic play without the suggestion or direction of adults.
7. *Answers will vary. See pages 633-634.*
8. Children use both large and small muscles. They practice eye-hand coordination, and are encouraged to listen, talk, and share. They express feelings and practice cooperation and teamwork.
9. Share favorite photographs and talk about families, favorite celebrations/childhood experiences.
10. *Answers will vary. See the bottom of page 636 to top of page 637.*

Answers to Section 27-3 Test

Matching:

1. B   3. E
2. F   4. D

Short Answer:

5. They learn to express their thoughts, ideas, and feelings.
6. What they are too young to experience in real life.
7. *Any three:* Housekeeping center, block center, sandbox, water table, and outside playground.
8. At least a 45-minute block of time.
9. Problem-solving skills and imagination—especially symbolic thought.
10. Care providers can model appropriate play skills for children who have trouble cooperating with others and can also help children join dramatic play by suggesting roles they can play.
11. *Answers will vary, but may include:* Specific furnishings including dolls, stuffed animals, prop boxes, and puppets.
12. Create different themes throughout the year.
13. Props add realism, detail, and interest.
14. *Any three:* Contents should be safe, clean, durable, easy to use, familiar, and real rather than toy objects.
15. Enhance self-worth, memory stimulation, and creation of peer support.

WORKPLACE CHALLENGE — *Any two:* Ask questions that are open-ended; prepare children for story and drama interactions by asking them age-appropriate questions before they interact with older adults; teach children how to ask questions of and listen respectively to older adults; ask the children to maintain eye contact with the older adults during the storytelling process.

Child & Adult Care Professionals Instructor Resource Guide

INSTRUCTIONAL PLAN

Developing Artistic Expression

Section **28-1**

FOCUS & PLANNING

Section Objectives

- ❑ List the goals of an art curriculum.
- ❑ Describe the stages of children's artistic development.
- ❑ Plan an art learning center for preschoolers.
- ❑ Explain appropriate methods for guiding children's art experiences.
- ❑ Plan and lead art activities for children.

Instruction & Student Practice

- ❑ **Reading.** Have students read *Section 28-1* on text pages 641-647. Assign the *Section 28-1 Knowledge Check* and *Mini Lab*.
- ❑ **Stages of Art Analysis.** Have students collect a family drawing from each preschool child in the fall and again in the spring. Have the student contrast the drawings and write an analysis of the child's artistic development.
- ❑ **Journal Entry.** Have students write a paragraph reacting to the phrase "process versus product" as it applies to children's art.
- ❑ **Lab Manual.** Assign the *Lab Activity 103* on page 199 of the Lab Manual.
- ❑ **Child & Adult Care Study Guides.** Assign *Study Guide 28-1* from the Student Motivation Kit.
- ❑ **Child & Adult Care Applications.** Assign *Activities 63* and *118* from the Student Motivation Kit.
- ❑ **Child & Adult Care Observations.** Assign *Observations C-29* and *C-30* as desired from the Student Motivation Kit.
- ❑ **Activity Cards for Children.** Assign *Activity Cards C-27* to *C-40* as desired from the Student Motivation Kit.
- ❑ **Child & Adult Care Career Profiles.** Assign *Career Profiles* as desired from the Student Motivation Kit.

Review & Student Performance

- ❑ **PowerPoint® Slides.** Use the *Section 28-1 PowerPoint®* slides on the Effective Instruction CD-ROM.
- ❑ **Section 28-1 Test.** Have students complete the *Section 28-1 Test* on pages 441-442 of this guide. Or, create your own test by using the **Exam**View® Test Generator found on the **Child & Adult Care Professionals** Effective Instruction CD-ROM.

KEY TERMS

- **proportion**
- **process versus product**
- **three-dimensional**
- **collage**

CARE PROVIDER TIP

It is important that one child's artwork not be compared with another's. Creating using paints, crayons, and other tools needs to be fun and a way for the child to experiment and develop fine motor skills.

(Continued on next page)

Answers to Section 28-1 Knowledge Check

1. A process where they experiment with art materials.
2. Use talc-free products and nontoxic products, have good ventilation, avoid dangerous art tools, do not let children use paints or markers on their skin.
3. Through scribbling, mark-making.

MINI LAB —*Activities and answers will vary.*

Answers to Section 28-1 Test

Matching:

1.	F	4.	H
2.	E	5.	A
3.	D		

Short Answer:

6. They build their vocabulary skills and learn to observe and listen to others' ideas.
7. Creativity, imagination, and thinking skills.
8. The representational stage (ages 4 to 7).
9. Invites children to select art activities on their own during choice time, according to their interests and abilities.
10. When the emphasis is on process, art experiences are less apt to aim for a specific result—allowing children to make decisions about their projects.
11. *Answers may vary, but should be similar to:* "You've been working hard. Please tell me about your picture."
12. These practices lower self-esteem and can stifle interest and creativity.
13. Construction paper seeds, fabric scraps, and string.
14. Add food coloring to cold cream, hand lotion, unscented shaving cream, or mild liquid soap.
15. Small motor skills and eye-hand coordination.

WORKPLACE CHALLENGE —*Any five:* Water-based tempera paint, which is inexpensive, washable, and nontoxic; easels that can be adjusted to children's height and big enough so that two to four children can paint at once; newsprint, which is the type of paper used for newspapers; painting tools, such as long-handled brushes, ½- to 1-inch wide (younger children may need wider brushes); materials such as plastic aprons and old shirts to keep children's clothes clean; an area where paintings can be placed for drying.

INSTRUCTIONAL PLAN ━━━━━━━━━━━━━━━━━━━━━

Developing Musical Expression

Section **28-2**

FOCUS & PLANNING

Section Objectives

❑ Identify the benefits of music to children.

❑ Plan a music learning center for preschoolers.

❑ Explain the care provider's role in music.

❑ Describe how basic skills and concepts are reinforced through music activities.

❑ Plan and lead music activities.

Instruction & Student Practice

❑ **Reading.** Have students read *Section 28-2* on text pages 648-653. Assign the *Section 28-2 Knowledge Check* and *Mini Lab*.

❑ **Sound Discrimination:** Have students make a sound bingo game to use with preschool children.

❑ **Musical Transitions:** Have students develop a card file of songs that may be used to signal transitions between activities. Have them practice using the songs with young children.

❑ **Lab Manual.** Assign the *Lab Activity 105* on page 202 and *Lab Activity 106* on page 203 of the Lab Manual.

❑ **Child & Adult Care Study Guides.** Assign *Study Guide 28-2* from the Student Motivation Kit.

❑ **Child & Adult Care Applications.** Assign *Activity 65* from the Student Motivation Kit.

❑ **Child & Adult Care Observations.** Assign *Observations C-35* and *C-37* as desired from the Student Motivation Kit.

❑ **Activity Cards for Children.** Assign *Activity Cards C-58* to *C-67* as desired from the Student Motivation Kit.

❑ **Child & Adult Care Career Profiles.** Assign *Career Profiles* as desired from the Student Motivation Kit.

Review & Student Performance

❑ **PowerPoint® Slides.** Use the *Section 28-2 PowerPoint®* slides on the Effective Instruction CD-ROM.

❑ **Section 28-2 Test.** Have students complete the *Section 28-2 Test* on pages 443-444 of this guide. Or, create your own test by using the **Exam***View*® Test Generator found on the ***Child & Adult Care Professionals*** Effective Instruction CD-ROM.

KEY TERMS

- lyrics
- tempo
- pitch
- melody
- rhythm instruments
- call-and-response songs

CARE PROVIDER TIP

Adults who are not musically trained are often self-conscious about teaching others to sing. Children enjoy the tune, rhythm, and rhyming words of songs. If you are uncomfortable teaching songs yourself, use CDs or tapes to assist you.

(Continued on next page)

Answers to Section 28-2 Knowledge Check

1. Infancy.
2. Recordings and a machine for playing them, a wide variety of recorded music, child-size versions of rhythm instruments, musical instruments for teachers to use as they lead activities, such as a piano or guitar.
3. Follow the same principles for guiding art experiences, consider the process more important than the performance, encourage children to explore and experiment, allow children to express themselves uniquely, and refrain from judging children or pressuring them to perform.

MINI LAB —*Activities and answers will vary.*

Answers to Section 28-2 Test

Matching:

1. B   3. D   5. G
2. H   4. C   6. A

Short Answer:

7. Large muscle development and refined motor coordination.
8. Music can calm frustration and provide outlet for anger, help children gain self-confidence with success in musical activities, and allow them to share songs from their culture, which affirms their heritage.
9. Friendliness, cooperation, honesty, and caring for family.
10. Prop boxes for dramatic play can have a musical theme, field trips allow children to see community music in action, musically talented visitors can show children how to play instruments, and musicians can perform for the children.
11. The developmental level, interests, and voice range of the children. Make sure songs have an identifiable beat or rhythm, have an interesting story to tell, have verses that repeat, and have understandable vocabulary.
12. *Any three:* Introduce instruments a few at a time; demonstrate how to use each instrument appropriately, so it does not break; show children where and how to store instruments; and set basic rules for playing with instruments to avoid misuse.

13. *Any three:* In greeting and farewell activities, as a calming transition from outside play, at nap time to ease children into sleep, and during lunch to encourage children to associate music with friendship and informality.
14. Obtain two aluminum pie tins and two empty thread spools. Glue the spools to the center of insides of pie tines. Use the spools as handles.
15. *Any two:* Consider developmental level, consider interests, select simple melodies within voice range, make sure songs have an identifiable beat, include songs with an interesting story, and songs with verses that repeat and have understandable vocabulary.

WORKPLACE CHALLENGE —Memory develops as children learn lyrics and follow directions to musical games; vocabularies grow and concepts become clearer as children sing songs about shape, color, and size; listening skills develop because children have to listen carefully to the sounds, words, and music before then can respond appropriately; attention span lengthens and concentration improves; children learn about music itself.

INSTRUCTIONAL PLAN ━━━━━━━━━━━━━━━━━━━━━━━━

Art for Older Adults

Section **28-3**

FOCUS & PLANNING

Section Objectives

❑ Describe art and art therapy in working with older adults.

❑ List the benefits of art activities for older adults.

❑ Plan intergenerational art activities for children and older adults.

Instruction & Student Practice

❑ **Reading.** Have students read *Section 28-3* on text pages 654-657. Assign the *Section 28-3 Knowledge Check* and *Mini Lab.*

❑ **Art Therapy Report.** Have students research the values of art therapy, call local adult centers to find where it is used, and report their findings to the class. If possible, have an art therapist visit the class and explain how art is used to improve the quality of life of many adults.

❑ **Service Learning.** Have students display the artwork produced by older adults at their center by matting and hanging flatwork and attractively arranging three-dimensional works.

❑ **Lab Manual.** Assign the *Lab Activity 107* on page 205 of the Lab Manual.

❑ **Child & Adult Care Study Guides.** Assign *Study Guide 28-3* from the Student Motivation Kit.

❑ **Child & Adult Care Applications.** Assign *Activities 81, 82,* or *90* as desired from the Student Motivation Kit.

❑ **Child & Adult Care Observations.** Assign *Observations OA-4* and *OA-12* as desired from the Student Motivation Kit.

❑ **Activity Cards for Older Adults.** Assign *Activity Cards OA-21 to OA-30* as desired from the Student Motivation Kit.

❑ **Child & Adult Care Career Profiles.** Assign *Career Profiles* as desired from the Student Motivation Kit.

Review & Student Performance

❑ **PowerPoint® Slides.** Use the *Section 28-3 PowerPoint®* slides on the Effective Instruction CD-ROM.

❑ **Section 28-3 Test.** Have students complete the *Section 28-3 Test* on pages 445-446 of this guide. Or, create your own test by using the **Exam***View®* Test Generator found on the ***Child & Adult Care Professionals*** Effective Instruction CD-ROM.

KEY TERMS

- **art therapy**
- **art therapist**

CARE PROVIDER TIP

Older adults will have a wide range of artistic abilities and talents. Some will have pursued artistic interests throughout life and others will be dabbling for the first time. It is important to make the art experiences fun, enabling all adults to benefit from the experience.

(Continued on next page)

Answers to Section 28-3 Knowledge Check

1. Art therapy is a human service profession that uses art media and the creative art process as helpful tools in treating people who experience developmental, medical, social, or psychological concerns.
2. Making dough beads to paint and string; painting ceramics; building and painting clay pots; making jewelry that may include working with metals and other materials to create earrings, bracelets, and other jewelry.
3. Successful programs include older adults in the planning of art-related activities.

MINI LAB —*Activities and answers will vary.*

Answers to Section 28-3 Test

Matching:
1. A
2. B

Short Answer:
3. Cognitive stimulation and active engagement in life.
4. Can bring communities together and provide older adults with a positive and healthy feeling about the aging process.
5. The Older Americans Act.
6. The creative art process helps them express their thoughts and emotions.
7. To establish a safe environment for older adults to be creative.
8. By noting and reinforcing older adults' creative choices.
9. Because they enjoy working and feeling needed.
10. Children and older adults can celebrate culture and build community.
11. They can practice teamwork and new skills and gain respect for one another.
12. Retired artists can teach art classes and coach both children and older adults in carrying out art projects.
13. Administrators, care providers, artists, older adults and their families, and parents of young children.
14. The goal is to help older adults increase communication with others and increase feelings of self-worth and self-confidence.
15. *Any three:* Physicians, psychologists, social workers, or teachers.

WORKPLACE CHALLENGE —Age-awareness training helps undo misunderstandings and stereotypes many people hold about older adults; age-awareness training positively influences the way people interact with older adults, eliminating poor relationships and interactions.

INSTRUCTIONAL PLAN ━━━━━━━━━━━━━━━━━━━━━

Music for Older Adults

FOCUS & PLANNING

Section Objectives

❏ Describe music therapy.

❏ List the benefits of music activities for older adults.

❏ Plan intergenerational musical activities.

Instruction & Student Practice

❏ **Reading.** Have students read *Section 28-4* on text pages 658-661. Assign the *Section 28-4 Knowledge Check* and *Mini Lab.*

❏ **Concert Calendar.** Have students find the dates, times, and costs of musical concerts in the community. Students should produce a monthly calendar to have available at adult centers.

❏ **Sing-Along.** Have students select familiar old-time songs that appeal to children as well as older adults. Students might arrange for an intergenerational sing-along using a karaoke machine.

❏ **Lab Manual.** Assign the *Lab Activity 108* activity on page 207 of the Lab Manual.

❏ **Child & Adult Care Study Guides.** Assign *Study Guide 28-4* from the Student Motivation Kit.

❏ **Child & Adult Care Applications.** Assign *Activities 81, 82,* or *90* as desired from the Student Motivation Kit.

❏ **Child & Adult Care Observations.** Assign *Observations OA-5* and *OA-12* as desired from the Student Motivation Kit.

❏ **Activity Cards for Older Adults.** Assign the *Activity Card OA-40* from the Student Motivation Kit.

❏ **Child & Adult Care Career Profiles.** Assign *Career Profiles* as desired from the Student Motivation Kit.

Review & Student Performance

❏ **PowerPoint® Slides.** Use the *Section 28-4 PowerPoint®* slides on the Effective Instruction CD-ROM.

❏ **Section 28-4 Test.** Have students complete the *Section 28-4 Test* on pages 447-448 of this guide. Or, create your own test by using the **Exam***View®* Test Generator found on the ***Child & Adult Care Professionals*** Effective Instruction CD-ROM.

KEY TERMS

- **recreational music**
- **music therapist**

CARE PROVIDER TIP

Music often jogs the memory for older adults. Listening to music that is representative of a time in history stimulates conversations about people, places, and events of the time.

(Continued on next page)

Answers to Section 28-4 Knowledge Check

1. Music to help meet the physical, psychological, cognitive, and social functioning of older adults.
2. Better quality of life, increased independence, reduced depression and stress, cognitive and sensory stimulation.
3. Sing-alongs, musical events, playing instruments, using a musical studio, and dancing.

MINI LAB—*Activities and answers will vary.*

Answers to Chapter 28 Review & Activities

1. Develop motor skills, stimulate language and thinking skills, encourage self-expression, teach basic concepts, encourage appreciation for diversity, develop social skills.
2. *See page 642.*
3. Stocked with a variety of art materials and tools on child-size shelving, placed over a washable surface with child-size tables, chairs, and easels, contains drying rack, placed near a water source for easy clean up.
4. Use talc-free, safety scissors, and nontoxic products; have good ventilation; do not let children use paints or markers on their skin.
5. Develop large and small muscles and coordination; develop language, memory, and social skills; learn basic concepts; develop friendships and self-expressions.
6. Provide an instrument, play and sing familiar music, conduct small group and individual music activities.
7. Benefits include a change in how much control older adults feel they have over their lives, increased ability to make decisions, change in identity from aging adult to creative person, increased socialization and communication, improved small-motor function and eye-hand coordination, an emotional outlet.
8. Helps older adults with stiff finger joints, increases dexterity, provides sense of accomplishment, and is relaxing.
9. Connects generations and cultures, builds relationships, allows children and older adults to celebrate culture and community, fosters teamwork and respect for one another.
10. *Any four. See pages 655-656.*

Answers to Section 28-4 Test

Matching:

1. C   2. A

Short Answer:

3. Sensory stimulation and social experiences.
4. They might sing, dance, and reminisce about their favorite music from years past.
5. Work closely with older adults and their families to offer meaningful music activities.
6. *Any three:* Physical disabilities, dementia, depression, severe pain, high blood pressure, and social isolation.
7. To use musical experiences to create positive changes in human behavior.
8. Because it is nonthreatening.
9. Their quality of life.
10. To plan music therapy activities for individuals or groups of people, assess the needs of older adults, design music sessions according to those needs, and participate in the activities.
11. Music.
12. A person who is a trained musician or someone with an interest in music.
13. A fun music activity and a good form of exercise.
14. New Jersey Intergenerational Orchestra, Encore Community Music Association, Lawrence Philharmonic, and Ridgewood Symphony Orchestra.
15. *Any three:* Better quality of life; increased independence; reduced depression and stress; cognitive and sensory stimulation; increased physical exercise; opportunities to share musical interests with youth; relaxation; increased social interaction; chance to explore personal feelings; improved attitude; increased problem-solving skills.

WORKPLACE CHALLENGE—*Any two:* Place the studio in an open area that is used for music, dance, and drama activities; design it to allow older adults and children to come together to engage in creative expression of ideas, thoughts, and feelings related to music; stock it with a stereo, musical recordings, and instruments.

Child & Adult Care Professionals Instructor Resource Guide

SECTION TESTS

Contents

Name _____ Course _____ Date _____

Understanding Child Development

Matching Directions: Read each description carefully. Then match it with the correct key term from the list on the right. Write the letter of the key term in the space provided. Do not use any term more than once. Check you answers before turning in your paper. **(6 points each)**

Descriptions

_____ **1.** Refers to how people think and learn.

_____ **2.** Learning through the use of our five senses.

_____ **3.** Experiences that involve the five senses.

_____ **4.** Typical way a child responds to people and situations.

_____ **5.** Includes people, culture, and physical and social surroundings.

_____ **6.** Passing of parents' qualities and traits through genes at their child's conception.

_____ **7.** Nerve cells in the brain.

_____ **8.** Electrical connections between neurons.

KEY TERMS

A. Cognitive

B. Environment

C. Heredity

D. Neurons

E. Sensorimotor

F. Sensory

G. Synapses

H. Temperament

Short Answer Directions: Read each question or statement carefully. Write your answer(s) in the space provided. Reread your answers before turning in your paper. **(6 points each)**

9. What do infants do to show they have developed large motor skills?

_____

10. Describe how children develop concepts.

_____

_____

_____

11. Why is it important for children to understand cause and effect?

_____

_____

(Continued on next page)

Child & Adult Care Professionals Instructor Resource Guide
Copyright © Glencoe/McGraw-Hill

12. How can care providers help children learn to think favorably of themselves?

_____

_____

13. What is one result of a child's lack of social skills and the acceptance that comes with it?

_____

_____

14. List two skills that allow a child to adjust to other people's ways.

_____

_____

15. Why do children learn faster than adults?

_____

_____

Workplace Challenge Directions: Explain the differences between the intelligence theories of Alfred Binet and Howard Gardner. **(10 points)**

_____

_____

_____

_____

_____

_____

_____

_____

_____

Child & Adult Care Professionals Instructor Resource Guide

Influences on Development

Section Test **1-2**

Matching Directions: Read each description carefully. Then match it with the correct key term from the list on the right. Write the letter of the key term in the space provided. Do not use any term more than once. Check you answers before turning in your paper. **(6 points each)**

Descriptions

_____ 1. An environment that interferes with a child's proper development and well-being.

_____ 2. Before birth health care.

_____ 3. A surgical delivery.

_____ 4. Resources and specialized help provided by a professional.

_____ 5. Sending the prospective parent to another resource other than family or friends.

KEY TERMS

A. At risk

B. Cesarean birth

C. Intervention services

D. Prenatal

E. Referral

Short Answer Directions: Read each question or statement carefully. Write your answer(s) in the space provided. Reread your answers before turning in your paper. **(6 points each)**

6. List two factors on which a child's growth and development depend.

_____

_____

7. List four traits of parents that are passed on to the child by the parents' genes.

_____

_____

8. List two factors that may slow down the typical development rate of a child.

_____

_____

9. What foods best provide children with fuel for growth and energy?

_____

_____

(Continued on next page)

10. During feeding times, what can a care provider do to communicate love and worth to a child?

_____

11. What factors have a great influence on a family's beliefs, traditions, and other practices?

_____

_____

12. List two possible effects of poor nutrition on a child.

_____

_____

13. What is a possible effect on a child if the family moves often?

_____

14. What topics do typical parent education programs include?

_____

_____

15. List two agencies that conduct grandparenting workshops and print newsletters about raising grandchildren.

_____

_____

Workplace Challenge Directions: List five factors that create a stable environment for a child. **(2 points each, 10 points total)**

◆ _____

◆ _____

◆ _____

◆ _____

◆ _____

Aging & Adult Development

Section Test 2-1

Matching Directions: Read each description carefully. Then match it with the correct key term from the list on the right. Write the letter of the key term in the space provided. Do not use any term more than once. Check you answers before turning in your paper. **(6 points each)**

Descriptions

_____ 1. Study of the aging process.

_____ 2. Study of society, its institutions, and social relationships.

_____ 3. Field of medicine that focuses on preventing or managing common diseases for older adults.

_____ 4. The power to generate or produce something of value.

_____ 5. People born between 1946 and 1964, following World War II.

KEY TERMS

A. Baby boomer

B. Generativity

C. Geriatrics

D. Gerontology

E. Sociology

Short Answer Directions: Read each question or statement carefully. Write your answer(s) in the space provided. Reread your answers before turning in your paper. **(6 points each)**

6. During psychological aging, what mental processes are most likely to change?

_____

_____

_____

7. Describe the basic responsibilities of a geriatric case manager.

_____

_____

_____

8. What are the positive and negative ends of the young adulthood stage of life, according to Erickson?

_____

_____

9. According to Erickson, older adults review their pasts to gain a sense of uniqueness, accomplishment, and fulfillment. What happens if this does not occur?

_____

(Continued on next page)

10. According to Levinson, what stage in life causes a life crisis for some people?

_____

11. What stage in life, according to Levinson, is usually more satisfying and productive than any other time in life?

_____

12. What does Roger Gould, a psychiatrist, say about change, emotions, and motivation during adulthood?

_____

13. What are the two major population shifts that the United States is experiencing?

_____

14. What does the Census Bureau predict life expectancy to be by the year 2050?

_____

15. What effect will the increase in life expectancy have on career options?

_____

Workplace Challenge Directions: As you consider a career as a geriatric care manager, you will probably encounter the following myths and stereotypes about aging. In the space provided, list the truth about each one. **(2 points each, 10 points total)**

◆ Older adults become intellectually impaired. _____

_____

◆ All older adults are senile. _____

_____

◆ Older adults are depressed and have every right to be. _____

_____

◆ Older adults have nothing to contribute to society. _____

_____

◆ Older adults do not respect young people, but yet they want younger people to respect them.

_____

_____

Child & Adult Care Professionals Instructor Resource Guide

Name_____ Course_____ Date_____

Basic Needs of Older Adults

Matching Directions: Read each description carefully. Then match it with the correct key term from the list on the right. Write the letter of the key term in the space provided. Do not use any term more than once. Check you answers before turning in your paper. **(6 points each)**

Descriptions

_____ **1.** A receipt or statement attesting to the expenditure or receipt of money.

_____ **2.** Money left after paying for basic needs.

_____ **3.** A person who assesses and directs the care of older adults.

_____ **4.** How people picture themselves.

_____ **5.** A facility or program with staff members who are trained to provide a caring environment that will meet the physical and emotional needs of the terminally ill.

KEY TERMS

A. Discretionary income

B. Family care manager

C. Hospice

D. Self-perception

E. Voucher

Short Answer Directions: Read each question carefully. Write your answer(s) in the space provided. Reread your answers before turning in your paper. **(6 points each)**

6. What are two new roles retirees may welcome?

_____

7. What are three general types of programs that are available to assist older adults in their homes?

_____

8. What agency serves as a clearinghouse for all government services for older adults who seek to remain in their homes?

_____

9. What may be an older adult's most important financial liability?

_____

10. To live in subsidized housing, residents must pay what percent of their adjusted income for rent?

_____

(Continued on next page)

Child & Adult Care Professionals Instructor Resource Guide
Copyright © Glencoe/McGraw-Hill

11. As a care provider, how can you assist older adults who must use public transportation?

_____

_____

12. As a care provider, what needs of older adults should you consider, other than their basic, functional needs?

_____

13. What two other relationship connections do older adults need in addition to their families' displays of appreciation and respect?

_____

_____

14. What is the objective of the grieving process?

_____

_____

15. In the denial stage of death and dying, what are two devices a dying person may use to cope with the idea of death?

_____

Workplace Challenge Directions: Several factors have an impact on how adults picture themselves. Name at least five. **(2 points each, 10 points total)**

◆ _____

◆ _____

◆ _____

◆ _____

◆ _____

Child & Adult Care Professionals Instructor Resource Guide

Caring for Children

Section Test
3-1

Matching Directions: Read each description carefully. Then match it with the correct key term from the list on the right. Write the letter of the key term in the space provided. Do not use any term more than once. Check you answers before turning in your paper. **(6 points each)**

Descriptions

_____ 1. A direction in which a society moves within a given time frame.

_____ 2. A person who owns and operates a business.

_____ 3. A nationally recognized credential program for early childhood professionals.

_____ 4. Required by law.

KEY TERMS

A. Child Development Associate (CDA)

B. Entrepreneur

C. Mandated

D. Trend

Short Answer Directions: Read each question or statement carefully. Write your answer(s) in the space provided. Reread your answers before turning in your paper. **(6 points each)**

5. What is the first step in the planning of your occupational career?

_____

_____

6. What did researchers find when they studied children's early childhood education experience?

_____

_____

7. What seems to be the most likely factor influencing the willingness of parents to enroll their children in child-care programs or centers?

_____

_____

8. For many families, what two factors have made two incomes a necessity?

_____

_____

(Continued on next page)

9. Where do child care providers most often work?

_____

_____

10. What can you do in high school to help confirm that you have the traits, attitudes, skills, and abilities to be an early childhood care provider?

_____

_____

11. All early childhood programs and centers, including private and government-run child care centers, must comply with which federal law?

_____

12. Through which classroom routines can care providers demonstrate their respect for an individual family's traditions and beliefs?

_____

13. Exposure to minor illnesses could be a cause of stress in a care provider's daily routine. List three of these illnesses.

_____

_____

14. What is a primary ability that a child care provider must have to successfully work in a care setting?

_____

15. How much education would you need to be qualified as a nanny?

_____

Workplace Challenge Directions: There are many questions people need to ask themselves if they are considering owning a child-centered business. List five that you believe apply specifically to you. **(2 points each, 10 points total)**

◆ _____

◆ _____

◆ _____

◆ _____

◆ _____

Caring for Older Adults Section Test 3-2

Matching Directions: Read each description carefully. Then match it with the correct key term from the list on the right. Write the letter of the key term in the space provided. Do not use any term more than once. Check you answers before turning in your paper. **(6 points each)**

Descriptions

_____ 1. Health insurance program for older adults.

_____ 2. Discrimination against older adults.

_____ 3. Physical or mental exhaustion due to long periods of stress and frustration.

_____ 4. Programs that involve two or more generations.

_____ 5. Health insurance program for low-income people.

_____ 6. A combination of two or more fields of study.

KEY TERMS

A. Ageism

B. Burnout

C. Intergenerational programs

D. Medicaid

E. Medicare

F. Multidisciplinary

Short Answer Directions: Read each question carefully. Write your answer(s) in the space provided. Reread your answers before turning in your paper. **(6 points each)**

7. How will future adult care professionals differ from those in the past?

_____

_____

8. As a result of the Older Americans Act, career opportunities in aging have grown in what agencies?

_____

_____

9. What model of an adult care center provides activities for its participants, such as helping physically challenged or frail adults with crafts?

_____

10. What intergenerational program model offers its employees the benefit of an on-site child care center?

_____

(Continued on next page)

11. What understanding and skills do you need to be successful in the field of gerontology or geriatric services?

_____

_____

_____

12. How should care providers address older adults?

_____

13. What must a worker do to sustain a career as a care provider?

_____

_____

14. What characteristics does a care provider with a positive attitude exhibit?

_____

_____

15. Why do states have adult protective services agencies?

_____

_____

Workplace Challenge Directions: Describe the oral communication skills needed by an older adult care provider. **(2 points each, 10 points total)**

◆ _____

◆ _____

◆ _____

◆ _____

◆ _____

Child & Adult Care Professionals Instructor Resource Guide

Preparing for Employment

Matching Directions: Read each description carefully. Then match it with the correct key term from the list on the right. Write the letter of the key term in the space provided. Do not use any term more than once. Some terms will not be used. Check you answers before turning in your paper. **(6 points each)**

Descriptions

_____ **1.** A personal commitment to do your very best.

_____ **2.** Put tasks in the order of importance.

_____ **3.** Paying attention to and interacting with the speaker.

_____ **4.** The ability to adapt willingly to changing circumstances.

_____ **5.** Communicates through what a person sees when he speaks or listens to you.

KEY TERMS

A. Active listening

B. Body language

C. Flexibility

D. Prioritize

E. Work ethic

F. Signing

Short Answer Directions: Read each question or statement carefully. Write your answer(s) in the space provided. Reread your answers before turning in your paper. **(6 points each)**

6. Why should you not use slang as a care professional?

_____

_____

7. Why should you smile when you speak on the telephone?

_____

_____

8. What are the two most common forms of business writing that you will do as a care provider?

_____

_____

9. If you have never met the person to whom you are writing, what is an effective way to begin your message?

_____

_____

(Continued on next page)

10. What determines your style of written communication?

_____

_____

11. Describe the reading skill of focusing.

_____

_____

12. What are five activities for which care directors use math skills?

_____

_____

13. What are the three kinds of thinking skills needed by a professional?

_____

_____

14. What behaviors show that you as an employee are committed to your job?

_____

_____

15. How would you practice honesty on the job?

_____

_____

_____

Workplace Challenge Directions: What are five characteristics of a person who shows responsibility on the job? **(2 points each, 10 points total)**

◆ _____

◆ _____

◆ _____

◆ _____

◆ _____

Child & Adult Care Professionals Instructor Resource Guide

Seeking Employment *Section Test* 4-2

Matching Directions: Read each description carefully. Then match it with the correct key term from the list on the right. Write the letter of the key term in the space provided. Do not use any term more than once. Some terms will not be used. Check you answers before turning in your paper. **(4 points each)**

Descriptions

_____ 1. Making use of all your personal and professional contacts to further your career goals.

_____ 2. A job lead.

_____ 3. Magazines and newsletters published for members of a professional organization.

_____ 4. Community service as part of your schoolwork.

_____ 5. A summary of your career objectives, work experience, job qualifications, education, and training.

_____ 6. Significant words that make it easier for employers to search for relevant information.

KEY TERMS

A. Keywords
B. Networking
C. Referral
D. Résumé
E. Service learning
F. Trade publications
G. Internship
H. Portfolio

Short Answer Directions: Read each question or statement carefully. Write your answer(s) in the space provided. Reread your answers before turning in your paper. **(4 points each)**

7. If someone gives you a job lead, how should you respond to the lead?

_____

_____

_____

8. List two job search tasks you can perform on the Internet.

_____

_____

_____

(Continued on next page)

9. List as least two job-search benefits that you may receive by joining a professional organization.

_____

_____

10. What is one advantage of working through a temporary employment agency?

_____

_____

11. When responding to a job lead by telephone, what should you write down?

_____

_____

12. When writing a letter requesting an application form or an interview, what should you include in the letter?

_____

_____

13. Describe appropriate dress and grooming for an interview.

_____

_____

_____

_____

_____

14. During the interview, what should you do after the interviewer introduces himself or herself to you?

_____

_____

_____

_____

(Continued on next page)

Child & Adult Care Professionals Instructor Resource Guide

15. During an interview, what three questions should you not hesitate to ask?

_____

_____

_____

16. If at the interview the employer promises to contact you but does not, what is an appropriate action on your part?

_____

_____

_____

17. If you are offered a job but decide that the job is not right for you, or you are offered a better job with another employer, what is an appropriate response to the offer?

_____

_____

_____

18. What is the proper behavior when talking with a receptionist or another person before meeting with the interviewer?

_____

19. Why is it advisable to maintain eye contact with the interviewer?

_____

_____

20. What name is usually given to a system of recording your job possibilities, interviews, and follow-up information?

_____

_____

(Continued on next page)

Workplace Challenge Directions: Name at least five tips to keep in mind when completing a job application. (4 points each, 20 points total)

◆ _____

_____

◆ _____

_____

◆ _____

_____

◆ _____

_____

◆ _____

_____

Child & Adult Care Professionals Instructor Resource Guide

On the Job Section Test 4-3

Matching Directions: Read each description carefully. Then match it with the correct key term from the list on the right. Write the letter of the key term in the space provided. Do not use any term more than once. Some terms will not be used. Check you answers before turning in your paper. **(6 points each)**

Descriptions

_____ 1. The skill of putting yourself in another's place.

_____ 2. Financial help to cover medical expenses and lost wages.

_____ 3. The lowest hourly amount a worker can earn.

_____ 4. Extra pay or time off for working overtime.

_____ 5. An organization of workers in a similar field.

_____ 6. Process of workers and employers agreeing to working conditions, contracts, and other job benefits.

_____ 7. Unfair treatment based on age, gender, race, ethnicity, religion, physical appearance, disability, or other factors.

_____ 8. A period in which an employer observes the employee's work and behavior to assess whether the employee is fit to remain with the company.

_____ 9. Your internal guidelines for distinguishing right from wrong.

_____ 10. Any unwelcome verbal or physical behavior of a sexual nature.

KEY TERMS

A. Collective bargaining

B. Compensatory time

C. Discrimination

D. Empathy

E. Ethics

F. Job insurance

G. Labor union

H. Minimum wage

I. Probation

J. Sexual harassment

K. Workers' compensation

Short Answer Directions: Read each question carefully. Write your answer(s) in the space provided. Reread your answers before turning in your paper. **(6 points each)**

11. What factors usually influence your pay on the job?

_____

_____

12. How do you demonstrate self-respect on the job?

_____

_____

(Continued on next page)

13. What can you do to show your boss that you use your time responsibly?

_____

_____

_____

_____

14. What things will an employer usually examine during an employee's performance evaluation?

_____

_____

_____

_____

15. After finding a new job, what is your responsibility to your present employer?

_____

_____

_____

_____

Workplace Challenge Directions: Federal, state, and local regulations require your employer to provide you with safe working conditions. List an employer's five responsibilities. **(2 points each, 10 points total)**

◆ _____

◆ _____

◆ _____

◆ _____

◆ _____

Child & Adult Care Professionals Instructor Resource Guide

Professional Communication

Section Test 5-1

Matching Directions: Read each description carefully. Then match it with the correct key term from the list on the right. Write the letter of the key term in the space provided. Do not use any term more than once. Some terms will not be used. Check you answers before turning in your paper. **(4 points each)**

Descriptions

_____ 1. Any obstacles that prevent people from sending or receiving information.

_____ 2. Communication with the general public about your program.

_____ 3. A combination of a person's ethnic background, customary beliefs, social practices, religious beliefs, and family values.

_____ 4. A set of beliefs.

_____ 5. An illness that affects the memory of aging adults.

KEY TERMS

A. Alzheimer's disease

B. Communication barriers

C. Culture

D. Philosophy

E. Public relations

F. Race

G. Senility

Short Answer Directions: Read each question or statement carefully. Write your answer(s) in the space provided. Reread your answers before turning in your paper. **(6 points each)**

6. What common medical factors cause communication barriers for children and older adults?

_____

7. List four common social factors that can influence a person's ability to communicate.

_____

_____

8. What can you do as a care provider to establish children's and older adults' trust in you?

_____

_____

9. In the process of developing a close partnership between you and the older adult in your care, what questions will you need to answer?

_____

_____

_____

(Continued on next page)

10. What are three criteria that will contribute to an effective presentation about your program to a local organization?

_____

_____

11. What are the advantages of using a Web site to communicate program information?

_____

_____

_____

_____

12. What are necessary precautions to take during an informal conversation with family members?

_____

_____

13. List two types of communication that encourage teamwork.

_____

_____

14. List two ways to treat your coworkers with professional respect.

_____

_____

15. List two effective techniques to use when discussing an older adult's problem with family members.

_____

_____

Workplace Challenge Directions: List four suggestions for minimizing conflicts between workers. **(5 points each, 20 points total)**

◆ _____

◆ _____

◆ _____

◆ _____

Child & Adult Care Professionals Instructor Resource Guide

Professional Ethics

Matching Directions: Read each description carefully. Then match it with the correct key term from the list on the right. Write the letter of the key term in the space provided. Do not use any term more than once. Some terms will not be used. Check you answers before turning in your paper. **(6 points each)**

Descriptions

_____ 1. Standards of right and wrong that apply to your professional behavior.

_____ 2. Rules for workplace dress.

_____ 3. Updating your career knowledge and acquiring new job skills.

_____ 4. Large gatherings at which members of specific professions exchange information about the latest findings, developments, and practices in their field.

_____ 5. The belief that the privacy of others must always be maintained.

KEY TERMS

A. Code of ethical conduct

B. Conferences

C. Confidentiality

D. Continuing education

E. Dress code

F. Professional ethics

G. Seminars

Short Answer Directions: Read each question or statement carefully. Write your answer(s) in the space provided. Reread your answers before turning in your paper. **(6 points each)**

6. List three character traits that ethical professionals should maintain.

_____

7. What guideline should you follow when wearing a T-shirt at work?

_____

8. What is a simple and inexpensive way to continue your education?

_____

9. Name the professional association that hosts a yearly conference of about 30,000 early childhood professionals.

_____

10. What are the advantages of obtaining the CDA credential?

_____

_____

(Continued on next page)

11. A director of an adult day services program may be required to have credentials and management experiences in any one of what areas?

_____

12. What two general precautions should all early childhood and adult care professionals take to protect program participants from harm?

_____

13. List four ways in which information can be shared with clients and family members.

_____

_____

_____

_____

14. List three ways family members of children and older adults can participate in programs.

_____

_____

_____

15. What is an advantage of cooperative planning among coworkers?

_____

Workplace Challenge Directions: Describe how you would maintain confidentiality with individual family information. **(10 points)**

_____

_____

_____

_____

_____

_____

Child & Adult Care Professionals Instructor Resource Guide

Advocacy

Matching Directions: Read each description carefully. Then match it with the correct key term from the list on the right. Write the letter of the key term in the space provided. Do not use any term more than once. Some terms will not be used. Check you answers before turning in your paper. **(6 points each)**

Descriptions

_____ 1. Process of pleading a cause to influence change for the best interests of others.

_____ 2. People who inform legislators (or policy makers) of their clients' needs and welfare.

_____ 3. Residents of a legislator's electoral district.

> **KEY TERMS**
>
> **A.** Advocacy
> **B.** Advocates
> **C.** Constituents
> **D.** Informers

Short Answer Directions: Read each question or statement carefully. Write your answer(s) in the space provided. Reread your answers before turning in your paper. **(6 points each)**

4. Give an example of a basic principle of democracy.

_____

_____

5. Before talking with others about a cause that you are promoting, what should you be sure to do?

_____

6. What should you do before visiting a legislator in person?

_____

7. Where can you locate addresses and telephone numbers for local, state, and federal legislators?

_____

8. What is the formal title for a legislator?

_____

9. How many issues should you limit yourself to when writing a letter to a legislator?

_____

10. What is a recommended finish for a letter to your legislator?

_____

(Continued on next page)

11. Why is it advisable to follow up your letter with a telephone call to the legislator's office?

_____

12. What should be the closure in a letter to your legislator?

_____

13. What is the purpose of the *Intergenerational Life History Project* of the Brookdale Center on Aging in New York City?

_____

_____

14. List two kinds of support offered by programs like the Foster Grandparent Program of The Senior Corps.

_____

_____

15. What does the *Youth in Service to Elders* (YIST) program, sponsored by Generations Together, encourage students to do?

_____

Workplace Challenge Directions: List at least five acts that provide the basis for laws by which human service professionals must abide. **(2 points each, 10 points total)**

◆ _____

◆ _____

◆ _____

◆ _____

◆ _____

Child & Adult Care Professionals Instructor Resource Guide

Health & Safety for Children

Matching Directions: Read each description carefully. Then match it with the correct key term from the list on the right. Write the letter of the key term in the space provided. Do not use any term more than once. Some terms will not be used. Check you answers before turning in your paper. **(4 points each)**

Descriptions

_____ 1. Disease-causing organisms.

_____ 2. Vaccines that protect children from certain diseases.

_____ 3. Infection-control guidelines staff must follow to protect themselves from infectious disease and limit its spread.

_____ 4. Materials that come into contact with bodily fluids.

_____ 5. A condition resulting when the body's temperature gets dangerously low.

_____ 6. The freezing of body tissue.

_____ 7. A condition of dizziness and fatigue resulting from loss of fluid and salt through profuse sweating.

_____ 8. Examinations given to a group of children to look for one specific health problem.

_____ 9. The statement of rules and procedures that protect children and staff.

_____ 10. Emergency procedures established in writing.

KEY TERMS

A. Biohazardous

B. Frostbite

C. Heat exhaustion

D. Hypothermia

E. Immunizations

F. Pathogens

G. Risk-management plan

H. Safety policy

I. Screenings

J. Universal precautions

K. Heat stroke

L. Disaster drills

Short Answer Directions: Read each question or statement carefully. Write your answer(s) in the space provided. Reread your answers before turning in your paper. **(4 points each)**

11. List two infectious diseases that are spread easily among children in group care.

_____

12. What information is usually included in a child's health record?

_____

_____

13. Under what conditions should you wear gloves when working with children?

_____

(Continued on next page)

14. Describe how you should prepare biohazardous materials for disposal?

_____

15. What are three ways to prevent heat exhaustion in children?

_____

_____

16. To what governmental agency should you report a contagious disease such as chicken pox?

_____

17. What procedures should a staff follow if a child needs professional medical treatment?

_____

_____

18. What are the common symptoms of an asthma attack?

_____

19. What procedures can be followed to prevent allergic reactions in children?

_____

20. Only under what conditions should a child be permitted to leave a program's care?

_____

Workplace Challenge Directions: List the six steps for washing your hands. **(3 points each)** Give two instances when staff or children should wash their hands. **(2 points) (20 points total)**

1. _____

2. _____

3. _____

4. _____

5. _____

6. _____

◆ _____

◆ _____

Child & Adult Care Professionals Instructor Resource Guide

Health & Safety for Older Adults

Section Test **6-2**

Matching Directions: Read each description carefully. Then match it with the correct key term from the list on the right. Write the letter of the key term in the space provided. Do not use any term more than once. Some terms will not be used. Check you answers before turning in your paper. **(6 points each)**

Descriptions

_____ **1.** A physician who provides care for children.

_____ **2.** A physician who provides care for older adults.

_____ **3.** Inconsistencies in health care among different groups in the population.

_____ **4.** The combining of medications.

_____ **5.** The tension people feel when they face a situation that is different, new, unpleasant, or threatening.

_____ **6.** A life-saving technique used when the heartbeat has stopped.

KEY TERMS

A. Cardiopulmonary resuscitation (CPR)

B. Disparities

C. Geriatrician

D. Pediatrician

E. Polypharmacy

F. Stress

G. Podiatrist

H. Discrimination

Short Answer Directions: Read each question or statement carefully. Write your answer(s) in the space provided. Reread your answers before turning in your paper. **(6 points each)**

7. What are the goals of *Healthy People 2010*?

_____

_____

8. What may be the result of too much unhealthful stress?

_____

9. List four key practices that help all people, including older adults, stay healthy.

_____

_____

_____

_____

10. List two factors that may prevent older adults from preparing nutritious meals.

_____

(Continued on next page)

Child & Adult Care Professionals Instructor Resource Guide
Copyright © Glencoe/McGraw-Hill

11. List the three principles of lifelong wellness.

_____

_____

12. Modifications are sometimes made to homes so that older adults can practice which independent living activities?

_____

13. What is the most common home accident of older adults?

_____

14. What is the first principle of first aid?

_____

15. What are three ways that older adults can improve their quality of life?

_____

_____

_____

Workplace Challenge Directions: Describe five ways care providers can prevent older adults from falling. **(2 points each, 10 points total)**

◆ _____

_____

◆ _____

_____

◆ _____

_____

◆ _____

_____

◆ _____

_____

Child & Adult Care Professionals Instructor Resource Guide

Name_____ Course _____ Date _____

Health & Safety for Staff

Matching Directions: Read each description carefully. Then match it with the correct key term from the list on the right. Write the letter of the key term in the space provided. Do not use any term more than once. Some terms will not be used. Check you answers before turning in your paper. **(6 points each)**

Descriptions

_____ 1. Proof that a foodservice manager has passed a state-administered test covering proper foodservice practices.

_____ 2. Harmful substances in certain products.

_____ 3. Training that helps care providers recognize and handle situations that cause stress on the job and at home.

_____ 4. Putting pressure on the diaphragm to dislodge an object that is blocking air through the windpipe or throat.

_____ 5. Gentle puffs of air given to the person along with compression of the chest to help the heart circulate blood.

_____ 6. An electrical shock that reestablishes a normal heart rhythm.

_____ 7. A feeling of being overwhelmed with life tasks.

KEY TERMS

A. Automated external defibrillation (AED)

B. Burnout

C. Cardiopulmonary resuscitation (CPR)

D. Electrocardiogram

E. Foodservice sanitation certificate

F. Heimlich maneuver

G. Stress management

H. Toxins

I. Trauma

Short Answer Directions: Read each question or statement carefully. Write your answer(s) in the space provided. Reread your answers before turning in your paper. **(6 points each)**

8. What are two certificates that staff members at child or adult day centers should obtain?

_____

_____

9. In addition to sick leave, the Family and Medical Leave Act of 1993 allows employees to have up to how many weeks of unpaid, job-protected leave?

_____

10. When a staff member is absent, whose responsibility is it to find another worker to fill the position?

_____

(Continued on next page)

Child & Adult Care Professionals Instructor Resource Guide

11. Which government agency certifies most foodservice staff in child and adult day centers to handle food?

_____

12. List the temperatures at which hot foods and cold foods should be served.

_____

13. How can you identify whether or not a person is choking?

_____

14. If an infant is choking but is still conscious, what first-aid procedure should you use?

_____

15. When evacuating infants from a child care facility during an emergency, what is the recommended procedure?

_____

_____

Workplace Challenge Directions: Describe the procedure certified staff members use in providing rescue breathing to someone who stops breathing, but has a heartbeat. **(10 points)**

_____

_____

_____

_____

_____

_____

_____

Child & Adult Care Professionals Instructor Resource Guide
Copyright © Glencoe/McGraw-Hill

Observing Children

Matching Directions: Read each description carefully. Then match it with the correct key term from the list on the right. Write the letter of the key term in the space provided. Do not use any term more than once. Some terms will not be used. Check you answers before turning in your paper. **(4 points each)**

Descriptions

_____ 1. Records facts rather than personal opinion or bias.

_____ 2. An observation based on personal judgments.

_____ 3. Observer watches children and records their natural behaviors as they occur.

_____ 4. Someone who interacts with children while observing.

_____ 5. A written description that focuses on a particular incident.

_____ 6. A record of how many times a particular behavior or situation occurs during a specific period of time.

_____ 7. A list of specific information for which a care provider is looking.

_____ 8. A method in which the observer assigns a verbal or numerical value to items.

_____ 9. A sequential record of anything that happens during a specific period of time.

KEY TERMS

A. Anecdotal record

B. Checklist

C. Frequency count

D. Maternalistic observation

E. Naturalistic observation

F. Objective observation

G. Participant observer

H. Point scale

I. Rating scale

J. Running record

K. Subjective description

Short Answer Directions: Read each question carefully. Write your answer(s) in the space provided. Reread your answers before turning in your paper. **(4 points each)**

10. What characteristics should you exhibit when you observe children in an activity?

_____

_____

11. If you are observing a child and the child questions what you are doing, what is an appropriate response?

_____

12. What precautions should you follow if your observations are used in research?

_____

(Continued on next page)

13. What do early childhood staff members usually look for when interpreting observations?

_____

14. Before you interpret facts contained in observations of a child, whom should you contact?

_____

15. If an observer has no choice but to sit in the same room with the children, what precautions should be taken?

_____

16. What is the main factor in determining which observation method you will use?

_____

17. Why are checklists useful for parent-teacher conferences?

_____

18. What personal qualities or skills are needed for good observations?

_____

19. Who must give written permission for a child's observations to be shared with people other than child care staff?

_____

20. What observation method would be effective in evaluating a center's environment?

_____

Workplace Challenge Directions: List at least four guidelines for an observer who conducts an observation in the same room with the children. **(5 points each, 20 points total)**

◆ _____

◆ _____

◆ _____

◆ _____

Child & Adult Care Professionals Instructor Resource Guide
Copyright © Glencoe/McGraw-Hill

Observing Older Adults

Section Test 7-2

Matching Directions: Read each description carefully. Then match it with the correct key term from the list on the right. Write the letter of the key term in the space provided. Do not use any term more than once. Some terms will not be used. Check you answers before turning in your paper. **(6 points each)**

Descriptions

_____ 1. Observers include their own personal ideas, thoughts, feelings, and attitudes in their records.

_____ 2. Requires that the observer leave any personal judgments out of the observation.

_____ 3. Condition when a person tends to get nervous or uptight.

_____ 4. Usually presented in a worksheet for recording details about an older adult's impairment, if he or she has one.

_____ 5. The pulse rate at the wrist.

KEY TERMS

A. Activities of Daily Living (ADL)

B. Agitated

C. Carotid pulse

D. Journaling

E. Objective reporting

F. Radial pulse

G. Subjective reporting

Short Answer Directions: Read each question or statement carefully. Write your answer(s) in the space provided. Reread your answers before turning in your paper. **(6 points each)**

6. Why is it important to observe older adults who participate in older adult centers?

_____

7. What are three skilled sensory techniques you can use to observe older adults?

_____

_____

8. When communicating with older adults, why is it important to identify in advance the topic that is to be discussed or observed?

_____

9. When communicating with an older adult, what can you ask the person to do so that you know he or she understands the intent of your communication?

_____

_____

(Continued on next page)

Child & Adult Care Professionals Instructor Resource Guide
Copyright © Glencoe/McGraw-Hill

10. What types of statements enable you to effectively communicate with older adults? Give two examples.

_____

_____

11. What is the most common method to use when performing objective observation and reporting?

_____

12. When observing older adults, why is it helpful for staff to use interval reporting?

_____

_____

13. What type of report is required for funding and for future program implementation?

_____

14. What is the value of measuring and recording vital signs of a participant?

_____

_____

15. List four factors affecting the pulse rate of an older adult.

_____

_____

_____

_____

Workplace Challenge Directions: Journaling is one way of recording subjective reports for an observation. Describe how you would keep a journal. **(10 points)**

_____

_____

_____

_____

Child & Adult Care Professionals Instructor Resource Guide
Copyright © Glencoe/McGraw-Hill

Child Abuse & Neglect  Section Test 8-1

Matching Directions: Read each description carefully. Then match it with the correct key term from the list on the right. Write the letter of the key term in the space provided. Do not use any term more than once. Some terms will not be used. Check you answers before turning in your paper. **(6 points each)**

Descriptions

_____ 1. When an intentional injury is inflicted on a child.

_____ 2. The failure to provide a child with the basic necessities of life, including food, clothing, shelter, and medical care.

_____ 3. What care providers do when making a confidential, written record of suspected abuse or neglect.

_____ 4. Provides 24-hour child care services to parents who feel they might hurt their child.

_____ 5. Occurs when children learn to cope with and eventually recover from the hardships of abuse and neglect.

KEY TERMS

A. Alternative nursery

B. Child abuse

C. Child neglect

D. Crisis nursery

E. Documenting

F. Hotline recording

G. Resilience

Short Answer Directions: Read each question or statement carefully. Write your answer(s) in the space provided. Reread your answers before turning in your paper. **(6 points each)**

6. Where does normal bruising occur if it is from a routine injury resulting from a child's own activity?

_____

7. Describe the suffering children experience when they are emotionally abused.

_____

_____

8. What do sexual abusers often use to keep children from telling anyone about the abuse?

_____

9. From what do parents and others who abuse or neglect children often suffer?

_____

10. What can an early childhood program do to help adults who abuse or neglect children?

_____

(Continued on next page)

11. What is the value of classroom routines for children who live in fear or in a confusing home?

_____

12. List one thing child care directors can do before hiring staff members to prevent child abuse.

_____

13. What happens internally when a child is frightened and stress hormones are released?

_____

_____

14. Which older adults are less likely to be abused?

_____

15. What can older adults do to discourage people from stealing their belongings?

_____

Workplace Challenge Directions: List five things that an early childhood professional can do to help build resilience in children. **(2 points each, 10 points total)**

◆ _____

◆ _____

◆ _____

◆ _____

◆ _____

Elder Abuse & Neglect Section Test 8-2

Matching Directions: Read each description carefully. Then match it with the correct key term from the list on the right. Write the letter of the key term in the space provided. Do not use any term more than once. Some terms will not be used. Check you answers before turning in your paper. **(6 points each)**

Descriptions

_____ 1. Being unable to defend oneself against acts of unkindness or mistreatment.

_____ 2. Any act that harms the health or welfare of an older adult.

_____ 3. Using an older adult's money or possessions without permission.

_____ 4. The intentional misrepresentation of something or someone to another person for financial gain.

_____ 5. People who are skilled at influencing others for their personal gain.

_____ 6. Being dishonest about medical claims, most often misrepresenting a medicine or device.

_____ 7. Agencies that receive and investigate reports of suspected abuse and neglect.

KEY TERMS

A. Adult protective services
B. Con artists
C. Elder abuse
D. False medical claims
E. Family abuse
F. Financial abuse
G. Fraud
H. Quackery
I. Swindle
J. Vulnerable

Short Answer Directions: Read each question or statement carefully. Write your answer(s) in the space provided. Reread your answers before turning in your paper. **(6 points each)**

8. What condition makes it easier for adults to be abused without the abuse being noticed?

_____

9. What actions constitute physical abuse of older adults?

_____

_____

_____

10. What usually drives the person who commits sexual abuse of adults?

_____

(Continued on next page)

11. Give three reasons why older adults are more frequently targeted for fraud and quackery than are younger people.

_____

_____

_____

12. What might cause older adults to lack the desire to maintain their health and strength?

_____

13. What federal act makes provisions for the protection against abuse and neglect of older adults?

_____

14. What is the best way to get information about agencies that help older people?

_____

15. List three reasons why older adults do not report abuse of themselves.

_____

_____

_____

Workplace Challenge Directions: List five actions care providers can take to help victims of abuse recover. **(2 points each, 10 points total)**

◆ _____

◆ _____

◆ _____

◆ _____

◆ _____

Child & Adult Care Professionals Instructor Resource Guide

Schedules & Routines for Children

Section Test 9-1

Matching Directions: Read each description carefully. Then match it with the correct key term from the list on the right. Write the letter of the key term in the space provided. Do not use any term more than once. Some terms will not be used. Check you answers before turning in your paper. **(6 points each)**

Descriptions

_____ 1. A plan for how time will be used.

_____ 2. Cooperating in class activities in an independent, cooperative fashion.

_____ 3. A regular, expected procedure that is followed to accomplish something.

_____ 4. A short activity or technique used to guide children smoothly from one activity, routine, or event to another.

_____ 5. Signals or short activities that prompt children to move from one place or routine to another.

_____ 6. A board that lists daily jobs for children to select.

_____ 7. A container filled with pieces of paper that show pictures of activities that children can perform.

_____ 8. A transition technique that lets children decide which activity they would like to participate in next.

> **KEY TERMS**
>
> A. Choice time
> B. Chore board
> C. Down time
> D. Job jar
> E. Provider-directed
> F. Routine
> G. Transition activity
> H. Transition techniques
> I. Schedule
> J. Self-directed

Short Answer Directions: Read each question carefully. Write your answer(s) in the space provided. Reread your answers before turning in your paper. **(6 points each)**

9. What are the last activities to take place in a child care program's daily schedule?

_____

10. What are some ways you can give individual attention to children?

_____

11. What is an advantage of balancing indoor and outdoor play for children?

_____

(Continued on next page)

12. How does a schedule save valuable time for staff and children?

_____

13. How can mealtimes encourage self-help skills in children?

_____

14. What is a recommended way to end a morning's arrival routine?

_____

_____

15. What are two advantages of having smooth transitions between activities?

_____

_____

Workplace Challenge Directions: Describe at least five transition techniques that you can use in an early childhood facility. **(2 points each, 10 points total)**

◆ _____

_____

◆ _____

_____

◆ _____

_____

◆ _____

_____

◆ _____

_____

Child & Adult Care Professionals Instructor Resource Guide

Name_____ Course_____ Date_____

Matching Directions: Read each description carefully. Then match it with the correct key term from the list on the right. Write the letter of the key term in the space provided. Do not use any term more than once. Some terms will not be used. Check you answers before turning in your paper. **(6 points each)**

Descriptions

_____ 1. A plan that shows task assignments for each staff member.

_____ 2. Tasks that are performed daily, weekly, or monthly.

_____ 3. Provides a full range of in-house services.

_____ 4. Includes the usual six home-management activities.

_____ 5. Person who works 40 hours per week.

KEY TERMS

A. Full-time employee (FTE)

B. Geriatric care manager

C. Gerontology care manager

D. Instrumental activities of daily living (IADL)

E. Routines

F. Schedule

G. Structure

Short Answer Directions: Read each question or statement carefully. Write your answer(s) in the space provided. Reread your answers before turning in your paper. **(6 points each)**

6. What major factor impacts the scheduling of activities for older adults?

_____

_____

_____

7. Why is it a good idea to list on the schedule all services offered at the center?

_____

_____

8. Who is responsible for creating a work schedule for the day center staff?

_____

9. What is the recommended maximum number of older adults per staff member?

_____

10. Which staff member helps older adults with their finances, such as insurance?

_____

(Continued on next page)

11. Why is it important for the center director to know why people participate in the programs and activities at an adult day service program?

_____

12. Why is a work plan necessary for care providers?

_____

13. How will the number of participants affect the scheduling of intergenerational activities?

_____

14. Give one example of a problem that may occur if a child has had little or no experience with older adults.

_____

15. Why have a backup plan for an intergenerational activity?

_____

_____

Workplace Challenge Directions: What program values and principles should all-day programs provide or adhere to in regard to personal care? **(2 points each, 10 points total)**

◆ _____

◆ _____

◆ _____

◆ _____

◆ _____

Child Nutrition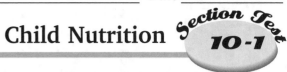

Matching Directions: Read each description carefully. Then match it with the correct key term from the list on the right. Write the letter of the key term in the space provided. Do not use any term more than once. Some terms will not be used. Check you answers before turning in your paper. **(3 points each)**

Descriptions

_____ 1. Substances in food that the body uses to function, grow, repair tissue, and produce energy.

_____ 2. Process through which the body uses the nutrients in food.

_____ 3. A plant material that doesn't break down when the body digests food.

_____ 4. Chemical compounds that make up proteins.

_____ 5. A protein that contains the essential amino acids.

_____ 6. A protein that doesn't contain all of the essential amino acids.

_____ 7. A severe shortage of, for example, a food nutrient.

_____ 8. A guide to daily food choices based on the recommendations of nutrition experts.

_____ 9. Food that will spoil if not refrigerated or frozen.

_____ 10. Person who periodically observes and evaluates a program's health practices, including the foodservice areas.

KEY TERMS

A. Absorption

B. Amino acids

C. Carbohydrates

D. Complete protein

E. Deficiency

F. Fiber

G. Food Guide Pyramid

H. Health department inspector

I. Incomplete protein

J. Nutrients

K. Nutrition

L. Perishable food

M. Regenerated protein

Short Answer Directions: Read each question or statement carefully. Write your answer(s) in the space provided. Reread your answers before turning in your paper. **(3 points each)**

11. Why is good nutrition important in a child's early years?

_____

_____

12. When does most of the brain's growth occur?

_____

(Continued on next page)

13. List four sources of complex carbohydrates.

_____

_____

14. List five sources of complete protein.

_____

_____

_____

15. What function does fiber perform in the body?

_____

_____

16. List five good sources of fats.

_____

_____

17. Why are vitamins important for good health?

_____

_____

18. With what two minerals does vitamin D combine to build and maintain strong bones and teeth?

_____

19. How do minerals help maintain good health?

_____

_____

20. What disease is caused by lack of vitamin D?

_____

21. Large amounts of which foods are not essential for good health and should be used sparingly?

_____

(Continued on next page)

Child & Adult Care Professionals Instructor Resource Guide

22. What is the recommended number of servings of each food group for children?

_____

_____

23. What is the recommended daily amount of milk or milk equivalent for children?

_____

24. Why should children's food be only lightly seasoned?

_____

25. What is the name of the child nutrition program in which many early childhood programs participate?

_____

26. What three factors could require dietary modifications for children?

_____

_____

_____

27. Why should fruits and vegetables be served raw, if possible?

_____

_____

28. Which two government agencies have established safe food-handling standards?

_____

_____

29. What is the minimum internal cooking temperature for meat? Poultry?

_____

30. What is the formula for a sanitizing solution for food-preparation areas?

_____

_____

(Continued on next page)

Child & Adult Care Professionals Instructor Resource Guide
Copyright © Glencoe/McGraw-Hill

Workplace Challenge Directions: Plan a healthful breakfast and lunch for a day at an early childhood center. In addition, plan healthful morning and afternoon snacks. **(10 points total)**

Breakfast (4 points):

_____

_____

_____

_____

Morning Snack (1 point):

_____

_____

Lunch (4 points):

_____

_____

_____

_____

Afternoon Snack (1 point):

_____

_____

Nutrition for Older Adults

Matching Directions: Read each description carefully. Then match it with the correct key term from the list on the right. Write the letter of the key term in the space provided. Do not use any term more than once. Some terms will not be used. Check you answers before turning in your paper. **(4 points each)**

Descriptions

_____ 1. A condition in which there are not enough red blood cells in the body to carry oxygen.

_____ 2. A disease in which bones become brittle and weak and can fracture easily.

_____ 3. Foods that provide a large amount of nutrients in relation to the number of calories.

_____ 4. The length of time a product remains healthful and safe to eat.

_____ 5. Helps older adults build a foundation for health.

_____ 6. The program that delivers meals to homebound older adults.

_____ 7. Meals served in group settings.

KEY TERMS

A. Anemia

B. Arthritis

C. Community meals

D. Congregate meals

E. Elderly Nutrition Program (ENP)

F. Meals on Wheels

G. Nutrient dense

H. Osteoporosis

I. Shelf life

Short Answer Directions: Read each question or statement carefully. Write your answer(s) in the space provided. Reread your answers before turning in your paper. **(4 points each)**

8. Older adults should obtain what percent of their calories from complex carbohydrate sources?

_____

9. What are three effects of lack of protein in an older adult's diet?

_____

_____

10. Which vitamins are referred to as the antioxidant vitamins?

_____

11. Intake of fats should be limited to what percent of a person's caloric intake per day?

_____

(Continued on next page)

12. What foods might care providers encourage older adults to eat to increase their intake of milk products?

_____

13. Which two vitamins work together with vitamin D to help the body make red blood cells?

_____

14. The mineral needs for older adults do not appear to change throughout life, except for which three minerals?

_____

15. What are some functions of zinc in the body?

_____

16. What are the nutritional effects of changes in the senses of smell and taste caused by aging or from medications?

_____

17. Give two examples of foods included in a soft diet.

_____

18. What system is used to modify diets for diabetics?

_____

19. Why are low-fat diets useful for some older adults?

_____

20. What agency administers the Elderly Nutrition Program?

_____

Workplace Challenge Directions: List five recommended guidelines for planning and preparing healthful meals for older adults. **(4 points each, 20 points total)**

◆ _____

◆ _____

◆ _____

◆ _____

◆ _____

Building Social Skills

Matching Directions: Read each description carefully. Then match it with the correct key term from the list on the right. Write the letter of the key term in the space provided. Do not use any term more than once. Some terms will not be used. Check you answers before turning in your paper. **(6 points each)**

Descriptions

_____ **1.** A person's ability to get along with others in acceptable and appropriate ways.

_____ **2.** The ability to understand another person's feelings.

_____ **3.** The ability to respond sensitively to others' feelings and experiences.

KEY TERMS

A. Compassion

B. Empathy

C. Positive social skills

D. Social competence

E. Sympathy

Short Answer Directions: Read each question or statement carefully. Write your answer(s) in the space provided. Reread your answers before turning in your paper. **(6 points each)**

4. List four social traits possessed by a young child that are classified as positive.

_____

_____

5. What is the foundation of social skills?

_____

6. What is the value of learning to see things from another's view?

_____

7. What can a care provider do to help build empathy and compassion in children?

_____

8. What are two activities for children that nurture cooperation and teamwork?

_____

9. What kinds of feelings must a child learn to manage appropriately to get along well with others?

_____

_____

(Continued on next page)

10. Name at least three activities that encourage social development in children.

_____

11. What can a care provider do to help build in infants a foundation for social attachment?

_____

_____

12. Name one technique that a care provider can use to help children learn to identify feelings and find appropriate ways to express them.

_____

13. Under which parenting style does a child have the greatest freedom in decision making?

_____

14. What is one advantage for a child to be reared in a multigenerational home?

_____

15. What are three childrearing decisions that multigenerational homes should cooperatively make?

_____

_____

Workplace Challenge Directions: List five ways that group activities benefit brain development in children. **(2 points each, 10 points total)**

◆ _____

_____

◆ _____

_____

◆ _____

_____

◆ _____

_____

◆ _____

_____

Child & Adult Care Professionals Instructor Resource Guide

Guiding Children

Matching Directions: Read each description carefully. Then match it with the correct key term from the list on the right. Write the letter of the key term in the space provided. Do not use any term more than once. Some terms will not be used. Check you answers before turning in your paper. **(3 points each)**

Descriptions

_____ 1. The ability to guide your own behavior.

_____ 2. A specific description of behavior, how it affects you, and your feelings about it.

_____ 3. Steering a child's disruptive behavior to a different, more acceptable activity that still meets the child's basic needs.

_____ 4. Events that occur as the result of a particular behavior.

_____ 5. A consequence that rewards a particular behavior, making it more likely to be repeated.

_____ 6. To deny a child a privilege for a short time.

_____ 7. A short period of time in which the child must sit apart from the other children and activities.

KEY TERMS

A. Consequences

B. Cool-down moment

C. I-messages

D. Open-ended activities

E. Positive guidance

F. Positive reinforcement

G. Redirection

H. Self-discipline

I. Withdrawal of privileges

Short Answer Directions: Read each question or statement carefully. Write your answer(s) in the space provided. Reread your answers before turning in your paper. **(3 points each)**

8. What are the criteria for care providers' expectations of children?

_____

9. List the steps in developing rules for children.

_____

_____

_____

10. What is the meaning of the term *positive guidance* when developing rules for children?

_____

11. What is one technique to use to help children remember the rules?

_____

(Continued on next page)

12. How can many potential behavior problems be prevented?

_____

_____

13. What can a care provider do to alleviate a child's stress when he or she is being separated from a parent?

_____

14. What might happen if activities are too difficult for a child?

_____

15. Why should a program provide an adequate amount of toys and equipment?

_____

_____

16. What is the advantage of having one-on-one or small-group time with children?

_____

_____

17. What can a care provider do to encourage good behavior in children?

_____

_____

_____

18. Why are "I-messages" effective in communicating behavior expectations and limits?

_____

_____

_____

19. List at least four factors that contribute to misbehavior in children.

_____

_____

(Continued on next page)

Child & Adult Care Professionals Instructor Resource Guide
Copyright © Glencoe/McGraw-Hill

20. What should be a care provider's goal in managing a child's misbehavior?

_____

_____

21. Why is it desirable to allow children to make age-appropriate decisions?

_____

_____

22. What are three positive traits of children that care providers should recognize and reinforce?

_____

_____

_____

23. With very young children, such as infants, what is the best method of reducing dangerous behavior?

_____

_____

24. When should natural consequences be used to discourage a repeated misbehavior?

_____

25. Once you state consequences of misbehavior, why should action be taken as soon as possible after the misbehavior?

_____

_____

26. What is the recommended maximum length of a cool-down moment?

_____

27. Who should bring the child back to classroom activities after a cool-down moment is over?

_____

_____

(Continued on next page)

28. What social skills are involved in resolving conflicts among children?

_____

_____

29. What should a care provider do if a child's behavior problems last for weeks or months?

_____

_____

_____

30. If a child bites and injures another child, what should a care provider do at the end of the day?

_____

_____

_____

Workplace Challenge Directions: List five actions a care provider can take to help prevent behavior problems. **(2 points each, 10 points total)**

◆ _____

_____

◆ _____

_____

◆ _____

_____

◆ _____

_____

◆ _____

_____

Child & Adult Care Professionals Instructor Resource Guide

Guiding Older Adults

Matching Directions: Read each description carefully. Then match it with the correct key term from the list on the right. Write the letter of the key term in the space provided. Do not use any term more than once. Some terms will not be used. Check you answers before turning in your paper. **(4 points each)**

Descriptions

_____ 1. Light, casual conversation.

_____ 2. Talk that occurs when a person is trying to find the right words to say in a conversation.

_____ 3. A defensive way of talking.

_____ 4. Using words that can be resentful to other people.

_____ 5. Using direct eye contact to show older adults that you care.

_____ 6. Using problem solving to identify the older adults' needs, fears, and goals and exploring patterns of interaction among those involved.

_____ 7. Provides written feedback, summarizes everyone's comments, and documents the solutions.

KEY TERMS

A. Action plan

B. Active listening

C. Back talk

D. Conflict-management plan

E. Nonverbal communication

F. Fight talk

G. Search talk

H. Small talk

I. Spite talk

Short Answer Directions: Read each question or statement carefully. Write your answer(s) in the space provided. Reread your answers before turning in your paper. **(4 points each)**

8. What can a care provider do to establish a relationship with an older adult, build her or his self-esteem, and help the older-adult maintain her or his dignity?

_____

_____

9. What are two factors that greatly affect an older person's behavior?

_____

10. What is the most common form of noncompliance in older adults?

_____

11. What are four emotional needs of older adults?

_____

(Continued on next page)

12. What can result from conflicts among older adults?

_____

13. Identify the most common causes of anxiety in older adults.

_____

14. List the most common causes of stress for older adults.

_____

_____

15. What is one of the most powerful and effective weapons people of any age can use against stress?

_____

16. What can care providers do to avoid career-related stress?

_____

17. What are the basic needs of a person, regardless of age?

_____

_____

18. What can a care provider do to help foster a solution to a conflict?

_____

19. What body movements are most noticeable when a person feels out of control?

_____

20. What is an effective technique to use to avoid conflicts?

_____

Workplace Challenge: Identify four guidelines for developing a conflict-management plan. **(5 points each, 20 points total)**

_____

_____

_____

_____

Child & Adult Care Professionals Instructor Resource Guide
Copyright © Glencoe/McGraw-Hill

Sensory-Appropriate Indoor Environments

Section Test **12-1**

Matching Directions: Read each description carefully. Then match it with the correct key term from the list on the right. Write the letter of the key term in the space provided. Do not use any term more than once. Some terms will not be used. Check you answers before turning in your paper. **(3 points each)**

Descriptions

_____ 1. List of desirable features that are considered part of high-quality early childhood programs.

_____ 2. Experienced through the senses.

_____ 3. Clearly defined spaces for specific types of play and investigation.

_____ 4. Furniture that is easy to care for, practical, and durable.

_____ 5. Direction children take as they go from one learning center to another.

_____ 6. Poisonous materials.

_____ 7. A separate room for children who become ill.

KEY TERMS

A. Accreditation criteria

B. Developmental design

C. Functional furniture

D. Intergenerational design

E. Isolation room

F. Learning centers

G. Sensory experiences

H. Texture pattern

I. Toxic materials

J. Traffic pattern

Short Answer Directions: Read each question or statement carefully. Write your answer(s) in the space provided. Reread your answers before turning in your paper. **(3 points each)**

8. What determines the range of areas to include in an indoor environment?

_____

_____

9. What is the first step in meeting the needs of children when designing classroom space?

_____

10. What are the basic child care needs to consider when designing classroom space?

_____

11. What are the advantages to having a good working environment for the staff?

_____

12. Why should cubbies be placed near an entrance?

_____

(Continued on next page)

13. What are the advantages to having an inviting and convenient building entrance?

_____

_____

14. What is required to keep sensory environments interesting to children?

_____

15. What effect do the colors blue and green have on children?

_____

16. What effect can fluorescent lights have on children?

_____

17. What are considered to be the core learning centers?

_____

_____

18. Describe the requirements for exit routes from an adult care facility.

_____

_____

19. List five examples of functional furniture.

_____

_____

20. What is the maximum recommended number of adults per table in the dining area?

_____

21. List the four common cognitive and sensory activity areas in an adult day center.

_____

22. What is the advantage of having a circular design for an intergenerational environment?

_____

(Continued on next page)

Child & Adult Care Professionals Instructor Resource Guide

23. In addition to meeting minimum space requirements set by state licensing agencies, what other qualities should an indoor intergenerational environment include?

_____

_____

_____

_____

24. What is the advantage of having the director's office near the building's entrance?

_____

25. Learning centers need at least how many boundaries?

_____

26. What play items are well-suited for lofts?

_____

_____

27. Why is it important to coordinate colors in an adult care center?

_____

_____

28. Why are high-contrast colors to be avoided in an adult care center?

_____

_____

29. What should be avoided when selecting a carpet for an adult care center?

_____

_____

30. In an effective furniture arrangement, at least how many older adults should be able to participate in a conversation at one time?

_____

(Continued on next page)

Child & Adult Care Professionals Instructor Resource Guide
Copyright © Glencoe/McGraw-Hill

Workplace Challenge Directions: List five space requirements for an early childhood facility. *Or*, list five space requirements for an older adult day care facility.

Early Childhood Facility Space Requirements (1 point each, 5 points total):

◆ _____

◆ _____

◆ _____

◆ _____

◆ _____

Older Adult Day Care Facility Space Requirements (1 point each, 5 points total):

◆ _____

◆ _____

◆ _____

◆ _____

◆ _____

Child & Adult Care Professionals Instructor Resource Guide

Sensory-Appropriate Outdoor Environments

Matching Directions: Read each description carefully. Then match it with the correct key term from the list on the right. Write the letter of the key term in the space provided. Do not use any term more than once. Some terms will not be used. Check you answers before turning in your paper. **(6 points each)**

Descriptions

_____ 1. Areas that help keep children from walking into swings and ensure that children fall onto soft, rather than hard, surfaces.

_____ 2. Not poisonous.

_____ 3. Tillable garden site, usually framed with wood, with a surface higher than ground level.

_____ 4. Activities that assist with healing.

_____ 5. Condition caused by lost water or body fluids.

KEY TERMS

A. Dehydration

B. Fall zones

C. Limited access

D. Nontoxic

E. Raised bed

F. Special-needs bed

G. Therapeutic

Short Answer Directions: Read each question or statement carefully. Write your answer(s) in the space provided. Reread your answers before turning in your paper. **(6 points each)**

6. How can color, texture, and aroma be introduced into outdoor play areas?

_____

7. What plants and trees provide good sensory experiences?

_____

8. Which law offers specific guidelines for providing safe, accessible play yards for all participants?

_____

9. List the two types of accessible routes connecting all entry and exit points to play components designed for children with disabilities.

_____

10. What construction features are used to provide access to elevated play components?

_____

(Continued on next page)

11. What are the requirements of each elevated ramp run?

_____

_____

_____

12. What is the maximum height of handrails on both sides of a ramp?

_____

13. What construction feature is required when the space between the barrier and the ramp is greater than one inch?

_____

14. What are the advantages of having a variety of areas and surfaces in a play yard?

_____

15. How can outdoor activities benefit the health of older adults?

_____

_____

Workplace Challenge Directions: List five of the minimum accessibility requirements for new or altered play areas as required by the Americans with Disabilities Act (ADA). **(2 points each, 10 points total)**

◆ _____

◆ _____

◆ _____

◆ _____

◆ _____

Child & Adult Care Professionals Instructor Resource Guide
Copyright © Glencoe/McGraw-Hill

Early Childhood Equipment & Supplies

Section Test 13-1

Matching Directions: Read each description carefully. Then match it with the correct key term from the list on the right. Write the letter of the key term in the space provided. Do not use any term more than once. Some terms will not be used. Check you answers before turning in your paper. **(6 points each)**

Descriptions

_____ 1. Type of items that fit children's abilities.

_____ 2. Not poisonous.

_____ 3. Cleaned in a way that will kill the organisms that can cause illness.

KEY TERMS

A. Developmentally appropriate

B. Goal-related

C. Nontoxic

D. Sanitized

E. Sterilized

Short Answer Directions: Read each question or statement carefully. Write your answer(s) in the space provided. Reread your answers before turning in your paper. **(6 points each)**

4. Why should equipment and supplies meet children's varying abilities and styles of learning?

_____

5. List two examples of early childhood classroom equipment that aids large muscle development.

_____

_____

6. How may a preschooler feel if activities and toys are not age appropriate?

_____

7. List a technique that a parent can use to help a child feel more at home in the classroom.

_____

8. What emergency supplies are recommended for each transportation vehicle?

_____

_____

9. List two results of poor choices in selecting indoor equipment.

_____

_____

(Continued on next page)

10. What is the result when children are provided a balance of commercially purchased toys and home-made toys?

_____

11. Give an example of a toy that provides success with small muscle coordination.

_____

12. What can result if there are too few materials for children to share?

_____

13. List four items that are appropriate for inclusion in a media station.

_____

_____

14. Why should there be separate outdoor play yards for infants and toddlers, preschoolers, and school-age children?

_____

_____

15. What are the basic requirements of an outdoor play area?

_____

_____

_____

Workplace Challenge Directions: Identify five categories of outdoor play equipment care providers should consider and give an example of each. **(2 points each, 10 points total)**

◆ _____

◆ _____

◆ _____

◆ _____

◆ _____

Child & Adult Care Professionals Instructor Resource Guide

Name_____ Course_____ Date_____

Adult Care Center Equipment & Supplies

Matching Directions: Read each description carefully. Then match it with the correct key term from the list on the right. Write the letter of the key term in the space provided. Do not use any term more than once. Some terms will not be used. Check you answers before turning in your paper. **(6 points each)**

Directions

_____ **1.** Supplies that can be used up.

_____ **2.** A detailed record of the quantity of supplies on hand.

_____ **3.** A pool designed for swimming in a small area.

> **KEY TERMS**
>
> **A.** Aerobics pool
> **B.** Consumable supplies
> **C.** Extra supplies
> **D.** Inventory
> **E.** Lap pool
> **F.** Operational record

Short Answer Directions: Read each question or statement carefully. Write your answer(s) in the space provided. Reread your answers before turning in your paper. **(6 points each)**

4. What equipment is usually included in an educational area of an adult day center?

_____

_____

5. What items should be in the fitness area of an adult day center?

_____

6. What should older adults do before starting a fitness program?

_____

7. What standards should the kitchen and dining area follow?

_____

_____

8. Where should sanitation and disinfecting rules for the kitchen be posted?

_____

9. How should the chairs and tables be arranged in the center dining room?

_____

_____

(Continued on next page)

Child & Adult Care Professionals Instructor Resource Guide
Copyright © Glencoe/McGraw-Hill

10. What provisions should be provided in the rest room of an adult day center?

_____

_____

11. What standards should be followed in equipping and maintaining storage areas?

_____

_____

12. List the basic items that should be included in the outdoor relaxation area.

_____

_____

_____

13. In addition to having appropriate equipment and facilities, what else can an adult day center do to provide a successful outdoor program?

_____

_____

14. What is the value of having cleaning procedures for the staff to follow?

_____

_____

15. What precautions should staff members follow when cleaning equipment?

_____

_____

Workplace Challenge Directions: Describe how a care provider should equip and maintain a nature area for an adult day care center. **(10 points)**

_____

_____

_____

_____

_____

Child & Adult Care Professionals Instructor Resource Guide

Program Types

Matching Directions: Read each description carefully. Then match it with the correct key term from the list on the right. Write the letter of the key term in the space provided. Do not use any term more than once. Some terms will not be used. Check you answers before turning in your paper. **(4 points each)**

Descriptions

_____ 1. Describes general beliefs, concepts, and attitudes the program has about how children learn.

_____ 2. Basic skills, concepts, and attitudes to develop and encourage in children.

_____ 3. Programs that are designed to bring in more income than they spend on their services.

_____ 4. Programs that have no stockholders who receive money from the program's income.

_____ 5. Specific groups that fund or manage an early childhood program.

_____ 6. Someone employed by parents or guardians to provide child care in their own homes.

_____ 7. A young person who comes from one country to live with a family in another country and exchange housework and child care for room and board.

_____ 8. Programs that are not required to obtain a license to operate legally.

_____ 9. Written notification to city or state officials of a care provider's name, address, telephone number, and intention to provide services.

KEY TERMS

A. Au pair

B. For-profit

C. Free

D. License-exempt

E. Nanny

F. Nonprofit

G. Objectives

H. Philosophy

I. Program goals

J. Program sponsors

K. Registration

L. Voluntary

Short Answer Directions: Read each question or statement carefully. Write your answer(s) in the space provided. Reread your answers before turning in your paper. **(4 points each)**

10. What is the defining feature of any early childhood program?

_____

11. What is the common aim of all early childhood programs?

_____

(Continued on next page)

12. List the four things that good child care centers provide.

_____

13. Child care services offered by individuals in their own homes usually have how many children enrolled?

_____

14. What do preschools and nursery schools emphasize in their programs?

_____

15. What is the primary purpose of prekindergarten programs?

_____

16. In what ways do children benefit from being in an intergenerational care center?

_____

17. How long does a child stay in a backup child care center?

_____

18. What is the purpose of the Head Start program?

_____

19. List two types of child care programs that do not have to be licensed to operate legally.

_____

_____

20. What is the best-known accreditation program for early childhood settings?

_____

Workplace Challenge Directions: List at least four program operation areas for which there are minimum state licensing requirements. **(5 points each, 20 points total)**

◆ _____

◆ _____

◆ _____

◆ _____

Child & Adult Care Professionals Instructor Resource Guide

Managing Program Services

Matching Directions: Read each description carefully. Then match it with the correct key term from the list on the right. Write the letter of the key term in the space provided. Do not use any term more than once. Some terms will not be used. Check you answers before turning in your paper. **(4 points each)**

Descriptions

KEY TERMS

_____ 1. A written list of duties and responsibilities for each staff member.

_____ 2. Equipment and supplies listed on a sheet when purchased.

_____ 3. A group of individuals who support the program's purpose but are not employed by the program.

_____ 4. The process of a director and a board making decisions about the program's policies and procedures.

_____ 5. A board that only gives directors recommendations on decisions to be made.

_____ 6. Boards that have full decision-making power.

_____ 7. Balancing income and expenses.

_____ 8. Actions taken to present a positive image of the program to the community.

A. Advisory board

B. Board

C. Financial management

D. Governing board

E. Inventory record

F. Job descriptions

G. Program governance

H. Program management

I. Public relations

Short Answer Directions: Read each question or statement carefully. Write your answer(s) in the space provided. Reread your answers before turning in your paper. **(4 points each)**

9. How often should a director reevaluate program philosophy and goals?

_____

10. What determines the number of staff, and their qualifications, for a program?

_____

11. How do directors sometimes encourage continuing education on the part of staff members?

_____

_____

12. On what factors should an employee's evaluation be based?

_____

(Continued on next page)

Child & Adult Care Professionals Instructor Resource Guide

13. Where would one find the requirements for a facility's equipment and supplies?

_____

14. What should be included in an organized inventory?

_____

15. What are some program decisions that a board helps make?

_____

_____

16. What document states the program's purpose and establishes conduct rules for the board?

_____

17. Once children are enrolled in a program, whose responsibility is it to maintain good relationships with the family?

_____

18. List one way that families can be involved in the program.

_____

19. Why do programs routinely undergo a variety of inspections and evaluations?

_____

20. Explain the process a director might follow before hiring a staff member.

_____

_____

_____

Workplace Challenge Directions: List five actions a staff member should follow if he or she detects a licensing violation. **(4 points each, 20 points total)**

◆ _____

◆ _____

◆ _____

◆ _____

◆ _____

Older Adult Activity Programs

Matching Directions: Read each description carefully. Then match it with the correct key term from the list on the right. Write the letter of the key term in the space provided. Do not use any term more than once. Some terms will not be used. Check you answers before turning in your paper. **(6 points each)**

Descriptions

_____ 1. A community-based facility usually sponsored by the city and county department on aging.

_____ 2. Programs where people meet other people of a similar age.

_____ 3. Printed information about a substance's properties, ingredients, hazards, and precautions for use.

_____ 4. The study of the aging process.

_____ 5. A field of medicine that focuses on preventing or managing common diseases for older adults.

KEY TERMS

A. Geriatrics
B. Gerontology
C. MSDS
D. Multipurpose senior center
E. Operator's manual
F. Pediatrics
G. Recreational programs

Short Answer Directions: Read each question or statement carefully. Write your answer(s) in the space provided. Reread your answers before turning in your paper. **(6 points each)**

6. How do programs in fitness and nutrition benefit participants?

_____

7. List one function of employee assistance services to older adults.

_____

8. What are two general service providers that fund adult activity programs?

_____

_____

9. List three types of facilities or nutritional centers that serve nutritious meals to older adults.

_____

_____

10. To whose policies and leadership does an older adult activity program adhere?

_____

(Continued on next page)

11. Who is responsible for overseeing how an older adult activity program follows policies and guidelines?

_____

12. What is the main responsibility of a program coordinator?

_____

_____

13. What general competencies are required of potential staff for an older adult activity center?

_____

_____

14. List four issues that are usually included in a program handbook for staff members.

_____

_____

15. Who is responsible for advertising and recruiting participants for a program?

_____

_____

Workplace Challenge Directions: Describe the organizational structure and function of an advisory board for an older adult activity model program. **(10 points)**

_____

_____

_____

_____

_____

_____

_____

_____

Social-Medical & Medical Model Programs

Section Test
15-2

Short Answer Directions: Read each question or statement carefully. Write your answer(s) in the space provided. Reread your answers before turning in your paper. **(6 points each)**

1. What is the term used to describe people who have funds invested in a center?

   _____

2. List the type of care that provides temporary relief for family members who care for a relative who is unable to function independently but does not require 24-hour nursing care.

   _____

3. What type of services does a social-medical activity program provide?

   _____

   _____

4. What is the major reason for the rapid growth of older adult day care centers?

   _____

   _____

5. What type of services does a respite care program provide?

   _____

   _____

6. What kinds of participant needs are met by quality older adult programs?

   _____

   _____

7. Why is an active fitness program important in an older adult program?

   _____

   _____

8. What are the in-house services provided by a high-quality adult care center?

   _____

   _____

9. Under the social-medical model, full-day service provides daytime care for people with what kinds of needs?

   _____

(Continued on next page)

10. Which individuals might be referred to a medical model center?

_____

11. Where would you find the rules for facility maintenance?

_____

12. If a care center cannot offer the needed service, what must it do?

_____

13. How often should the governing body of a center meet during a year?

_____

14. What is the staff ratio for most social-medical and medical model centers?

_____

15. What is the makeup of a care management team?

_____

_____

Workplace Challenge Directions: Assume you are an older adult care provider in charge of scheduling meetings with potential participants. Your job also includes accepting applications and making referrals. You have scheduled a meeting with a potential participant. Identify five types of information you will include in the application packet for this individual. **(2 points each, 10 points total)**

◆ _____

_____

◆ _____

_____

◆ _____

_____

◆ _____

_____

◆ _____

_____

Intergenerational Care Program Basics

Section Test 16-1

Matching Directions: Read each description carefully. Then match it with the correct key term from the list on the right. Write the letter of the key term in the space provided. Do not use any term more than once. Some terms will not be used. Check you answers before turning in your paper. **(8 points each)**

Descriptions

_____ **1.** Something created when separate programs plan activities to bring participants together.

_____ **2.** Result of programs simultaneously caring for young children and older adults.

_____ **3.** Older adults' individual stories.

KEY TERMS

A. Community

B. Family history

C. Integrated services

D. Life history

E. Partnership

Short Answer Directions: Read each question or statement carefully. Write your answer(s) in the space provided. Reread your answers before turning in your paper. **(8 points each)**

4. Identify two concepts that provide a foundation for planning intergenerational programs.

_____

_____

5. What are three ways that types of intergenerational programs can vary?

_____

_____

6. List three characteristics of partnership programs between early childhood and older adult programs.

_____

_____

_____

7. Describe the administration system for integrated programs.

_____

_____

_____

(Continued on next page)

8. How should integrated program facilities be designed to promote frequent interactions between all ages?

_____

9. Identify two ways that children benefit from intergenerational programs and two ways that older adults benefit from these programs.

_____

_____

_____

_____

10. List one benefit of sharing oral histories.

_____

Workplace Challenge Directions: Assume you have an opportunity to start a new intergenerational program. Which type of program would you choose—a partnership or an integrated service program? Give at least four points to support your choice. **(20 points)**

_____

_____

_____

_____

_____

_____

_____

_____

_____

Child & Adult Care Professionals Instructor Resource Guide

Managing Intergenerational Programs *Section Test* 16-2

Matching Directions: Read each description carefully. Then match it with the correct key term from the list on the right. Write the letter of the key term in the space provided. Do not use any term more than once. Some terms will not be used. Check you answers before turning in your paper. **(6 points each)**

Descriptions

_____ 1. One who specifically plans, coordinates, and leads activities for children and older adults.

_____ 2. Training in the needs and development of both age groups—young and old.

_____ 3. Being a problem solver and knowing how to continue to develop the program for participants.

Short Answer Directions: Read each question or statement carefully. Write your answer(s) in the space provided. Reread your answers before turning in your paper. **(6 points each)**

KEY TERMS

A. Cross-training

B. Intergenerational coordinator

C. Intergenerational developer

D. Proactive

E. Reactive

4. What factor determines the staffing of an intergenerational program?

_____

5. What is the source of child care and adult care staff qualifications and training requirements?

_____

6. List the knowledge all staff must have for both age groups, young and old.

_____

_____

_____

7. What key factor influences schedules for intergenerational programs?

_____

8. In preparing to accommodate the special needs of program participants who have physical disabilities or vision and hearing loss, what factors should program staff consider?

_____

_____

_____

(Continued on next page)

9. Identify at least five types of activities that are included in the daily schedule for intergenerational programs.

_____

_____

10. What influences how often intergenerational activities are planned for program participants?

_____

11. What law establishes requirements for a program site when accommodating disabled participants?

_____

12. What accommodations should be made for children and older adults who use mobility equipment?

_____

_____

13. What determines the amount of time participants spend in various activities?

_____

14. List four standard forms used for evaluating intergenerational programs.

_____

_____

15. What are two responsibilities of a supervisor for an intergenerational care program?

_____

_____

Workplace Challenge Directions: Identify five factors you should keep in mind when creating intergenerational care schedules. **(2 points each, 10 points total)**

◆ _____

◆ _____

◆ _____

◆ _____

◆ _____

Child & Adult Care Professionals Instructor Resource Guide

Services & Referrals

Section Test **17-1**

Matching Directions: Read each description carefully. Then match it with the correct key term from the list on the right. Write the letter of the key term in the space provided. Do not use any term more than once. Some terms will not be used. Check you answers before turning in your paper. **(6 points each)**

Descriptions

_____ 1. All family members approved by the child's legal guardian can visit the program any time.

_____ 2. People with similar needs who meet regularly to discuss common concerns.

_____ 3. Connecting families to the assistance they need.

_____ 4. A reference guide for staff members in making referrals.

KEY TERMS

A. Community service directory

B. Involvement center directory

C. Open door policy

D. Open house policy

E. Referrals

F. Support groups

Short Answer Directions: Read each question or statement carefully. Write your answer(s) in the space provided. Reread your answers before turning in your paper. **(6 points each)**

5. What is the first step in building good partnerships with participants' families?

_____

6. How can care providers promote family involvement in early childhood programs?

_____

_____

7. What are two reasons why an open door policy is beneficial to family members?

_____

_____

8. How often do early childhood providers usually schedule a conference to privately discuss a child's development and behavior?

_____

9. What is the value of allowing siblings and other family members to visit a child?

_____

(Continued on next page)

Child & Adult Care Professionals Instructor Resource Guide
Copyright © Glencoe/McGraw-Hill

10. What are two values of potluck meals?

_____

11. List the benefits of having family members volunteer at older adult care facilities.

_____

_____

12. What are two examples of support groups?

_____

13. If a child has delayed motor skills, to whom should you refer the child?

_____

14. What opportunities exist for family-member volunteers in older adult day care programs?

_____

_____

15. What are four types of referrals often made for older adults?

_____

_____

Workplace Challenge Directions: As an older adult care provider, describe the details you would include for every service listed in a community service directory. **(2 points each, 10 points total)**

◆ _____

_____

◆ _____

_____

◆ _____

_____

◆ _____

_____

◆ _____

Child & Adult Care Professionals Instructor Resource Guide

Legal Issues *Section Test* 17-2

Matching Directions: Read each description carefully. Then match it with the correct key term from the list on the right. Write the letter of the key term in the space provided. Do not use any term more than once. Some terms will not be used. Check you answers before turning in your paper. **(6 points each)**

Descriptions

_____ 1. A written contract stating the days and hours of a child's attendance, costs for services, payment procedures, and penalties for late-paid bills.

_____ 2. A document that gives one or more people the authority to handle finances, property, or other personal matters in case a dependent family member becomes unable to take care of his or her business.

_____ 3. A document that states how an individual wants his or her medical decisions made if he or she becomes unable to make these decisions.

_____ 4. A document that allows a person to state the type of medical care he or she wants (or does not want) if unable to make a decision.

_____ 5. Area of law affecting older adults.

KEY TERMS

A. Advanced directive

B. Durable power of attorney

C. Elder law

D. Fee agreement contract

E. Future directive

F. Living will

G. Temporary power of attorney

Short Answer Directions: Read each question carefully. Write your answer(s) in the space provided. Reread your answers before turning in your paper. **(6 points each)**

6. What are three nonbiased enrollment practices?

_____

7. What procedures must be followed if enrollment ends for any client?

_____

_____

8. Who may share a child's files or information about his or her behavior while in the program?

_____

9. What is required before sharing information about a child with someone who is not affiliated with the child care program staff?

_____

(Continued on next page)

10. How can an older adult legally give an adult child or other family member access to his or her bank account?

_____

11. What should an older adult do before preparing an advanced directive?

_____

12. Other than legal expertise, what should an attorney who works with older adults bring to his or her practice?

_____

13. How do employment and enrollment practices for adult day care centers differ from senior activity centers?

_____

_____

_____

14. To be in compliance with laws, for what information must adult day programs that offer medical and health services be accountable?

_____

15. What types of information should be kept for each participant in a day care program offering medical and health services?

_____

_____

_____

Workplace Challenge Directions: List five issues for which an adult day program could offer legal aid services to help older adults. **(2 points each, 10 points total)**

◆ _____

◆ _____

◆ _____

◆ _____

◆ _____

Child & Adult Care Professionals Instructor Resource Guide
Copyright © Glencoe/McGraw-Hill

Family Care Management

Matching Directions: Read each description carefully. Then match it with the correct key term from the list on the right. Write the letter of the key term in the space provided. Do not use any term more than once. Some terms will not be used. Check you answers before turning in your paper. **(6 points each)**

Descriptions

_____ 1. Process through which family members and service providers work together as a team to manage the care of a dependent family member.

_____ 2. Person who best understands the wants and needs of the dependent family member and speaks on his or her behalf.

_____ 3. Positive, caring, and respectful relationships that involve effective communication and conflict resolution skills.

KEY TERMS

A. Family care management

B. Family care manager

C. Family relationship

D. Interpersonal relationship

E. Mutual respect

F. Spouse

Short Answer Directions: Read each question or statement carefully. Write your answer(s) in the space provided. Reread your answers before turning in your paper. **(6 points each)**

4. List possible members of the care team for a dependent family member.

_____

5. What roles does the family care manager follow to effectively carry out the care plan goals?

_____

_____

_____

6. What are two resource needs that an older adult may have that a family care manager can best identify?

_____

7. List two groups with which a family care manager might network.

_____

8. List two examples of legal and financial papers the family care manager would maintain.

_____

(Continued on next page)

Child & Adult Care Professionals Instructor Resource Guide
Copyright © Glencoe/McGraw-Hill

9. What can a family care manager do to reduce conflict among family members who share the care of a dependent older adult?

_____

10. If family members feel overwhelmed with providing care, what is a wise action for them to take?

_____

11. What is an effective technique to follow to lessen the stress of providing care for a dependent family member?

_____

12. What should a family care manager do to avoid conflicts in assigning caring roles to family members?

_____

13. List a task that children can assume in the care of a dependent family member.

_____

14. After assigning roles, what should the family care manager do with the list?

_____

15. In addition to the family, who else can be involved in the care of the dependent older adult?

_____

Workplace Challenge Directions: Identify five resources that a family care manager may activate for a dependent family member. **(2 points each, 10 points total)**

◆ _____

◆ _____

◆ _____

◆ _____

◆ _____

Child & Adult Care Professionals Instructor Resource Guide

Development & Care

Matching Directions: Read each description carefully. Then match it with the correct key term from the list on the right. Write the letter of the key term in the space provided. Do not use any term more than once. Some terms will not be used. Check you answers before turning in your paper. (**4 points each**)

Descriptions

_____ **1.** Instinctive, involuntary reactions to a stimulus.

_____ **2.** Skills that require the coordination of vision, intellect, and movement.

_____ **3.** The ability to move the hands and fingers precisely in relation to what is seen.

_____ **4.** The time frame during which infants develop their intellect.

_____ **5.** The understanding that an object continues to exist even when out of sight.

_____ **6.** Sounds that imitate adult language.

_____ **7.** A sign of bonding when the infant shows signs of pleasure when his or her preferred care provider appears and signs of distress when that person leaves.

_____ **8.** A person's inborn style of reacting to the environment.

_____ **9.** A characteristic of children that makes them see everything only from their own point of view.

_____ **10.** An infant's fear of unfamiliar people, usually expressed by crying.

KEY TERMS

A. Attachment behavior

B. Egocentric

C. Eye-hand coordination

D. Introvert

E. Object permanence

F. Perceptual motor skills

G. Personality

H. Reflexes

I. Sensorimotor period

J. Stranger anxiety

K. Temperament

L. Vocalizations

Short Answer Directions: Read each question or statement carefully. Write your answer(s) in the space provided. Reread your answers before turning in your paper. (**4 points each**)

11. What three factors allow infants to have the best possible start in life?

_____

12. What are two factors that contribute to healthy prenatal and lifelong development of a child?

_____

_____

13. Under what conditions does a child's brain function best develop?

_____

(Continued on next page)

14. What strengthens an infant's learning power?

_____

15. How much sleep does an infant require per day to sustain rapid growth and development?

_____

16. Identify two actions a care provider can take to encourage sensory development in infants.

_____

17. What is an example of beginning eye-hand coordination in infants?

_____

18. What type of learning has occurred when an infant sees that pulling a string on a toy will make the toy move?

_____

19. Why is the emotional development called bonding important?

_____

20. What two factors form the basis for personality development during infancy?

_____

Workplace Challenge Directions: In preparing children and older adults for intergenerational activities, describe the actions you should take in each of the following areas to make these experiences successful. **(5 points each, 20 points total)**

Consider Backgrounds: _____

_____

Evaluate Physical Health: _____

_____

Consider Emotional Health: _____

_____

Provide Training and Direction: _____

_____

Child & Adult Care Professionals Instructor Resource Guide

Managing Infant Programs
Section Test 18-2

Matching Directions: Read each description carefully. Then match it with the correct key term from the list on the right. Write the letter of the key term in the space provided. Do not use any term more than once. Some terms will not be used. Check you answers before turning in your paper. **(6 points each)**

Descriptions

_____ 1. Rate at which employees leave their jobs.

_____ 2. Routines for infants conducted according to each child's individual needs.

_____ 3. Form used to organize and record the routine care provided.

_____ 4. Form used to detail the infant's activities and behavior before arrival at the center.

Short Answer Directions: Read each question or statement carefully. Write your answer(s) in the space provided. Reread your answers before turning in your paper. **(6 points each)**

KEY TERMS

A. By schedule

B. Care provider report form

C. Child report form

D. On demand

E. Parent report form

F. Staff turnover

5. What is the primary cause of the great demand for high-quality infant care services?

_____

6. How does success as an infant care provider start?

_____

7. List three types of paperwork required in a properly managed infant care program.

_____

_____

_____

_____

8. When a team approach is used to provide infant care, how are assignments made?

_____

9. What are the numbers of infants and care providers in a typical care group?

_____

(Continued on next page)

10. To promote bonding and attachment, how many children are assigned to one primary care provider?

_____

11. What information is generally included on a care provider report form?

_____

_____

_____

12. As a care provider, what can you do to encourage an infant's overall development?

_____

_____

13. During the first year of an infant's life, what are the major goals for physical development?

_____

14. What are three ways that care providers can nurture intellectual development in infants?

_____

_____

_____

15. Identify two ways that care providers can help infants develop socially.

_____

_____

Workplace Challenge Directions: As a care provider, identify five ways that you can promote healthy emotional development in infants. **(2 points each, 10 points total)**

◆ _____

◆ _____

◆ _____

◆ _____

◆ _____

Child & Adult Care Professionals Instructor Resource Guide

Development & Care

Section Test 19-1

Matching Directions: Read each description carefully. Then match it with the correct key term from the list on the right. Write the letter of the key term in the space provided. Do not use any term more than once. Some terms will not be used. Check you answers before turning in your paper. **(4 points each)**

Descriptions

_____ 1. Skills that allow children to help take care of their personal needs.

_____ 2. Time spent focused on one activity.

_____ 3. The understanding that one thing can stand for something else.

_____ 4. The development period that covers ages two to seven.

_____ 5. General ideas formed from other information.

_____ 6. Taking in new information and trying to make it fit with what is already known and understood.

_____ 7. Changing thinking to make the new information fit.

_____ 8. A sense of independence.

_____ 9. When a child plays alone, rather than with other children.

_____ 10. Children playing near each other but not with each other.

KEY TERMS

A. Accommodation

B. Assimilation

C. Attention span

D. Autonomy

E. Concepts

F. Group play

G. Memory span

H. Parallel play

I. Preoperational period

J. Self-help skills

K. Solitary play

L. Symbolic thinking

Short Answer Directions: Read each question or statement carefully. Write your answer(s) in the space provided. Reread your answers before turning in your paper. **(4 points each)**

11. What are three physical changes that occur as infants become toddlers?

_____

_____

12. Which skills contribute to improved eye-hand coordination and other perceptual skills?

_____

13. List three self-help skills for toddlers.

_____

_____

(Continued on next page)

14. What are three factors that impact intellectual development in toddlers?

_____

_____

15. How does increasing memory help intellectual development?

_____

16. How do children exhibit symbolic thinking?

_____

17. According to Piaget, what is the difference between assimilation and accommodation?

_____

_____

18. List three examples of how a toddler asserts his or her independence.

_____

_____

19. How do fears often develop in children?

_____

20. What are two ways that care providers can promote independence and responsibility?

_____

_____

Workplace Challenge Directions: List the recommended steps to follow in toilet training a child. **(20 points)**

_____

_____

_____

_____

_____

Name_____ Course _____ Date_____

Managing Toddler Programs

Matching Directions: Read each description carefully. Then match it with the correct key term from the list on the right. Write the letter of the key term in the space provided. Do not use any term more than once. Some terms will not be used. Check you answers before turning in your paper. **(6 points each)**

Descriptions

_____ **1.** Ability to understand words spoken by others.

_____ **2.** Ability to use words to express oneself.

_____ **3.** Fear of separation from familiar people.

_____ **4.** Refusing to do what is asked or doing just the opposite.

_____ **5.** An episode in which a child shows anger or frustration in an aggressive or destructive way.

KEY TERMS

A. Negativism
B. Normal language
C. Obstructionism
D. Productive language
E. Receptive language
F. Separation anxiety
G. Temper tantrum

Short Answer Directions: Read each question or statement carefully. Write your answer(s) in the space provided. Reread your answers before turning in your paper. **(6 points each)**

6. What is the result of following a consistent schedule and routine with toddlers?

_____

7. Why should programs for toddlers ask parents for information about their child's development?

_____

_____

8. Identify three activities that help children develop small motor skills.

_____

_____

9. If a child spends a lot of time watching others play, should a care provider be overly concerned? Why or why not?

_____

_____

(Continued on next page)

10. What can care providers do to help toddlers build self-esteem?

_____

11. What can care providers do to reduce negativism in toddlers?

_____

_____

12. What can care providers do to minimize toddlers' frustrations and reduce the chances of temper tantrums?

_____

_____

_____

13. If a child has a temper tantrum at the center, what procedures should you follow in communicating with the parents?

_____

_____

14. In what size group do toddlers share more easily?

_____

15. What procedures should a care provider follow if disputes occur among toddlers?

_____

_____

Workplace Challenge Directions: List five steps care providers should take to eliminate safety hazards for toddlers at a center. **(2 points each, 10 points total)**

◆ _____

◆ _____

◆ _____

◆ _____

◆ _____

Development & Care

Matching Directions: Read each description carefully. Then match it with the correct key term from the list on the right. Write the letter of the key term in the space provided. Do not use any term more than once. Some terms will not be used. Check you answers before turning in your paper. **(4 points each)**

Descriptions

_____ 1. Thought process that limits children's focus to one characteristic at a time.

_____ 2. The ability to organize objects according to increasing or decreasing size.

_____ 3. Reciting numbers in order.

_____ 4. When counting objects, each item is counted once.

_____ 5. Understanding that the last number counted in a group represents the entire number of objects.

_____ 6. Understanding that an object's physical weight and properties remain the same, even when its appearance changes.

_____ 7. The language spoken in a child's home.

_____ 8. The ability to speak more than one language.

_____ 9. Playing together and agreeing on play activities and themes.

_____ 10. The belief that children learn their culture's beliefs, customs, and skills through social interactions with skilled peers and adults.

KEY TERMS

A. Basic counting

B. Bilingual

C. Centration

D. Conservation

E. Cooperative play

F. Native language

G. One-to-one correspondence

H. Parallel play

I. Rational counting

J. Rote counting

K. Seriation

L. Sociocultural theory

M. Social play

Short Answer Directions: Read each question or statement carefully. Write your answer(s) in the space provided. Reread your answers before turning in your paper. **(4 points each)**

11. Contrast the abilities of a three-year-old and a five-year-old in playing with a ball.

_____

12. What is the favorite physical activity of preschoolers?

_____

(Continued on next page)

13. What can preschool children understand about the concept of time?

_____

14. What can care providers do to help children develop their language ability more quickly?

_____

15. When a child leaves long pauses between words, or repeats a sound or word many times before continuing a sentence, what is the problem?

_____

16. What increasing range of emotions do preschoolers experience?

_____

17. How do preschool children show development of empathy and compassion?

_____

18. In terms of developing self-help skills, what can children do by age four?

_____

19. At what age do children begin to form close-knit groups of preferred playmates?

_____

20. What should a care provider do if a child frequently engages in name-calling?

_____

Workplace Challenge Directions: List five actions a care provider can take to encourage bilingual development. **(4 points each, 20 points total)**

◆ _____

◆ _____

◆ _____

◆ _____

◆ _____

Managing Preschool Programs

Short Answer Directions: Read each question or statement carefully. Write your answer(s) in the space provided. Reread your answers before turning in your paper. **(6 points each)**

1. What is literacy?

   _____

2. Define cooperative learning.

   _____

3. What do preschoolers require as their skills develop?

   _____

4. What changes in activities take place due to a preschooler's increased physical size?

   _____

5. What type of physical development allows preschoolers to do more complicated art activities?

   _____

6. What is the future result of a child's ability to hold crayons and markers?

   _____

7. A preschooler's increasing physical skills aids in what type of development?

   _____

8. As the brain develops, preschoolers are better able to grasp what kind of thinking skills?

   _____

9. How can a care provider use books to foster literacy in preschoolers?

   _____

   _____

   _____

10. List some ways a care provider can show children how literacy relates to real life.

    _____

    _____

(Continued on next page)

11. What skills help preschoolers deal more effectively with frustrations?

_____

12. What is one new emotional reality faced by preschool children?

_____

13. What can care providers do to support children's emotional development?

_____

_____

14. What can care providers do to help children when they experience conflict?

_____

_____

15. How do preschoolers benefit from learning about the community?

_____

_____

Workplace Challenge Directions: List five preparations care providers must make to ensure safe evacuation of classrooms and facilities during an emergency. **(2 points each, 10 points total)**

◆ _____

◆ _____

◆ _____

◆ _____

◆ _____

Child & Adult Care Professionals Instructor Resource Guide
Copyright © Glencoe/McGraw-Hill

Development & Care

Matching Directions: Read each description carefully. Then match it with the correct key term from the list on the right. Write the letter of the key term in the space provided. Do not use any term more than once. Some terms will not be used. Check you answers before turning in your paper. **(4 points each)**

Descriptions

_____ 1. A point at which younger school-age children reach slow and steady growth.

_____ 2. The transition stage when children undergo a series of physical changes and begin to look like adult men and women.

_____ 3. The ability to judge distance and see objects in perspective.

_____ 4. When children are no longer bound to learning through their senses.

_____ 5. The desire to perform skills, succeed at tasks, and make social contributions.

_____ 6. A feeling of not having met expected standards.

_____ 7. Only seeing things from one's own point of view.

_____ 8. Conditions or actions, such as fatigue, apathy, depression, aggressiveness, or fingernail biting.

_____ 9. Qualities that people have that make them different from one another.

_____ 10. Chemical substances carried in the blood that impact growth and development.

KEY TERMS

A. Concrete operations period

B. Depth perception

C. Diversity

D. Egocentric

E. Fatigue

F. Growth plateau

G. Hormones

H. Inclusion

I. Industry

J. Inferiority

K. Puberty

L. Stressors

M. Work ethic

Short Answer Directions: Read each question carefully. Write your answer(s) in the space provided. Reread your answers before turning in your paper. **(4 points each)**

11. At about what age do children begin losing their baby teeth?

_____

12. How much earlier do girls begin puberty than boys?

_____

13. At puberty, why do girls usually weigh slightly more than boys weigh?

_____

(Continued on next page)

14. By age ten, what types of large motor movement is possible?

_____

15. By age eight to ten, what sports can school-age children learn to play?

_____

16. What can school-age children understand about the passage of time?

_____

_____

17. What is the result of improved empathy in school-age children?

_____

18. What do school-age children need to prevent feelings of inferiority from developing?

_____

_____

19. Why do school-age children form friendships?

_____

_____

20. What are younger school-age children's attitudes towards rules?

_____

_____

Workplace Challenge Directions: As a care provider, summarize five key ways you can help school-age children deal with peer pressure. **(4 points each, 20 points total)**

◆ _____

◆ _____

◆ _____

◆ _____

◆ _____

Child & Adult Care Professionals Instructor Resource Guide

Managing School-Age Programs

Short Answer Directions: Read each question or statement carefully. Write your answer(s) in the space provided. Reread your answers before turning in your paper. **(6 points each)**

1. Define latchkey children.

   _____

2. Name two types of special activities often provided through school-age care programs.

   _____

3. What are some dangers facing children who are left at home without adult supervision?

   _____

4. What are the advantages of school-age care programs for children and their parents?

   _____

   _____

5. Most of the children in school-age programs are between what ages?

   _____

6. What are the operating hours for a typical school-age program?

   _____

7. What are three ways a care provider can accommodate all age levels in a program?

   _____

   _____

8. List the benefits of field trips.

   _____

   _____

9. List three activities that develop and use large motor skills.

   _____

   _____

(Continued on next page)

10. List three activities that strengthen small motor skills and develop eye-hand coordination.

_____

11. What are three ways children can apply creativity and imagination?

_____

12. How can care providers help school-age children examine their emotions?

_____

_____

13. What is the advantage of allowing school-age children to make more decisions and assume greater responsibilities?

_____

_____

14. List three activities that can help school-age children develop socially.

_____

_____

15. What is the advantage of permitting school-age children to help create rules?

_____

Workplace Challenge Directions: Describe five components of a daily routine for a typical school-age program. **(2 points each, 10 points total)**

◆ _____

_____

◆ _____

_____

◆ _____

_____

◆ _____

_____

◆ _____

_____

Child & Adult Care Professionals Instructor Resource Guide

Development & Care

Matching Directions: Read each description carefully. Then match it with the correct key term from the list on the right. Write the letter of the key term in the space provided. Do not use any term more than once. Some terms will not be used. Check you answers before turning in your paper. **(6 points each)**

Descriptions

KEY TERMS

_____ 1. Refers to circumstances that cause a child's physical, cognitive, and behavioral development to vary significantly from the norm.

_____ 2. Changes made in a classroom.

_____ 3. A disorder that affects the way the brain processes information.

_____ 4. A language impairment that affects a child's use of speech and understanding of language.

_____ 5. Causes a child to have trouble learning to recognize letters of the alphabet and have difficulty reading.

_____ 6. A disorder causing a child to be unable to count objects or recognize basic shapes.

_____ 7. Professionals trained to identify learning disorders and those who help children overcome them.

_____ 8. A disorder of the central nervous system that is caused by a lack of certain brain chemicals.

_____ 9. Disorder affecting communication and social interaction.

A. Accommodations

B. Adjustments in routine

C. Aphasia

D. Attention deficit hyperactivity disorder (ADHD)

E. Autism

F. Dysfunction

G. Dyscalcula

H. Dyslexia

I. Learning disability

J. Learning specialists

K. Special needs

L. Special needs team

Short Answer Directions: Read each question or statement carefully. Write your answer(s) in the space provided. Reread your answers before turning in your paper. **(6 points each)**

10. What law guarantees free special education and related services to all children with disabilities ages three to 21?

_____

11. What helps a child with a hearing impairment learn concepts?

_____

(Continued on next page)

12. What is the first step in making accommodations for children with physical and motor impairments?

_____

_____

13. List two characteristics of a child with a cognitive impairment.

_____

_____

14. List two causes of learning disabilities.

_____

_____

15. What may happen if gifted children are not challenged at their developmental levels?

_____

_____

Workplace Challenge Directions: List two ways that care providers can respond to the special needs of gifted children. **(5 points each, 10 points total)**

◆ _____

_____

_____

◆ _____

_____

_____

Child & Adult Care Professionals Instructor Resource Guide

Name _____ Course _____ Date _____

Managing Inclusive Programs

Matching Directions: Read each description carefully. Then match it with the correct key term from the list on the right. Write the letter of the key term in the space provided. Do not use any term more than once. Some terms will not be used. Check you answers before turning in your paper. **(6 points each)**

Descriptions

_____ 1. Integrating children with special needs into regular education classrooms.

_____ 2. Person who makes sure the child participates in all routines and activities in a meaningful way.

_____ 3. An assistance program for children younger than age three that is sponsored by local public schools.

_____ 4. A plan created by early intervention programs to make sure goals are set to meet a child's overall needs.

_____ 5. A school's written plan that outlines how to encourage development in a child who has special needs.

_____ 6. Making the environment easily usable by those with disabilities.

Short Answer Directions: Read each question or statement carefully. Write your answer(s) in the space provided. Reread your answers before turning in your paper. **(6 points each)**

7. In what kind of environment do children with special needs learn best?

_____

8. What is one source of information, assistance, and referral to help locate items needed for serving children who have disabilities?

_____

9. With what does successful inclusion of children with special needs begin?

_____

10. How should care providers treat children with special needs?

_____

11. What people are usually involved in creating an Individualized Education Program for a child?

_____

> **KEY TERMS**
>
> **A.** Accessible
>
> **B.** Assistant care provider
>
> **C.** Cooperative inclusion programs
>
> **D.** Early intervention programs
>
> **E.** Inclusion
>
> **F.** Individualized Education Program (IEP)
>
> **G.** Individualized Family Service Plan (IFSP)
>
> **H.** Primary care provider

(Continued on next page)

12. List three types of information that must appear on an Individualized Education Plan (IEP).

_____

_____

_____

13. What curriculum adaptations can be made to make sure children with special needs are not isolated?

_____

_____

14. How does a program's routine schedule make provisions for children with disabilities?

_____

_____

15. What should care providers do to make sure proper provisions are made for children who require special health care in their daily routine?

_____

_____

Workplace Challenge Directions: Describe how a care provider should handle the situation when a child with epilepsy or cerebral palsy has a seizure. **(10 points)**

_____

_____

_____

_____

_____

_____

_____

_____

_____

Physical Care

Section Test
23-1

Matching Directions: Read each description carefully. Then match it with the correct key term from the list on the right. Write the letter of the key term in the space provided. Do not use any term more than once. Some terms will not be used. Check you answers before turning in your paper. **(6 points each)**

Descriptions

_____ 1. A health problem for which there is no cure.

_____ 2. The ability of older adults to take care of themselves and manage their environments.

_____ 3. When an adult must rely on others for help with basic activities.

_____ 4. Refers to people who lose their ability to do things because someone takes over.

KEY TERMS

A. Avoidable helplessness

B. Chronic condition

C. Functional ability

D. Functionally dependent

E. Severe condition

F. Learned helplessness

Short Answer Directions: Read each question or statement carefully. Write your answer(s) in the space provided. Reread your answers before turning in your paper. **(6 points each)**

5. By the year 2030, how many Americans will be older than 65 years of age?

_____

6. Which disease is the leading cause of death in older adults?

_____

7. Why do older adults who become ill sometimes take longer to recover?

_____

_____

8. What causes a heart attack?

_____

9. A blood pressure reading is 140/90. What does the 140 represent? The 90?

_____

_____

(Continued on next page)

10. What are three common problems that get in the way of a person carrying out typical daily activities?

_____

_____

_____

11. What are everyday self-care tasks sometimes called?

_____

12. List two problems resulting from hearing loss.

_____

_____

13. A care plan for an older adult with functional limitations should include what two types of information?

_____

_____

14. How can a care provider promote independence for an older adult?

_____

_____

15. Describe how a care provider can give assistance to an older adult with impaired vision.

_____

_____

_____

Workplace Challenge Directions: In addition to awareness of which type of disease an older adult might have, list five care issues with which a care provider should be concerned. **(2 points each, 10 points total)**

◆ _____

◆ _____

◆ _____

◆ _____

◆ _____

Social, Emotional & Cognitive Care

Section Test
23-2

Matching Directions: Read each description carefully. Then match it with the correct key term from the list on the right. Write the letter of the key term in the space provided. Do not use any term more than once. Some terms will not be used. Check you answers before turning in your paper. **(4 points each)**

Descriptions

_____ 1. The idea that older adults continue to build on their lifetime of experiences, preferences, likes, and dislikes.

_____ 2. The extent to which an older person is involved and active with others and with the environment.

_____ 3. Paying care providers to care for and support others.

_____ 4. Nonpaid support that includes helping provide for social and emotional needs, as well as assisting with ADLs and IADLs.

_____ 5. Family members serving as care providers for older adults.

_____ 6. The older adult has the opportunity to make choices, based on his or her likes and dislikes.

_____ 7. Refers to thinking and includes memory, learning, reasoning, and problem solving.

_____ 8. Having feelings of sadness, hopelessness, helplessness, and worthlessness over a period of time.

_____ 9. Extreme or unrealistic worry about something for a prolonged period of time.

_____ 10. Extreme sadness related to a loss.

KEY TERMS

A. Anxiety

B. Cognitive ability

C. Consumer-directed care

D. Continuity theory

E. Depression

F. Engagement

G. Formal support

H. Grief

I. Informal support

J. Intergenerational support

K. Psychomotor ability

L. Self-directed care

Short Answer Directions: Read each question carefully. Write your answer(s) in the space provided. Reread your answers before turning in your paper. **(4 points each)**

11. What measures a person's ability to function and helps to identify needed help and services?

_____

12. In addition to helping meet older adults' physical activity needs, of what other needs should care providers be aware?

_____

_____

(Continued on next page)

13. What questions could a care provider ask an older adult to determine preferences for social interaction and activity?

_____

_____

14. If older adults show concern that they may be burdening care providers, what can care providers do to relieve that concern?

_____

_____

15. What can care providers do to help replace a loving family?

_____

16. What are three ethnically appropriate physical activities for older adults?

_____

_____

17. What are two advantages of having stimulating games for older adults?

_____

18. What are three mental health disorders that affect older adults?

_____

19. What is one way that care providers can help an older adult overcome the loss of a loved one?

_____

20. What is an advantage of having older adults participate in activities that require thinking skills?

_____

Workplace Challenge Directions: Describe five ways to help support older adults' efforts to cope with memory loss. **(4 points each, 20 points total)**

◆ _____

◆ _____

◆ _____

◆ _____

◆ _____

Child & Adult Care Professionals Instructor Resource Guide

Teaching Children

Section Test
24-1

Matching Directions: Read each description carefully. Then match it with the correct key term from the list on the right. Write the letter of the key term in the space provided. Do not use any term more than once. Some terms will not be used. Check you answers before turning in your paper. **(6 points each)**

Descriptions

_____ 1. Toys and materials that children can operate and change with their hands.

_____ 2. The ratio between mental age and chronological age.

_____ 3. The belief that people vary in terms of intelligence and learning strengths.

_____ 4. Helping bring play about without controlling it.

_____ 5. Unplanned opportunities for learning.

_____ 6. Items that can be used in a variety of ways, with no single correct outcome.

_____ 7. Items that are to be used primarily in one way, with an expected result.

KEY TERMS

A. Close-ended materials

B. Creative moments

C. Direct

D. Facilitate

E. Flexible materials

F. Intelligence quotient

G. Manipulatives

H. Multiple intelligences

I. Open-ended materials

J. Teachable moments

Short Answer Directions: Read each question or statement carefully. Write your answer(s) in the space provided. Reread your answers before turning in your paper. **(6 points each)**

8. Why do children learn differently than adults?

_____

_____

9. What are four key principles that early childhood professionals should keep in mind when planning activities for children?

_____

_____

_____

_____

(Continued on next page)

10. What does Howard Gardner believe about human intelligence?

_____

_____

11. List three types of grouping often used in early childhood classrooms.

_____

_____

12. What often determines group size for early childhood activities?

_____

13. What is the general rule in determining the size of a group?

_____

14. What is the advantage of an open-ended approach to play?

_____

15. Contrast the values of open-ended and close-ended play materials.

_____

_____

_____

_____

Workplace Challenge Directions: Choose one type of human intelligence as identified by Howard Gardner. Then list two activities that allow children to engage their own unique intelligences. **(5 points each, 10 points total)**

Type of Human Intelligence: _____

◆ _____

_____

_____

◆ _____

_____

_____

Curriculum Planning for Children

Section Test
24-2

Matching Directions: Read each description carefully. Then match it with the correct key term from the list on the right. Write the letter of the key term in the space provided. Do not use any term more than once. Some terms will not be used. Check you answers before turning in your paper. **(4 points each)**

Descriptions

_____ 1. The experiences and activities that support and guide children's learning.

_____ 2. Includes activities that are geared to the specific abilities and levels of development in a group of children.

_____ 3. Outcomes for children to achieve or experience through participation in a specific curriculum activity.

_____ 4. A ranking of educational objectives for cognitive development.

_____ 5. An in-depth investigation of a specific topic.

_____ 6. Curriculum is project based.

_____ 7. One central topic.

_____ 8. A detailed, written explanation of how an activity is to be taught.

_____ 9. Questions that require more than a yes or no answer.

Short Answer Directions: Read each question or statement carefully. Write your answer(s) in the space provided. Reread your answers before turning in your paper. **(4 points each)**

KEY TERMS

A. Bloom's Taxonomy

B. Curriculum

C. Developmentally appropriate curriculum

D. Essay questions

E. Goals

F. Lesson plan

G. Objectives

H. Open-ended questions

I. Project approach

J. Reggio Emilia Approach

K. Theme

10. What is the key to a strong curriculum?

_____

11. What are objectives designed to support?

_____

12. Successful team planning requires what kind of staff relationships?

_____

13. Whose final approval is required for selected curriculum and activities?

_____

(Continued on next page)

14. What factors should care providers and teachers keep in mind when using the project approach?

_____

_____

_____

15. What is the basis for the selection of a theme?

_____

16. Regardless of the curriculum approach used, curriculum is implemented to do what?

_____

17. List three ways to creatively encourage learning.

_____

18. What do care providers and teachers apply when planning developmentally appropriate learning experiences for children?

_____

19. How does a care provider's teaching style impact lesson activities?

_____

20. What is the value of a child's exposure to different teaching styles?

_____

Workplace Challenge Directions: List at least five resources suitable for a project on pets. **(4 points each, 20 points total)**

◆ _____

◆ _____

◆ _____

◆ _____

◆ _____

Child & Adult Care Professionals Instructor Resource Guide

Teaching Older Adults

Matching Directions: Read each description carefully. Then match it with the correct key term from the list on the right. Write the letter of the key term in the space provided. Do not use any term more than once. Some terms will not be used. Check you answers before turning in your paper. **(6 points each)**

Descriptions

_____ 1. A process used to strengthen and increase learning.

_____ 2. Ability to remember information.

_____ 3. Ability to use the information taught in an activity in a different setting.

> **KEY TERMS**
>
> A. Connected learning
> B. Motivation
> C. Original learning
> D. Reinforcement
> E. Retention
> F. Transfer learning

Short Answer Directions: Read each question or statement carefully. Write your answer(s) in the space provided. Reread your answers before turning in your paper. **(6 points each)**

4. What is one of the most beneficial educational activities for older adults?

_____

5. List two factors that impact the selection of activities for older adults.

_____

6. What do adults use to process new information and make decisions?

_____

7. What are four characteristics of adult learners?

_____

_____

8. Identify two ways that care providers can meet the slowing cognitive abilities of some older adults.

_____

_____

9. What are three factors that motivate older adults to learn?

_____

_____

(Continued on next page)

10. What kind of materials help older adults understand topics?

_____

11. What are two factors that impact reinforcement of newly learned skills for older adults?

_____

12. What determines how much information older adults retain?

_____

13. What can care providers and family members do to help older adults retain the information that they learn?

_____

14. For older adults, when is transfer of learning most likely to occur?

_____

15. What kind of information do many older adults want to learn?

_____

Workplace Challenge Directions: Describe one way you could teach older adults with the following learning styles how to log-on to the Internet. **(5 points each, 10 points total)**

Auditory Learners: _____

_____

_____

Kinesthetic Learners: _____

_____

_____

Program Planning for Older Adults

Section Test
24-4

Short Answer Directions: Read each question or statement carefully. Write your answer(s) in the space provided. Reread your answers before turning in your paper. **(6 points each)**

1. Identify four ways that developmentally appropriate programs for older adults improve well-being.

   _____

   _____

   _____

   _____

2. What two actions can care providers take to ensure that learning activities meet each individual's plan of care?

   _____

   _____

   _____

3. What role do older adults play in ensuring that programs are successful?

   _____

4. On what does program design depend?

   _____

5. What increases the probability that older adults will participate and assume responsibility for their learning?

   _____

6. List two criteria to follow to help ensure older adults' participation in activities.

   _____

   _____

7. What are five types of activities care providers can plan with and for older adults?

   _____

   _____

(Continued on next page)

8. What categories should you include in an activity plan for older adults?

_____

_____

_____

9. What are the benefits of gardening activities to older adults?

_____

10. What is a key benefit of intergenerational activities to young people and older adults?

_____

11. Give an example of an intergenerational community service project.

_____

12. What are the basic steps a care provider should take in involving older adults in program planning?

_____

_____

13. How does humor contribute to a desirable informal environment?

_____

14. What can care providers do to provide problem-solving support for older adults?

_____

15. How do older adults learn best?

_____

Workplace Challenge Directions: Describe a procedure for program evaluation. **(10 points)**

_____

_____

_____

_____

_____

Child & Adult Care Professionals Instructor Resource Guide

Developing Language Skills

Matching Directions: Read each description carefully. Then match it with the correct key term from the list on the right. Write the letter of the key term in the space provided. Do not use any term more than once. Some terms will not be used. Check you answers before turning in your paper. **(4 points each)**

Descriptions

_____ 1. Includes activities that teach children to listen, speak, read, and write.

_____ 2. Understanding and speaking two languages.

_____ 3. The gradual development of children's literacy skills.

_____ 4. Settings that use printed materials throughout the classroom in meaningful ways.

_____ 5. Including reading and writing in meaningful classroom activities.

_____ 6. Hearing similarities and differences in sounds and words.

_____ 7. Accompanying a song with specific hand motions.

_____ 8. Learning to notice similarities and differences in shapes and alphabet letters.

_____ 9. Spelling a word the way it sounds.

KEY TERMS

A. Advancing literacy

B. Auditory discrimination

C. Bilingual

D. Emergent literacy

E. Finger plays

F. Invented spelling

G. Language arts

H. Print-rich environment

I. Sound discrimination

J. Visual discrimination

K. Whole language

Short Answer Directions: Read each question or statement carefully. Write your answer(s) in the space provided. Reread your answers before turning in your paper. **(4 points each)**

10. How can a care provider best help build a child's readiness to master language skills?

_____

_____

11. What are three ways that care providers can encourage language learning?

_____

_____

12. Give an example of a print-rich environment.

_____

(Continued on next page)

13. What are the key components of the language arts center in an early childhood classroom?

_____

14. What types of books interest infants and toddlers? Preschoolers? School-age children?

_____

_____

15. List three types of listening and speaking activities.

_____

_____

16. How do small motor skills impact a child's writing ability?

_____

17. What can a care provider do to help children recognize their names?

_____

18. What are two small motor activities that help prepare children to use writing tools?

_____

19. What activities help children develop the eye-hand coordination needed for writing?

_____

_____

20. What should you do if you cannot read a child's invented spelling?

_____

_____

Workplace Challenge Directions: List at least five suggestions for success when reading stories to children. **(4 points each, 20 points total)**

◆ _____

◆ _____

◆ _____

◆ _____

◆ _____

Child & Adult Care Professionals Instructor Resource Guide
Copyright © Glencoe/McGraw-Hill

Developing Social Responsibility

Section Test
25-2

Short Answer Directions: Read each question or statement carefully. Write your answer(s) in the space provided. Reread your answers before turning in your paper. **(6 points each)**

1. What does the social studies curriculum area teach?

   _____

   _____

2. Define social responsibility.

   _____

3. How do care providers help children become good community members?

   _____

4. How do care providers build self-esteem in children?

   _____

   _____

5. What is the first step toward developing a well-rounded personality?

   _____

6. How can care providers help develop a child's self-pride?

   _____

   _____

7. List at least two types of hands-on activities that help introduce children to a world of diversity.

   _____

   _____

8. Name two things that a social studies curriculum teaches children about families.

   _____

   _____

9. What may cause children to have misconceptions about aging?

   _____

(Continued on next page)

10. What is an effective way to begin a study with children about land characteristics, plants, and animals?

_____

11. What are the three "Rs" of conservation?

_____

12. What is one way for children to learn to become productive members of society?

_____

13. Describe how a care provider can help ensure that children obey rules.

_____

14. List two ways that care providers can give children an opportunity to make a decision.

_____

_____

15. Describe two ways that children can be included in classroom tasks.

_____

_____

Workplace Challenge Directions: Identify five ways that care providers can reflect diversity throughout the classroom. **(2 points each, 10 points total)**

◆ _____

_____

◆ _____

_____

◆ _____

_____

◆ _____

_____

◆ _____

_____

Child & Adult Care Professionals Instructor Resource Guide

Social Wellness for Older Adults

Section Test 25-3

Matching Directions: Read each description carefully. Then match it with the correct key term from the list on the right. Write the letter of the key term in the space provided. Do not use any term more than once. Some terms will not be used. Check you answers before turning in your paper. **(6 points each)**

Descriptions

_____ 1. Having meaningful relationships and maintaining a network of supportive friends.

_____ 2. Having a positive attitude about life and having the ability to cope with change.

_____ 3. Information gathered from an older adult as the older adult speaks about past life events.

KEY TERMS

A. Normal aging

B. Oral history

C. Personal history

D. Positive aging

E. Social well-being

Short Answer Directions: Read each question or statement carefully. Write your answer(s) in the space provided. Reread your answers before turning in your paper. **(6 points each)**

4. What does achieving emotional wellness allow a person to do?

_____

5. List three things an older adult can do to stay emotionally well.

_____

_____

6. What can care providers do to help adults deal with living on a fixed retirement income?

_____

7. What can care providers do to help older adults learn to cope with problems of daily life?

_____

8. What qualities do older adults have who experience positive aging?

_____

_____

9. Why is maintaining social skills important for older adults?

_____

_____

(Continued on next page)

10. What are the possible rewards for children who listen to an older adult talk of past events?

   _____

11. Describe the procedure for gathering information for an oral history project.

   _____

12. Describe food and craft activities that allow older adults to learn about other cultures.

   _____

   _____

13. List an example of how culture can be shared through music.

   _____

14. How might a care provider help older adults participate in and enjoy their communities?

   _____

   _____

15. How can children benefit from being involved in a diverse intergenerational environment?

   _____

Workplace Challenge Directions: List five ways care providers can help older adults keep a positive attitude. **(2 points each, 10 points total)**

◆ _____

   _____

◆ _____

   _____

◆ _____

   _____

◆ _____

   _____

◆ _____

   _____

Education & Technology for Older Adults

Section Test
25-4

Short Answer Directions: Read each question or statement carefully. Write your answer(s) in the space provided. Reread your answers before turning in your paper. **(6 points each)**

1. What is household automation?

   _____

2. Define assistive technology.

   _____

   _____

3. What is the fastest-growing group of technology users?

   _____

4. What are two ways that older adults can use the Internet to maintain their independence?

   _____

   _____

5. Describe the advantage of an automated teller machine (ATM) for older adults.

   _____

6. What type of telephone is suitable for people with limited vision or mobility problems?

   _____

7. How do household technologies primarily benefit older adults?

   _____

   _____

8. What can a care provider do to help older adults feel comfortable with various types of technology?

   _____

   _____

9. What helps older adults feel happy and stay healthy?

   _____

(Continued on next page)

10. What is the advantage of wheelchair sensing systems?

_____

11. What type of lighting helps reduce the possibility of seasonal depression for older adults?

_____

12. What can care providers do to help address the needs of all older adults in the use of technology?

_____

13. What can care providers do to help foster reading hobbies of older adults?

_____

14. What can care providers do to assist older adults who want to use on-line book clubs?

_____

15. What can older adults use in place of check writing when shopping?

_____

Workplace Challenge Directions: List five ways care providers can help older adults perform cooking tasks. **(2 points each, 10 points total)**

◆ _____

◆ _____

◆ _____

◆ _____

◆ _____

Child & Adult Care Professionals Instructor Resource Guide

Math Skills for Children

Matching Directions: Read each description carefully. Then match it with the correct key term from the list on the right. Write the letter of the key term in the space provided. Do not use any term more than once. Some terms will not be used. Check you answers before turning in your paper. **(6 points each)**

Descriptions

_____ 1. Words that express numbers, quantities, shape, size, or volume.

_____ 2. Identifying size relationships between objects.

_____ 3. Memorizing and reciting numbers in order.

_____ 4. Recognizing the numerical symbols that represent quantities and placing them in sequential order.

_____ 5. Written symbols that represent numbers.

> ### KEY TERMS
>
> **A.** Mathematical concepts
>
> **B.** Mathematical vocabulary
>
> **C.** Numerals
>
> **D.** Rational counting
>
> **E.** Rote counting
>
> **F.** Sequence counting
>
> **G.** Seriation

Short Answer Directions: Read each question or statement carefully. Write your answer(s) in the space provided. Reread your answers before turning in your paper. **(6 points each)**

6. In what age range does a true understanding of math occur?

_____

7. What is the goal of a math curriculum for young children?

_____

8. What is the best way to lead children to math mastery?

_____

9. How can care providers determine a child's level of readiness for a new concept?

_____

_____

10. What can a care provider do to encourage children to see relationships between shapes?

_____

_____

(Continued on next page)

11. Describe at least one activity that can be used to teach counting skills.

_____

_____

12. What is one activity that a care provider can use to teach rational counting?

_____

_____

13. Describe an activity care providers can use to help children learn to recognize numerals.

_____

_____

14. What can be used to allow children to relay mathematical information they gather?

_____

_____

15. What is one activity that can be used to strengthen the skill of ordering numerals?

_____

_____

Workplace Challenge Directions: Explain five ways that visiting a supermarket helps children learn about math. **(2 points each, 10 points total)**

◆ _____

_____

◆ _____

_____

◆ _____

_____

◆ _____

_____

◆ _____

_____

Science Skills for Children

Section Test 26-2

Matching Directions: Read each description carefully. Then match it with the correct key term from the list on the right. Write the letter of the key term in the space provided. Do not use any term more than once. Some terms will not be used. Check you answers before turning in your paper. **(6 points each)**

Descriptions

_____ 1. Table with a boxlike, hollow top that can hold water, sand, beans, or other substances.

_____ 2. A low table with a plastic, white cover. Beneath the cover are low-wattage light bulbs.

_____ 3. A recipe that illustrates ingredients and directions with picture symbols.

KEY TERMS

A. Light table

B. Picture recipe

C. Rebus recipe

D. Sensory table

E. Science table

Short Answer Directions: Read each question or statement carefully. Write your answer(s) in the space provided. Reread your answers before turning in your paper. **(6 points each)**

4. Under what conditions do children discover science best?

_____

5. How do care providers guide science learning?

_____

_____

6. What kind of questions best help focus children's thinking?

_____

7. List two basic scientific laws that await children's discovery.

_____

_____

8. What are three goals for a science curriculum?

_____

_____

_____

(Continued on next page)

9. What must happen before a care provider can develop science activities for children?

_____

10. What is the best approach in capturing children's interest in science activities?

_____

11. What guides a care provider's organization of science learning opportunities?

_____

12. List at least four science concepts that are of interest to children.

_____

_____

_____

13. Where is a recommended location for a science area in a classroom?

_____

14. What are five types of science materials to include in a science learning center?

_____

_____

_____

15. What should a care provider do before using a recipe with children?

_____

Workplace Challenge Directions: List at least five skills that young children can practice through science activities. **(2 points each, 10 points total)**

◆ _____

◆ _____

◆ _____

◆ _____

◆ _____

Child & Adult Care Professionals Instructor Resource Guide

Nature & Gardening Activities

Section Test 26-3

Matching Directions: Read each description carefully. Then match it with the correct key term from the list on the right. Write the letter of the key term in the space provided. Do not use any term more than once. Some terms will not be used. Check you answers before turning in your paper. **(6 points each)**

Descriptions

_____ **1.** Teaching about the environment and life on earth.

_____ **2.** A book for identifying natural items, such as flowers, insects, birds, or trees.

_____ **3.** Watching birds.

Short Answer Directions: Read each question or statement carefully. Write your answer(s) in the space provided. Reread your answers before turning in your paper. **(6 points each)**

> **KEY TERMS**
>
> **A.** Birding
>
> **B.** Physical education
>
> **C.** Field guide
>
> **D.** Nature education
>
> **E.** Nature guide

4. What is the benefit of studying nature to young and old people?

_____

5. What are the benefits of grandparents and grandchildren participating in an Elderhostel™ program that includes hands-on, nature activities?

_____

_____

6. What are two activities that young and old alike can do to learn about textures?

_____

_____

7. What are three activities that young and old alike can do to learn about the effects of climate and weather?

_____

_____

8. Name at least five tools for nature exploration.

_____

_____

_____

(Continued on next page)

9. What is the main value of having classroom pets?

_____

_____

10. How do pets address people's social needs?

_____

_____

11. What type of dog is recommended for children and older adults as a pet?

_____

12. What skills can be refined in the process of learning to identify birds?

_____

13. List the items needed to attract birds.

_____

14. Describe how gardening shows the dependence of plants and insects on each other.

_____

_____

15. What are the long-term health benefits of gardening for adults?

_____

_____

Workplace Challenge Directions: As a care provider, name five indoor gardening activities that you could plan that are appropriate for people of all ages. **(2 points each, 10 points total)**

◆ _____

◆ _____

◆ _____

◆ _____

◆ _____

Finances for Older Adults

Short Answer Directions: Read each question carefully. Write your answer(s) in the space provided. Reread your answers before turning in your paper. **(6 points each)**

1. What is a daily money manager?

   _____

   _____

2. Why do older adults often become targets of commercial exploitation?

   _____

   _____

3. On what is an older adult's financial status based?

   _____

4. What is the value of setting financial goals?

   _____

5. What can care providers do to assist older adults in using their money wisely?

   _____

   _____

   _____

6. List a way care providers can help older adults organize and keep track of their financial records.

   _____

7. Where is a good place to keep insurance policies?

   _____

8. How can an older adult be made to feel more secure concerning care and finances?

   _____

   _____

(Continued on next page)

Child & Adult Care Professionals Instructor Resource Guide

9. What can care providers do to assist family members of older adults?

_____

_____

10. How can family members assist older adults with their spending?

_____

_____

11. What can adult day care providers do to help in the selection of a daily money manager?

_____

12. What is the difference between a debit card and a credit card?

_____

_____

13. How do unethical people financially abuse older adults?

_____

14. How can care providers help older adults be aware of schemes used to take advantage of them?

_____

15. Describe a financial filing system for older adults.

_____

_____

Workplace Challenge Directions: List two factors that impact the financial stability of older adults of which care providers should be aware. **(5 points each, 10 points total)**

◆ _____

_____

◆ _____

_____

Child & Adult Care Professionals Instructor Resource Guide

Motor Development & Fitness

Section Test
27-1

Matching Directions: Read each description carefully. Then match it with the correct key term from the list on the right. Write the letter of the key term in the space provided. Do not use any term more than once. Some terms will not be used. Check you answers before turning in your paper. **(6 points each)**

Descriptions

_____ 1. Responding to music or a mental image through physical movement.

_____ 2. The way a person walks.

_____ 3. The way people change their movements to be safe.

_____ 4. Moving body joints evenly and consistently to avoid stiffness and pain.

Short Answer Directions: Read each question or statement carefully. Write your answer(s) in the space provided. Reread your answers before turning in your paper. **(6 points each)**

> **KEY TERMS**
>
> A. Creative movement
> B. Dancing
> C. Gait
> D. Joint mobilization
> E. Locomotion compensation
> F. Pace
> G. Physical therapy

5. What three components promote a healthy lifestyle and allow individuals to participate in activities of their choice?

_____

6. What kind of activities help children learn to make their bodies do what they want them to do?

_____

7. What is the key to children's mastery of motor skills?

_____

8. What is the importance of body awareness activities?

_____

_____

9. What three problems can cause older adults to experience changes in their gait?

_____

(Continued on next page)

10. What physical problems can lead to falls?

_____

11. List at least three environmental hazards that can lead to falls for older adults.

_____

12. List one device that can be used by older adults to achieve locomotion compensation.

_____

13. What kind of activities can be instrumental in maintaining body strength and balance in older adults?

_____

14. List at least three stretching exercises that older adults can perform.

_____

_____

15. List three benefits of water exercise for older adults.

_____

_____

Workplace Challenge Directions: List two broad-based activities that help children become aware of their bodies. **(5 points each, 10 points total)**

◆ _____

_____

◆ _____

_____

Child & Adult Care Professionals Instructor Resource Guide
Copyright © Glencoe/McGraw-Hill

Active Play & Recreation

Matching Directions: Read each description carefully. Then match it with the correct key term from the list on the right. Write the letter of the key term in the space provided. Do not use any term more than once. Some terms will not be used. Check you answers before turning in your paper. **(6 points each)**

Descriptions

_____ **1.** A deliberately confusing series of pathways.

_____ **2.** Activities that engage children in fun physical participation.

_____ **3.** Therapy that helps older adults with illnesses or disabilities and helps maintain their physical, mental, and emotional health and well-being.

KEY TERMS

A. Active play

B. Healthful play

C. Maze

D. Obstacle course

E. Physical therapy

F. Recreational therapy

Short Answer Directions: Read each question or statement carefully. Write your answer(s) in the space provided. Reread your answers before turning in your paper. **(6 points each)**

4. What kind of games help develop children's problem-solving and goal-setting skills?

_____

5. What emotional changes occur in children as they master physical skills?

_____

6. What can care providers do to conduct indoor active play experiences in a limited space?

_____

_____

7. Describe how safety rules should be stated.

_____

_____

8. What criteria should active play materials meet?

_____

_____

(Continued on next page)

9. List three games that help develop large motor and perceptual motor skills.

_____

10. What are three games that are especially good for developing eye-hand coordination and perceptual motor skills?

_____

11. When should care providers encourage older adults to stop exercising?

_____

12. Why are recreational activities and fitness important for older adults?

_____

13. What can recreational therapy do for older adults who experience depression, anxiety, stress, or limited mobility?

_____

14. What are the benefits of positive experiences in recreational therapy for older adults?

_____

15. List three sports that are not recommended for school-age children in a child care setting.

_____

_____

Workplace Challenge Directions: In addition to age and skill level, what are two factors that older adult care providers should consider in planning activities for older adults? **(5 points each, 10 points total)**

◆ _____

_____

_____

◆ _____

_____

_____

Child & Adult Care Professionals Instructor Resource Guide

Self-Expression Through Drama

Section Test 27-3

Matching Directions: Read each description carefully. Then match it with the correct key term from the list on the right. Write the letter of the key term in the space provided. Do not use any term more than once. Some terms will not be used. Check you answers before turning in your paper. **(6 points each)**

Descriptions

_____ **1.** When children create realistic or fantasy situations and act them out.

_____ **2.** Children engage in dramatic play without the suggestion or direction of adults.

_____ **3.** Items that suggest themes for dramatic play.

_____ **4.** A container for storing items used in a specific drama theme.

KEY TERMS

A. Drama box

B. Dramatic play

C. Paraphernalia

D. Prop box

E. Props

F. Spontaneous dramatic play

G. Unplanned play

Short Answer Directions: Read each question or statement carefully. Write your answer(s) in the space provided. Reread your answers before turning in your paper. **(6 points each)**

5. What can children learn through make-believe play?

_____

6. What does dramatic play safely allow children to explore?

_____

7. List three common sites for dramatic play.

_____

8. How much time do children need to decide on a theme and their roles, put on costumes, enact the scene, and then put away the equipment and materials?

_____

9. What intellectual skills do children develop as they try to create drama plots?

_____

10. What is the value of having care providers participate with children in dramatic play?

_____

_____

(Continued on next page)

11. Describe how a dramatic play learning center should be designed.

_____

12. What can care providers do to ensure there is a variety of daily activities in the dramatic play learning center?

_____

13. What purposes are served with the use of props?

_____

14. List three criteria for a prop box.

_____

_____

15. What is the value of dramatic storytelling for older adults?

_____

_____

_____

Workplace Challenge Directions: List at least two guidelines for planning and implementing intergenerational dramatic storytelling activities. **(5 points each, 10 points total)**

◆ _____

_____

_____

◆ _____

_____

_____

Child & Adult Care Professionals Instructor Resource Guide

Name_____ Course _____ Date _____

Developing Artistic Expression

Matching Directions: Read each description carefully. Then match it with the correct key term from the list on the right. Write the letter of the key term in the space provided. Do not use any term more than once. Some terms will not be used. Check you answers before turning in your paper. **(6 points each)**

Descriptions

_____ **1.** The size or relationship of the parts.

_____ **2.** Principle that states that what children learn is more important than the art product they create.

_____ **3.** Stage of development when children use lines and shapes and represent real objects with shapes.

_____ **4.** Shapes and objects that have height, width, and depth.

_____ **5.** A picture or design made by gluing or pasting many different pieces of material to a backing.

KEY TERMS

A. Collage

B. Realistic stage

C. Paste-up

D. Symbolic stage

E. Process versus product

F. Proportion

G. Sequence

H. Three-dimensional

Short Answer Directions: Read each question or statement carefully. Write your answer(s) in the space provided. Reread your answers before turning in your paper. **(6 points each)**

6. How does participation in art help children develop language skills?

_____

7. As children make decisions about their art projects, what intellectual skills do they develop?

_____

8. At what stage of children's art do drawings and symbols become more recognizable to others?

_____

9. What is the advantage to children of having a well-stocked art learning center?

_____

10. What is the value in focusing on the "process" rather than the "product" with art experiences for children?

_____

_____

(Continued on next page)

11. Rather than asking, "What is it?" and risk discouraging young artists, what would be an appropriate response to a child's piece of artwork?

_____

_____

12. Why is it inappropriate to grade children's art or to label it bad or ugly?

_____

13. What are three suitable materials for a collage?

_____

14. Describe how you would create finger-paint substitutes.

_____

_____

15. What skills can children practice and develop when they mold and shape dough or clay?

_____

Workplace Challenge Directions: Assume you have been given the task of equipping the art center with supplies for painting activities. Name at least five types of materials and supplies you would put in the art center. **(2 points each, 10 points total)**

◆ _____

_____

◆ _____

_____

◆ _____

_____

◆ _____

_____

◆ _____

_____

Child & Adult Care Professionals Instructor Resource Guide

Developing Musical Expression

Matching Directions: Read each description carefully. Then match it with the correct key term from the list on the right. Write the letter of the key term in the space provided. Do not use any term more than once. Some terms will not be used. Check you answers before turning in your paper. **(6 points each)**

Descriptions

_____ **1.** Words to songs.

_____ **2.** The speed at which a song is sung.

_____ **3.** The highness or lowness of musical sounds.

_____ **4.** The tune of a song.

_____ **5.** Musical instruments that allow children to experiment with making their own rhythms.

_____ **6.** Songs in which an adult sings questions and children sing back the answers.

KEY TERMS

A. Call-and-response songs

B. Lyrics

C. Melody

D. Pitch

E. Question-and-answer songs

F. Rhythm

G. Rhythm instruments

H. Tempo

I. Verses

Short Answer Directions: Read each question or statement carefully. Write your answer(s) in the space provided. Reread your answers before turning in your paper. **(6 points each)**

7. What type of physical development occurs when children move rhythmically to music?

_____

8. List positive effects of music on emotional development.

_____

_____

_____

9. What social values are developed from the singing of folk songs?

_____

10. List three examples of how music can be related to other curriculum areas.

_____

_____

_____

(Continued on next page)

11. What guidelines should be considered when choosing songs for group singing?

_____

12. List at least three procedures or guidelines for using instruments.

_____

_____

_____

13. List three ways care providers can incorporate music into classroom routines.

_____

_____

_____

14. Describe how you can construct your own cymbals.

_____

_____

15. What are two guidelines for group singing?

_____

Workplace Challenge Directions: List five cognitive areas that develop when children sing. (**2 points each, 10 points total**)

◆ _____

_____

◆ _____

_____

◆ _____

_____

◆ _____

_____

◆ _____

_____

Child & Adult Care Professionals Instructor Resource Guide

Art for Older Adults

Section Test **28-3**

Matching Directions: Read each description carefully. Then match it with the correct key term from the list on the right. Write the letter of the key term in the space provided. Do not use any term more than once. Some terms will not be used. Check you answers before turning in your paper. **(6 points each)**

Descriptions

_____ 1. A human service profession that uses art media and creative art process as helpful tools in treating people who experience developmental, medical, social, or psychological concerns.

_____ 2. Professionals trained in the field of art therapy at the master's level following the requirements established by the American Art Therapy Association.

KEY TERMS

A. Art therapy

B. Art therapist

C. Psychological therapy

D. Psychologist

E. Social therapy

Short Answer Directions: Read each question or statement carefully. Write your answer(s) in the space provided. Reread your answers before turning in your paper. **(6 points each)**

3. What does art, as a creative medium, encourage in older adults?

_____

4. As people age, what does art appreciation and participating in art activities accomplish?

_____

_____

5. Which federal act recognizes and supports art therapy?

_____

6. Of what value is participation in art therapy to older adults who may not be able to express themselves verbally?

_____

7. What is the role of art therapists?

_____

8. In what way do art therapists encourage independence in older adults?

_____

(Continued on next page)

9. Why do many older adults volunteer in local community organizations?

_____

10. In an intergenerational art program, what is the value of building relationships?

_____

11. What are three benefits of shared experiences to children and older adults?

_____

12. How can care providers make use of retired artists in an intergenerational art program?

_____

_____

13. List the suggested members of an intergenerational art program planning team.

_____

14. What is the goal of art therapy?

_____

_____

15. List three other professionals who may be on the team with art therapists.

_____

_____

_____

Workplace Challenge Directions: Describe two benefits of age-awareness training for children, older adults, and professional volunteer artists. **(5 points each, 10 points total)**

◆ _____

_____

_____

◆ _____

_____

_____

Music for Older Adults *Section Test* 28-4

Matching Directions: Read each description carefully. Then match it with the correct key term from the list on the right. Write the letter of the key term in the space provided. Do not use any term more than once. Some terms will not be used. Check you answers before turning in your paper. **(6 points each)**

Descriptions

_____ 1. Music that is purely for social and personal enjoyment.

_____ 2. Uses music to help meet the physical, psychological, cognitive, and social functioning of older adults.

Short Answer Directions: Read each question or statement carefully. Write your answer(s) in the space provided. Reread your answers before turning in your paper. **(6 points each)**

KEY TERMS

A. Music therapy

B. Psychological therapy

C. Recreational music

D. Therapy music

3. How is recreational music of benefit to older adults?

_____

_____

4. What are three activities that older adults might perform during planned music functions?

_____

5. What procedures should care providers follow in planning musical activities for older adults?

_____

6. List three health problems in which music therapy may be useful.

_____

7. What is the goal of music therapy?

_____

8. Why can music therapy be used successfully with people in all stages of development?

_____

9. Like art, what does music help older adults maintain?

_____

(Continued on next page)

10. Describe the role of a certified music therapist.

_____

_____

11. What is considered to be an effective bridge between generations?

_____

12. Who is considered qualified to conduct intergenerational music activities?

_____

_____

13. Describe the benefits of dancing.

_____

_____

14. Name two nationally known music groups that offer intergenerational programs.

_____

_____

15. Name three benefits of music for older adults.

_____

_____

Workplace Challenge Directions: Describe two key ways that care providers can design a musical studio to benefit children and older adults. **(5 points each, 10 points total)**

◆ _____

_____

_____

◆ _____

_____

_____

Child & Adult Care Professionals Instructor Resource Guide